North America's
GREATEST
Fishing
Lodges

A **SPORTS AFIELD** GUIDE

North America's
GREATEST
Fishing
Lodges

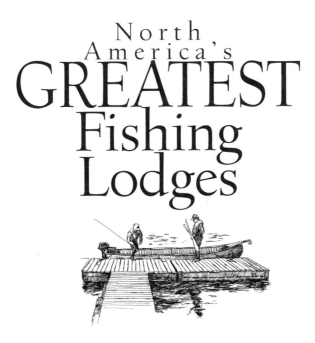

More than 250 Hotspots in the
U.S., Canada & Caribbean Basin

BY JOHN ROSS & KATIE ANDERS

Printed in the United States of America

DESIGNED BY GARY GRETTER

Maps and Illustrations by R. L. Gretter

Cover Photograph by Rob Bossi

Library of Congress Cataloging-in-Publication Data
Ross, John, 1946-
    North America's greatest fishing lodges : more than 250 hotspots
  in the U.S., Canada & Caribbean Basin / by John Ross & Katie Anders.
      p. cm.
    Includes index.
    ISBN 1-57223-105-X (alk. paper)
    1. Fishing lodges --North America--Guidebooks. 2. North America--
Guidebooks. I. Anders, Katie. II. Title.
SH462.R685 1997
799.1' 0257--dc21   97-16540
                                                                  CIP

EDITED BY JAY CASSELL

Published by
WILLOW CREEK PRESS
PO Box 147
Minocqua, WI 54548

Acknowledgements

WERE IT NOT FOR THAT wonderfully selfless connector, Marilynne Herbert, who introduced John to Jay Cassell, articles editor at *Sports Afield*, a couple of years ago, this book would not have happened.

Cassell championed the idea from the beginning and, along with Lorraine Loughran, his wife, edited the manuscript. Cassell's insights and extensive experience as an outdoor journalist brought depth and perspective. Loughran, also a career journalist, added a healthy dose of common sense with her copy edits.

Thanks too must go to *Sports Afield*'s design director, Gary Gretter, who designed this book; and to Sid Evans, associate editor, who helped cement the dealings between *Sports Afield* and Willow Creek Press.

They go as well to Tom Helgeson, editor of *Midwest Fly Fishing,* who introduced us to Bob Linsenman, author and steelheader (probably not in that order), whose input has been invaluable. So has that of John Sherman, the finest innkeeper in all of Paris.

Staff in Canadian provincial fisheries and tourism agencies and Frank LaFleche of the Canadian Embassy in Washington, D.C., provided timely and effective information and assistance.

Much research went into the project and references are listed in each regional introduction. To the authors of all those regional guides, we owe a debt. Their books make our fishing better. *Great Rivers—Great Hatches* by Charles Meck and Greg Hoover (Stackpole, 800/732-3669) and *The Traveling Angler*, elegantly written by Ernest Schwiebert and sadly out of print, are also excellent resources. They belong in every angler's library.

C o n t

e n t s

_Anglers who fish the "golden triangle"
centered in West Yellowstone, Montana,
catch huge brown trout (these came from
the Big Hole), rainbows and cutthroats._

INTRODUCTION

SHELVES IN BOOKSTORES are stuffed with good books about fishing. In addition to volumes on tackle craft and technique, you'll find scores about the fishing in North America and its wonderfully diverse regions. But missing is a book that brings the fishing together with information about where to stay when you do it. That's where *Sports Afield* comes in. *Sports Afield*'s editors and writers roam the continent to bring you stories about the best fishing everywhere. In the process, they've come to know places where the angling is fantastic and accommodations are fabulous. You'll find plenty of those places in this book.

Here we've profiled more than 250 great fishing lodges. What makes a lodge great? It's a matter of taste and priorities. When Katie and I took our first trip to Alaska, I told her we would be staying in "upscale" wilderness lodges. For me, the fisherman, that meant warm, dry, screens on windows and doors, and a bath with hot water. For Katie, former senior editor of *Country Inns* magazine, "upscale" meant more. Her mind sees rooms decorated with quality furnishings and coordinated fabrics, plus amenities. She believes an upscale room should soothe the senses of its guests. I thought rooms were for sleeping when it was too dark to fish. There you have the Ross and Anders approach to angling accommodations. Needless to say my perceptions have changed. So have Katie's.

Of primary importance to traveling anglers is not so much the accommodations: Plush places are available in lots of locales where there are no fish. It's the fishing that's most important. Yet scattered throughout North America and included in this book are places where good fishing is complemented by lodges, inns, bed and breakfasts, and camps that offer lodging experiences that will suite varying tastes and pocketbooks. If you're looking for classic lodges of honey-toned log, where tablefare is haute cuisine, and the wine cellar is extensive, you'll find them here. You'll also find snug camps where you bring your own grub and gear.

While the fishing may be great most of the time in most of the lodges listed, some of the time the fishing will be slow, or worse. Such is fishing. But in the places we've described, unless you live on the Henry's Fork or the upper Delaware, the fishing is normally much better than what you have at home. One travels to catch fish of size and quantity and to rendezvous with other similarly inspired anglers.

We have made no attempt to rate these lodges. Tastes and needs are personal, and the true measure of the greatness of a lodge is how well it suits you, not us. This is a guide to a variety of places—but by no means all—where angling and accommodations are highly regarded. We hope it starts you on your way to the fishing vacation of your dreams.—*John Ross and Katie Anders, Upperville, Virginia, 1997.*

HOW TO PICK A LODGE

RESEARCHING FISHING LODGES IS FUN. For one thing, you can let your imagination run wild. One moment you're on a skiff casting to tailing bonefish in the Bahamas, the next you're waist deep in a brawling river, wrestling an Alaskan rainbow. And you can do it all from the comfort of home. No doubt about it, dreaming is great tonic for midwinter (or anytime) blues. Turning those fantasies into reality is not difficult, either. Yet too many angling vacations fall, somehow, short of the mark. The hype of promotional videos, quick summaries in books and magazines, glib recommendations from friends, and, unfortunately, professional advice, all heighten your expectations, perhaps unrealistically.

To keep expectations and reality in harmony, remember:

❖ IF IT'S POUNDS OF FISH YOU WANT, VISIT A FISH MARKET. Nobody can guarantee that you'll catch any fish, or lots of fish, or lots of big fish. Credible lodge operators, and the guides who work for them, do their best to put you on fish. But the variables in the equation—weather and angler skills, primarily—are too great to ensure success. Lodge operators stack the odds in your favor but, after all, it's still called fishing.

❖ PLAN THOROUGHLY. Determine what you and those who are going with you want to gain from a vacation (or business meeting) at an angling lodge. Write down your objectives and priorities. Do as much of your own research as you can. The more you know about a place before you get there, the better the trip will be.

❖ BE REASONABLE. Most of us have become accustomed to basic amenities when we travel: rooms with private baths, TV, maid service, room service, laundry service, telephone, data ports, extensive menus. You'll find these at some lodges, but not at most. Accommodations are generally in the bush, and may be fairly primitive by normal standards. Those that aren't charge a premium.

Planning the perfect trip

Jot down the following questions and answer them.

❖ WHO WILL BE JOINING YOU ON THIS VACATION (OR BUSINESS TRIP)? Make a list. The makeup of your group will determine the kind of fishing experience you ultimately have. Is your spouse or significant other joining you? What about your boss or best client? Kids? Your lifelong fishing buddy? Or is it just you? Your needs are very different when you travel solo than when you travel with someone else. If you can, gather your potential trip partners together and tackle the next three questions as a group. If not, try conference calls. Everybody should participate.

❖ WHAT KIND OF FISHING EXPERIENCE DO YOU WANT? Variables include species, geography, terrain, climate, type of fishing, kind of accommodations and level of service. The possibilities are endless—casting for monster pike, trolling for lakers, spinning for smallmouths, fishing dries for savvy browns. Lakes, rivers, streams, saltwater flats, blue water: All hold fish. Do you prefer to wade, fish from a driftboat or troll under power? Does choppering into an isolated rapid whet your imagination? Would you prefer to fish, one-on-one, with a personal guide, or would you rather explore new water on your own? Do it your way; all the options are out there.

❖ WHAT ACCOMMODATIONS DO YOU EXPECT? In a similar vein, does a room with fireplace, whirlpool bath, queen-size bed, balcony with a river view and fine dinners accompanied by '85 Chateau Latour, slake your thirst for total comfort? Or are you more comfortable in a tent camp on barren tundra with an air mattress and sleeping bag and meals eaten around a fire? How important are private baths, daily maid service, and collateral activities such as horseback riding, tennis or golf? Is it necessary to be near a town with restaurants and shopping?

❖ HOW MUCH TIME AND MONEY DO YOU HAVE TO SPEND? Time is harder to find than money. You'll need one or two days to travel to most fly-in or remote lodges and an equal amount of time to return. The final legs of most flights into lodges depart from hub airports early in the morning. That invariably means an overnight stay en route. And while flights out from lodges depart in the mornings, they frequently fail to connect with anything other than red-eye returns. It is a law of nature.

Many lodges offer two- or three-day packages. There's some attraction to these. If you haven't been to a lodge or region before, it may make sense to opt for a shorter stay rather than a full week. That way you can check out the lodge and the fishing, and see if they are really what you want. If you decide to go this route, keep in mind that much depends on the weather. Heavy rains and high water may mean that a three-day stay isn't enough to really explore an area. (Since you haven't used all of your vacation, you may be able to do a second quick trip somewhere else.)

Despite the vagaries of weather, fishing is better at some times during a season than it is in others. Most fish behave in reasonably consistent annual cycles. Most anglers want to time trips to coincide with the best fishing. Those dates fill up early. On the other hand, most Americans vacation in the summer, so the weeks from mid-July through the end of August are extremely popular. Often spring (before June) and fall (after August) fishing is spectacular, and lodges may offer discounts for these periods. In the Caribbean, better fishing is frequently not found in January, but in October and November or March and April. To secure prime weeks, you'll need to book early, sometimes as far as a year in advance.

A week at a truly first-class lodge in the Rockies can cost $4000 or more with travel. For similar accommodations and fishing in Alaska, the tab will nudge $5000. The same is true of the Caribbean. But for $3000 or so, including travel, you can find many full-service lodges where the fishing is superb; meals, hearty; and rooms, comfortable. If you're willing to do your own cooking, a week in Canada or Maine can cost less than $1000. Plush surroundings, daily fly outs, full-time guides and gourmet cuisine all add to the cost. But they can make your angling vacation truly the trip of a lifetime. Prepare a budget that's comfortable and try to stick to it. When you're interviewing lodge operators, be sure to ask for an estimate of the total cost, including tips, licenses, fees for processing and shipping fish and extra costs such as bar tabs and charges for flies or lures.

Once you've answered the previous questions, you're ready to move to the next steps.

❖ SETTING PRIORITIES. Get everybody who's going on the trip together some evening (or spring for another conference call), and kick these questions around. Write up a list of priorities for your trip. A week later get back together and review your list. Any second thoughts? There should be. What's changed? Revise the priorities and move to do the next step: gathering information.

❖ GATHERING INFORMATION. Sources of information about lodges are legion. Magazines, books, the world wide web (a search for "fishing lodges" will keep you online for a week), agents, booths at fishing shows, governmental game and fish agencies, chambers of commerce and tackleshops are all ready sources. So, too, are your friends and acquaintances who may have fished the area you plan to visit. Ask around.

❖ ABOUT BOOKING AGENTS. There are two schools of thought about whether to book a trip through an agent. On the plus side: Agents know many more lodges than most of us. They have inspected the lodges and understand the clientele that the lodge serves. And they know about the fishing. In most cases, you'll pay the same price for a week at a lodge whether you book through an agent or do it yourself. (If you book through an agent, the lodge pays the agent a fee; it costs you the same either way.)

On the down side, some agents have exclusive relationships with one or more lodges. There's a quid pro quo in this. In exchange for being the sole representative of a lodge in, say, the U. S., the agent pledges to provide the lodge with so many guests per year. If an agent is the sole representative for a lodge, you can bet that his priority is filling that lodge with guests. Sure, he wants guests to be satisfied. That keeps him and the lodge in repeat business. But rest assured that he's going to try and sell you on that lodge.

Agents who represent many lodges have a different perspective. Their bread and butter comes from establishing relationships with clients who may not want to go to the same lodge year after year. In the main, their job is to help you find the fishing vacation of your dreams—and then book it. If things go awry on your trip, as they sometimes to do, and if you booked it through an agent, you'll have greater opportunity for redress than you will if you've booked it directly. Agents are generally current on international travel and airline regulations, and will provide you with a wealth of practical information that will facilitate your fishing vacation.

You might want to think of a booking agent as a kind of travel consultant. Some, such as Off the Beaten Path, specialize in designing custom angling (and other) vacations. You'll pay an additional fee—about $200 for a single destination trip or $70 per hour for one that's more complex—but in return you receive a personal itinerary, background on each destination, and savings on airfares, car rentals and en route lodging.

If you're working with an agent, you should talk directly with prospective lodges as well. And beware of the agent who tries to prevent you from doing it. Remember, it's your trip and your money, and you must satisfy yourself that this trip is going to meet your expectations. At the same time, if you're working with an agent who has recommended a lodge, it's frankly unethical to book the lodge on your own.

Selecting an agent is similar to picking a lodge. We've included a list of some of the best. Call them, ask about their services, discuss their relationships with the lodges they represent and obtain and use a list of references, particularly people who live near you.

❖ APPROVALS, ENDORSEMENTS AND RATINGS. We Americans like to rate things...our colleges, cities, computers, cake mixes, everything. While no uniform rating system exists for angling lodges, you can get some hints in terms of quality by looking at ratings that do exist. Some tourism agencies in the provinces of Canada rate angling lodges in terms of service, accommodations and food. Stars are awarded. Call the tourism office in the province you're headed to and ask to see a list of the rankings. The North American Fishing Club (612/939-9449) "approves" fishing lodges based on member reports. Also based on subscriber reports, Don Causey's (305/670-1361) newsletter, *The Angling Report,* provides details on lodges and regions, but he does not approve or endorse lodges. Orvis (800/778-4778) endorses a number of angling lodges that meet fairly strict standards and pay a promotional fee. How valuable are the ratings? They add a bit of useful information, but should not be the determining factor in your choice of a lodge.

❖ MAKING THE FINAL CHOICE. After you've identified several lodges that appear to meet your criteria, how do you make a final choice? First, organize your information, one lodge to a file folder. Then assemble your group and get out your list of priorities, along with the answers to the questions we discussed at the beginning of this chapter. Pass the files around and have each member grade (A, B, C, etc.) each lodge. Then sit back and discuss why you graded them as you did. Also, agree on the dates you want to travel. By the end of the evening, you'll have settled on one you like best and a couple of alternatives. Elect one person to contact the agent or lodge and arrange the booking.

❖ AFTER YOU RETURN. One night, after you return and you've gotten your pictures back, gather everyone together and debrief. Take a look at your priorities when you started preparing for the trip. What was really great? What didn't work? How could the trip have been better? Make notes. Before you know it, you'll be planning for next year.

BOOKING AGENTS

ANGLING DESTINATIONS
330 N. Main St., Sheridan, WY 82801;
800/211-8530

◆

CABELA'S OUTDOOR ADVENTURES
812 13th Ave., Sidney, NE 69160;
800/346-8747, http://www.cabelas.com

◆

FISHABOUT
PO Box 1679, Los Gatos, CA 95031;
800/409-2000,
http://www.wmc.com/fishabout

◆

FRONTIERS INTERNATIONAL
305 Logan Rd., PO Box 959, Wexford,
PA 15090-0959; 800/245-1950,
http://www.frontierstrvl.com

◆

GAGE OUTDOOR EXPEDITIONS
Northstar East Building, 608 Second
Ave. S., Suite 166, Minneapolis, MN
55402; 800/888-1601

◆

KAUFMANN'S STREAMBORN
PO Box 23032, Portland, OR 97281-
3032; 800/442-4359,
http://www.kman.com

◆

BOB MARRIOTT'S FLYFISHING STORE
2700 W. Orangethorpe Ave., Fullerton,
CA 92633; 800/535-6633,
http://www.bobmarriotts.com

◆

JIM MCCARTHY ADVENTURES
4906 Creek Dr., Harrisburg, PA 17112;
717/652-4374

PAUL MERZIG'S ADVENTURE SAFARIS LTD.
38 W. 581 Sunset Dr., St. Charles, IL
60175; 630/584-6836,
http://www.merzig@artcom.com

◆

OFF THE BEATEN PATH
27 E. Main St., Bozeman, MT 59715;
800/445-2995,
http://www.offbeatenpath.com

◆

PAN ANGLING TRAVEL SERVICES
180 North Michigan Ave., Chicago, IL
60601; 800/533-4353,
http://www.spav.com/panangling/

◆

SHOOTING AND ANGLING DESTINATIONS
3220 Audley, Houston, TX 77098;
800/292-2213, jbooth@detailco.com

◆

THE FLY SHOP
4140 Churn Creek Rd., Redding, CA
96002; 800/669-3474,
http://www.theflyshop.com

◆

TIGHTLINE DESTINATIONS
248 Spring St., Hope Valley, RI 02832;
800/933-4742

◆

WORLD CLASS ADVENTURES
270 Corporate Ave., Suite 800, Kalispell,
MT 59901; 800/515-7988

SUCCESSFUL TRAVEL TIPS

MY FIRST VISIT to a fishing lodge was a disaster. I packed everything I thought I'd need—rods, reels, tackle, three changes of clothing, raingear, cameras, tripods, laptop—and arrived at the airport with four pieces of ungainly luggage plus my carry-on bag. Schlepping the stuff required the efforts of three men. Today, I'm learning to travel light, prompted in part by airlines that are increasingly stringent about luggage size and weight requirements. I'm also finding that some of the gear I thought I could never leave behind is less and less important.

The Essentials. When packing for a fishing vacation, ask yourself: "What are the most important items I must, and I mean MUST, have with me at all times?"

❖ MEDICATIONS AND PRESCRIPTION GLASSES. Lay in an emergency supply of medications. Carry one supply with you, pack the other in your luggage. Be sure to have current copies of prescriptions. In addition to prescription sunglasses, take a spare pair of glasses and extra sets of contact lenses, if you use them. My spare glasses travel in my carryon.

❖ MONEY. Traveler's checks, ATM cards and credit cards have reduced the need for cold cash on the road. But not entirely. It's a good rule of thumb to have the equivalent of $100 (US) in local currency and another $300 to $500 in traveler's checks for each week you'll be on the road. In addition, take two or three personal checks. And take only two or three credit cards (American Express, Discover, MasterCard or Visa). Many lodges won't take plastic, but will accept personal or business checks in payment. Keep $200 in emergency cash and traveler's checks and a list of all your credit cards (card numbers and phone numbers if you have to cancel them) in a place separate from where you carry your main funds. That way you won't be out of luck if someone steals your wallet. Pay attention to laws governing the amount of currency you may bring into a country. I know that convenience has its price, but I usually change money at the airport when I enter or leave a country.

❖ IDENTIFICATION. If you're traveling out of the U.S., get a passport. Waiting time can be up to five weeks. If you plan to travel sooner than that, you can expedite the process by paying an additional fee and sending along other evidence, such as a copy of your plane ticket, with the application. To initiate the passport process, contact your county courthouse or the largest post office in your county. You may also contact the National Passport Information Center at 900/225-5674. Operated by the U.S. Department of State, the center will give you the name of the closest office where you can apply for a passport and provide information on the status of a passport application. Automated service is available for 35 cents per minute, and live operators, $1.05 per minute.

You don't really need a passport to travel to the Bahamas, Canada or Mexico. A photo ID such as a driver's license and your birth certificate will suffice. Be aware that regulations do vary from country to country. Belize, for instance, wants to see your round-trip plane ticket and proof of sufficient financial resources equal to $50 for each day you plan to be in the country. Half of that must be in cash. The lodge that you are booking into or your travel agent should be able to tell you precisely what's required.

❖ AIRLINE TICKETS. Booking a flight at the best price is like playing the lottery. Travel agents can often get you a good deal, but sometimes you can do better on your own. It depends, mainly, on whether you're willing to spend the time to do it. Advance-purchase tickets can save you a bundle, but not if the no-refund, no-alteration policy is so strict as to limit flexibility in case of missed connections due to weather, primarily on the return leg of your trip. Beware of connections that are too tight, particularly at international airports. Though baggage may be checked through, you'll have to take it through customs yourself. Even when entering Canada, two hours between planes isn't too much. Booking agents have shepherded thousands of clients through the intricacies of international travel. If you're new to the traveling angler game, they can be a big help.

Tickets do get lost or stolen. Make copies of them before leaving home; keep one with your stash of emergency cash, the other folded in your wallet. If your ticket vanishes mysteriously, the copy will help you cancel the ticket and may help secure a replacement. And don't carry your ticket sticking out of a travel bag. Sure, it's convenient, but it's also easily swiped.

❖ INSURANCE. Lodges book far in advance and require payment of up to 50 percent to hold a reservation. In some cases the balance is due in advance, while others may want it on arrival or just prior to departure. In any event, you will have contracted for services; should you not be able to make the trip, you'll be liable for the full cost. If you cancel more than 60 days in advance, there's a fairly good chance that the lodge or your booking agent will be able to fill the space. (Each lodge has its own refund policies. Check them out thoroughly.) Travel insurance is something to consider, too. Should illness, accident or a death in the family prohibit you from making the trip, the insurance will pay up to the full amount of your obligations. Available coverage varies extensively among insurance companies, as do premiums. Expect to pay about 5 percent of the total coverage, or roughly $350 for a policy worth $6500.

If you're traveling to another country, you'll also want to check with your medical insurance carrier to determine coverages. If you're stricken with an acute medical problem while in the bush, will your insurance pay for your evacuation to the closest hospital? It's also a good idea to determine the applicability of automobile insurance and loss/theft provisions of your homeowner's or business insurance in foreign countries.

The Basics. If you've taken care of the essentials, you'll survive your trip and most likely won't go broke. But what about luggage, clothing and traveling tackle?

❖ BAGGAGE. Add up all your gear: waders, wading boots, rainjacket, sweaters, rods, reels, etc., etc. None of it's light and most of it's bulky. While baggage weight limits in the U.S. are not too stringently enforced, you can bet that when you fly internationally, you'll be charged for excess weight or size. In some cases, you'll be charged per pound. In others, you'll be charged a flat fee that will vary depending on your destination and length of the flight. Check baggage limits with each carrier that you plan to fly with. If you're headed for a fly-in lodge, the lodge operator can provide weight and size restrictions.

Anglers (and other tourists) are obvious prey for baggage thieves. Use tough, nondescript bags when you plan to check your luggage. Attach a tag with your name, address and phone number on each bag; put one inside as well. Even if you're in love with a long two-piece rod, consider getting shorter travel or packrods. (While three- and four-piece travel rods used to be extremely stiff because of the extra joints, today's space-age graphite rods fish almost as well as their two-piece siblings.) You can hide packrods in your duffel bag, or stow them in carry-on luggage.

Checked baggage does get lost. Because of this, I pack things that I absolutely cannot do without in my carry-on luggage: medications, extra glasses, Gore-Tex hat (wear the jacket), mini-shaving kit, camera, a couple paperbacks, waders, ultralight wading shoes, fingerless gloves, flashlight, extra batteries for camera and light, two reels with floating and sinking lines, and a Ziploc bag with a pair of heavy socks and lightweight polypropylene long underwear. The shortest traveling rod I own, a Thomas & Thomas Vagabond, straps on top, and whatever tackle (nippers, forceps, flies, leaders and so) I need, I cram in the side pockets. All this, crammed into an old large waterproof Fisherman's Kit Bag from Orvis, weighs about 25 pounds and slings comfortably over my shoulder. It fits most overhead bins and can be stuffed under most seats.

Wherever I fish, it rains. Instead of a waterproof fishing jacket, I prefer to use a lightweight Gore-Tex parka shell. It's comfortable and attractive enough to wear as a jacket. Rather than packing it, I tend to wear it when I travel. The same is true with my walking boots and, in winter, a heavy Polarfleece or woolen sweater. (Leave cotton sweaters at home. They're bulky, heavy and soak up moisture like sponges.)

Finally, consider wearing a sportpouch to carry spare medication, emergency money, identification, glasses, small flashlight and a Swiss army knife with scissors, screwdriver, corkscrew and file. Unobtrusive and secure, you'll forget you're even wearing the pouch, but you'll be glad you have it in an emergency.

❖ CLOTHING. Each lodge will provide you with a list of things to bring. If you have questions, call and talk with the operator. Fashionable clothing at most lodges fits into the old and comfortable category. At some of the more posh places in the states and islands, you may want a jacket for dinner. Here, too, the lodge management can provide guidance. Otherwise, keep it simple. Remember that many lodges have laundries; if they don't, you can always wash clothing in the sink and drape it over a hot water line to dry.

❖ BATTERIES. So many of our devices are powered by batteries that we hardly give them a thought until they die, which is usually at the worst possible time. Before you leave, replace or charge batteries in everything that you intend to take along (watch, flashlight, tape player, camcorder, camera). Carry spares if you can. Many lodges sell common batteries, but don't count on finding the ones you need for your watch or camera in their supply.

❖ INSECT REPELLENT. The best times to fish usually occur during the height of insect season, especially in the North, where blackflies and mosquitoes grow to bird-like proportions. Don't let them ruin your trip. Carry lots of your favorite insect repellent, and use it liberally when astream. The same applies to suntan lotion and lip balm.

❖ TACKLE. As with clothing, outfitters will tell you what to bring. Some supply gear, and it's usually in pretty good shape. Still, you'll want to use your own when you can. Take at least two rods, but no more than three (unless you'll be fishing in a number of different situations—flyrodding for grayling, casting for big king salmon, bottomfishing for halibut). Drag systems on reels fail more frequently than rods. A couple of spare reels are very good insurance. Put fresh, new line on all of your reels before your trip. Stock up on leader materials, and don't forget wire leader if you're after pike, bluefish or other toothsome gamefish. Lures and flies will generally be available from the lodge or guides. Still, take those that have worked for you in similar situations, or which you intuitively feel will catch fish. They don't weigh much.

❖ SHIPPING FISH HOME. With the exception of saltwater and salmon lodges in Alaska and British Columbia, most fishing is now catch-and-release. What you bring home are photos and memories, or perhaps a fishprint (gyotaku) made in the Japanese style. Most catch-and-keep lodges will clean and package your fish in insulated boxes. You'll be responsible for additional charges for shipping them home.

❖ DEMON RUM. A toddy at the end of a day's fishing can be very welcome. Most lodges have a BYOB policy, though some have open bars with complimentary drink and others operate lounges where you pay as you go. If it's important to you to imbibe 25-year-old Kings Crest, you'd best bring it with you. Plastic bottles travel well, but you may want to use aluminum or stainless bottles sold by camping stores for fuel. These are virtually indestructible and do not impart significant flavor to your favorite potion.

VITAL STATISTICS

EACH LODGE PROFILE includes a Vital Statistics section. We offer it as guidance only. You should contact lodges that interest you for the latest data. The Vital Statistics information is abbreviated, so a little explanation may be useful.

❖ CONFERENCE GROUPS. Many lodges host business groups that want to combine work with pleasure. In some cases the companies use lodges as sites for planning retreats or team building. In others, it's a reward for a job well done. Most lodges do not have the kinds of multi-media or communications equipment you'd expect at a first-class conference center. Some do; call and check out their facilities.

❖ MEALS. American plan includes breakfast, lunch and dinner; modified American plan, breakfast and dinner; European plan, meals may be available at additional cost.

❖ RATES. Figures given here are generally the least expensive price for staying at the lodge. Those marked (CDN) are in Canadian dollars. Rates listed are for the 1996-1997 season and may increase, as you would expect. Most lodges price accommodations in the price per person for two in a room. That works well for lodge owners because one guide can usually serve two anglers, and two is the number of anglers who can fish most comfortably from a small boat.

❖ GUIDES. Guide fees are generally listed, except as otherwise noted, as the price for a full-day for two anglers.

❖ GRATUITIES. Tipping a guide is always an issue. A good rule of thumb is 10 percent to 15 percent of the price of the service. Tips are expected, but keep in mind that they should reward service that is above and beyond. In some cases lodges collect tips based on a percentage of the cost of the total package and then divide it with kitchen, wait, room and guide staff. If the tip covers the package, we've tried to note it.

❖ PREFERRED PAYMENT. While some lodges take credit cards and some personal checks, the largest majority, but not all, will accept cash or traveler's checks.

❖ CONTACT. The world wide web is a font of information about lodges, but it's still very much a frontier. We've made every effort to verify the addresses, but websites, like people, move. Only websites move more often. If you can't connect, call the lodge.

THE EAST

CONNECTICUT, MAINE, MASSACHUSETTS,
NEW HAMPSHIRE, NEW JERSEY, NEW YORK,
PENNSYLVANIA, RHODE ISLAND, VERMONT

G LACIERS rounded the mountains, pushed up the hills, hollowed out the lakes, bent the rivers, and laid down vast plains dimpled with kettle ponds. Fish for native brookies in remote beaver ponds or high mountain streams. Try for lake trout and landlocked salmon when ice leaves the lakes. Rapacious smallmouth bass swim swift rivers, while creeks and streams harbor finicky browns. The traditions of American freshwater angling were born in the waters of Pennsylvania, New York and Maine. Many of these fisheries have been restored, and near them, you'll find camps, lodges, country inns and bed and breakfasts that cater to anglers.

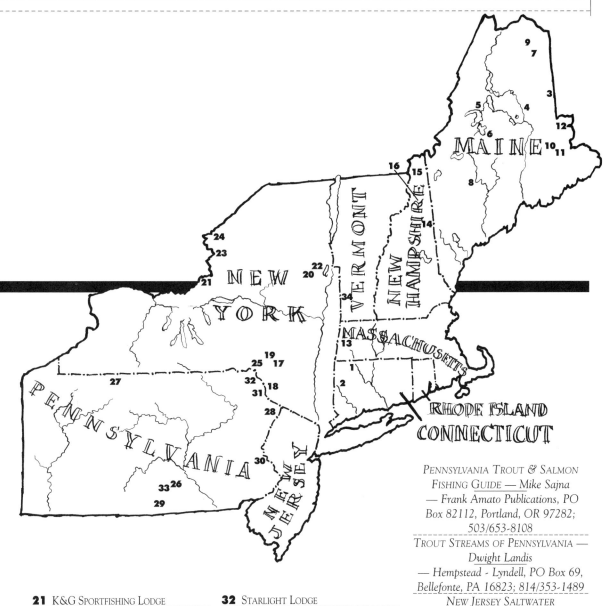

References:

Trout Unlimited Guide to Pennsylvania Limestone Streams — A. Joseph Armstrong
Surf Fishing the Atlantic Coast — Eric B. Burnley — Stackpole Books, Cameron & Keller Sts., PO Box 1831, Harrisburg, PA 17105; 800/732-3669

Pennsylvania Trout & Salmon Fishing Guide — Mike Sajna — Frank Amato Publications, PO Box 82112, Portland, OR 97282; 503/653-8108
Trout Streams of Pennsylvania — Dwight Landis — Hempstead - Lyndell, PO Box 69, Bellefonte, PA 16823; 814/353-1489
New Jersey Saltwater Fishing Guide — Pete Barrett — The Fisherman Library, 1622 Beaverdam Rd., Pt. Pleasant, NJ 08742; 908/295-8600
Good Fishing in Lake Ontario and its Tributaries — Rich Giessuebel
Good Fishing in the Catskills — Jim Capossela
Good Fishing in the Adirondacks — Dennis Aprill
Good Fishing in Western New York — C. Scott Sampson
Fishing Vermont's Streams and Lakes — Peter E. Cammann

References & Resources

PENNSYLVANIA TROUT STREAMS AND THEIR HATCHES — *Charles Meck* — *Backcountry Publications, The Countryman Press, Rt. 2, PO Box 748, Woodstock, VT 05091; 802/457-4826*

NORTHEAST GUIDE TO SALTWATER FISHING & BOATING — *Vin T. Sparano, Editor* — *International Marine/McGraw-Hill Companies, Customer Service Department, PO Box 547, Blacklick, OH 43004; 800/822-8158*

Resources:

CONNECTICUT DEPARTMENT OF ENVIRONMENTAL PROTECTION, *Fisheries Div. 79 Elm St., 6th Floor, Hartford, CT 06106; 860/424-3474, website http://dep.state.ct.us/*

MAINE DEPARTMENT OF INLAND FISHERIES AND WILDLIFE, *284 State St., Augusta, ME 04333; 207/287-8000, website http://www.state.me.us/ifw/ homepage.htm*

MASSACHUSETTS DIVISION OF FISHERIES AND WILDLIFE, *Field Headquarters, Westborough, MA 01581; 508/792-7270, website http://www.state.ma.us/dfwele*

NEW HAMPSHIRE FISH AND GAME DEPARTMENT, *Div. Public Affairs, 2 Hazen Dr., Concord, NH 03301; 603/271-3211, website http://www.wildlife.state.nh.us/*

NEW JERSEY DIVISION OF FISH, GAME AND WILDLIFE, *Information & Education Div., CN 400; Trenton, NJ 08625; 609/292-9450, website http://www.state.nj.us/dep/fgwweb/html /welcome.htm*

NEW YORK DIVISION OF FISH, WILDLIFE AND MARINE RESOURCES; *50 Wolf Rd., Albany, NY 12233; 518/457-5420, website http://www.iloveny.state.ny.us/outdoor /fishing.html*

PENNSYLVANIA FISH AND BOAT COMMISSION, *Bureau of Boating and Education, Box 67000, Harrisburg, PA 17106- 7000; 717/657-4518, website http://www.dcnr.state.pa.us/*

RHODE ISLAND DIVISION OF FISH AND WILDLIFE, *Stedman Government Center, 4808 Tower Hill Rd., Wakefield, RI 02879- 2207; 401/789-3094*

VERMONT FISH AND WILDLIFE DEPARTMENT, *103 South Main St., Waterbury, VT 05671; 802/241-3700, website http://www.state.vt.us/anr*

For more than 100 years, anglers have fished for rare blueback trout found in ponds and lakes close to Red River Camps near Portage, Maine. — page 25.

Old Riverton Inn
R i v e r t o n ,   C o n n e c t i c u t

Hidden northwest of Hartford is one Connecticut's premiere trout streams.

VITAL STATISTICS:

KEY SPECIES:
Brown trout

Season:
All year

Accommodations:
OLD COLONIAL INN
NUMBER OF GUEST ROOMS: 12
MAXIMUM NUMBER OF GUESTS: 24 to 28

Conference Groups: Yes

Meals: Basic room rate includes breakfast. Lunch and dinner additional

Rates:
From $45 per person per night, single occupancy

Guides: Available for $150

Gratuities: Client's discretion

Preferred Payment:
American Express, Discover, MasterCard

Getting There:
About 3 hours by car from New York and Boston, 45 minutes from Bradley Field at Hartford.

Other Activities:
Biking, canoeing, golf, hiking, bird watching, antiquing, wildlife photography, skiing.

Contact:
Mark or Pauline Telford Old Riverton Inn, PO Box 6, Riverton, CT 06065; 860/379-8678, fax 860/379-1006.

FOR 200 YEARS, travelers have been lodging at the Old Riverton Inn, reputedly a stage stop on the Albany Post Road. Among tourists today are growing numbers of anglers looking to combine an evening in a late 18th century inn, replete with four posters and vintage Hitchcock tables and chairs, with trout fishing on the West Branch of the Farmington.

The West Branch is a tailwater fishery with flows controlled by releases from Goodwin Dam about a mile upstream from the inn. Four miles downstream in People's State Forest is a three-mile catch-and-release section which, oddly enough, can be fished with bait as well as lures. Flyfishers should try Church Pool, a half mile of riffles, runs and a long quiet flat. That's the most interesting water according to guide Don Butler (860/583-2446), who recommends flies as small as 24s to 26s and 8X tippet on a 2-weight system. Particular doesn't even begin to describe these browns that range up to 16 inches. There's also good trout fishing across the street from the inn. In midsummer water temperatures stay in the 60s, thanks to the dam, and that brings trout upstream from warmer waters.

Unless it's a party you want, it's best to avoid the third Saturday in April, Connecticut's opening day. That's when the Riverton Country Store throws its annual fishing soiree, a tradition since 1950. From 6:00 to 10:00 a.m. this old New England mill town and 63 houses rocks with anglers seeking limits of stocked trout. The madness passes and summer bucolia settles over the Farmington. That's when the fishing is best. Inn owner Mark Telford will arrange for a guide if you want. Licenses (as well as necessities) can be bought down the street at the country store.

If you're interested in history, this inn has more than a bit. An enclosed porch is floored with stones quarried 100 years ago in Nova Scotia, and used to grind world-famous Collins machetes made downstream in Collinsville. The Hitchcock Chair Company was founded across the river from the inn. Shoppers will like the company's outlet store and numerous antique shops nearby.

With 12 guest rooms, many with fireplaces, all with private baths, the Old Riverton is small enough to be intimate, yet large enough to offer all the amenities including a very good restaurant. Try the Yankee chicken pot pie. The price of a room includes breakfast; numerous packages with dinner are also available.

The Boulders

N e w   P r e s t o n ,   C o n n e c t i c u t

A luxurious country inn, deep in the Litchfield Hills, offers excellent trout and smallmouth fishing nearby.

VITAL STATISTICS:

KEY SPECIES:
Brown trout; smallmouth and largemouth bass

Season:
All year

Accommodations:
CLASSIC LAKE LODGE WITH ADJACENT GUEST HOUSES
NUMBER OF GUEST ROOMS: 17
MAXIMUM NUMBER OF GUESTS: 38

Conference Groups: Yes
Meals: Modified American plan (MAP) or bed and breakfast

Rates:
From $200 for 2 (MAP)
Guides: From $200 for 2 per day
Gratuities: 20%
Preferred Payment:
American Express, MasterCard, Visa

Getting There:
Take US 7/220 north from Danbury, stay on 220 to New Preston, follow Rt. 45 north to the inn.

Other Activities:
Golf, tennis, canoeing, swimming, hiking, bird watching, antiquing, biking, wildlife photography, skiing.

Contact:
Kees Adema
The Boulders, East Shore Rd. (Rt. 45), New Preston, CT 06777;
860/868-0541, fax 860/868-1925.

CONNECTICUT'S LITCHFIELD HILLS remind one of the Berkshires, yet they are an hour closer to New York City. Gentle mountains, rounded by glaciers and heavily forested, crest at about 1500 feet. In the valleys between the mountains are a number of small rivers—the Appentuck and its East Branch, the Bantam above and below Bantam Lake, and the Shepaug—that are stocked with trout and provide limited, but productive, angling. Small lakes offer fishing opportunities as well: Bantam Lake for largemouth and smallmouth bass; the pond in Mount Tom State Park, largemouths and trout; South Spectacle Pond, largemouths; and Waramaug Lake, largemouths and smallmouths. Most of these waters are governed by special regulations.

Connecticut's premiere trout water is the Housatonic, a "western river misplaced in the East," according to guide Rob Nicholas (860/672-4457). While 50 miles of fishable water flows south through the westernmost portion of the state from Massachusetts to the tidal estuary at Bridgeport, the best trout fishing begins 10 miles north of The Boulders at Cornwall Bridge. Fish upstream for nine miles. You'll find long riffles, pocket water and deep pools. Nicholas suggests paying particular attention to the hatch of the Housatonic Quill...a white mayfly that comes off in evenings. You'll also want to fish the Alder Fly in June and Blue-Winged Olives in September and October. In the lower sections south of Cornwall Bridge, smallmouth bass are increasingly present. A float from the bridge down to Kent Falls can produce 30 to 50 smallmouths, many in the 15- to 16-inch range, per trip.

While it bills itself as a country inn, The Boulders is actually the quintessential lakefront lodge. Native rock defines the deep porch and the massive chimney of the weathered shingle lodge. It sits amidst maples on the slope of a hill. When nights are balmy, dinners are served on a semi-circular terrace and deck with a lovely view of the lake across the road. Meals are exquisite. Start with roasted portobello mushroom with polenta and umbreco cheese. Move on to crisp skinned duck breast with Asian black bean salad. Rooms, some with fireplaces and all with private baths, are furnished with antiques and comfortable overstuffed chairs and sofas for lounging or reading. Directly behind the inn, four guest houses offer lake views, private decks and fireplaces. Fireplaces are also featured in the three rooms in the carriage house. Slip down to the inn's dock early in the morning, untie a canoe and work the shore for smallies.

Bear Mountain Lodge
Smyrna Mills, Maine

VITAL STATISTICS:

SPECIES:
Brook trout; landlocked salmon

Season:
May through mid-July

Accommodations:
LODGE AND FUNCTIONAL CABINS
NUMBER OF GUEST ROOMS: 6 in lodge; 4 in cabins
MAXIMUM NUMBER OF GUESTS: 30

Conference Groups: Yes

Meals: Various plans

Rates:
From $20 per person per night

Guides: $100 per party per day

Gratuities: 15%

Preferred Payment:
Cash or check

Getting There:
About 110 miles north of Bangor on Rt. 11.

Other Activities:
Canoeing, boating, swimming, hiking, bird watching, antiquing, biking, wildlife photography.

Contact:
**Carroll P. Gerow
Bear Mountain Lodge,
Moro Plantation, RR 1,
Box 1969, Smyrna Mills,
ME 04780; 207/528-2124.**

This old-style Maine lodge hasn't been fancied up; neither has its price.

FISHING LODGES IN MAINE come in essentially two flavors. There are those of coordinated decor and sophisticated cuisine, and others of the down-home, Down-East variety. At the latter, accommodations are utilitarian: a couple of beds in a room or cabin with screened windows and door, a place to hang up your clothes, lights, hot and cold water and a privy that's often, but not always indoors. Food is basic and plentiful. At down-home lodges, the operative philosophy is pure Maine: "Make do, do without, use it up, wear it out." The advantages: These camps tend to be very affordable. A housekeeping cabin may cost only $20 per night per person; room and board for a week will set you back only $350 or so. Here you can hire a guide if you wish (and it's a good idea for a day or two), but you can fish on your own and figure it out for yourself. Some see virtue in that.

Bear Mountain Lodge in southern Aroostook County is one such camp. Run by registered Maine guide Carroll Gerow and his wife, Deanna, most of the year it houses hunters after bear, deer, moose and birds. But from ice-out on the first of May through mid-July when the water warms, the camp fills with anglers in search of brook trout and landlocked salmon. Brookies aren't huge—a 14-incher is a good fish—but they're brightly colored and eager to hit your lure, bait or fly. Dozens of small 10- to 12-acre ponds dimple this country, and are often connected by good-size streams that hold fair fish. You can work the ponds and their flowages by using canoes, starting with land-locked salmon that begin to feed on smelts as soon as the ice is out. Troll spoons or flies in Rockabema, Pleasant or Mud lakes or in Shin Ponds for fish up to 20 inches.

Anglers at Bear Mountain Lodge stay in four cabins with private baths or in rooms (some with private baths) in the lodge. Buildings are wood with some log, and by no means fancy. You can either do your own cooking or have roast beef, steak, ham, turkey or meat loaf family-style in the lodge. Bear Mountain also operates an outpost camp at Rockabema Lakes and another at Skitacook Lakes. Here you'll be heating with wood and cooking with gas. The outhouse is 'round the back.

Dad's Camps
L i n c o l n ,   M a i n e

VITAL STATISTICS:

KEY SPECIES:
Smallmouth bass; brook trout

Season:
May through November
Accommodations:
HOUSEKEEPING CABINS
NUMBER OF GUEST ROOMS: 6 cabins sleeping 6 to 12
MAXIMUM NUMBER OF GUESTS: 53
Conference Groups: Yes
Meals: Various plans
Rates:
From $30 for 2 per day
Guides: $150 for 2 per day
Gratuities: $20 per day
Preferred Payment:
Cash or check
Getting There:
Bangor is the closest airport; rent a car or the lodge will provide transportation for $40 each way.
Other Activities:
Golf, canoeing, swimming, boating, hiking, bird watching, wildlife photography, mountain climbing, hunting.

Contact:
Raymond Thibodeau Dad's Camps, PO Box 142, W. Enfield, ME 04493; 207/746-7278, fax 207/557-3237.

Would you believe that the camp record 6-pound 3-ounce smallmouth was caught by a 13-year-old?

ANY CAMP NAMED DAD'S may be the ultimate family camp. Owners Raymond and Therese Thibodeau, married 33 years, have eight children, and at last count as many grandkids. Ray, a logger who's semi-retired, always wanted a camp on the Penobscot, a river he's loved since he was a boy. On 400 acres, he built six housekeeping cabins, all fronting the river, and in 1991 opened the camp.

The main attraction is smallmouth bass. Down East, smallmouths have always been the stepchild to salmon, landlocked and Atlantic, and brook trout. Only now are they coming into their own. Because of relatively stable flows and diverse habitat, the Penobscot is one of the country's finest smallmouth rivers. During the season, May through October, the average fish caught is in the two-pound-plus range. Many are larger—four pounds or so—and once in a while someone catches a whopper, like the 6-pound 3-ounce camp record caught right in front of the cabins by a 13-year-old girl. Fishing is best in May, prior to the spawn, and in September and October. Topwater lures work well, as do crankbaits and lead-headed jigs. Flyrodders will also find plenty of action on Dahlberg divers and big Woolly Buggers. Though some of the water is wadeable, you'll want a boat or canoe to fish the river, and Dad's rents both. While smallmouths will demand your attention, don't overlook brookies of up to three pounds found in the nearby lakes. Thibodeau will tell you where to find them, or hook you up with a guide.

Dad's cabins, 75 feet from the river's edge, accommodate up to 12 people and are fully equipped for housekeeping (bring your own sheets, blankets and towels). Charcoal grills are provided for the do-it-yourself cooks. But if you don't feel like messing with pots and pans, Therese will fix meals for you, family-style. The menu? "I usually ask guests to name the foods they do not like, and I make sure I don't serve them," she says. If there's a chill on the river, you may find a New England boiled dinner—ham, carrots and potatoes—or chicken pot pie. After dinner, loll on the screened porch and watch the river darken with the falling dusk.

Gentle Ben's Lodge

R o c k w o o d ,   M a i n e

Down-home lodging with landlocked salmon, brook trout and lake trout on the doorstep.

VITAL STATISTICS:

KEY SPECIES:
Landlocked salmon; brook and lake trout

Season:
All year

Accommodations:
FRAME HOUSE ON LAKE
NUMBER OF GUEST ROOMS: 3
MAXIMUM NUMBER OF GUESTS: 12

Conference Groups: Yes

Meals: American plan

Rates:
$50 per person, $300 per week, double occupancy

Guides:
$225 for up to 4 for a full day

Gratuities: $25

Preferred Payment:
Credit cards

Getting There:
Bangor, Maine is the closest commercial airport. Rent a car and follow Rt. 15 to Rockwood; less than a 2-hour drive.

Other Activities:
Canoeing, swimming, boating, hiking, bird watching, wildlife photography, fall hunting (bear, moose, deer, grouse).

Contact:
Bruce Pelletier
Gentle Ben's Lodge, PO Box 212, Rockwood, ME 04478; 800/242-3769, fax 207/534-2236.

MOOSEHEAD LAKE has long been a favored angling destination. Loaded with landlocked salmon, lake trout and brookies, this 175,000-acre lake has been a steady performer for generations. A number of resorts are located on the lakeshore, but few are as down-home and Down East as Gentle Ben's. Owners Bruce and Cheryl Pelletier only book two to four fishing guests at one time. "We don't mix parties," says Bruce, "we only have one group at a time." With a weekly rate including meals of $300 per person, Gentle Ben's hosts a lot of families. Guided fishing runs $225 per full day for groups up to four.

Moosehead opens up with ice-out in late April to early May. Ten days after ice-out, smelt run into the mouths of the Moose and Roach, the two rivers that feed the lake. Smelt turn on the salmon. Trolling wobblers or copper and chrome Sutton spoons brings strikes near the surface. Flyrodders use traditional patterns such as the Grey Ghost or Joe's Smelt. Lake trout are occasionally taken too, but they tend to be deeper. When Pelletier has to pick a "best time" to fish these species, he'll tell you early June. After that the salmon and lake trout move to cooler and deeper water and become less active.

Not so with the brook trout. They are feisty from Memorial Day on. Flyfishing for them in the tributaries can be very productive at this time, as can trolling or casting with spinning gear. Moosehead brookies run up to two-pounds-plus, but your chances of catching a trophy improve if you opt for a fly out to a remote lake. A Cessna or workhorse Beaver, depending on the size of the group and whether you're carrying a boat, will ferry you, your partner and guide to one of a number of lakes unreachable by road. Brookies in these are in the three-pound class. The area also provides unlimited stream fishing for brook trout.

With typical Maine practicality, the lakeside lodge is comfortable but not tricked up. Fishing parties will have the run of three bedrooms and a shared bath upstairs in the house. Meals, hearty and family-style, are served in the dining room downstairs. Special diets can be accommodated with advance notice.

Greenville Inn
Greenville, Maine

VITAL STATISTICS:

KEY SPECIES:
Landlocked salmon; lake and brook trout; smallmouth bass

Season:
All year

Accommodations:
VICTORIAN MANSION WITH OUTLYING COTTAGES
NUMBER OF GUEST ROOMS: 12
MAXIMUM NUMBER OF GUESTS: 28

Conference Groups: Yes
Meals: Bed and breakfast, dinner is extra

Rates:
From $105 for 2 per day
Guides: $250 for 2 per day
Gratuities: 10% to 30%
Preferred Payment:
Discover, MasterCard, Visa

Getting There:
Drive north from Bangor (about a 1-hour drive).

Other Activities:
Moose watching, golf, tennis, canoeing, rafting, swimming, boating, hiking, bird watching, antiquing, biking, wildlife photography, skiing.

Contact:
Michael Schnetzer Greenville Inn, PO Box 1194, Norris St., Greenville, ME 04441; 888/695-6000, fax 207/695-2206, email gvlinn@moosehead.net, website http://www. maineguide.com/moos head/greenvilleinn

With hand-carved paneling, this inn is the epitome of Victoriana; the fishing isn't bad either.

U NTIL A FEW YEARS AGO, most of Maine's fabled fisheries were in decline. Landlocked salmon of more than 16 inches elicited a "nice" fish comment, brookies of eight to 10 inches were considered "good," and the blue char was (and still is, sadly) all but extinct. Two things happened. First, the flyfishing revolution sent armies of East Coast anglers out West, cutting back seriously on the state's tourism dollars. This, in turn, put pressure on those who control sportfisheries via legislation or fiat. Also, with few salmon or trout to fish for, Maine guides chuckled up their sleeves and sold their sports on smallmouth bass instead. The laugh was on the guides, as smallmouths proved to be hard-fighting game-fish that everyone took a liking to.

All this resulted in a win-win situation. Trout and salmon are now making substantial comebacks, particularly in isolated ponds, lakes and rivers. And Maine guides, perhaps even more set in their ways than fish commissioners, have found that smallmouth bass are big-time fun. One of the best places to avail yourself of these happy circumstances is in Greenville, on the shores of Moosehead Lake. Fishing at Moosehead is improving, as catches of lake trout in the three- to 12-pound range attest. The best angling is right after ice-out in May. So it is, too, with landlocked salmon that run from two to six pounds. And you'll find scrappy smallmouths up to three pounds or so on top in June. But the better fishing is found in the myriad small lakes and streams that connect them. These are the headwaters of the mighty Kennebec and Penobscot rivers. To check them out, contact guide Dan Legere (207/695-2266), who for years has championed enlightened management of Maine's freshwater fisheries.

Fishing is an increasingly important staple in Maine's economic base, which once depended largely on forest products. The latter brought lumber baron William Shaw to Greenville and in 1895 he built a monumental, gracious home, embellished with carved cherry, mahogany and oak paneling. Light on the stairway filters through boughs of a graceful spruce painted on the panes of the tall leaded glass window. Half a dozen fireplaces are framed with mosaic and English tile. Guests rooms and cottages are equally well appointed with stylish period furniture. Rooms come with breakfasts, but most guests stay for gourmet dinners as well: quail with herb sausage stuffing and potato pancakes. To rise early after such fare as this demands abnormal dedication even for a die-hard angler.

Libby Camps
A s h l a n d ,   M a i n e

Will the real Lake Millinocket please stand up?
That's where you'll find Libby's.

VITAL STATISTICS:

KEY SPECIES:
Brook and lake trout; landlocked salmon

Season:
May through October

Accommodations:
RUSTIC LOG CABINS AND OUTPOST CAMPS
NUMBER OF GUEST ROOMS: 7
MAXIMUM NUMBER OF GUESTS: 27

Conference Groups: Yes

Meals: American plan

Rates:
From $105 per person per day, double occupancy

Guides: $150 for 2 per day

Gratuities: $35 per day

Preferred Payment:
MasterCard, Visa

Getting There:
Fly to Presque Isle, Maine. Round-trip transfer to lodge by air is $220 per planeload, or $175 per load via van with $20 gate fee per person.

Other Activities:
Canoeing, swimming, boating, hiking, bird watching, wildlife photography.

Contact:
Matt or Ellen Libby, Libby Sporting Camps, PO Box Drawer V, Ashland, ME 04732; 207/435-8274, fax 207/435-3230, email libbycam@libbycam.sd. agate.net, website http://www.spav.com/sa /progc.html

Represented By:
Tightlines, 800/442-4359.

MATT LIBBY'S FLOATPLANE is a time machine. It picks you up in Presque Isle and flies you 75 miles and 100 years back into the Maine wilderness where Teddy Roosevelt fished for three-pound squaretails and landlocked salmon of five pounds or more. Within 20 miles of Libby's main camp on Lake Millinocket are 46 ponds, 18 lakes, 12 streams and four rivers.

Maine has at least two lakes named "Millinocket." (This is, no doubt, a carefully orchestrated strategy by the Libby clan to divert attention from their secret fishery. They even went so far as to create a town in the center part of the state by the name of Millinocket to throw anglers off the track.) Matt Libby's Millinocket is in the headwaters of the Aroostook watershed. Fishing is outstanding for lake trout (two to 12 pounds) right after ice-out, generally around May 1. The same goes for landlocked salmon of up to six pounds. Trolling streamers and spoons is the most effective tactic, though casting from shore can sometimes produce results. Brook trout, up to four pounds or so, also open in May, but the fishing doesn't really get going until June and July. Low shallow waters warm earliest and those that are higher and deeper peak last. During August, brookies school up in springholes and when you find them, fishing can be fabulous. As water cools in September, the fishery revives with the onset of the spawn.

For four generations the Libby family has run the camps. Here you'll find oil lamps, wood stoves, ice cut from the lake, seven up-to-date log guest cabins, and Ellen Libby's scrumptious cooking served in the rustic stone lodge with the open, double-sided stone fireplace. Get a copy of her cookbook. The family also maintains eight spike camps on seven other lakes for overnight trips. The lodge is Orvis-endorsed.

Libby's offers three packages: The basic plan includes room, maid service, home-cooked meals and boat, motor or canoe. You can add every-other-day fly outs or overnights at remote spike camps (you'll fly in with your own food, which you'll prepare in these fully equipped log cabins). Guides are also available. Essentially, Libby's will configure a vacation just for you. Then all you have to do is the fishing part.

Northern Outdoors
The Forks, Maine

*Trout anglers are welcome here,
but only if they'll learn to fish for smallmouths.*

VITAL STATISTICS:

KEY SPECIES:
Smallmouth bass

Season:
All year

Accommodations:
LODGE ROOMS, EFFICIENCIES AND CABINS
NUMBER OF GUEST ROOMS: 24 housing units plus camping
MAXIMUM NUMBER OF GUESTS: 300

Conference Groups: Yes

Meals: A la carte

Rates:
From $19 to $55 per person per night

Guides: $198 for 1 or 2 per day

Gratuities: $40

Preferred Payment:
Major credit cards

Getting There:
Fly to Bangor and rent a car or arrange for a representative of the lodge to pick you up for $200 round trip.

Other Activities:
Paddle tennis, whitewater rafting, swimming, boating, hiking, wildlife photography, rock climbing, leadership development courses.

Contact:
**Chris Russell
Northern Outdoors,
PO Box 100, The Forks,
ME 04985; 800/765-
7238, fax 207/663-2244,
email rafting@northern
outdoors.com, website
http://www.northern
outdoors.com**

I N SOME PARTS OF MAINE, *Micropterus dolomieui* gets top billing as the freshwater species of choice. How come? With their tailwalking and deep runs, smallmouth bass bring light tackle fans constant action. And smallmouths thrive in the state's lakes and rollicking rivers. Both facts aren't lost on outfitter Wayne Hockmeyer, who with his wife, Suzie, created Northern Outdoors and its comfortable resort at The Forks about 50 miles north of Waterville on Route 201.

Northern Outdoors offers whitewater and wilderness adventures. In addition, primarily because Hockmeyer is an angler (he invented the Banjo Minnow lure), the outfitter runs fishing trips for smallmouths only. "We literally turn away trout fishermen," he says. "The trout fishing isn't that good anymore, and I don't want them to be disappointed." In the watersheds Hockmeyer fishes—the Kennebec, Penobscot and Androscoggin—everyone can be successful on smallmouths. The key is knowing the water. Bass in the two- to three-pound range are common, and four-pounders frequent enough not to be too surprising.

As you would suspect for a master Maine guide, Hockmeyer knows the area and he guides clients on a number of tributaries to larger and well-known streams, although the drive to the best water may be as long as 50 miles. Strictly catch-and-release, protecting the resource is his first concern. Second comes the success of his guests. They fish from bassboats on larger waters and float tubes or rafts where lakes are small and inaccessible. Small streams are waded. June is the best month, but smallies of size and quantity can be found into the fall. Spinning or fly tackle is preferred. Hockmeyer is a topwater fan and likes to fish the minnow of his own creation ("a soft plastic jerkbait that swims"). Other effective lures include small Slugos, Rapalas and stickbaits. Northern Outdoors also offers a two-and-a-half-day flyfishing school.

The Forks Resort Center is a full-service recreation spot, complete with platform tennis, swimming pool, lounges and bars. It offers a variety of accommodations, from modern lodge rooms with two double beds and a bunk bed, to cabins for groups or families with separate bedrooms, living room, dining area and full kitchen. Or you can rough it in gas-lit cabins, cabin tents and campsites. All accommodations have private baths.

Red River Camps
Portage, Maine

VITAL STATISTICS:

KEY SPECIES:
Blueback and brook trout; landlocked salmon

Season:
May through October
Accommodations:
RUSTIC AND HISTORIC LOG CABINS
NUMBER OF GUEST ROOMS: 9
MAXIMUM NUMBER OF GUESTS: 41
Conference Groups: Yes
Meals: American plan or housekeeping
Rates:
From $35 per person house-keeping; $80 American plan
Guides: $100 for up to 4 anglers per day
Gratuities: Client's discretion
Preferred Payment:
Cash or check
Getting There:
Presque Isle is the closest air-port. Rent a car, or for an additional fee, the camp van will come and get you.
Other Activities:
Canoeing, swimming, boating, hiking, bird watching, wildlife photography.

Contact:
Mike or Rhonda Brophy Red River Camps, PO Box 320, Portage, ME 04768; 207/435-6000 (summer); 207/528-2259 (winter).

Marooned when glaciers left the country, rare blueback trout are still found in Red River's ponds.

FOR NEARLY A CENTURY, there's been a camp where the Red River flows out of Pushineer Pond. Of local log, the camp has grown to 17 buildings. One, a single cottage on a small island, can be used as a honeymoon suite, family getaway or just a place to hide out. The only way to reach this cabin under venerable pines, with its big stone fireplace, large living room and master bedroom with modern bath and kitchenette, is by canoe. You'll ground the canoe on the stony beach, climb the knoll to the cabin and bask in the solitude. In the morning, you'll rig your flyrod, slip down the hill, launch the canoe and work nymphs or streamers for brook trout.

Red River Camps fishes some 15 lakes and ponds ranging in size from 12 to 300 acres. Nine of the ponds are restricted to flyfishing only; four permit trolling with spinners; one is artificials only, and one, Togue Pond, allows use of bait. Brook trout, or "speckled trout" in local lingo, are the primary quarry here. Fishing for them is best in late June and July. When air temperatures climb into the 90s and the surface temperature of the water reaches 70°F or so, brookies hug bottom. At this time, successful anglers use high-density sinking lines (weighted nymphs and split-shot on leaders may be illegal—check the regs) and relatively short, stout leaders to get streamers and big nymphs down to springholes. The mouths of feeder creeks can also produce. Brook trout come back up to feed in September as the water cools.

Of special interest here is the blueback trout (*Savelinus oquassa*), another member of the char family that was once quite common in Maine waters and is now all but extinct. They seem to be thriving in a few of the lakes near Red River Camps. The most likely time to catch them is just after ice-out and again in late September, when landlocked salmon are hitting as well. You'll find both species up to 22 inches or so. Guides are available but not required. Fly outs to remote lakes can also be arranged.

Fishing here is via canoe or boat. Bring your own or rent the lodge's. Use of motors is restricted on some of the ponds. In addition to the island camp, guests stay in nine other hand-hewn log cabins of varying size. All feature gas lights, wood stoves and private baths. Electricity is provided for three hours in the morning and three hours in the late evening (bring a flashlight). Home-baked beans, chicken, turkey, roast beef and ham are centerpieces of family-style dinners. Anglers are sent out with generous packed lunches or fixings for shore dinners.

The Pines

G r a n d   L a k e   S t r e a m ,   M a i n e

VITAL STATISTICS:

KEY SPECIES:
Smallmouth bass; lake trout

Season:
May through October

Accommodations:
FRAME LODGE WITH SURROUNDING CABINS
NUMBER OF GUEST ROOMS: 7 cabins, 3 lodge rooms
MAXIMUM NUMBER OF GUESTS: 25

Conference Groups: No
Meals: American plan
Rates:
$60 per person per day, single or double occupancy
Guides: $125 for 2 per day
Gratuities: Client's discretion
Preferred Payment:
Cash or check
Getting There:
Drive tote roads from Grand Lake Stream or drive south from Springfield on Rt. 6.
Other Activities:
Hiking, swimming, boating, bird watching, wildlife photography.

Contact:
**Steve or Nancy Norris
The Pines, PO Box 158,
Grand Lake Stream, ME
04637; 207/825-4431
(winter); 207/796-5006
(summer).**

Stay at a serene old camp in Maine's deep woods, on a lake where salmon and smallmouth abound.

EVER POPULAR WITH ANGLERS, some of Maine's waters can become pretty crowded. But not Lake Sysladobsis, 12 miles west of the village of Grand Lake Stream. On eight-acre Norway Point, a peninsula that juts into the lake, Steve and Nancy Norris operate a lodge that's been known forever, simply, as The Pines. From the upper deck of the double porch on this 1880s vintage frame lodge, you can see smallmouths rising across the lake; and at night, you'll hear the echoes of loons calling from somewhere out in the darkness. As soon as you arrive, stow your watch in your bags. Let the sun tell you the time until Nancy rings the farm bell, calling you to dinner at 6:00 p.m.

Roughly seven miles long and a mile or so wide, Sysladobsis fishes best from ice-out (about May 1) through June, when the bass leave their beds. One trolls for land-locked salmon with flies or hardware early. Most fish run two to three pounds, with some larger ones likely. Smallmouth action picks up again when waters warm in late June, with fish typically running a pound or two. They are plentiful, though; 30-fish days are not at all unusual. And among the bunch will be one or two in the three-pound-plus category. Crankbaits, spinners, spinnerbaits and topwater plugs all work, as do flyrod poppers, streamers and Woolly Buggers.

In addition to fishing local ponds and flowages for brook trout, flyfishermen will enjoy a trip over to Grand Lake Stream, where three miles of flyfishing-only water runs from West Grand Lake to Big Lake. Landlocked salmon, running up to 20 inches in length, readily take streamers and, on occasion, dries. The best fishing is in the first two weeks of October, when these Maine woods burn bright with chromium yellows, russet and red.

Since the days of Calvin Coolidge and Andrew Carnegie, families have been coming to The Pines. They find a serenity, as if transported to an earlier generation when life's complexities were focused on subsistence: filling the woodbox by the stove, preparing meals, trimming the lamps in the growing dusk. If that sounds attractive, rent one of The Pines' two island housekeeping cabins. Comfortable as only a split log cabin can be, these are the real McCoys: Plumbing is "out back." You'll bring your own provisions and use your own or rent a boat and motor from the lodge. Here you're on your own schedule, but if you get lazy and would rather not cook dinner, just boat over to the lodge when you hear the dinner bell. At the lodge, guests stay in modernized versions of the lake cabins with private lavatories but a shared shower house or in three rooms (shared bath) upstairs.

Weatherby's

Grand Lake Stream, Maine

*Generations of anglers have been coming back
to this Maine lodge for its fine fishing and good food.*

**VITAL
STATISTICS:**

KEY SPECIES:
Brook trout; landlocked
salmon; smallmouth
bass; pickerel

Season:
April through mid-October
Accommodations:
INDIVIDUAL CABINS
NUMBER OF GUEST ROOMS: 5
MAXIMUM NUMBER OF GUESTS: 45
(2 handicapped accessible)
Conference Groups: No
Meals: Modified American
plan
Rates:
From $85 per person per day,
double occupancy
Guides: $125 for 2 for a
full day
Gratuities: 12%
Preferred Payment:
MasterCard, Visa
Getting There:
Fly to Bangor and rent a car,
take Rt. 9 to US 1 near the
Canadian border, then go north
through Princeton to the turnoff
to Grand Lake Stream.
Other Activities:
Tennis, swimming, boating, hik-
ing, bird watching, antiquing,
biking.

Contact:
**Charlene Sassi
Weatherby's, RR 1, Box
2272, Kingfield, ME
04947; 207/237-2911
(winter); Box 69, Grand
Lake Stream, ME 04637;
207/796-5558 (sum-
mer).**

THE TOWN IS TINY, a village really, clustered at the mouth of the rapid little river draining West Grand Lake into Big Lake. Landlocked salmon run in the river that flows past the lodge. Early in the season—10 days after ice-out on the lakes in late April—the fishing is superlative. Two to five hookups per evening are not unheard of. If river fishing doesn't suit your style, troll the lakes with spoons or flies. The gentle purr of an outboard-powered canoe will lull you into a bit of a stupor until your rod tip suddenly points at the water and your drag wakes up and sings.

Later in spring, as sun warms the shallows, smallmouth bass feed lustily before going onto their beds to spawn. Flies or lures cast toward the rocky shore can bring fierce strikes. Bass run between one and four pounds. Ultralight and flytackle are the order of the day here. Brook trout also strike readily at this time of year. Fish for them in the many brooks and lakes in May and June. Spinners and small plugs will work for ultralight anglers, while streamers, bead-head nymphs and attractors will do the job for flyfishermen. In midsummer, the fishing slows as waters warm and fish go deep. Try casting a popper along bouldery shores at dusk, however, and you'll be surprised at the great topwater action you can have with pickerel. In mid to late August, as the sun angle declines and nights cool, the fishing picks up again. September brings some of the best salmon and smallmouth action. Most anglers fish with guides (not only for their expertise, but for their stories as well) either in canoes or wading in the rivers.

For more than 20 years, Ken and Charlene Sassi have owned Weatherby's, a lodge that traces its ancestry back to the turn of the century. This is everything you'd expect a Down East resort to be. A long front porch, some of it open and other parts screened and glassed, wraps three sides of the white clapboard inn. Paneled in pine with hooked rugs on hardwood floors and a mounted salmon above the mantle, graced by a pair of oil lamps over the fireplace, this is a fish camp at its finest. Guests stay in cabins (private baths) of similar decor that are scattered under the trees around the main lodge. The cabins have screened porches and deep Adirondack chairs, meant for lazing away the afternoon before dinner of lobster, lamb or turkey, followed by the evening hatch.

Wheaton's Lodge and Camps
Forest City, Maine

Here you'll get into some of the best smallmouth and salmon fishing in the state.

"NOBODY FISHES FOR THEM 'round here" was the word on smallmouth bass in northern Maine 20 years ago. Today smallmouths have come into their own and, along with landlocked salmon and brookies, are the favorite quarry of Down East freshwater anglers. Isolated and lightly fished, Maine may have more top-notch smallmouth water than any state. Twenty-five-mile-long East Grand Lake, along the New Brunswick border, is one of the best. At the east end you'll find Wheaton's Lodge, with its 10 rustic cottages scattered under the pines.

"We offer fishin', not wishin'," says owner Dale Wheaton. He and his wife, Jana, have been in the business for 25 years, and run one of the finest outfits in the state.

Guests stay in quaint cottages scattered in a grove of pines along Grand Lake. Each has a screened porch and private bath. Dining is American plan, but guests order from menus and the food is scrumptious. Reservations need to be made early in the year because Wheaton's fills up fast.

Open from ice-out in May through September, Wheaton's offers excellent smallmouth action from June through August. The bass will attack plugs, poppers, small spinners, streamers and nymphs in the shallows early in the season. Later, fish for them at dusk and dawn with crankbaits off points, or down deep with bait. Then, when the first chill of fall spices the air, the bronzebacks go on a feeding binge. Each season, Wheaton's guests catch and release 20 smallies more than four pounds. In its beginning, salmon season coincides with smallmouth, and you have to choose between the two. Landlocks are caught trolling. Early in the season they hit spoons and flies near the surface, but as the water warms, they too go deep. For fun, tie a bit of ultrathin wire leader to your ultralight or fly leader and cast small spinnerbaits or streamers for pickerel. Take your own boat, rent a boat or hire a guide and his canoe for $120 per day for two. That's a deal.

VITAL STATISTICS:

KEY SPECIES:
Landlocked salmon; smallmouth bass; pickerel

Season:
May through September

Accommodations:
CABINS WITH SCREENED PORCHES
NUMBER OF GUEST ROOMS: 10
MAXIMUM NUMBER OF GUESTS: 30

Conference Groups: Yes

Meals: American plan

Rates:
$75 per person per day, single occupancy (minimum 3-day stay)

Guides: $120 for 2 per day

Gratuities: 15%

Preferred Payment:
Cash or check

Getting There:
Fly to Bangor and rent a car. The camp is 2 hours north.

Other Activities:
Canoeing, swimming, boating, hiking, bird watching, antiquing, biking, wildlife photography.

Contact:
Jana Wheaton
Wheaton's Lodge and Camps, HC81, Box 120, Forest City, ME 04413; 207/448-7723 (summer); 207/843-5732 (winter).

The Williamsville Inn

W e s t   S t o c k b r i d g e ,   M a s s a c h u s e t t s

The Williams River, across from the Williamsville Inn, is one of Massachusetts' best-kept trout fishing secrets.

VITAL STATISTICS:

KEY SPECIES:
Brook, brown and rainbow trout

Season:
All year

Accommodations:
COLONIAL INN
NUMBER OF GUEST ROOMS: 6
MAXIMUM NUMBER OF GUESTS: 37

Conference Groups: Yes

Meals: Breakfast included, dinner available

Rates:
From $105 for 2 per day

Guides: $200 per day

Gratuities: Client's discretion

Preferred Payment:
American Express, MasterCard, Visa

Getting There:
Nearest commercial airports are in Albany, New York and Hartford, Connecticut. Best bet is to drive. You'll want a car to poke around in the Berkshires.

Other Activities:
Tennis, swimming, hiking, symphony, theater.

Contact:
**Govane Lohbauer
The Williamsville Inn, Rt. 41, West Stockbridge, MA 01266; 413/274-6118, fax 413/274-3539.**

THE WILLIAMSVILLE INN has something of a tradition of serving anglers in the spring. "My father was an avid flyfisherman," says Govane Lohbauer, general manager of the inn. "He fished all over the country. The Williams and the Green were two of his favorite trout streams in the 1970s."

The Williams is a secret river, overshadowed by the Housatonic a few miles to the east. Flowing out of Shaker Mill Pond north of West Stockbridge, the Williams runs under the Mass Pike, breaks to the west and then turns south, paralleling, but hidden from the Great Barrington Road. It winds through a narrow valley until crossed by the Great Barrington Road just north of the Cobb Road intersection. After passing through a small pond, the Williams plays tag with the road until it eventually enters the Housatonic east of Van Deusenville. Public access is limited, the best being a path across the road from The Williamsville Inn.

Here the river is about 25 feet wide. Its bottom is gravel and in late summer and fall it can be quite shallow. Some of its pools, however, are 10 feet deep and provide holding areas for trout. While boulders create some pocket water, in the main the Williams is slow and steady. Wading is the way to fish it. Rick Moon (413/528-4666), who guides and operates an outdoor sports store in Great Barrington, recommends an Elk-Hair Caddis with a green body on a No. 14 or 16 hook. Browns up to 22 inches, small brook trout and a few rainbows inhabit the river, as do rock bass and carp. Because of pollution problems in the past, the Williams has been a kind of self-maintained catch-and-release fishery. In the early 1990s a new sewage treatment plant went on line in West Stockbridge, and water quality in the Williams is now suitable for swimming and fishing.

As one would expect, here in the Berkshires the Williamsville Inn is thoroughly colonial. Prior to the signing of the Declaration of Independence, Christopher French began purchasing parcels between the Williams River and Tom Ball Mountain to the west. After the Revolutionary War, he built the house that in 1952 became the Williamsville Inn. Wing chairs sit on wide, polished pine board floors in front of the fireplace in the parlor. The restaurant, recommended by *Bon Appetit*, serves scrumptious breakfasts and dinners that verge on gourmet.

Nereledge Inn
North Conway, New Hampshire

VITAL STATISTICS:

KEY SPECIES:
Brook, brown and rainbow trout

Season:
All year

Accommodations:
WHITE FRAME COUNTRY COLONIAL
NUMBER OF GUEST ROOMS: 11
MAXIMUM NUMBER OF GUESTS: 25

Conference Groups: Yes

Meals: Bed and breakfast

Rates:
From $59 for 2

Guides: From $175 per day

Gratuities: $25

Preferred Payment:
Major credit cards

Getting There:
Drive from Boston or Portland.

Other Activities:
Golf, canoeing, whitewater rafting, swimming, hiking, climbing, bird watching, antiquing, biking, wildlife photography, skiing.

Contact:
Valerie or Dave Halpin
Nereledge Inn, River Rd., PO Box 547, North Conway, NH 03860; 603/356-2831, fax 603/356-7085, website http://www.nettx.com/ nereledge.html

Catch colorful native brook trout in Presidential streams of the North Country.

STREAMS IN THE White Mountains have always held a fascination. The water in many of them is so clear that you can see into their depths, and pick out the trout whose backs take on the pale gray or tan of the granite boulder bottoms. Streams like this, which flow down unchecked from the cirques and tarns of the Presidential Range, are crystalline. Creeks from beaver flowages are another matter. They originate in tannin lakes with deep-brown beds. Native brook trout taken from these waters have midnight-black backs, scores of red spots haloed in faint blue and flanks that grade from dark blue to orange to white. Orange fins are piped in white and blue. These are the wildflowers of troutdom.

Sadly, acid rain continues to take its toll on brook trout in high mountain ponds. But Jon Howe of North Country Angler in North Conway (603/356-6000) knows about Sawyer and Mountain ponds, and he will take you to them to fish. You may fish them in May when the swamp maples are in flower or in early fall when the same maples change color and begin to blush red. He will also take you to the Saco and Ellis rivers, big freestone streams that drain the Presidentials, where brookies, browns and rainbows take Red Quills, caddis and stoneflies. Fish range in the eight- to 12-inch class, but occasionally a 20-incher succumbs to fly or spinner. With his MacKenzie driftboat, a welcome addition to these waters, Howe will float you down the Androscoggin for browns, brookies, landlocked salmon and rainbows, or run you over to the Connecticut for a drift from West Stewardstown to Colebrook, a great brook trout tailwater.

The place to stay while you're doing all this is Nereledge Inn, a traditional bed and breakfast, white framed with gaily striped awnings, on the outskirts of North Conway, New Hampshire's biggest ski and mountain tourism resort town. Built in 1787, the inn exudes traditional country charm. Cane-bottom rockers and other period pieces accent light and airy guest rooms. Flowered, eiderdown quilts grace spindle beds. You'll find a score of outstanding restaurants in town. And the following morning, in the cozy and sunny breakfast room, you'll have your choice of eggs, pancakes or French toast, topped off with warm apple pie with vanilla ice cream. Think you could get away with that at home?

Tall Timber Lodge

Pittsburg, New Hampshire

VITAL STATISTICS:

KEY SPECIES:
Landlocked salmon; brown and brook trout; smallmouths

Season:
All year

Accommodations:
RUSTIC LODGE WITH CABINS
NUMBER OF GUEST ROOMS: 25
MAXIMUM NUMBER OF GUESTS: 65

Conference Groups: Yes

Meals: Breakfast and dinner included

Rates:
From $63 per person per day, single occupancy

Guides: From $125 per day

Gratuities: $20 per day

Preferred Payment:
MasterCard, Visa

Getting There:
Drive from Manchester, New Hampshire or Boston, Massachusettts.

Other Activities:
Golf, tennis, canoeing, boating, hiking, bird watching, biking, wildlife photography and skiing.

Contact:
**Cindy Sullivan
Tall Timber Lodge, 231 Beach Rd., Pittsburg, NH 03592; 800/835-6343, fax 603/538-8562, website http://www.spav. com/progc/talltimber/**

Fish for wild landlocked salmon and trout in the North Country.

YOU'LL FIND THE TALL TIMBER about as far north as you can go and still be in New Hampshire. Located on Back Lake, the lodge is at the threshold of the upper Connecticut River watershed. Lakes are numerous, ponds are plentiful, streams abound and the main river provides a range of angling opportunities.

Troll for landlocked salmon and lake trout as soon after ice-out as you can. When water warms in June and July, caddis, mayfly and stonefly hatches provide good dry fly fishing for browns and brookies. In the dog days of August, dredging nymphs through spring holes will entice big browns. And when the maples reach their glorious reds and yellows in late September, that's the time for equally colorful brookies and browns on the spawn. Salmon return to the rivers then, and the wise angler who slips a 20-gauge into his duffel can unlimber it on partridge and woodcock.

Anglers who prefer spinning tackle can have a field day here, as ultralight gear is ideal for the rivers and streams. Use small spinners and spoons. In the lakes, the smallmouths hit minnow and crayfish imitations. Troll spoons with heavier spinning gear just after ice-out, and you'll get solid hits from landlocked salmon and lake trout.

The Tall Timber has been serving anglers for 50 years. Local guides are available for guests who want them, and the lodge's staff—plus angling guests themselves—provide helpful hints on where to go and what to use. Licenses, tackle and flies are available at the lodge.

Seventeen cabins with two to five bedrooms line the lake near the main lodge. All feature private baths and porches. The main lodge itself includes eight guest rooms, two with private baths. Owners Cindy Sullivan and Judith Caron take their food seriously. You'll find pot roast, steak and pork on the menu with homemade soups, breads and enticing desserts. It isn't a place to lose weight, but vegetarian diets are available on request.

Getting to the Tall Timber requires a drive. Manchester, New Hampshire is the closest major airport, though fares may be lower if you fly into Boston, an additional hour's drive south. Rent a car, drive up Interstate 93 through Franconia Notch, and take Route 3 north. No matter when you do it, the ride is one of the prettiest in the East, so allow yourself a day to enjoy it.

The Balsams

Dixville Notch, New Hampshire

Politics and fish are on the menu at this White Mountain resort.

VITAL STATISTICS:

KEY SPECIES:
Brook, rainbow and brown trout; smallmouth bass

Season:
Late May through October

Accommodations:
GRAND VINTAGE RESORT HOTEL
NUMBER OF GUEST ROOMS: 212
MAXIMUM NUMBER OF GUESTS: 400

Conference Groups: Yes

Meals: American plan

Rates:
From $85 per person per night, double occupancy

Guides: From $200 for 2 per day

Gratuities: Client's discretion

Preferred Payment:
Major credit cards

Getting There:
It's a lovely drive from Portland, Maine or Boston, Massachusetts.

Other Activities:
Golf, tennis, canoeing, swimming, boating, hiking, antiquing, biking, wildlife photography, skiing, children's programs.

Contact:
Jerry Owen
The Balsams, Lake Gloriette, Rt. 26, Dixville Notch, NH 03576; 603/255-3400, fax 603/255-4221, email theBALSAMS@AOL.COM, website http://www. thebalsams.com

EVERY FOUR YEARS the hamlet of Dixville Notch makes big news; it's the first precinct in the nation to close its polls and count its votes in presidential elections. This tiny town is also host to one of the world's finest hotels. Since 1866, travelers have found a warm hearth and friendly lodging in the glacial-carved notch between Dixville Peak and Sanguinary Mountain. The Balsams is one of the last great Victorian resorts (the "New Wing" was completed in 1918), and its rooms and amenities have been continually updated without sacrificing the classic vintage hotel charm.

Lake Gloriette, in front of the hotel, is stocked, but that isn't the fishing attraction. Nor are the numerous small creeks and ponds that hold native brook trout. The real action is east, down Route 26 at Errol. That's where the Androscoggin River flows out of the dam impounding Lake Umbagog. Much farther south the Androscoggin falls victim to paper plants at Berlin, but its upper end is simply an amazing fishery. The upper section from Bog Brook to the Umbagog dam (about 20 miles) is big pocket water broken by long flats, particularly those between Bragg Bay and Mollidgewock Brook. The flats are deep and hold huge browns. In the heavy water, you'll find brookies, rainbows and browns, as well as smallmouths and a few landlocked salmon. The salmon are thin because the river lacks smelt, the staple of their diet. All but the three-quarters of a mile below the dam can be fished with any tackle during the season, which runs January 1 through October 15. Guide Ken Hastings floats anglers down this stretch in his MacKenzie driftboat.

Flyfishers will enjoy the tailwater of Umbagog Dam. Though favored by kayakers, this rolling pocket and pool water holds rainbows and brook trout up to five pounds. You'll also find some browns. Best fishing in the spring begins in mid-April. Use Black Ghosts and Mickey Finns or ask Wayne Underwood at Luc Cote's store in Errol for a couple of his Picket Pins or Brown Owls. Woolly Buggers and black and brown stonefly nymphs are good, too. While the fishing is better than good all summer, Umbagog is big and shallow and warms easily. In July and August fishing is an early and late proposition. But when fall comes, the waters cool and angling becomes as glorious as the foliage. While the flyfishing-only section of the Androscoggin commands attention, not to be overlooked are trout in Clear Stream, the river followed by Route 26 on the way up to the Balsams; native brookies in the Swift Diamond River; or browns in the Connecticut River west above Colebrook.

Beaverkill Valley Inn
Lew Beach, New York

*Get away to this 19th century country inn
and fish the only open water on the upper Beaverkill.*

VITAL STATISTICS:

KEY SPECIES:
Brook and brown trout

Season:
All year

Accommodations:
COUNTRY INN
NUMBER OF GUEST ROOMS: 20
MAXIMUM NUMBER OF GUESTS: 40

Conference Groups: Yes

Meals: American plan

Rates:
From $260 for 2 per night

Guides: From $175 for 1
per day

Gratuities: Client's discretion

Preferred Payment:
American Express, MasterCard,
Visa

Getting There:
Stewart International in
Newburgh, New York has the
best commercial service. Rent a
car, take I-84 west to Rt. 17
west, to Lew Beach exit.

Other Activities:
Tennis, swimming, hiking,
bird watching, antiquing,
biking, wildlife photography,
cross-country skiing, croquet,
children's programs.

Contact:
**Darlene O'Dell
Beaverkill Valley Inn,
136 Beaverkill Rd., Lew
Beach, NY 12753;
914/439-4844, fax
914/439-3884.**

SO FULL IS THE LITERATURE of flyfishing with references to the Beaverkill, that the stream takes on mythic proportions. Spirits of Theodore Gordon, Sparse Grey Hackle and Lee Wulff haunt its pools and pocket waters. Shaded and cool in the height of summer, the upper Beaverkill supports natural propagation of browns and brookies. Fishing is delicate and precise. Today the upper Beaverkill is largely private water, but guests at the Beaverkill Valley Inn have access to a mile of it. That's reason enough to book into this 100-year-old lodge with 20 rooms of country antique decor. A short walk across the meadow puts you on the stream.

Here the Beaverkill is shallow and little more than 30 feet wide. Begin fishing the bottom of the long pool and gently work your way upstream, casting to rising trout. On the right, the pool runs hard against a rock retaining wall that shores-up county Route 54. The water is deeper, and the rocks provide cover for browns, some in excess of 16 inches. Below this pool is a sharp bend where the stream beats against big boulders as it turns into a short hole. Nymphs, particularly at dusk, can produce fish after fish. The upper reaches of the inn's mile is classic pocket water. Overhanging trees make casting challenging. A 7 1/2-foot 3-weight rod is ideal.

While much of the upper Beaverkill is tied up by fishing clubs and landowners, two sections of the river are open to public angling. The uppermost can be found near the state campground at Covered Bridge, and the lower section runs from the Sullivan/Delaware County line down to Roscoe. Pressure is heavy on both sections throughout the summer, but anglers who fish before the campground opens and in fall will find a bit of seclusion. A short drive from the inn will take you to the Willowemoc, which boasts greater public access than the upper Beaverkill, and to the East and West Branches of the Delaware. These are superb tailwater fisheries.

Several local flyshops sell patterns specific to the river, and the Catskill Fly Fishing Center and Museum in nearby Livingston Manor displays memorabilia from the legendary flytiers, the Darbees and the Dettes; an extensive collection of Lee Wulff's innovations and many exhibits depicting the angling heritage of the region. If you want to improve your fishing and casting skills, explore programs at the Wulff School of Fly Fishing (914/439-4060), just up the road from the inn. The school is run by champion flycaster and author Joan Wulff, who has introduced hundreds of women, as well as men, to the sport. Her students stay at the lodge.

Eldred Preserve

E l d r e d ,   N e w   Y o r k

Stocked ponds and preserve hunting make this an ideal site for cast-and-blast weekends.

VITAL STATISTICS:

KEY SPECIES:
Largemouth and hybrid bass; trout; catfish

Season:
All year

Accommodations:
LOG MOTEL
NUMBER OF GUEST ROOMS: 26
MAXIMUM NUMBER OF GUESTS: 55

Conference Groups: Yes

Meals: Restaurant

Rates:
Room: $85 for 2 per night. Fees are charged for fishing, hunting and sporting clays.

Guides: $150 for 2 per day

Gratuities: 15%

Preferred Payment:
Major credit cards

Getting There:
Take I-84 east from Pennsylvania, west from New York, to Port Jervis. Follow Rt. 97 north to Barryville, turn right onto Rt. 55 and go six miles.

Other Activities:
Canoeing, swimming, boating, hiking, bird watching, antiquing.

Contact:
Bonnie Robertson
Eldred Preserve, 1040 Rt. 55, Eldred, NY 12732; 914/557-8316, fax 914/557-8733, email eldred@warwick.net, website http://www. eldredpreserve.com

J UST NORTH of the Delaware River near the little town of Eldred, the Eldred Preserve offers anglers a choice of bass, trout or catfish from a series of carefully managed lakes and ponds, all surrounded by forests and fields that belie its location less than two hours from New York City. In addition, you'll find five-stand sporting clays and hunting for stocked chukar and pheasant as well as native whitetails and turkeys. Along with this is a comfortable log cabin lodge with 26 modern, motel-style rooms and a restaurant famous for its trout dinners.

The prime attraction at Eldred is a pair of bass lakes, each offering a different kind of angling. Sunrise Lake contains 75 acres of submerged weedbeds, timber and deep structure. Steges Lake is bigger, 85 acres, shallower and known for rafts of lily pads that hide good fish. A strict catch-and-release policy applies, and that's why large-mouths in the four- to six-pound class are not unusual. You'll fish from a 16-foot bass-boat powered by a bow-mounted trolling motor with a raised casting deck and swivel seats. The fee is $75 per day for the boat and two anglers.

You may also want to check out Eldred's catch-and-release trout ponds. Brown, brook, rainbow, tiger and golden trout to six pounds are more difficult to catch than you think on barbless flies. If it's a mess of fish you're wanting, switch to the catch-and-keep pond and fill your creel with one- and two-pounders. These ponds are excellent for introducing kids to fishing and catching, something that doesn't always go hand in hand. Along with the trout ponds, you'll find others set aside for catfish and hybrid striped bass in the 10-pound range. Any bait that works is legal in these waters.

Air-conditioned rooms feature private baths, phones and cable TV. On the menu at Angler's Rest Cafe are trout any way you want them: preserve-style with capers, lemon and tomatoes; almandine; baked with seasoned bread crumbs and herbs; stuffed with crab; fried in cornmeal; blackened; and char-broiled. And there's steak for those who want. In addition to your appetite and fishing tackle, bring your shotgun and shoot sporting clays. This is one place where you can do it all without busting the bank.

Huff House
R o s c o e ,   N e w   Y o r k

This resort—only three hours from Manhattan—caters to families, corporate groups and individuals interested in angling.

VITAL STATISTICS:

KEY SPECIES:
Brook, brown and rainbow trout

Season:
All year

Accommodations:
FRAME LODGE AND MOTEL ROOMS
NUMBER OF GUEST ROOMS: 45
MAXIMUM NUMBER OF GUESTS: 100

Conference Groups: Yes
Meals: Bed and breakfast or American plan

Rates:
From $105 for 2 per day, bed and breakfast; $170 for 2 per day, American plan

Guides: From $145 for 1 per day

Gratuities: $20 to $ 50

Preferred Payment:
Major credit cards

Getting There:
Fly to Binghamton or Stewart, New York, rent a car and drive to the lodge.

Other Activities:
Golf, tennis, swimming, boating, canoeing, bird watching, hiking, antiquing, biking, wildlife photography.

Contact:
Joe or Joanne Forness Huff House, 100 Lake Anawanda Rd., Roscoe, NY 12776; 800/358-5012, 607/498-4200.

HIGH UP IN THE CATSKILL MOUNTAINS is Huff House, a 188-acre resort with tennis, a nine-hole par-3 golf course, swimming pool and fine restaurant. Three ponds, one stocked with rainbows and the others with largemouths and pickerel, provide some fishing action for guests. "The kids have names for all the bass," says owner Joe Forness, laughing. This is a great place to teach kids to fish, to hold a corporate retreat or to hang your hat when you're fishing the region's famous and very well-known trout waters.

Roscoe—Trout Town USA—is six miles down the mountain. Two fine flyshops, the Beaverkill Angler and Donegal's, sit opposite each other on the town's main street. Down the block is the Little Store and, as its name suggests, it has a little bit of everything that an angler might need.

The Willowemoc flows through the southern edge of the town, meeting the Beaverkill at Junction Pool. Public easements extend from the hamlet of Willowemoc down below the campground at the covered bridge. Brookies are being replaced by browns in this section. From Livingston Manor downstream to Roscoe, the Willow is generally open to public fishing. Browns, mostly stocked but some wild, predominate. The river passes the Catskill Flyfishing Center and Museum here. Check out its flytying, casting and children's programs, all of which are excellent and inexpensive.

The upper mileage of the Beaverkill is held privately and the first public water, about a mile, begins at the Covered Bridge campground. It's heavily pressed in summer, but in early spring can yield a semblance of solitude along with browns of 12 to 16 inches. The second stretch of public water runs from Cat Hollow Road to Roscoe, about two miles. The lower Beaverkill below the Junction Pool is open to public fishing.

These rivers are the stuff of legend—Theodore Gordon tied the first "American" dry flies here—and Huff House is a convenient headquarters from which to explore the region. Of white frame, the main house is a restored Victorian farm decorated with antiques. The four guest rooms in the house and the 41 rooms in nearby motel-style accommodations provide comfort and quiet for traveling anglers. While the dinner menu is not extensive, the range of appetizers and entrees (thick grilled tuna with balsamic vinaigrette or sauteed chicken breast coated with walnuts and bread crumbs) will please any taste.

At the Beaverkill Valley Inn in Lew Beach, New York,
anglers can fish a private mile of the legendary upper Beaverkill,
home of dry fly fishing in America. — page 33.

Steelhead, lake-run browns, walleyes and
king salmon make up the bill of fare at The
Wild River Inn in Pulaski, New York. — page 40.

Hungry Trout Motor Inn

Whiteface Mountain, New York

Picture this: dinner, breakfast and a day on the only private catch-and-release section of the Ausable for less than $80!

VITAL STATISTICS:

KEY SPECIES:
Brown, rainbow and brook trout

Season:
All year

Accommodations:
Motel rooms
Number of Guest Rooms: 22
Maximum Number of Guests: 40

Conference Groups: Yes

Meals: Modified American plan

Rates:
From $79 per person per day, double occupancy

Guides: $220 per day for 2

Gratuities: $10 per angler

Preferred Payment:
Major credit cards

Getting There:
Fly to Saranac Lake, New York and rent a car; or drive following directions provided by the inn.

Other Activities:
Golf, tennis, canoeing, rafting, swimming, boating, hiking, bird watching, antiquing, biking, wildlife photography, skiing, hunting.

Contact:
Jerry Bottcher
Hungry Trout Motor Inn, Rt. 86, Whiteface Mountain, NY 12997; 518/946-2217, fax 518/946-7418, email hungrytrout@white face.net, website http://www.hungry trout.com

A FEW MILES ABOVE the ski jump towers at Lake Placid, Marcy and South Meadow brooks join to form the West Branch of the Ausable, one of the more storied trout streams in America. Its place in angling tradition is overshadowed in the East only by the legendary Beaverkill far to the south in the Catskills. From its origins to its union with the East Branch at Ausable Forks, the West Branch presents about 35 miles of good to outstanding trout water.

Deeply shaded as it runs through narrow gorges, well oxygenated by many falls (the tallest is the 100-foot-plus High Falls at Wilmington Notch State Campground) and blessed with consistent hatches and an ample population of baitfish, the West Branch maintains all the ingredients of a blue-ribbon trout stream. As it wrestles its way down from the mountains, it surges over thousands of boulders that provide excellent cover for big trout, but which make wading difficult. Felt soles are essential here, a wading staff is wise and it's best not to fish this river without a buddy within hailing distance. Though a bit of a drive from the population centers of New York State, the stream sees a good deal of fishing pressure from summer tourists. To meet the demand, it is heavily stocked. Rainbows and browns predominate, some in the four- to eight-pound range. Brook trout are available as well.

The West Branch is generally open all year (check the regulations before you fish), but regulars take more large trout in the weeks of early spring, just after ice leaves the river, and in fall, when the color of autumn scenery is at its glorious peak. Bait anglers have access to much of the river and they do well. A special trophy area is set aside for use of artificials. Early in the season brown and black stonefly patterns work well. Later in spring, try Hendricksons, Light Cahills and caddis. From mid-June to mid-July, there's a Green Drake hatch, and in the middle of summer, the usual sulphurs and tricos appear. Streamers such as the Hornburg and Woolly Bugger are also consistent performers.

Among the best sources for information about fishing on the West Branch is Jerry Bottcher, owner of the Hungry Trout Motor Inn. Bottcher is a flyfisher par excellence. Not only will you find comfortable rooms at his motor inn, with views of Whiteface Mountain, but a very good restaurant (trout, venison, salmon) and a watering hole that may well be the only one in the East that serves up fishing videos and boasts a flytying bench. If that weren't enough reason to book into the Hungry Trout, there's a mile of private catch-and-release water reserved for guests at the inn.

K & G Sportfishing Lodge

O s w e g o ,   N e w   Y o r k

Boat to first-rate salmon and trout fishing from Oswego, a tiny port on Lake Ontario.

VITAL STATISTICS:

KEY SPECIES:
Brown and lake trout; chinook salmon; steelhead

Season:
All year

Accommodations:
MODERN CABINS
NUMBER OF GUEST ROOMS: 12
MAXIMUM NUMBER OF GUESTS: 33

Conference Groups: Yes

Meals: Housekeeping or American plan

Rates:
Multiple packages from $25 per person per night, single occupancy

Guides: Included in many packages

Gratuities: 15%

Preferred Payment:
Cash or traveler's check

Getting There:
Drive up from Syracuse.

Other Activities:
Golf, antiquing.

Contact:
**Greg or Kris Gehrig
K & G Sportfishing Lodge,
94 Creamery Rd.,
Oswego, NY 13126;
800/346-6533.**

LAKE ONTARIO'S BROWNS, steelhead and salmon can be fickle, but Greg and Kris Gehrig have figured out the charter trips that put anglers on fish and get them in the boat. In addition, the Gehrigs have half a dozen cabins that provide clean and utilitarian accommodations for itinerant fisher folk. In spring and summer you'll fish the lake; in fall and winter you're on the Oswego River.

The Gehrigs' guests troll the lake from two 33-foot sportfishermen, an Egg Harbor and a Viking. Both are equipped with outriggers and downriggers. In April, as the surface warms, brown trout averaging six pounds become active near the surface. Use custom noodle rods with Garcia 6500 reels spooled with 8-pound-test line to troll stickbaits and small flutter spoons. Lake trout and steelhead fall for the same setup when they become active in May. By June the fish have moved down to 40 or 50 feet, but on still days when there's little wave action to mix temperature layers, Gehrig looks for thermobars, flows of warm water riding on the surface of the cold. When he finds them, you'll find steelhead and lots of them. If thermobars are not present, Gehrig trolls with "jingle bell" rigs on downriggers for lake trout averaging 13 pounds.

In September, focus shifts to the salmon run on the Oswego. Steelhead averaging 10 pounds and browns in the six-pound-plus range follow later in October. You'll fish from jet or driftboat, or wade, depending on your preference and river conditions. The jetboat allows anglers to cover more of the river with greater thoroughness than with other types of watercraft. And it's an incredible aid to flyfishers because it's easier to follow big fish. Fishing improves as the weather deteriorates, and an enclosed cockpit provides welcome relief from freezing rain. You can also find smallmouths and walleyes in both the river and lake.

After the trip, you'll head for your cabin. It's furnished for practicality, with two full beds in each of two bedrooms, a private bath, fully-equipped kitchen and living room. If one of your party is a passable cook, you might rustle up your own grub. If not, you may want to take advantage of the Gehrigs' novel meal plans. For $35 additional per day, you can take your pick of anything on the menu at Dahl's Diner (the place for breakfast in Oswego), and the same thing goes for dinner at the Little While, a good Italian-American Restaurant, and Admiral Woolsey's on the waterfront.

Lake Placid Lodge
Lake Placid, New York

The epitome of regional architecture, furnishing and fine cuisine, here you'll fish waters of legend.

VITAL STATISTICS:

KEY SPECIES:
Lake, rainbow, brown and brook trout

Season:
All year

Accommodations:
CLASSIC ADIRONDACK LODGE
NUMBER OF GUEST ROOMS: 38
MAXIMUM NUMBER OF GUESTS: 75

Conference Groups: Yes

Meals: Bed and breakfast, dinners prix fixe or ala carte

Rates:
From $200 for 2 per night

Guides: From $225 for 2 per day

Gratuities: Client's discretion

Preferred Payment:
Major credit cards

Getting There:
Off Rt. 86 just west of Lake Placid.

Other Activities:
Golf, tennis, canoeing, swimming, hiking, boating, bird watching, antiquing, biking, wildlife photography, skiing.

Contact:
Charlie Levitz
Lake Placid Lodge, PO Box 550, Lake Placid, NY 12946; 518/523-2700, fax 518/523-1124, website http://www.lplodge. com

THE SIGNATURE of the Adirondack style is the use of bent twigs and branches in furniture and embellishments. One look at the railing on the balcony of this lodge tells you where you are in space and in time: Thin limbs, bent and curved, form the letters "Lake Placid Lodge" in the railing of the balcony over the front porch. The Shroeder family built this as their summer camp in 1882. In the 1940s it became Lake Placid Manor, and in 1993 it was purchased and thoroughly renovated in the Adirondack tradition by David and Christine Garrett.

Carved by glaciers and filled by icy streams running down the folds of the mountains, Lake Placid has brook, lake and rainbow trout, smallmouth bass and northern pike. As with all northern waters, the lake's best fishing for lake trout occurs just after ice goes out, usually in late April or early May. Trolling is the most productive tactic. In 1986 the state record laker of 34 pounds 8 ounces was taken with a deeply trolled spoon. Brook trout also fish best just after ice-out, with small spoons, spinners, streamers and big nymphs all producing. Rainbows seem to come to life later in the year when the water temperature exceeds 55°F. Smallmouths in the two- to three-pound range respond to crankbaits cast shoreward in June. But don't be surprised if a four- or five-pounder nails your plug. And, of course, not to be overlooked is the nearby Ausable River with its mix of rainbows and browns. Don Jones at Jones Outfitters, Ltd. (518/523-3468), a flyfishing shop in Lake Placid, reports that the Ausable fishes well with nymphs and big streamers early in the season. By late June, fishing pressure on the river has tapered off but angling is still good particularly for browns. Blue-Winged Olive hatches in September and early October can trigger the best dry fly fishing of the year. Lake Placid Lodge recommends guides depending on the angling interests of each guest.

Stone and wood and richly woven fabrics are tastefully orchestrated in the traditional northwoods decor of Lake Placid Lodge. Overstuffed chairs sit on oriental rugs over gleaming wooden floors before floor-to-ceiling hearths of round river rock. Snowshoes and moose heads and old wicker creels adorn mantles and walls of spruce and pine. Guest rooms, whether in the lodge or nearby log cabins, are spacious, private, appointed with Adirondack antiques and frequently have private fireplaces. Dining is strictly gourmet: Try the grilled Appalachian quail on rosemary branches with shittake fritters and blackberry vinaigrette, and follow it with stone roasted arctic char and fennel hush puppies. Bon appetit.

The Wild River Inn

Pulaski, New York

VITAL STATISTICS:

KEY SPECIES:
Steelhead; king salmon; brown trout; walleyes; smallmouth bass

Season:
All year

Accommodations:
HOUSEKEEPING EFFICIENCIES
NUMBER OF GUEST ROOMS: 5
MAXIMUM NUMBER OF GUESTS: 20

Conference Groups: Yes

Meals: Cook for yourself or eat in nearby restaurants

Rates:
From $45 for 2 per night

Guides: Wading: $220; driftboat: $240 for 2 anglers

Gratuities: $30 to $50 per day

Preferred Payment:
Discover, MasterCard, Visa

Getting There:
Fly to Syracuse, rent a car and drive north on I-81 to Pulaski.

Other Activities:
Icefishing, whitewater rafting, canoeing, wildlife photography, biking, hunting.

Contact:
Todd or Ann Marie Sheltra
The Wild River Inn, 7743 State Rt. 3, Pulaski, NY 13142; 315/298-4195, fax 315/298-4459, email wildriverinn@juno.com

Fish with a Western guide for Eastern steelhead, king salmon, brown trout and walleyes.

HOW DOES IT FEEL to be chest deep in the freezing black water of New York's Salmon River when there's three feet of snow on the ground? Great, if you've got your arms wrapped around a 16-pound steelhead. No doubt about it, the adrenal rush of a strike and hookup instantly thaws frigid fingers and toes, even if the landscape is fading fast under a torrential snow squall blown in from Lake Ontario.

The worse the weather, the better the fishing, at least for steelhead in tributaries to Lake Ontario. With the first snow flurries, bright fish start spawning migrations in October. The run reaches full force in November and spawning begins in December, reaching its zenith near Christmas. The Salmon is not the only river used by these lake-run steelies, but because of discharges from the hydroelectric dam impounding the Salmon River Reservoir, the river never clogs with ice and snow nor does it freeze. Wading, however, is less than fun—even if steelhead are hammering your egg sacks or trashing your lure. The current is swift, river rocks slippery and the prospect of a fall always at hand.

The alternative is to float the river with a knowledgeable guide like Todd Sheltra who, with wife Ann Marie, owns and operates The Wild River Inn, a western-style lodge one mile north of the Salmon River near Pulaski. Holding a pace slightly slower than the river, Sheltra drifts clients over likely water. Hookups are frequent enough to keep you on your toes, and fish run between 10 and 20 pounds. The best angling is in November and December and in the more hospitable months of April and May. In addition, Sheltra trolls Lake Ontario for king salmon up to 35 pounds from July through September and walleyes in May and June. He also guides for brown trout (up to 15 pounds) from April through November; smallmouths (two to three pounds) from June to September; and river-run salmon (up to 35 pounds) from late September to early November.

Lured east by the river and its fishing, the Sheltras came to Pulaski from Colorado a decade ago. You'll notice their western heritage—elk antlers over the front door—but it's not overplayed. The recreation room of the lodge is unabashedly Early American, with some antiques and other pieces of period furniture. Guest rooms are really efficiencies containing stove, refrigerator and sink, as well as private baths. You can whip up your own meals or eat in any of a number of restaurants in downtown Pulaski.

Thousand Islands Inn

Clayton, New York

Stay at an old-time inn that offers good fishing off the front porch, plus is home of the famous salad dressing.

VITAL STATISTICS:

KEY SPECIES:
Largemouth and small-mouth bass; northern pike; muskellunge; walleyes

Season:
May through November

Accommodations:
SMALL RESORT HOTEL
NUMBER OF GUEST ROOMS: 14
MAXIMUM NUMBER OF GUESTS: 25

Conference Groups: Yes

Meals: Full service restaurant

Rates:
Multiple packages from $43.50 per person per day, double occupancy

Guides: $300 for 2 for a full day

Gratuities: Included in package price

Preferred Payment:
Cash, check, credit card

Getting There:
Syracuse, 85 miles to the south, is the closest city with a major airport.

Other Activities:
Golf, tennis, canoeing, swimming, boating, hiking, bird watching, antiquing, biking, wildlife photography.

Contact:
Allen or Susan Benas Thousand Islands Inn, 335 Riverside Dr., PO Box 69, Clayton, NY 13624-0069; 800/544-4241, email tiinn@ 1000islands.com, website http://www. 1000islands.com/inn

WHERE LAKE ONTARIO NARROWS into the St. Lawrence River, half a million acres of rock bars and shoals, headlands, drop-offs, deep channels, grassy shallows and islands by the score provide largemouth and smallmouth action in such profusion from June through October that no angler can ever know it all. Add to that northern pike from early May through November; walleyes from mid-August through October; and muskies in mid-June through December, and you've got a full plate.

Tackle is your choice. Fly and spinfishers will find bass and pike in the shallows early in their seasons. Everything goes deep during summer with the exception of small-mouths on the shoals after dark. Best fishing for walleyes and muskies is in fall, and that means jigging and trolling with fairly stout gear. The St. Lawrence fishery is so varied that you'll need an expert to help you sort it out.

Coming as close as anyone is Allen Benas, who with wife, Susan, owns the Thousand Islands Inn. Since 1978 he's guided anglers for bass and pike on the St. Lawrence. Among the better ways to get to know the water is to book a trip with Benas on his "office," a custom headboat designed to carry a maximum of 15 anglers to drift-fish for walleyes. Benas' office also carries flyrodders in search of bass and northern pike. Numerous other fishing packages are available, including fall hunts for trophy muskies. Many trips include a shore lunch: appetizer, salad, corn on the cob, boiled potatoes, fresh fish and dessert. The nap afterwards is optional.

Dating from 1897, the inn is one of the few remaining small resort hotels that were once prolific in towns along the St. Lawrence. To celebrate its centennial, the Benases have redone its 14 rooms with private baths in turn-of-the-century country style. When dining in the restaurant, check out the venison, quail and walleye entrees. And, in case you didn't know it, the salad dressing of the same name was invented right here. Anglers with their own boats can launch and dock them across the street from the inn.

West Branch Angler

D e p o s i t ,   N e w   Y o r k

Among the finest Eastern tailwaters, the West Branch flows a stone's throw from your cabin door.

VITAL STATISTICS:

KEY SPECIES:
Brown and rainbow trout

Season:
All year

Accommodations:
LODGE, GUEST HOUSE AND HOUSE-KEEPING CABINS
NUMBER OF GUEST ROOMS/GUESTS:
WILD RAINBOW: 6/14
WEST BRANCH: 23/75

Conference Groups: Yes

Meals:
WILD RAINBOW: Custom catered or eat out
WEST BRANCH: Cook for yourself or eat out

Rates:
WILD RAINBOW: $85 for a minimum of 8 guests per night
WEST BRANCH: From $70 per night

Guides: $275 for 2 per day

Gratuities: $20 per day

Preferred Payment:
MasterCard

Getting There:
Drive from New York City or Binghamton, New York.

Other Activities:
Canoeing, boating, hiking, bird watching, biking, wildlife photography.

Contact:
Harry Batschehet
West Branch Angler, 150 Faulkner Rd., Deposit, NY 13754; 607/467-5525.

ALONG WITH THE UPPER SECTION of the East Branch, the West Branch of the Delaware River in New York and, downstream, along the Pennsylvania-New York border must rank among the finest tailwater fisheries in the East. Once ravaged by pollution, flooding and low warm summer flows, the upper Delaware and its branches are now stable, coldwater rivers, thanks to dams at Cannonsville (1968) on the West Branch and Pepacton (1955) on the East. These impoundments provide water for New York City, which in turn operates the reservoirs to maintain the quality of the fishery.

The West Branch runs from Stilesville 16 miles downstream to Hancock, where it joins the East Branch to form the main stem of the Delaware. Just downstream from Hale Eddy, the West Branch becomes the border between New York and Pennsylvania. New York Route 17 follows the course of the river closely and anglers use pull-offs for parking. Easy access can mean crowds, but it's no worse than popular streams in the West. Cobbles and gravel make up the bottom, providing good spawning grounds as well as easy wading. Browns up to 20 inches predominate in the upper section of the West Branch above Hale Eddy, and rainbows of the same size hang out below. Flyfishing and spinfishing are permitted. The section from Hale Eddy south is open year-round; but upstream to the dam, the river is only fished from April 1 through September 30. Hatches are prolific throughout the season. Start with Hendricksons in April, then fish caddis, stones and sulphurs. Blue-Winged Olives come off throughout the year.

Harry Batschehet operates two lodges on the Upper Delaware: West Branch Angler and Sportsman's Resort at Hales Eddy; and Wild Rainbow Lodge a couple miles below Hancock. Wild Rainbow, which is ideal for a group of eight to 10 anglers, is a log-sided house with four bedrooms and a broad deck on a low terrace just above the river. Nearby is an intimate cabin. Inside, the house and cabin are stylishly modern. Guest rooms have private baths. Meals will be prepared if desired or they may be eaten in town. At West Branch Angler, guests stay in 18 riverfront log housekeeping cabins or in the lodge. All rooms have private baths. Meals are served a la carte in the restaurant (a new one is under construction) at the resort. At the resort is a fully stocked fly-shop, and guides are available for wade or float trips; one of the best bets is an overnight float to a tent camp on an island in the main river, where big trout take flies at night. The Beaverkill and Willowemoc are less than an hour away.

Allenberry Inn

B o i l i n g   S p r i n g s ,   P e n n s y l v a n i a

Match the hatch with a play at this country inn and Equity theater on the Yellow Breeches.

VITAL STATISTICS:

KEY SPECIES:
Brown and rainbow trout

Season:
All year

Accommodations:
COUNTRY INN AND CABINS
NUMBER OF GUEST ROOMS: 64
MAXIMUM NUMBER OF GUESTS: 128

Conference Groups: Yes
Meals: Various plans
Rates:
From $84 for 2 per night
Guides: $200 for up to 2 per day
Gratuities: Client's discretion
Preferred Payment:
Major credit cards
Getting There:
Harrisburg is the closest airport. Rent a car there and drive. From I-81 at Carlisle, follow signs to Boiling Springs.
Other Activities:
Tennis, swimming, hiking, antiquing.

Contact:
Jere Heinze
Allenberry Resort Inn and Playhouse, PO Box 7, Rt. 174, Boiling Springs, PA 17007; 717/258-3211, fax 717/258-1464.

Represented By:
Cabela's, 800/346-8747.

JOE HUMPHREYS WILL TELL YOU that the best time to fish the Yellow Breeches in central Pennsylvania is not during its famed white mayfly hatch in August. Too crowded, he says. Come, instead, during the first three weeks of May. "Hatches and stream conditions are good then, and trout (browns and rainbows) are active." Flowing through bucolic farm country known for its colonial houses of thick limestone block, the river draws its name from the color that it turned the white britches of British soldiers during the Revolution.

Hessian soldiers, quartered nearby at what is now Carlisle Barracks, might have recognized fish in today's Yellow Breeches. German browns from 12 to 18 inches predominate, but you'll also find ample rainbows in the same size, and a few brook trout as well. Unlike the Letort, Falling Spring and Big Spring nearby, the Yellow Breeches is not a spring creek. Though fed by huge springs at Huntsdale and Boiling Springs, this freestone stream warms quickly in July and August, sending fish in search of cooler waters.

That's what makes Allenberry so special. A mile upstream from the inn, the massive spring boils out of the ground in the center of a quaint one-time summer resort community and pours cold water into the Breeches, dropping its temperature even in the sultry heat of summer. Trout thrive, and you can fish for them year-round in the catch-and-release section from the spring to just below Allenberry. An old mill dam backs up the creek into a long, deepish pool. Below the dam, riffles and runs characterize the water until it is again impounded by a low dam just upstream from Brandtsville. The Breeches is an ultralight angler's dream, where Rooster Tails, Panther Martins and 00 Mepps turn the trick. Flyfishers will enjoy sulphur, trico and white fly hatches. And novices and experienced anglers alike can learn from Humphreys, Ed Shenk and Norm Shires at their flyfishing schools ($365 per person, double occupancy) at Allenberry.

Uphill from an old mill dam on the Breeches, you'll find Allenberry's two major buildings, remodeled limestone barns that date from the late 1700s. In addition to a pair of fine restaurants, comfortable but not elegant guest rooms in three lodges, extensive conference facilities, tennis courts and an Olympic-size pool, Allenberry's Equity playhouse has been drawing audiences for nearly 50 years. A little more than two hours from Washington, Baltimore and Philadelphia, Allenberry is a perfect spot for an angling getaway weekend. Many guests match the hatch with a play.

Big Moore's Run

Coudersport, Pennsylvania

This is the consummate center for learning how to snake big trout out of small water.

VITAL STATISTICS:

KEY SPECIES:
Brook, brown and rainbow trout

Season:
March through October

Accommodations:
MODERN LOG LODGE
NUMBER OF GUEST ROOMS: 6
MAXIMUM NUMBER OF GUESTS: 10

Conference Groups: Yes

Meals: American plan

Rates:
Numerous packages from $675 per person for 3 nights and 2 days fishing, double occupancy. Three-day group school $395; private school $595; plus $235 optional room, board and fishing per person.

Guides: Included in some packages

Gratuities: $30 per day

Preferred Payment:
Discover, MasterCard, Visa

Getting There:
Off I-80, specific directions sent on request.

Other Activities:
Hiking, biking, bird watching, wildlife photography.

Contact:
**Barbara Haldaman
Big Moore's Run, RR 3, Box 204A, Coudersport, PA 16915; 814/647-5300, fax 814/647-9928.**

THE SIGN ON THE HIGHWAY says "Welcome to Potter County, God's Country." This is as close to wilderness as you'll find anywhere in the East. Deeply incised valleys cut the heavily forested plateau. Rivers are freestone, narrow, clear and cold-running year-round. They produce abundant trout in sizes that are surprising; while trout are measured in inches in many nearby waters, here the tendency is to use pounds.

The fishing is not easy, and that's where Bill Haldaman's Big Moore's Run comes into play. Set on 300 acres with two ponds and a headwater stream meandering through it, Big Moore's may be one of the finest places in the country to learn to fish small waters for big trout. It's like a kindergarten and college rolled into one. Anglers who've recently taken up the flyrod will learn the basics of reading streams, selecting flies, casting and playing fish in group schools held most weekends from the end of March through September. Students learn techniques over casting ponds and try out their newly developed skills solo on the stream. For those with a few years of experience, Haldaman's three-day private schools may be the ticket. You will become proficient in snaking lunkers out of tight lies with Haldaman's special brand of headwater's fishing: downstream rollcast presentations and controlled drifts. You learn at your own pace, generally one-on-one with a guide, in the privacy of your own beat.

Not only does Big Moore's offer quality instruction, but the waters are pristine and browns, brookies and Kamloops rainbows propagate naturally. The ponds are incredibly fertile, one of the few places in the East where Specklewing mayflies—*Callibaetis*—hatch with regularity. Much more common on lakes and slow rivers of the West, a Specklewing hatch can last for hours and bring fish to a state of near indiscriminate feeding. At Big Moore's, you have five or six weeks to catch the hatch—early April into May. Bring your Blue Duns or buy them at Haldaman's Orvis shop. Taking eight-pound Kamloops on dries in Pennsylvania is not to be missed. Call to check on specific dates.

The deep-brown modern log lodge snuggles on the side of a wooded hill with a large deck overlooking a manicured yard, the lake and forest beyond. Guests stay in simply furnished, comfortable rooms with private baths. Family-style dinners include duck, pheasant, quail and trout, as well as steaks.

Cliff Park Inn
Milford, Pennsylvania

Relax at an elegant country colonial inn that's only 10 minutes from the best smallmouth water on the Delaware.

VITAL STATISTICS:

KEY SPECIES:
Smallmouth bass; shad; muskellunge; walleyes

Season:
All year

Accommodations:
COLONIAL RESORT
NUMBER OF GUEST ROOMS: 18
MAXIMUM NUMBER OF GUESTS: 36

Conference Groups: Yes

Meals: Bed and breakfast, dinners are extra

Rates:
From $93 for 2 per night off-season, $125 in-season

Guides: About $160 for 2 per day

Gratuities: Client's discretion

Preferred Payment:
Major credit cards

Getting There:
Drive to Milford, Pennsylvania via US 209, US 206 or I-84. The inn is 1 1/2 miles from town. Call for directions.

Other Activities:
Golf, canoeing, rafting, swimming, hiking, antiquing, biking, cross-country skiing.

Contact:
John Curtin
Cliff Park Inn, RR 4, Box 7200, Milford, PA 18337; 800/225-6535, fax 717/296-3982, email cpi@warwick.net, website http://www. inbook.com/cliff.html

IN 1820 GEORGE BUCHANAN built a farmhouse high on the palisades above the Delaware River. Across the river rises the Kittatinny Mountains. As far as your eye can see, the gently rolling mountains are tufted with oaks, maples, beeches and firs. Hard to believe that you're only 70 minutes from Newark, New Jersey. And that the river you see below offers some of the finest fishing in the East.

Below Milford, some 40 miles south to the Delaware Water Gap, the Delaware River flows through a national recreation area, a primitive land of cornfield bottoms and hardwood ridges. The river, a tailwater controlled by dams 80 miles upstream above Hancock, New York, is a favorite with canoeists, tubers, rafters and, above all, anglers. The season begins with shad on light spinning or flytackle in May. Smallmouth bass become active at the end of the month, lull a bit at the height of summer and turn on in August and September. Winter finds the walleyes hitting, particularly in the deep pool at the Milford access. And muskies, fished either with live suckers or big stickbaits, become vicious feeders from October through December.

The most pleasant way to fish the river is by canoe. The water is not difficult, consisting mostly of gentle riffles and runs. Start your float at Tri-State Canoe, and fish the heads of the pools as you drift down. Cast crankbaits that imitate crayfish or minnows into rocky cover and breaks in the grassbeds along the banks. Ultralight spinning tackle with 4-pound-test line is all you need. Flyfishers will find better success if they pull over and cast Zonkers, Woolly Buggers or crayfish patterns out into the fast water and let them wash down.

While you wouldn't call the Cliff Park Inn a fishing lodge, many of its guests fish the Delaware and the scores of trout streams in the surrounding Pocono Highlands. The three-story white frame homestead is a classic. Sit on the wide, white-columned front porch and survey the one-time fields, now a nine-hole golf course. Guest rooms in the inn and nearby cabins are full of country charm, with a diverse collection of French provincial, Victorian and art deco accents. This feels a little like spending the night at grandma's, and no wonder; Buchanans have been filling the place with family heirlooms for 170 years. The menu is as diverse as the decor: stuffed quail in truffle sauce, lemon sole wrapped in spinach. If it's a sense of historic country elegance you're seeking, with outstanding fishing nearby, there are few better places so close to New York City.

Falling Spring Inn
C h a m b e r s b u r g ,   P e n n s y l v a n i a

Wild rainbows and browns thrive in the spring creek, thanks to a group of anglers and streamside residents.

VITAL STATISTICS:

KEY SPECIES:
Brown and rainbow trout

Season:
All year

Accommodations:
HISTORIC STONE HOUSE
NUMBER OF GUEST ROOMS: 7
MAXIMUM NUMBER OF GUESTS: 14

Conference Groups: Yes
Meals: Bed and breakfast
Rates:
From $59 for 2 per night
Guides: $200 for 2 per day
Gratuities: Client's discretion
Preferred Payment:
Major credit cards

Getting There:
Chambersburg is on I-81, about a 3-hour drive from Philadelphia and Washington, D.C.

Other Activities:
Golf, tennis, swimming, hiking, bird watching, antiquing, biking, wildlife photography, skiing.

Contact:
Adin L. Frey
Falling Spring Inn, 1838 Falling Spring Rd., Chambersburg, PA 17201; 717/267-3654, fax 717/267-2584.

THE GREAT LIMESTONE RUNS of south-central Pennsylvania are the laboratories where many of the mysteries of spring creek fishing have been uncovered. Anglers such as Vincent Marinaro, Charles Fox and Ross Trimmer pioneered new patterns and techniques to seduce the skittish browns of the Letort below Carlisle. And because of their work, the Letort is perhaps the most famous spring creek in the East. Yet 30 miles south and west down the Cumberland Valley near Chambersburg is a 2.4-mile section of Falling Spring Run, the near equal of the Letort in every aspect.

Falling Spring is best known for its trico hatches, though they are much less profuse than in the 1960s. Development along the upper reaches and constrictions of its flow have increased sedimentation and inhibited propagation of aquatic insects. But thanks to the stream work by concerned anglers and area residents, united in the Falling Springs Greenway project, the creek and its hatches appear well on the way to recovery. You'll find trout feeding on No. 24 tricos in the mornings from June through October.

Perhaps the best hatch on Falling Spring is the sulphur hatch that begins in May, reaches full force in June and early July, and continues off and on into fall. Blue-Winged Olives, caddis imitations and Cahills in Sizes 14 to 20 round out the basic dry fly collection for Falling Spring. If you choose to fish in winter, casting large dark streamers such as Black Sculpins, Woolly Buggers and Marabou Muddlers can bring vicious strikes from browns or rainbows of more than 20 inches.

Six miles of Falling Spring Run are considered fishable, with the flyfishing-only section in the middle. Across a country lane from Greenway Meadow in the heart of the stream restoration area is a quaint stone farmhouse that dates from the 1850s. Adin and Janet Frey raised their six children in the home while running a prosperous dairy farm. In the 1990s, with children grown and gone, they retired from active farming and opened a bed and breakfast to anglers and others attracted by the somnolent countryside. Six guest rooms, all with private baths, are country-comfortable and inviting. Around the breakfast table, you may talk with flyfishers from Europe and Asia who have come to fish this stream of international repute.

Golden Pheasant Inn

E r w i n n a ,   P e n n s y l v a n i a

VITAL STATISTICS:

KEY SPECIES:
Smallmouth bass; shad; striped bass; muskies

Season:
All year

Accommodations:
RIVERSIDE COUNTRY INN
NUMBER OF GUEST ROOMS: 6
MAXIMUM NUMBER OF GUESTS: 12

Conference Groups: Yes

Meals: Bed and breakfast

Rates:
From $85 for 2

Guides: From $125 additional

Gratuities: Client's discretion

Preferred Payment:
Major credit cards

Getting There:
Drive from Philadelphia via I-95 and Rt. 32 or from New York via I-78 to Easton and then south on Pennsylvania Rt. 611 and Rt. 32.

Other Activities:
Swimming, boating, hiking, bird watching, antiquing, biking, wildlife photography, cross-country skiing.

Contact:
Barbara Faure
Golden Pheasant Inn,
763 River Rd., Erwinna,
PA 18920; 610/294-
9595, fax 610/294-9882,
website http://www.
goldenpheasant.com

Had Lafayette been an angler, he'd have fished these waters and been at home in the kitchen.

IT ISN'T OFTEN THAT ONE FINDS elegant accommodations and exquisite cuisine on a river where the fishing is first rate. But that happy situation occurs on the lower Delaware, and it's within a few hours' drive of both Philadelphia and New York City. Pennsylvania's Route 32 winds along the west bank of the Delaware through quaint and historic river towns largely bypassed by suburban sprawl. The village of Washington's Crossing provides a glimpse of the Revolutionary War period. Farther north, above New Hope, numerous inns reflect the region's heritage rooted in commerce borne on the river and, later, the Delaware Canal. Once stops for mule-pulled barges, several of these fine circa-1850s structures have been reincarnated as country inns. None is more charming than the Golden Pheasant.

You'll find canopied beds, period furniture, electrified oil lamps and fresh flowers in the six bedrooms. Each has a private bath. A fire fills the grate in the stone-walled, open-beamed dining room, which blends colonial decor with a French country accent. You have the feeling that Lafayette would be comfortable here, and well he should. His countryman, Michel Faure, from Grenoble, owns the inn with his wife, Barbara, and is at work in the kitchen turning out truite fume maison, sauce raifort (smoked filet of trout, creamed horseradish), crouette de chair de crabe Brittany (lump crab cake with a light mustard hollandaise) and canard roti Michel Faure (roast boneless duck with a raspberry, ginger and rum sauce).

Arrive about 4:00 p.m. on Friday, which gives you time to scout the river, noting water level, clarity and access (not a problem). Plan your approach for the next day's angling. If you go in April, you'll no doubt want to fish shad. Known as "Poor Man's Salmon," they'll hit one-eighth-ounce darts cast out and bumped along bottom or fished behind an anchored boat. Shad are valiant fighters that, after a lightning run or three, settle down to duke it out with you. Striped bass move into the river to spawn in June. Crankbaits and Clousers work on them, for spin and flyfishers respectively. Smallmouth bass are standard fare, running one to three pounds, with fish of four pounds possible. Fish them early in the morning or as the sun sets. And don't pass up muskies up to 12 pounds. Though few and far between, those that smack your plug or bait will bend your rod double before you get it sorted out. Guides are not available at the Golden Pheasant, but you might try J.B. Kasper (215/295-1502). He lives in Morrisville, across the river from Trenton, and knows the Delaware with great intimacy.

Roebling Inn on the Delaware

L a c k a w a x e n ,   P e n n s y l v a n i a

VITAL STATISTICS:

KEY SPECIES:
Smallmouth bass; shad; rainbow trout; walleyes

Season:
All year

Accommodations:
TURN-OF-THE-CENTURY COUNTRY INN
NUMBER OF GUEST ROOMS: 5 plus cottage
MAXIMUM NUMBER OF GUESTS: 15

Conference Groups: No

Meals: Bed and breakfast

Rates:
$65 midweek for 2. Slightly higher on weekends and from April to October.

Guides: $100 to $150 additional from Angler's Roost

Gratuities: 15% to 20%

Preferred Payment:
American Express, Discover, MasterCard, Visa

Getting There:
About 3 hours from New York via I-80 and New York Rt. 97.

Other Activities:
Tennis, canoeing, rafting, swimming, boating, hiking, bird watching, antiquing, wildlife photography, skiing.

Contact:
**Don or JoAnn Jahn
Roebling Inn on the Delaware, Scenic Dr., Lackawaxen, PA 18435; 717/685-7900, fax 717/685-1718.**

Fish for smallmouth bass and shad in Zane Grey's front yard.

IF YOU'RE A FAN OF ZANE GREY'S freshwater fishing stories, this is the place to visit. His first published story, *A Day on the Delaware,* tells of smallmouth fishing not far from this inn. Other yarns such as *Mast Hope Brook in June* and *Lord of Lackawaxen Creek* recount trout fishing nearby. Two doors up from the inn is Grey's old house, now a National Park Service museum devoted to this most prolific author of westerns, baseball and children stories, and fishing yarns. He's buried in the cemetery next to the inn, and out front flows his beloved Delaware River.

In Grey's day the Delaware was quite different from the present. Then it was a free-flowing warmwater river known for smallmouths, shad and an occasional striped bass. Trout were a rarity in those days, restricted pretty much to the Lackawaxen, Mast Hope Brook, and other streams that drain the Pocono Highlands to the west. But since the late 1950s, with the construction of New York City water supply reservoirs in its headwaters, the Delaware has become a classic tailwater fishery.

Upstream, above Calicoon, are hard-fighting rainbows that act for all the world like steelhead, yet they feed like trout. In the pool in front of Grey's place, you'll have a field day with shad in the spring and walleyes when the weather is raw in autumn and better suited to ducking. Riffles up and downstream are great for smallmouths in late summer and fall. Lackawaxen Creek, also controlled by an upstream hydro plant, is a poor vestige of what it once was. On summer days, water temperatures can reach the high 70s. Trout fishing here is essentially a marginal put-and-take operation.

Come for the shad and smallmouths, and stay in the Roebling Inn, a white frame Greek Revival house dating from 1870. Owners Don and JoAnn Jahn offer six comfortable guest rooms with private baths, and a basic breakfast. An adjacent cottage with kitchen and bath provides accommodations for two. Fish early and late, and in between sit in a rocker on the inn's front porch and read Grey's stories. Or walk down to the oldest wire suspension bridge in the U.S. Built in 1849 by John Roebling to carry a canal over the Delaware, this bridge is the precursor to the Brooklyn Bridge. Also nearby is Angler's Roost, source of licenses, tackle and flies as well as tubes, canoes and rafts for riding the river.

Starlight Lodge
Starlight, Pennsylvania

Fish for trout and shad on the main-stem Delaware,
while staying at a bed and breakfast in the Pennsylvania hills.

VITAL STATISTICS:

KEY SPECIES:
Brown and rainbow trout; shad

Season:
All year

Accommodations:
Log lodge
Number of Guest Rooms: 6
Maximum Number of Guests: 14

Conference Groups: Yes

Meals: Breakfast only

Rates:
$75 per person per day

Guides: $275 for 2 per day

Gratuities: $25

Preferred Payment:
Cash or check

Getting There:
If you want to fly, go to Binghamton, New York and rent a car. Otherwise follow US 17 to Hancock, take PA 191 south and follow the signs.

Other Activities:
Canoeing, bird watching, skiing.

Contact:
Pat Schuler
Starlight Lodge, PO Box 86, Starlight, PA 18461;
717/798-2350.

THREE HOURS WEST of New York City and not much farther from Boston and Philadelphia flows the upper Delaware River, one of the best stretches of water in the East. Rainbows grow to 24 or more inches and browns hit 16 to 18 with no trouble at all. American shad, earning the sobriquet "Poor Man's Salmon" from their lightning runs and stunning leaps, fill the river in late May and early June. Add a smattering of smallmouth bass and walleyes, perhaps an errant muskellunge, and you get the picture.

The upper Delaware begins at Hancock, New York, an old lumbering town that could be a tourist mecca like Jackson, Wyoming. But it's not. The fishing's good enough, but there's no skiing and no dude ranches. What there is is a good diner, groceries and gas. Anglers meet their guides at the diner. This is the jumping-off point for the Delaware's east and west branches. From Pepacton Dam down to the village of East Branch, the eastern fork of the river is an excellent brown trout fishery. At the village it joins the Beaverkill, which in its lower reaches can be tragically warm in summer. The West Branch is shorter (about 18 miles long compared to 31 miles for the East Branch), and more heavily influenced by dam releases. This, too, is brown trout water.

The two streams join at Hancock to form the main river. For about 18 miles south to Hankins, this section is a superb coldwater fishery. Rainbows, stocked by accident, outnumber the browns. Hatches, all the Eastern standards, are prolific and fish rise readily. And when nothing's coming off, big stoneflies and streamers such as Woolly Buggers work well. Unfortunately, in the past few years much of the bank has been bought up and access is not as easy as it once was. The season generally runs from April through October, but specific dates vary.

River guide Pat Schuler's bed and breakfast, Starlight Lodge, is the place to stay when you're fishing the main stem. A massive, honey-colored log home perched high on the flank of a Pennsylvania hill, Starlight caters to anglers. You know it the minute you enter. Pegs hold scores of rods on the walls, decorated here and there with frames of flies tied in classic Delaware style. There's a drying room for waders and boots, and upstairs, a large living room with stone fireplace. A tier's bench is handy. So is a library and collection of fishing videos. Rooms are spartan, but comfortable. Breakfast is served on a tiled island in the kitchen. On occasion you can see turkeys working across the backyard, and deer in the meadow before the lodge.

The Yellow Breeches House

B o i l i n g   S p r i n g s ,   P e n n s y l v a n i a

Learn to flyfish in the heart of limestone country while staying at a vintage bed and breakfast.

VITAL STATISTICS:

KEY SPECIES:
Brown and rainbow trout

Season:
All year

Accommodations:
1890s TOWN HOUSE
NUMBER OF GUEST ROOMS: 5
MAXIMUM NUMBER OF GUESTS: 10

Conference Groups: Yes
Meals: Bed and breakfast
Rates:
From $90 for 2 per day
Guides: $285 for 2 per day
Gratuities: $40 to $50
Preferred Payment: Major credit cards

Getting There:
Harrisburg, 25 miles away, has regular commercial service. Shuttle to the inn or taxi service is available at extra cost.

Other Activities:
Tennis, swimming, hiking, bird watching, antiquing, biking, wildlife photography, skiing.

Contact:
Matt Zito
The Yellow Breeches House, 213 Front St., PO Box 221, Boiling Springs, PA 17007; 800/258-1639, fax 717/258-9882, email flyfish@pa.net, website http://www.pa.net/flyfish/

Represented By:
The Gillie, 888/244-5543.

BLACK DIKES OF IGNEOUS ROCK once rose vertically through folded and faulted limestone, interrupting the subterranean flow of water and forcing it to boil to the surface in what was to become a quaint town named for the huge spring in its center. The outflow of the spring joins the Yellow Breeches, a freestone stream that winds its way from west to east through bucolic Cumberland. A mile of water from the spring downstream to below the old mill dam at Allenberry is state-designated catch-and-release water. You'll find a mixture of browns and rainbows and the odd brook trout. Some are wild and others stocked. Fishable all year, this section sees lots of anglers in midsummer when the rest of the stream warms and fish hug deeper, cooler holes. Above and below the special regs area the use of spinners and bait is permitted. Ultralight anglers who like to flip little Panther Martins or Mepps into riffles and runs will find good fish. The smallest stickbaits can also be killers.

There are plenty of trout in these waters, and that makes them ideal for the schools run by The Yellow Breeches House. Its Learn to Flyfish Program attracts students of all ages, but never more than six at a time. You'll learn about rods, reels, lines, leaders, and how these components work in harmony to deliver fly to fish. You'll learn to cast—not those long, sinuous casts that look so lovely—but the short practical casts that take fish in nearby streams. You'll learn how to read the water and how to select flies. Your classroom will move from the inn's backyard to the Yellow Breeches; there's nothing like practicing over live trout. After dinner in the local tavern—generally very good, by the way—you'll tie your first fly, which you'll use in the morning. The remainder of Sunday is free to fish on the Breeches. Advanced schools, two students to an instructor, focus on techniques for success on the Letort, Big Spring or Yellow Breeches.

The inn is one of several 1890s vintage houses across a shady street from Boiling Springs Lake, once the heart of a summer resort community. Now a bed and breakfast, the inn also includes a small tackleshop, a fishing library with flytying bench, a guest kitchen where you can whip up a bag lunch and a 35-foot porch ideal for goofing off. Rooms have been modernized and are comfortable, not fancy. Two of the five share a bath. A short walk around the lake brings you to Yellow Breeches Outfitters, an outstanding flyfishing emporium. Walk around the lake the other way, and you're at the head of the special regs section of the Yellow Breeches.

The Inn at Manchester
Manchester, Vermont

VITAL STATISTICS:

KEY SPECIES:
Brown and brook trout

Season:
All year
Accommodations:
VICTORIAN INN WITH CARRIAGE HOUSE
NUMBER OF GUEST ROOMS: 18
MAXIMUM NUMBER OF GUESTS: 40
Conference Groups: Yes
Meals: Bed and breakfast
Rates:
From $95 for 2 per day
Guides: Available through
Orvis at $300 per day
Gratuities: Client's discretion
Preferred Payment:
American Express, Discover,
MasterCard, Visa
Getting There:
Drive from Albany, New York,
an hour to the west.
Other Activities:
Golf, canoeing, swimming, hiking, antiquing, biking, skiing,
falconry.

Contact:
**Stan Rosenberg
The Inn at Manchester,
Historic Rt. 7A,
Manchester, VT 05254;
800/273-1793, fax
802/362-3218, website
http://www.vtweb.com/
innatmanchester**

Orvis and the Battenkill are within easy walking distance of this bed and breakfast.

WHILE THE INN AT MANCHESTER is not a fishing lodge, per se, it is a place where anglers stay. Why? For one, the Orvis headquarters store is within walking distance. So is the Battenkill, one of America's most storied trout streams. Plan to arrive at the inn on a Friday night. Next morning, after pushing yourself away from breakfast at the inn, stroll down to Orvis and test a handful of their rods on the pond behind the store. Watch monster brookies and rainbows take your hookless fly. Talk with the staff in the fishing department about water conditions and hatches on the Battenkill.

That afternoon, put your freshly gathered intelligence to work on wild brook trout below town. Walk down Union Street, past the golf course, and you'll come to a bridge spanning the Battenkill. Downstream from the bridge, stretching for almost a mile, is the flyfishing-only section. To fish it, you'll need a permit which you can get at Orvis. June evenings bring out sulphurs. Midsummer afternoons are ideal for ants and small 'hoppers. Mornings from late July through early August are ideal for Blue-Winged Olives and tricos. The trico hatch is one of the most important on this section of the river. Fish through dusk, treat yourself and someone special to dinner in one of the many excellent restaurants in this colonial town, sleep well and be on the stream with the next day's sun.

Though the fishing within walking distance of the inn is respectable, it gets better downstream near Arlington and from there to the New York state line. The water is bigger and browns are heavier there. The Battenkill has not been stocked since the early 1970s. Brookies predominate on the upper stretches, and browns farther down where the water warms and slows. As a bonus, while you fish you may recognize scenes found in the art of John Atherton and Ogden Pleissner.

A white Victorian, The Inn at Manchester dates from the 1880s, when the town was in its prime as a summer vacation resort. With 18 guest rooms (four in the carriage house), all with private baths, the inn offers turn-of-the-century serenity. It is a bed and breakfast, to be sure, but in late afternoons tea is served along with such delights as apricot/cheese pound cake and plum cake, all made by innkeeper Harriet Rosenberg.

SOUTH/SOUTHEAST

*ALABAMA, DELAWARE, FLORIDA, GEORGIA,
KENTUCKY, LOUISIANA, MARYLAND, MISSISSIPPI,
NORTH CAROLINA, SOUTH CAROLINA, TENNESSEE,
TEXAS, VIRGINIA, WEST VIRGINIA*

THE SOUTH has it all: brisk Appalachian streams and frigid tailwaters teeming with browns and rainbows; foothill rivers alive with smallmouth bass; flats where bonefish and permit cruise; and, of course, sprawling lakes and reservoirs with record-class largemouth bass. If this isn't enough, there are landlocked striped bass, muskies, walleyes, sauger and huge blue and flathead catfish. Bluefish, striped bass and sea trout highlight fishing off northern beaches. Snook, tarpon and redfish predominate around Florida and into the Gulf. Offshore, it's tuna, marlin, cobia, wahoo and sharks. Accommodations vary from quiet marina motels to elegant lodges.

Lodges:

Alabama
1 WHITE OAK PLANTATION

Florida
2 ANGLER'S MARINA
3 BASS HAVEN LODGE
4 BIENVILLE PLANTATION
5 CHEECA LODGE
6 FARO BLANCO RESORT
7 FLAMINGO LODGE
8 HAWK'S CAY RESORT AND MARINA
9 ROLAND MARTIN'S LAKESIDE RESORT
10 THE ROD & GUN CLUB
11 'TWEEN WATERS INN

Georgia
12 CALLAWAY GARDENS
13 GILLIONVILLE PLANTATION
14 HIGHLAND MARINA AND RESORT
15 THE LODGE AT LITTLE ST. SIMON'S

Kentucky
16 LAKE BARKLEY STATE RESORT PARK

North Carolina
17 FONTANA VILLAGE RESORT
18 HIGH HAMPTON INN AND COUNTRY CLUB

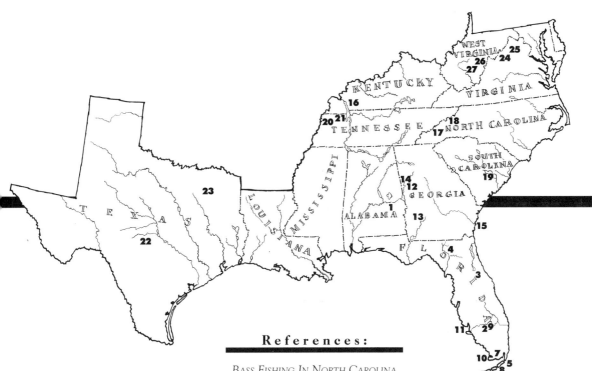

References:

BASS FISHING IN NORTH CAROLINA
FLYFISHING IN NORTH CAROLINA
TAR HEEL ANGLER
— *Buck Paysour*
INSHORE FISHING
THE CAROLINAS' COASTS
— *Bob Newman*
Down Home Press, PO Box 4126,
Asheboro, NC 27204; 910/672-6889
NORTHEAST GUIDE TO SALTWATER
FISHING & BOATING
SOUTHEAST GUIDE TO SALTWATER
FISHING & BOATING
— *Vin T. Sparano, Editor*
International Marine/McGraw-Hill
Companies, Customer Service
Department, PO Box 547, Blacklick,
OH 43004; 800/822-8158
SMOKY MOUNTAINS
TROUT FISHING GUIDE
SMOKY MOUNTAIN FLY FISHING
— *Don Kirk*
Menasha Ridge Press, PO Box 59257,
Birmingham, AL 35259; 205/324-
2964

TROUT FISHING IN THE
SHENANDOAH NATIONAL PARK
— *Harry W. Murray*
— Shenandoah Publishing Co., PO
Box 156, Edinburg, VA 22824;
703/984-4212
VIRGINIA TROUT STREAMS
— *Harry Slone*
TAILWATER TROUT IN THE SOUTH
TROUT STREAMS OF SOUTHERN
APPALACHIA
— *Jimmy Jacobs*
Backcountry Publications, The
Countryman Press, Rt. 2, PO Box
748, Woodstock, VT 05091;
802/457-4826
FRESHWATER FISHING IN VIRGINIA
— *Gerald Almy*
Virginia Heritage Publications, Casco
Communications, PO Box 933,
Warrenton, VA 22186; 540/347-1568

South Carolina

19 SANTEE STATE PARK

Tennessee

20 HAMILTON'S RESORT
21 MANSARD ISLAND RESORT & MARINA

Texas

22 777 RANCH
23 LAKE FORK LODGE

Virginia

24 INN AT NARROW PASSAGE
25 SHENANDOAH LODGE

West Virginia

26 CHEAT MOUNTAIN CLUB
27 CLASS VI RIVER RUNNERS

References & Resources

FISHING IN FLORIDA
— Kris Thoemke
Falcon Press, PO Box 1718, Helena,
MT 59624; 800/582-2665

Resources:

ALABAMA DEPARTMENT OF CONSERVATION
AND NATURAL RESOURCES,
Information Section, 64 North Union
St., Montgomery, AL 36130;
334/242-3151, website
http://www.wrldnet.net/~agfd

DELAWARE DIVISION OF
FISH AND WILDLIFE,
Fisheries Section
PO Box 1401, Dover, DE 19903;
302/739-3441, website
http://www.state.de.us

FLORIDA GAME AND FRESH WATER
FISH COMMISSION,
Office of Information Services, 620 S.
Meridian, Tallahassee, FL 32399-
1600; 904/488-4676;

FLORIDA DIVISION OF MARINE
RESOURCES
Office of Fisheries Management,
3900 Commonwealth Blvd., Mail
Station 240, Tallahassee, FL 32399-
3000; 904/922-4340, website
http://www.state.fl.us/gfc/gfchome.html

GEORGIA STATE
GAME AND FISH DIVISION,
2123 U.S. Hwy. 278 SE, Social

Circle, GA 30279; 770/918-6418,
website http://www.dnr.state.ga.us/

KENTUCKY DEPARTMENT OF FISH
AND WILDLIFE RESOURCES,
Div. of Fisheries, #1 Game Farm Rd.
Frankfort, KY 40601; 502/564-4336,
website http://www.state.ky.us/
agencies/fw/homepage.htm

LOUISIANA DEPARTMENT
OF WILDLIFE AND FISHERIES,
PO Box 98000, Baton Rouge, LA
70898-9000; 504/765-2887, website
http://www.wlf.state.la.us

MARYLAND DEPARTMENT OF
NATURAL RESOURCES,
Fisheries Div.,
Tawes State Office Bldg., 580 Taylor
Ave., Annapolis, MD 21401;
410/974-8480, 800/688-3467, website
http://www.gacc.com/dnr

MISSISSIPPI DEPARTMENT OF
WILDLIFE, FISHERIES AND PARKS,
Div. of Information Services &
Marketing, PO Box 451, Jackson, MS
39205; 601/364-9515, 800/467-
2757, website http://www.mdwfp.com

NORTH CAROLINA WILDLIFE
RESOURCES COMMISSION,
Boating and Inland Fisheries Div., 512
N. Salisbury St., Raleigh, NC 27604-
1188; 919/733-3633, website
http://www.state.nc.us/wildlife/boating

SOUTH CAROLINA DEPARTMENT OF
NATURAL RESOURCES,
Wildlife and Freshwater Fisheries Div.,
Box 167, Columbia, SC 29202;

803/734-3886, website
http://water.dnr.state.sc.us

TENNESSEE WILDLIFE
RESOURCES AGENCY,
Box 40747, Nashville, TN 37204;
615/781-6500, website
http://www.state.tn/

TEXAS PARKS AND
WILDLIFE DEPARTMENT,
4200 Smith School Rd., Austin, TX
78744; 800/792-1112, website
http://www.tpwd.state.tx.us/

VIRGINIA DEPARTMENT OF GAME
AND INLAND FISHERIES,
4010 W. Broad St., Box 11104,
Richmond, VA 23230-1104;
804/367-1000, website
http://www.state.va.us/~dgif/index.htm

WEST VIRGINIA DIVISION OF
NATURAL RESOURCES,
Building 3, Rm. 819, 1900 Kanawha
Blvd. E., Charleston, WV 25305;
304/558-2771, website
http://www.wvweb.com/travel__
recreation/fishing/fishing.html

White Oak Plantation

Tuskegee, Alabama

All those ponds that water White Oak's trophy bucks hold scores of big bass.

VITAL STATISTICS:

KEY SPECIES:
Largemouth bass

Season:
All year
Accommodations:
WOODEN LODGE
NUMBER OF GUEST ROOMS: 9
MAXIMUM NUMBER OF GUESTS: 18
Conference Groups: Yes
Meals: Various plans
Rates:
From $125 per person per day
with meals
Guides: $100 per day
Gratuities: Client's discretion
Preferred Payment:
Major credit cards
Getting There:
Drive from either Atlanta or
Montgomery.
Other Activities:
Hunting, sporting clays, golf,
tennis, hiking, swimming, bird
watching, antiquing, wildlife
photography.

Contact:
Robert Pitman
White Oak Plantation,
5215 County Rd. 10,
Tuskegee, AL 36083;
334/727-9258, fax
334/727-3411.

WHITE OAK PLANTATION and largemouth bass don't generally get mentioned in the same breath. When you think of White Oak, in Alabama's Black Belt, your mind turns to trophy whitetails. A select few, those who've had the pleasure of visiting the plantation in April, have seen its turkey harvest. If you've been there, you've admired the great woods and fields and the lodge, cozy dining room and comfortable cabins, and you've walked around the ponds. Maybe you've shot some sporting clays there as well.

The bass in those ponds, largemouths, average two to four pounds. Once a week someone gets hot and boats one that pushes eight pounds, and every season a lunker of 10-pounds-plus gets caught and released. When he was building the resort, Bo Pitman put in the eight ponds and stocked them with largemouths. Ranging in size from an acre and a half to 15 acres, they weren't fished for a while so the bass could become acclimated and grow. Today the fishing pressure is not what you'd call heavy. Some guests bring rods (or you may rent them at the plantation), and walk the banks in the evening, tossing crankbaits or topwater plugs at the cover. You don't need a boat, but a few with electric motors are available. Along with bass, shellcrackers, bluegills and catfish also live in these waters. Pitman is working closely with biologists from Auburn University to develop a balanced fishery. In addition to casual angling, White Oak also holds schools on flyfishing for bass. Bring your 8 weight.

If you go to White Oak to fish (or plan to fish while you hunt), you might want to take some of those old lures, the one's your daddy and granddaddy used. If you've got an old steel rod and a vintage levelwind reel, take that too. Pitman is into antique tackle. In fact he's planning a bass tourney wherein gear from the 1950s and earlier will be the only legal tackle. How's that for a backlash?

The lodge, low and long, is not large. This is not a classic Southern plantation house, but its nine paneled rooms are appointed with turn-of-the-century country furniture and gives you that warm, down-home feeling. All rooms have private baths and open onto the covered front porch. Meals, good Southern cooking, are served in the restaurant. Various hunting, shooting, youth conservation and fishing packages are available.

Angler's Marina

C l e w i s t o n ,   F l o r i d a

VITAL STATISTICS:

KEY SPECIES:
Largemouth bass; crappies; bluegills; shellcrackers

Season:
All year

Accommodations:
Condos and motel rooms
Number of Guest Rooms: 38
Maximum Number of Guests: 152

Conference Groups: Yes

Meals: Cook for yourself or eat nearby

Rates:
Rooms from $41.25, condos from $85 for 2 per night

Guides: $200 per day for 2

Gratuities: 10% to 15%

Preferred Payment:
Discover, MasterCard, Visa

Getting There:
Ft. Myers has the closest airport with commercial service. Rent a car and drive from there.

Other Activities:
Golf, tennis, swimming, boating, hiking, bird watching, wildlife photography.

Contact:
Reservations
Angler's Marina, 910 Okeechobee Blvd., Clewiston, FL 33440; 941/983-2128, fax 941/983-4613.

This full-service marina offers condos, guides and big bass on sprawling Lake Okeechobee.

AMONG BASS LAKES, few are as well known as sprawling Lake Okeechobee in the center of South Florida. About an hour and a half by car from each coast, Clewiston is a bit of "Old Florida," light years removed from the glitz and glitter of Miami and the retirement meccas on the Gulf Coast. From their big cattle, cane and vegetable spreads south and west of the city, ranchers and farmers bump elbows with anglers who come for big bass in the Big O.

While smaller Florida lakes grow bigger bass, Okeechobee grows largemouth bass in huge numbers in its 750 square miles of lily pads, grass, reefs and channels. Average bass run in the three- to five-pound range. That means you'll catch a lot of one- to three-pound bass, but you're bound to pick up a few in the seven- or eight-pound range to equal things out. A 10-pounder is a good fish in Okeechobee, just like it is anywhere else. The lake fishes well all year, too. During cooler weather, bass are on the move and maybe a little more aggressive. When temperatures climb, and central south Florida can feel like an inferno, bass hang out in the coolest, shadiest water they can find. You can catch bruisers in summer, but they are harder to locate. That's where a good guide comes in. Most anglers use casting tackle, but flyrodders find success. Light tackle fans will have field days on bluegills, crappies and shellcrackers.

One more word about the weather. The lake is big and open and passing cold fronts in winter and spring can push up good-size waves. That's why locally built lake boats sport high, dorylike bows. Fronts are less intense and less frequent in summer, but afternoon thunderstorms are almost an everyday occurrence and squalls associated with them can sweep the lake with gale force winds. Wise anglers fish with an eye particularly peeled for the weather.

Protected from big blows by its location on the Intercoastal Waterway at the west gate to the lock through the Okeechobee dike, Angler's Marina offers full boating services including launch, slips, rentals (14-footers and pontoon boats) and sales and service. Tackle and guides are also available. Surrounding the marina are 26 rental condominiums and a dozen efficiency motel rooms, all clean, quiet and tastefully decorated. Condos have two bedrooms and two baths, as well as a kitchen; and the motel units include kitchenettes. If you don't feel like cooking, drive over to the Clewiston Inn for dinner or check out the quaint Old South barbeque for its fried catfish and hush puppies.

Bass Haven Lodge
Welaka, Florida

Pull in to Bass Haven and be prepared to kick back and fish the "Old Florida" way.

VITAL STATISTICS:

KEY SPECIES:
Largemouth and striped bass; crappies; bream

Season:
All year

Accommodations:
MOTEL-STYLE ROOMS AND SUITES ALONG THE RIVER
NUMBER OF GUEST ROOMS: 10
MAXIMUM NUMBER OF GUESTS: 25

Conference Groups: Yes

Meals: Restaurant

Rates:
From $41 for 2 per night

Guides: $225 per day for 2 anglers

Gratuities: Client's discretion

Preferred Payment:
MasterCard, Visa

Getting There:
Drive from Jacksonville.

Other Activities:
Golf, boating, bird watching.

Contact:
Cher Hooten
Bass Haven Lodge, PO Box 458, Welaka, FL 32193; 904/467-8812.

SPANISH MOSS waves from live oak branches sprawled over Bass Haven Lodge on the St. John's River. Scruffy palms erupt here and there along the river. Across it broods the Ocala National Forest. Though only 65 miles from Jacksonville and 80 miles from Orlando, Florida here seems to have failed to escape the 1960s. Good thing too. People come to Bass Haven to get away from it all, and to catch bass while they're doing it.

The St. John's rises in the swamps above Lake Hell 'n Blazes just east of Melbourne on the Atlantic Coast and flows north through a series of lakes before entering Lake George, the largest. Below Lake George, the river channel narrows at Welaka, where the lodge is located on a low bluff. Largemouths of five or six pounds are common and bigger ones hit frequently here. Fish the eelgrass beds before the spawn in February and March, then move to similar cover in water that's a little deeper. The warmer the weather, the deeper the bass. Work moving water in summer and fish early and late in the day. Striped bass are also found in these waters, especially in February and March. One spot worth trying is the "Croaker Hole," a big spring where bass congregate. Crappies, bream and shellcrackers are plentiful in the St. John's, too.

In these parts, you won't find a fancy tackleshop loaded with the latest rods, reels and lures. But up the road at Welaka Bait and Tackle (904/467-3845), there's plenty of fresh live bait: shiners, grass shrimp, crickets and minnows, a limited selection of plugs, and a number of helpful folks who'll put you in touch with a local guide. Most guides fish out of fully equipped Ramblers or Gamblers, comfortable bassboats that will put you over fish in these good-size waters.

In addition, the weathered marina at Bass Haven rents fishing boats with outboard motors and provides slips where you can dock your own. You can buy bait and gas there. Up the hill and shaded by the trees, the lodge's ranch houses offer air-conditioned guest rooms, quaintly furnished with period reproductions and patchwork quilts. Several include kitchenettes. All offer river views. The restaurant, reputed to be one of the best in rural Florida, offers regional cuisine: fried okra and catfish, as well as Alfredo of shrimp, scallops and crab.

Bienville Plantation

_W h i t e   S p r i n g s ,   F l o r i d a_

VITAL STATISTICS:

KEY SPECIES:
Largemouth bass

Season:
All year

Accommodations:
Log lodge
Number of Guest Rooms: 25
Maximum Number of Guests: 50

Conference Groups: Yes

Meals: American plan

Rates:
From $475 per person per day

Guides: Included

Gratuities: From $25 per day

Preferred Payment:
American Express, MasterCard, Visa

Getting There:
Fly to Jacksonville, rent a car and drive west; about a 2-hour drive.

Other Activities:
Hunting, golf, boating, wildlife photography.

Contact:
Steve Barras
Bienville Plantation,
111 Orange St., Macon,
GA 31211; 912/755-
0705, fax 912/744-9672.

The golden age of bass fishing is flourishing at a preserve just opened to the public.

MANY SAY THAT THE GOLDEN AGE of Florida largemouth fishing is over, but don't bet on it. Bass fishing in the Sunshine State is hard to beat, particularly in lakes and ponds that have recently been opened to the public. Such is the case of Bienville Plantation, just north of the intersection of interstates 75 and 10. Formerly a private corporate preserve, its 6000 acres of lakes are now open to anyone, for a fee. Bring your liniment: A day's fishing can easily include 30 to 40 bass in the three- to five-pound range with a number of six- and seven-pounders thrown in for good measure. Bream here run up to 1 1/2 pounds, crappies to three.

It wasn't always this way. What appears to be lush forest overgrown with vines and moss was, a few years ago, a vast phosphate mine. In the recent past, white piles of ore stood stark against blue skies and water that collected in abandoned pits looked like bile. Enter a group of entrepreneurs who bought the land and planned to cut its pine timber. While inspecting the property, though, they found that some of the older pits had reverted to ponds, and contained huge bass that had never seen a lure. The group quickly realized that with catch-and-release fishing, they could earn revenue far and above anything to be gained from lumbering the land.

Each angler fishes with a guide equipped with a first-class bassboat. Depending on the kind of fishing you like—casting, fly, spinning—the weather, and what's hot, you'll pick a lake. If that one's only producing three- or four-pounders, go try another. Bassin' is best in February and March, and again in November and December. Guests stay in a cozy palm-shaded 25-room lodge with private baths. Bienville also offers packages that combine duck, deer or quail hunting with bass.

Cheeca Lodge

Islamorada, Florida

You'll find tranquil elegance and fine fishing on a 27-acre estate halfway down Florida's Keys.

VITAL STATISTICS:

KEY SPECIES:
Bonefish; tarpon; blue marlin; sailfish; redfish; kingfish

Season:
All year

Accommodations:
RESORT ESTATE
NUMBER OF GUEST ROOMS: 203
MAXIMUM NUMBER OF GUESTS: 550 plus

Conference Facilities: Yes

Meals: Several plans but none include room

Rates:
From $185 per person per day

Guides: From $325 for 2 for a full-day of backcountry fishing

Gratuities: 20%

Preferred Payment:
Credit cards

Getting There:
About a 2-hour drive from Miami.

Other Activities:
Diving, golf, tennis, canoeing, swimming, boating, bird watching, biking, wildlife photography.

Contact:
Cheeca Lodge Reservations, Mile Marker 82, PO Box 527, Islamorada, FL 33036; 305/664-4651, fax 305/664-2893, email cheecalodge@aol.com, website http://www. travelweb.com/thisco/ coastal/51321/51321_b. html

Represented By:
Booking available through any travel agent.

THE KEYS. A nip of the Caribbean strung out below mainland Florida, this string of limestone islands rises up just enough to separate warm and shallow Florida Bay from the Atlantic shelf and the Gulf Stream farther out. Flushed and nourished by tides, mangrove roots and submerged sea-grass beds are incredible nurseries for immature gamefish. So too are the coral reefs that stretch down the Keys' Atlantic side. But the Keys do hustle. Everyone's havin' fun up from Alabama Jack's on the Card Sound Road down the highway to Mallory Square in Key West, where Bacchanalia never ends.

But out on the flats it's different. You, your guide, a 17-foot skiff. The motor's off. Pole and push, eyes squinting to pick up the tail of a bone, or perhaps that gray smudge as it noses the marl. Maybe just the faint shadow, a darkness on the yellow flat. You can't look at the water to see bones, you look through it. There! Where? More left. I see 'em. Cast now. No, wait. The boat gains 10 feet. Now. You cast and the Crazy Charlie hits the water eight feet ahead of the tailing bone. Good. Watch him come. Get ready. His fins quiver and you think he's got it and eagerly set the hook. Nothing there but a muddy swirl where he was. The breeze blows in from the sea, a perpetual cooling fan, as you wipe your face with a rag. There'll be other bonefish.

March through June and August through October are best for bones on the backcountry flats, plus tarpon. November brings sailfish and kingfish on the Atlantic side and reds in the backcountry. Sailfish peak at the end of the year, but they're still around the reefs in January before moving offshore. Marlin pick up in May and peak in June.

Cheeca Lodge, about halfway down the Keys on Islamorada, is in the center of this fishery. A full day's offshore trip for up to six runs from $600 to $700. A full day for two for bones, tarpon or reds in the backcountry is about $325. Or, fish for snapper from a partyboat for $50 per day. Winner of the American Automobile Association's Four Diamond Award, Cheeca is an island of tranquility in the frenzy of the Keys. Rooms, either ocean view or garden view, are located in the main lodge or in island-style villas close by. All are air-conditioned, and many are cooled as well by ceiling fans and large windows opening onto private balconies. Dining is first class, whether in the award-winning Atlantic's Edge or Ocean Terrace Grill.

Faro Blanco Resort
M a r a t h o n ,   F l o r i d a

VITAL STATISTICS:

KEY SPECIES:
Bonefish; tarpon; permit

Season:
All year
Accommodations:
COTTAGES, HOUSEBOATS AND LIGHTHOUSE
NUMBER OF GUEST ROOMS: 125
MAXIMUM NUMBER OF GUESTS: 250
Conference Groups: Yes
Meals: Various packages
Rates:
From $89 per person per day; packages from $1250 per person for 3 nights and 2 day's fishing, double occupancy
Guides: Included in packages, otherwise per $350 per day for 2
Gratuities: $50 to $100
Preferred Payment:
Major credit cards
Getting There:
Fly to Marathon or drive from Miami (about a 2-hour drive).
Other Activities:
Diving, golf, tennis, boating, swimming, bird watching, biking.

Contact:
Gregg Kenney
Faro Blanco Resort, 1996 Overseas Hwy., Marathon, FL 33050; 800/759-3276, fax 305/743-2918, website http://www.westrec.com

Sleep in a lighthouse and fish for a grand slam at this unique resort.

YOU'LL SEE IT IN THE DISTANCE, a tall white lighthouse sticking up above everything else that lines the Overseas Highway linking Florida's Keys. Faintly New England in style, the lighthouse is now a navigation aid, but it wasn't always. Built in the post–World War II real-estate boom, the marker guided tourists to a modest fishing resort on this thin strip of land that separates the Atlantic from the Gulf of Mexico.

Extremely popular even in the height of summer (a perpetual breeze makes even the hottest days bearable), Marathon is overrun by anglers in spring. They have just cause. From April through June you can take your pick of bonefish, permit or tarpon on the flats. Offshore there's dolphin, sailfish, blackfin tuna and a few marlin. Reefs and wrecks hold snapper and grouper, and an hour's boat ride will cover the 22 miles up to Flamingo in Florida Bay for backcountry snook, redfish and weakfish.

Because of the crowds of anglers, flats fishing in the Keys is often disparaged in favor of the Bahamas a few score miles east and south. True, huge schools of three- to five-pound bonefish are more prevalent in the islands than on flats off the Keys. Here a big school is 50 fish. But in the Keys are a number of bones in the 10-pound range and your chances of a hookup are very good. Fishing is normally from flats boats, poled by a guide. In all but a few places, the bottom is too soft to wade with comfort. While resident tarpon are plentiful, bigger fish move onto the flats in spring. Permit are also present, especially over wrecks, but also on the edges of flats. A flyfisherman out for a grand slam stands about a 25 percent chance, and the odds for spinfishermen are even better.

Long a destination for winter-weary anglers, but short on all-inclusive fishing packages, Faro Blanco is now offering three-, five- and seven-night trips that include a variety of accommodations. Stay in stuccoed cottages on the Gulf side, an elegant three-bedroom, two-bath condo or the lighthouse itself. In the harbor, a pair of floating two-story houseboats permanently moored to the dock feature spacious apartments on each floor, with or without kitchenette, but all with cable TV, phone and private bath. Four restaurants cater to every palate. Packages include guided fishing, either on the flats or offshore; meals from the resort's restaurants; licenses and gratuities. They'll even throw in a bottle of sunscreen and a ball cap. For those on a budget, you can book rooms, housekeeping cottages, rent a boat and motor and buy licenses and tackle at the resort.

Flamingo Lodge
Flamingo,   Florida

VITAL STATISTICS:

KEY SPECIES:
Snook; tarpon; redfish; sea trout; snapper

Season:
All year

Accommodations:
MOTEL ROOMS AND HOUSEKEEPING CABINS
NUMBER OF GUEST ROOMS: 120
MAXIMUM NUMBER OF GUESTS: 250

Conference Groups: Yes

Meals: Continental breakfast in summer

Rates:
From $65 for 2 in summer and $87 in winter per day

Guides: From $265 for 2 per day, plus bait

Gratuities: 10%

Preferred Payment:
Major credit cards

Getting There:
Fly to Miami, rent a car at the airport and drive to the lodge.

Other Activities:
Canoeing, bird watching, sight-seeing by boat and tram, boating, hiking, biking, wildlife photography, interpretative programs.

Contact:
Reservations,
Flamingo Lodge ,
1 Flamingo Dr.,
Flamingo, FL 33034;
941/695-3101, fax
941/695-3921, email
evergldfll@aol.com

Try for snook, tarpon, redfish and sea trout, an hour south of Miami, in the Everglades.

WARS TO EVICT THE SEMINOLES brought white men deep into the Everglades for the first time, and when a truce was signed in 1859, dreamers envisioned vast plantations on drained swampland. A crude little town was established around a trader's store where the 'glades dipped into Florida Bay. In the days before screens, smudge fires smoldered in houses built on stilts and front doors were often made of cloth to keep the smoke inside. Residents, who were reluctant to wash, took on a brown patina, protection against malarial mosquitoes. Plumes from egrets, roseate spoonbills and wood storks were the primary cash crop, along with charcoal, tomatoes and fish. Lots of fish.

Around the turn of the century, word got out and sports began braving the swampy 38-mile wagon track that carried them to Flamingo and its fabulous fishing. They found tarpon, snook (once known as soapfish), redfish (channel bass), sea trout (weakfish), snappers, groupers, jacks, pompanos; the list of species is lengthy. The fish are still there. Inshore waters, often only a few inches deep at low tide, gave birth to the open-decked flats boat. Sportfishermen make longer runs to deeper waters. A dam and lock at Flamingo gives boaters access to a network of canals, including the 99-mile wilderness waterway that wends through a maze of brackish lakes and rivers to Everglades City on the western edge of the national park.

You'll need a boat to fish the area near Flamingo, as shore fishing is virtually non-existent. You can charter a guide for either bay or backcountry fishing. Other options include renting a houseboat, aluminum boat and motor or canoe. The season for snook, the premiere fish here, is closed from December 15 to January 31 and again from June through August. Other species are available year-round. Angling for redfish is best from August to December, tarpon from May to August. Sea trout turn on in spring and snapper in fall and winter.

Flamingo Lodge is open all year. You'll find cheerful motel-style rooms that open onto the bay and a colony of housekeeping cabins. The full-service restaurant in the visitor's center features regional cuisine. A screened pool keeps ever-present mosquitoes at bay, but outside in the summer (when the fishing's best, naturally), you'll be glad you wore long-sleeve light-colored cotton shirts and poplin trousers.

Hawk's Cay Resort and Marina

D u c k   K e y ,   F l o r i d a

Luxury and fishing go hand in hand on this private isle.

VITAL STATISTICS:

KEY SPECIES:
Sailfish; yellowtail; cobia; dolphin; tarpon; bonefish

Season:
All year

Accommodations:
ISLAND RESORT HOTEL WITH VILLAS
NUMBER OF GUEST ROOMS: 195
MAXIMUM NUMBER OF GUESTS: 994

Conference Groups: Yes

Meals: Multiple packages

Rates:
From $165 to $700 per person per day in midseason, double occupancy

Guides: Offshore: $700 for 4 per day; backcountry: $375 for 2 per day

Gratuities: 15%

Preferred Payment:
Major credit cards

Getting There:
Marathon Airport has regular service, but you may wish to come through Miami, rent a car and drive down.

Other Activities:
Golf, tennis, swimming, boating, bird watching, biking, wildlife photography, water skiing, para sailing, snorkeling, diving.

Contact:
Christopher R. Ferguson Hawk's Cay Resort and Marina, Mile Marker 61, Duck Key, FL 33050; 305/743-9000, fax 305/743-3198.

LIKE SOME SORT OF TAIL on the state of Florida, the Florida Keys are a remnant of an ancient reef. The Gulf Stream courses between the Keys and the Bahamas to the east, and north and west of the Keys the famed river of grass known as the Everglades filters fresh water into the shallows of Florida Bay. In the Keys the deep ocean, coral reefs, marl flats and mangrove swamps coalesce into a wonderfully rich marine environment that offers anglers an almost infinite number of gamefish to choose from. And in the middle of it all is Hawk's Cay Resort and Marina.

Offshore, sailfish of 30 to 60 pounds and kingfish of 10 to 20 are most active in January and February. Yellowtails of one to five pounds hit well from November to March. Cobia up to 80 pounds seem to be best in March and April, while dolphin in the five- to 50-pound range hit year-round but are best in summer. Rates for offshore angling vary, but a party of four can expect to pay $550 for a half day or $700 for a full day for a sportfisherman, with captain and mate.

Backcountry guiding is a little more expensive, running around $375 per day for two. Using fly, spin or baitcasting tackle, you will fish flats for bonefish in the six- to 15-pound range from September through November and February through April. April through May marks the height of tarpon (40 to 150 pounds) season, with permit (10 to 40 pounds) tops in May. Late April is the best month to try for a grand slam: a tarpon, bone and permit all in one day. Connecting on all three is incredibly tough. Permit are hard to find and more difficult to catch. For a change, spend a day in the backcountry (Florida Bay waters) casting for snook and redfish.

Hawk's Cay Resort and Marina keeps a staff of five skippers and guides on hand for both offshore and backcountry fishing. And when you're not out on the water you can expect to be pampered. The flavor of the Caribbean permeates this tropical inn, its colorful public areas complete with paddle fans, wicker and lush foliage. Your room may feature bamboo or rattan furnishings and will include a refrigerator and private balcony. Some view the Atlantic; others the Gulf. The range of accommodations and packages is extensive. So too are dining opportunities. Four restaurants are located within the 60-acre island and menus range from gourmet regional cuisine to quick bites.

Roland Martin's Lakeside Resort
Clewiston, Florida

VITAL STATISTICS:

KEY SPECIES:
Largemouth bass; crappies; bream

Season:
All year

Accommodations:
MOTEL ROOMS, CONDOS AND EFFICIENCIES
NUMBER OF GUEST ROOMS: 52
MAXIMUM NUMBER OF GUESTS: 128

Conference Groups: Yes
Meals: Restaurant at resort
Rates:
From $66 for 2 per night
Guides: $225 per day for 2
Gratuities: Client's discretion
Preferred Payment:
Credit cards
Getting There:
Drive from West Palm Beach or Ft. Myers.
Other Activities:
Golf, boating, swimming.

Contact:
Reservations Manager, Roland Martin's Lakeside Resort, 920 E. Del Monte Ave., Clewiston, FL 33440; 941/983-3151, fax 941/983-2191.

Despite what you may hear, the Big O is far from fished out.

WITH ABOUT 750 SQUARE MILES, Lake Okeechobee in south Florida offers some of the hottest bass action in the country. Contrary to most other largemouth lakes, midsummer is one of the best times to fish the Big O. Though midday temperatures will near 100°F and the fishery shuts down, early mornings and evenings provide fabulous action for bass in the two- to four-pound class. Even though bass action can be furious during summer, don't overlook November through April, when temperatures are more moderate.

A famed fishery since the turn of the century, Okeechobee was once extremely shallow. A dike system designed to prevent flooding deepened the lake (maximum about 17 feet) and provided more natural structure. Anglers work grass islands, submerged reefs, flooded stumps, stands of reeds and lily pads. Also productive are man-made structures: boat docks, rocky sides of the dikes, numerous channels and marina mouths.

Tackle for Okeechobee can be as simple or sophisticated as you want. Minnows account for a lot of big bass. So do Baby Zara Spooks, Tiny Torpedoes and other topwater plugs. Black weedless spoons dressed with skirts and Texas-rigged worms are still good producers, as are buzzbaits, spinnerbaits and crankbaits fished with slow jerk/pause cadences. Poppers and hairbody bugs do the job for flyfishermen. And for those not too proud, a little popper or light-colored stonefly nymph can attract bream that will put a good bend in a 6-weight rod.

While it's tempting to fish worms and crankbaits on relatively light tackle, you do so at your own risk. Fish from eight to 10 pounds are relatively common, and you'll need stout gear to horse them out of peppergrass flats.

In this area, hostelries that combine quality lodging, dining, bait and tackle, and a full-service marina are scarce. Among the best is Roland Martin's Lakeside Resort, which accommodates 128 guests in appealing motel rooms, efficiencies and condos. The decor is bright and cheerful, with tasteful contemporary furniture. Porches, a swimming pool and waving palms complete the package. The dock is steps from your door, and tennis and golf are nearby. RV sites are available as well.

The Rod & Gun Club

E v e r g l a d e s   C i t y ,   F l o r i d a

VITAL STATISTICS:

KEY SPECIES:
Snook; tarpon; redfish

Season:
All year

Accommodations:
BUNGALOWS
NUMBER OF GUEST ROOMS: 17
MAXIMUM NUMBER OF GUESTS: 40

Conference Groups: Yes

Meals: Restaurant in hotel

Rates:
From $50 per room per night

Guides: From $300 per day
for 2 anglers

Gratuities: Client's discretion

Preferred Payment:
Cash or check

Getting There:
Drive from Miami or Ft. Myers,
each 90 minutes away.

Other Activities:
Swimming, boating, wildlife
photography, bird watching.

Contact:
Pat Bowen
**The Rod & Gun Club, PO
Box 190, Everglades City,
FL 34139; 941/695-
2101.**

*Boom and bust and bust again left
Everglades City with little but fabulous fishing.*

I N 1922, NEW YORK advertising magnate Barron G. Collier had a dream: to create a port city in southwest Florida to rival Miami. He bought a million acres in the area, and set to work. At the center of his empire was the Storter House, an expanded country store that boarded, among others, anglers who came to fish for tarpon and snook among the Ten Thousand Islands separating the Everglades from the Gulf of Mexico. He laid out boulevards, built a block of stores with apartments above them (New York style), erected a Romanesque bank and city hall across a traffic circle from each other, and then watched the hurricane of 1926 blow his dream away. In the next 50 years, little changed. Storter House became The Rod & Gun Club. A few commercial fishermen moved to the isolated town, and when the market for fish sagged in the 1970s, many of them switched to running drugs. That attracted the Feds who, one night, arrested almost everyone in the whole town.

Today Everglades City is a quiet little village, deeply overshadowed in glitz and glamour by Marco Island and Naples to the west. Those in the know find their way to The Rod & Gun Club. Stubby cane rods, levelwind reels, and leathery snook and tarpon mounts fill the lobby. But the old frame hotel no longer houses guests. Instead you'll stay in rooms (private baths) in modern bungalows across the drive under the ficus trees. Sometimes breakfasts are served on the long screened hotel porch that fronts on the Barron River. You can lunch there too on great hamburgers and cold beer. Dinners are more formal and are served inside the high-ceilinged dining room. You'll find more modern accommodations in the area, to be sure, but none that articulates Everglades angling tradition as strongly as The Rod & Gun.

Rent a boat or hire a guide like John Carlisle (941/695-2244) who's fished these waters for half-a-century. Tarpon in the 80- to 130-pound range are his game. If you want to cast flies with a 12-weight rod, that's fine with him. He'll deck you out in red and white, chartreuse, and yellow and white tarpon flies and take you to the passes where fish are running. He's equally at home with anglers who use spinning or casting gear. Tarpon fishing picks up in mid-March and continues as long as the water temperature is above 70°F. In spring and fall snook fishing is unparalleled. Redfish, open all year, and sea trout (season varies, check when you get there) are making comebacks, thanks to new slot limits. Most of the waters you'll fish are part of the Everglades National Park.

'Tween Waters Inn
Captiva, Florida

*Experience a bit of pre-boom Florida fishing
and the white, sandy, shell-filled beaches of Sanibel.*

VITAL STATISTICS:

KEY SPECIES:
Snook; tarpon; redfish;
sea trout; grouper

Season:
All year

Accommodations:
'TWEEN WATERS: MODERN ROOMS AND EFFICIENCIES
THE CASTAWAYS: COTTAGES
NUMBER OF ROOMS/GUESTS:
'TWEEN WATERS: 137/330
THE CASTAWAYS: 40/120

Conference Groups: Yes

Meals: Restaurant or cook for yourself

Rates:
'TWEEN WATERS: From $150 for 2 per night
THE CASTAWAYS: From $90 for 2 per night

Guides: $400 for 2 per day

Gratuities: 10%

Preferred Payment:
Major credit cards

Getting There:
Fly to Fort Myers, rent a car and drive to the inn.

Other Activities:
Tennis, canoeing, swimming, boating, bird watching, biking, wildlife photography, shelling.

Contact:
Jeff Shuff
'Tween Waters Inn, PO Box 249, 15951 Captiva Dr., Captiva, FL 33924; 941/472-5161, fax 941/472-0249.

FAR REMOVED FROM THE HUSTLE and hype of high-pressure tourism, but still in the orb of civilized accommodations, is the 'Tween Waters Inn on Captiva Island. A narrow sand spit eroding with each tide, Captiva separates the Gulf of Mexico from Pine Island Sound. To the south, nourished by Captiva's sands, is larger Sanibel Island. Both are known as the best shelling beaches in Florida and for the wonderful wildlife sanctuary, a memorial to J.M. "Ding" Darling, pioneer conservationist and one-time director of the U.S. Fish and Wildlife Service.

Captiva and Sanibel have been destinations ever since Teddy Roosevelt's days. He fished from these islands for snook, tarpon and redfish. Much has changed since then, of course. But here, particularly in Pine Island Sound and San Carlos Bay to the west, it's possible to recapture a bit of the tranquility of "Old Florida." Snook fishing is particularly good. These voracious linesides, the saltwater equivalent of smallmouth bass, will top 20 pounds. Florida has established a split season—February through May and September through December—to protect them during their spawn in midsummer and in midwinter when they become almost dormant. The fishing is best in April and May and again in September.

In May and June, you'll also find tarpon averaging 60 to 80 pounds with some going to 150 pounds or better. Redfish (seven to 12 pounds) are best in summer. Sightcasting to these species is especially exciting. Weakfish or sea trout (closed from November through December) provide fast light-tackle action. As for bottomfish, there are groupers up to 20 pounds. Charters and guides are available through Orvis-endorsed Sanibel Light Tackle Outfitters.

Anglers have been fishing from 'Tween Waters since 1905, then a private fish camp. In the 1930s, guests began staying at "The School House," now the Old Captiva House restaurant (regional cuisine) at 'Tween Waters. Today, this full-service resort and marina offers a range of gulf- and bay-view rooms and efficiencies with kitchenettes. Each is furnished in modern hotel style and typically includes at least one queen-size bed. You'll find such amenities as hair dryers and complimentary coffee and tea. For a nominal fee you can stay in shape at the private gym. Boats can be launched and moored at the marina. To sample a bit of "Old Florida," check out the housekeeping cottages at The Castaways at Blind Pass, also operated by 'Tween Waters on the northern tip of Sanibel.

Callaway Gardens

P i n e   M o u n t a i n ,   G e o r g i a

VITAL STATISTICS:

KEY SPECIES:
Largemouth bass

Season:
All year

Accommodations:
LUXURY HOTEL ROOMS, COTTAGES AND VILLAS
NUMBER OF GUEST ROOMS: 789
MAXIMUM NUMBER OF GUESTS: 1342

Conference Groups: Yes
Meals: Many packages
Rates:
From $118 for 2 per day
Guides: $175 per half day for 2
Gratuities: 10% to 14%
Preferred Payment:
Major credit cards
Getting There:
About 70 miles southwest of Atlanta off I-85.
Other Activities:
Golf, tennis, canoeing, boating, hiking, bird watching, antiquing, biking, wildlife photography.

Contact:
Reservations
Callaway Gardens, US Hwy. 27, Pine Mountain, GA 31822-2000; 800/CALLAWAY, fax 706/663-5068, email vicki@mindspring.com, website http://www. callawaygardens.com

Fishing, flowers, golf and tennis are all featured at this garden resort.

ONE JULY AFTERNOON, some 60 years ago, Cason Callaway took a walk in the west Georgia woods and came across a bright red azalea. He'd never seen one like it before, and neither had anyone else. It was a rare native species that grew only in pine woods. Today, thanks to careful management, you'll see it in abundance throughout the 14,000 acres of Callaway Gardens.

Long renowned for its profuse and carefully tended vistas of flowering trees, shrubs and other plants, Callaway Gardens is also achieving a reputation for bass fishing. The largest of its 13 lakes, Mountain Creek, has been open to fishing since the 1960s, but the other dozen have been closed to the public. They contain largemouths in the 10- to 12-pound range, shellcrackers to three pounds and bluegills that nudge two. Mountain Creek Lake's 175 acres is a catch-and-keep fishery. For $20 you can rent a johnboat for half-a-day and fill a stringer with largemouths that average three pounds. Use artificial lures on spinning, casting or flytackle. The smaller lakes (three to 40 acres) are used exclusively for flyfishing schools and privately guided sessions. The angling pro shop at Callaway Gardens' boat house provides everything you'll need. Just sign up, meet your guide, pick up your rod and tacklebag, and go to it.

Spring and fall are traditionally the best months to fish these lakes. Summer evenings produce topwater action on deer-hair divers, Sneaky Petes and cork poppers. Winter angling is coming into its own as well. Carter Nelson, manager of the fishing program, has been dredging up two- to three-pound bass with a flyrod, floating line, 12-foot leader and a big, weighted streamer such as a bead-head Woolly Bugger.

Along with fishing and flowers, the garden is famous for its collection of butterflies, three 18-hole courses (No. 15 on Mountain View was rated the fourth most difficult par five on the PGA Tour by *USA Today*.) and a par-three executive course. Add tennis (among the top 50 such clubs in the country according to *Tennis Magazine*), swimming and hiking along the many paths winding through the orchards and gardens. This is one of the most comprehensive resorts in the Southeast. Accommodations range from elegant to luxurious in Callaway Gardens Inn (rooms and suites), Callaway Country Cottages (two-bedroom cottages) and private Mountain Creek Villas, which feature large living/dining areas with fireplace, kitchen, washer/dryer, screen porch and private bath for each bedroom. The inn features both casual and fine Southern cuisine.

Gillionville Plantation

Albany, Georgia

This antebellum plantation sets the standard for Southern hospitality, largemouth-style.

VITAL STATISTICS:

KEY SPECIES:
Largemouth bass

Season:
April through September

Accommodations:
CLASSIC SOUTHERN PLANTATION
NUMBER OF GUEST ROOMS: 7
MAXIMUM NUMBER OF GUESTS: 10

Conference Groups: Yes

Meals: American plan

Rates:
$450 per person per day

Guides: Included

Gratuities: $25 per day

Preferred Payment:
MasterCard, Visa

Getting There:
Albany has commercial service, and the lodge van will pick you up.

Other Activities:
Trap shooting, sporting clays, horseback riding, swimming, bird watching, antiquing, biking, wildlife photography.

Contact:
Jesse Jackson
Gillionville Plantation,
326 New Thompson Rd.,
Albany, GA 31707;
912/439-2837, fax
912/439-9263.

LUXURY AND LARGEMOUTHS go hand in hand beneath the live oaks in southern Georgia. The core of the plantation was assembled in the early 1800s, it survived the Civil War without major damage and for the past 125 years has been in the same family. Recognizing that bird hunters constituted a cash crop, the plantation launched a private quail shooting club on 14,000 acres in 1984. Several trophy bass ponds were also on the property, and five years later Gillionville unveiled The Anglers Club, offering first-class accommodations, superb cuisine and largemouths of trophy proportions. In short order, Gillionville sought and received recognition as the first Orvis-endorsed bass club in the country.

Only 10 anglers at a time are guests at Gillionville. Personal service is taken literally. Each angler enjoys the undivided attention of a knowledgeable guide. Guests have their choice of some 30 lakes. Each is different and no matter what the weather, some will be hot. Some offer bass that weigh in the double digits, others record numbers of four- to eight-pounders. Want to fish flooded timber where strands of Spanish moss dangle over the water? How about working reedy shallows or clay pits? Spinning and casting fans are as welcome as flyfishers. Guides choose waters where anglers stand the best chance of achieving their dreams. Most fish from 20-foot johnboats, others are poled or paddled in canoes and some wade. Days of 50 fish are not completely out of the ordinary at Gillionville, and on occasion someone ties into a behemoth of 12 to 15 pounds.

Largemouths, of course, have no manners. They'll thrash you and trash your tackle if given half a chance. Doing battle with 50 bass a day does wear a body down. Fear not, the staff at Gillionville will minister to your needs, restoring your soul, and providing nourishment for the flesh. Upon arrival at this oak-shaded bastion of Southern gentility, with its white columns, porticoes and tall windows framed by green shutters, you are greeted by a butler. Your bags are whisked off to your room, while you are ushered to the veranda or fireside, depending on the weather, and offered the libation of your choosing. Conversation will range widely—business, banking, politics and, of course fishing—over cocktails and hors d'oeuvres. The serving of dinner slows the talk, as it should when the likes of pork loin in red plum sauce or beef Wellington graces the table. But it picks up afterwards, and is only dampened when one wanders down the hall to bed in one of seven guest rooms, one of which shares a bath.

Highland Marina and Resort
L a G r a n g e ,   G e o r g i a

Fish the flooded timber of West Point Lake for bass up to eight pounds.

VITAL STATISTICS:

KEY SPECIES:
Largemouth and hybrid bass; crappies

Season:
All year

Accommodations:
COTTAGES
NUMBER OF GUEST ROOMS: 33 cottages, from 1 to 3 bedrooms
MAXIMUM NUMBER OF GUESTS: 150 plus

Conference Groups: No

Meals: Restaurant at marina

Rates:
From $54 per day for a 1-bedroom cottage

Guides: $250 per day for 2 anglers

Gratuities: $10

Preferred Payment:
Major credit cards

Getting There:
A 55-mile drive from Atlanta via I-85.

Other Activities:
Water skiing, boating, hiking.

Contact:
**George Marovich
Highland Marina and
Resort, 1000 Seminole
Rd., LaGrange, GA
30240; 706/882-3437,
fax 706/845-2968.**

ON THE ALABAMA BORDER, West Point Lake has earned kudos from pros and amateurs for its steady production of largemouths in the six- to eight-pound class. The reasons: great spawning grounds, lots of flooded timber, ample creekmouth channels and a management program tuned to grow big bass. When the U.S Army Corps of Engineers impounded this stretch of the Chattahoochee River, it created a 34-mile-long lake of 27,000 acres. Highland Marina and Resort in LaGrange is the major full-service boating and fishing facility on the lake. It also provides housekeeping cottages.

Like so many other southern bass lakes, West Point fishes best in spring. Later in the year, hot water temperatures drive bass down deep. In those balmy days of February and March, work the drowned valleys of the feeder streams. Highland is located on Yellow Jacket Creek, an arm of the lake that offers outstanding fishing, but because of its proximity to the marina, Yellow Jacket is often crowded. You might be better off running up to the New River, a tributary on the upper end of the lake, or ducking into others such as Veasy, Wehatkee or White Water. While largemouth is the name of the game here, a resident population of hybrids has also taken root. Live bait is the best bet, but shadlike lures and topwater plugs work well too. Hybrids average four pounds or so and can be caught year-round, though February and March are definitely the best months. As you'd suspect, crappies of a pound to a pound and a half are also plentiful, with the catching best in December and February. The crappie, hybrid and largemouth seasons are closed in January, with largemouths shut down in December as well.

Tucked in the woods above the lake, Highland Marina's 34 ranch-like cottages range from one to three bedrooms, all with kitchens, decks and grills, central heat and air, cable television and phones, and some with private docks. Highland has all the amenities you'd expect at a quality lakefront resort. Rent a fully-equipped bassboat, launch your own, stock up on bait and tackle, have your boat serviced or engage a guide at the marina. The waterfront restaurant offers hearty fare; check out the Sunday breakfast buffet. A shaded campground on the resort's 200 acres provides hookups for the RV crowd.

The Lodge at Little St. Simon's Island

St. Simon's Island, Georgia

On this isolated nub of an island is a rustic retreat with every amenity, and great fishing too.

VITAL STATISTICS:

KEY SPECIES:
Redfish; sea trout; flounder

Season:
All year

Accommodations:
RUSTIC CABINS
NUMBER OF GUEST ROOMS: 15
MAXIMUM NUMBER OF GUESTS: 30

Conference Groups: Yes

Meals: American plan

Rates:
From $300 for 2 per day

Guides: $100 per day per angler

Gratuities: 15%

Preferred Payment:
MasterCard, Visa

Getting There:
Jacksonville is the closest airport; from there, drive about an hour north to the Hampton River Club marina on St. Simon's Island and catch the ferry.

Other Activities:
Horseback riding, canoeing, swimming, boating, bird watching, biking, wildlife photography, nature treks and lectures.

Contact:
Deborah McIntyre
The Lodge at Little St. Simon's Island, PO Box 21078, St. Simon's Island, GA 31522; 912/638-7472, fax 912/634-1811, email 102.063.467@com puserve.com, website http://www.pactel.com. au/lssi

EMBRACING THE NORTHERN TIP of its larger sibling, Little St. Simon's Island is a private and secluded 10,000-acre barrier island. Its thick scrub-oak forest and salt marshes are cut by a score or more tidal rivers and creeks. Owned by the Berolzheimer family since the early 1900s, the island has been left largely as nature made it. A few shell roads wind through the trees, passing ponds where herons and wood storks fish, on their way to the beach.

From August through November and sometimes as late as the end of January, redfish, weakfish and flounder are abundant in the surf and the salt creeks that meander through the island. Redfish of up to six pounds are found in the deeper holes of the creeks and in their mouths. At times you will see them tailing in the shallows. Stalk them, then cast ahead so your Clouser or Deceiver strips across their noses. You will also encounter redfish in the surf, but will need a bigger rod, like a 10-foot 8 weight, to reach them. Fishing for reds is best in September and October. Weakfish or speckled sea trout also school up in holes in the creeks and cruise the beach. They begin to show up in midsummer, and by September the concentrations are dense enough to provide good fishing. The lodge provides guides and Carolina skiffs, or you may fish from the beach if you wish. While tarpon are not as large or as plentiful as they are farther south, they are occasionally caught in summer in Altamaha Sound north of the river. And flounder can be picked up in the island's creeks and surf much of the year. Anglers and their guides can plan custom excursions before arrival on the island, and then fine tune them based on weather conditions. In addition, Little St. Simon's, an Orvis-endorsed lodge, hosts a number of flyfishing schools throughout late summer and fall.

Dating from 1917, the Hunting Lodge is the heart of guest activities on Little St. Simon's. Heads of deer and other game adorn the richly paneled walls of the rustic, yet elegant, living room. If you come in late October or November, a fire will be crackling in the hearth, and the chef may have prepared a hearty chowder to open dinner, which features fine regional cuisine. Two guest rooms, each with private bath, are located in the Hunting Lodge. A nearby bungalow, Michael Cottage, is light and airy and has a pair of bedrooms served by a private bath as well as a living room with fireplace. This is a favorite with families and honeymooning couples. Cedar House and River Lodge round out the accommodations. Each has four bedrooms with private baths, living room with fireplace and a screened porch.

Lake Barkley State Resort Park

C a d i z ,   K e n t u c k y

Stay at a first-class resort that features hotel, cabins, campgrounds, plus out-of-this-world bass fishing.

VITAL STATISTICS:

KEY SPECIES:
Largemouth and Kentucky bass; crappies; bluegills; catfish

Season:
All year

Accommodations:
RAMBLING MODERN RESORT
NUMBER OF GUEST ROOMS: 148
MAXIMUM NUMBER OF GUESTS: 400

Conference Groups: Yes
Meals: Restaurant
Rates:
From $50 per person per night
Guides: Available through marina
Gratuities: Client's discretion
Preferred Payment:
Credit cards
Getting There:
From US 68 at Cadiz, drive west to Kentucky Rt. 1489 and turn north.
Other Activities:
Hunting, bird watching, bicycling.

Contact:
Reservations Office, Lake Barkley State Resort Park, Box 790, Cadiz, KY 42211; 800/325-1708, fax 502/924-0013.

WHEN HAROLD KNIGHT of Knight & Hale Game Calls isn't hunting, he's bass fishing on Lake Barkley. Barkley is the impoundment of the Cumberland River and it is close kin to Kentucky Lake on the Tennessee River. They're separated by Land Between the Lakes, a 170,000-acre wilderness area managed by the Tennessee Valley Authority in cooperation with the state wildlife agencies of Kentucky and Tennessee. The two lakes cover nearly 250,000 acres, but they are different. Kentucky is broad, shallower and tends to be more turbid. Barkley at 57,920 acres is smaller, narrower, a little deeper and a bit clearer. Of the two, there are those who say Barkley is the better bass fishery.

Barkley is known for largemouth and Kentucky bass that run in the four- to five-pound range. You'll also find crappies of a pound or more, catfish and plenty of bluegills. Bigger bass begin hitting in March as the water starts to warm. Fish the stumps and brushpiles and the north side of the bank. Bass begin to move to spawning areas in April, and that's the best time for consistent action. Look for flooded Buttonball willows. From the bow of your boat flip a jig and pig against the bank and work it through the submerged brush. They're still in the shallows during May and June, but retreat into deeper pockets from mid-June to September, when water temperatures reach the 80s.

If you come to fish the lake, check out the 3600-acre Lake Barkley State Resort Park, one of the top state parks in the nation and recipient of the American Automobile Association's Four Diamond Award. Guests stay either in Barkley Lodge, a rambling contemporary hotel of cedar, with 120 rooms and four suites, or in nearby Little River Lodge with 10 rooms and one suite. In addition, 13 two-bedroom cabins, four of them log and all with screened porches or decks, are available. The resort also includes a convention center. A half-mile from the lodge is the 172-slip marina where boats may be launched and rented. In addition, the resort includes a trap range, tennis courts and year-round campground with 78 sites complete with utility hookups.

Fontana Village Resort

Fontana Dam, North Carolina

Tucked deep in the Smokies, Fontana offers prime bass fishing; its creeks, excellent trout fishing.

VITAL STATISTICS:

KEY SPECIES:
Smallmouth, white and largemouth bass; brown and rainbow trout

Season:
All year

Accommodations:
HOUSEKEEPING COTTAGES AND A MAIN LODGE
NUMBER OF GUEST ROOMS: 91 in main lodge, 150 in cottages
MAXIMUM NUMBER OF GUESTS: 1300
Conference Groups: Yes
Meals: Various plans available
Rates:
$49 for 2 per night
Guides: $180 per day for 2
Gratuities: Client's discretion
Preferred Payment:
Major credit cards
Getting There:
Fly to Knoxville, Tennessee or Asheville, North Carolina and rent a car, a scenic 2-hour drive.
Other Activities:
Golf, tennis, canoeing, rafting, boating, hiking, bird watching, antiquing, biking, wildlife photography, skiing.

Contact:
Scott Waycaster
Fontana Village Resort,
Hwy. 28, Box 68,
Fontana Dam, NC 28733;
800/849-2258, fax
704/498-2209.

FONTANA DAM rises 480 feet above the Little Tennessee River hard by the southwest end of the Great Smoky Mountains National Park. Built to power Tennessee's aluminum plants in Alcoa and the atom bomb project at Oak Ridge, the dam created a deep and sinuous lake that stretches 29 miles along the eastern flank of the Smokies. The lake is isolated, accessible only to those who hike, ride horseback or boat in. This limits fishing pressure on Eagle, Hazel and Forney creeks, three gems among Smoky Mountain trout streams. The short tailwater below Fontana Dam is known for lunker browns, and the lake itself is outstanding for smallmouths, largemouths and walleyes.

The best time to fish here is spring, when redbud, then dogwood blossoms on the lower hills and spring beauties and trillium carpet the forest floor. When the sun climbs the ridge, it warms your back as you cast gray and brown jigs, spinnerbaits and crawdad imitations to the rocky shore exposed by the fluctuating lake pool. The lake is filling with spring rains, recovering from the winter drawdown on its way to full pool.

Hazel Creek is special for three reasons, two of which (trout and easy access) most anglers know, and the other, all but obscured by the laurels along this freestone stream. Hazel, once heavily stocked, is now a wild trout stream thickly populated with browns and rainbows in the 12- to 16-inch range. Like all park waters, it's fishable all year. It's best in spring when rainbows come up out of the lake to spawn, and again in fall when browns do likewise. A road, an old railroad grade, runs along the creek for three or four miles, providing easy access. In summer, you'll find lots of anglers here, but there's ample stream to absorb them all. Horace Kephart is Hazel Creek's secret. Once a scholarly librarian, in the early 1900s Kephart blew into Hazel Creek wreathed in moonshine fumes, lived there in a rude mountain cabin and later wrote *Our Southern Highlanders* (reprints: University of Tennessee Press), a book that helped create the park and an absolute must-read for those who fish these streams and Fontana.

The resort's marina will shuttle anglers to the mouth of Hazel Creek, rent boats and provide guides. Tackle, bait and licenses are available here as well. Less than two miles away is Fontana Village Resort, a collection of remodeled cottages that once housed workers building the dam. Cottages have been augmented by attractive motel-style accommodations, close to the main stone lodge where meals are served in both cafeteria and a la carte manner. Numerous flyfishing schools are held at the resort.

High Hampton Inn and Country Club
C a s h i e r s ,   N o r t h   C a r o l i n a

The ravages of modernization have bypassed this large log hotel deep in North Carolina's mountains.

VITAL STATISTICS:

KEY SPECIES:
Brook, brown and rainbow trout; largemouth bass

Season:
April 1 through November
Accommodations:
MOUNTAIN LODGE AND RUSTIC CABINS
NUMBER OF GUEST ROOMS: 125
MAXIMUM NUMBER OF GUESTS: 300
Conference Groups: Yes
Meals: American plan
Rates:
From $74 per person per day, double occupancy
Guides: $150 per day per angler
Gratuities: $20 to $50
Preferred Payment:
Major credit cards
Getting There:
Asheville, North Carolina and Greenville, South Carolina are the closest airports; rent and car and enjoy the drive.
Other Activities:
Golf, tennis, swimming, hiking, antiquing, bird watching, wildlife photography, canoeing, rafting, wildflower workshops.

Contact:
Reservations
High Hampton Inn and Country Club, PO Box 338, Cashiers, NC 28717-0338; 800/334-2551 or 704/743-2411, fax 704/743-5991.

MOST OF THE GRAND OLD HOTELS in the southern Appalachians have been modernized. Not so High Hampton. Here, air-conditioning means you open your window and sleep to the deep sigh of mountain winds. You won't be kept awake by your neighbor's television. He doesn't have one and neither do you. A wooden booth by the front desk holds public phones for the 30-room main lodge and 15 outlying cabins.

Opened in 1922 as a golf club (it was the 1400-acre estate of Confederate General Wade Hampton), now one out of every four guests comes to fish. Brookings (704/743-3768), an anglers' shop up the road in Cashiers, provides guides and runs fly-fishing schools at the inn's practice pond. Between the lush green links and heavy forest rising to 4300-foot granite-faced Rock Mountain are two lakes. With bait and bobbers, kids catch rainbows, bream and an occasional largemouth up to four pounds. The kitchen will gladly prepare your fish for lunch or dinner.

Sophisticated anglers should not overlook the lakes. Nearby they'll also find a plethora of trout water, mostly freestone mountain streams and small rivers. Some high mountain creeks, hidden by laurel slicks, hold bright native brookies. Then there's the Davidson, one of Trout Unlimited's top 100 rivers. It's known for exceptionally large brook trout—up to 18 inches—by mountain standards. Try a No. 16 Gold-Ribbed Hare's Ear, recommends guide John Druffel. Also tempting are the Nantahala, South Mills and Whitewater rivers, with their populations of browns and rainbows. An hour's drive takes you into the Smoky Mountains and its best trout waters: Forney, Deep and Hazel creeks. Best months to fish? April through June and September through October.

High Hampton is a family place. For your stay, you'll have your own table in the restaurant (southern mountain cooking). From 9:00 a.m. until 2:00 p.m., the Kid's Club offers activities for youngsters from 5 to 12. Organized playgroups are also available for toddlers from 2 to 4. Hiking and fitness trails lace woods carpeted with wildflowers from early spring into fall. And then there are those sturdy oak rockers deep in the shade on the front porch. Rooms in the lodge are basic: double beds, nightstand, bureau, private bath. Similarly appointed rooms and suites are available in 19 cottages, most fronting on the course or on the lakes. Or guests can chose from 45 private homes, available for rent during various periods of the year.

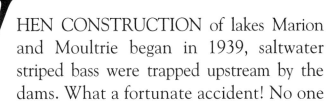

Santee State Park
Santee, South Carolina

In this sleepy Southern lake, where Spanish moss floats from live oaks, a 30-pound striper is waiting to slam your bait.

VITAL STATISTICS:

KEY SPECIES:
Landlocked striped bass and largemouth bass; crappies; catfish

Season:
All year

Accommodations:
OCTAGONAL CABINS
NUMBER OF GUEST ROOMS: 30
MAXIMUM NUMBER OF GUESTS: 180

Conference Groups: Yes

Meals: Housekeeping or restaurant

Rates:
From $64.20 per day

Guides: About $200 per day for 2

Gratuities: Client's discretion

Preferred Payment:
MasterCard, Visa

Getting There:
Drive from Columbia, South Carolina.

Other Activities:
Golf, tennis, swimming, hiking, bird watching, boating, biking, wildlife photography, water skiing, sailing.

Contact:
Mike Spivey
Santee State Park, 251 State Park Rd., Santee, SC 29142; 803/854-2408, fax 803/854-4834, website http://www. prt.state.sc.us/sc

WHEN CONSTRUCTION of lakes Marion and Moultrie began in 1939, saltwater striped bass were trapped upstream by the dams. What a fortunate accident! No one knew it at the time, but stripers can thrive in fresh water. Today, more than 50 years later, these lakes are producing huge fish. The world-record landlocked striper of 55 pounds came out of these waters and it may be no more than a matter of time until a bigger one comes to boat. Lake Moultrie, about half the size of Marion, is the better of the two lakes for stripers. Fish spawning runs in early spring or when they begin to school up in fall. The diversion canal between the two is a favorite spot for striper anglers, particularly during the spawn. Afterwards, the fish disperse throughout the lakes and trolling becomes the most effective tactic. In fall, flights of feeding sea gulls will often signal striper activity near the surface. A gentle approach will sometimes put anglers into fantastic topwater action.

Spreading hydrilla, vast forests of flooded cypress and plentiful submerged stumps and logs are key factors in Lake Marion's steadily improving largemouth fishery. And fishing pressure for black bass, according to state biologist Miller White, "is relatively light. We have more big fish than other lakes with similar fish densities," he adds. Cast spinnerbaits and crankbaits as close to cypress as possible. In late spring, don't bypass weedbeds, and in summer fish worm rigs, except early and late when topwaters can pay off big time. Bass ranging from six to eight pounds are common, and 12-pounders are not infrequent. One hotspot on Lake Marion is Jack's Creek across from Santee State Park.

The park, just west of Interstate 95, offers 30 octagonal lakeside housekeeping cabins that sleep six. Ten, built on piers over the water, have private docks. The 20 land-based cabins have decks and grills. All are fully furnished with cooking utensils, linens, cable TV and private baths. From June through August, cabins are rented for periods of not less than one week. At other times, they may be engaged on a nightly basis. In addition, there's a restaurant, marina, and tackle and bait shop, as well as all the activities associated with a top-quality state park.

Hamilton's Resort

H o r n b e c k ,   T e n n e s s e e

You can't beat the price of this budget resort, located in the center of Reelfoot Lake's best bass and crappie fishing.

VITAL STATISTICS:

KEY SPECIES:
Largemouth and white bass; crappies; catfish

Season:
All year

Accommodations:
MOTEL WITH KITCHENETTE
NUMBER OF GUEST ROOMS: 16
MAXIMUM NUMBER OF GUESTS: 50

Conference Groups: No

Meals: Restaurant on the property

Rates:
Packages from $99 per person for 4 nights and 3 days with boat, double occupancy

Guides: $125 for 2 per day

Gratuities: Client's discretion

Preferred Payment:
Cash or check

Getting There:
Drive from Memphis on US 51.

Other Activities:
Swimming, boating, bird watching, antiquing, wildlife photography.

Contact:
Jamie or Bonnie Hamilton
Hamilton's Resort, Rt. 1, 4992 Hamilton Rd., Hornbeck, TN 38232; 901/538-2325.

RESORT CAN MEAN a lot of things, but here on the banks of Reelfoot Lake in west Tennessee, it means warm and friendly hospitality, a clean and comfortable motel room with kitchenette and a ringside seat on some of the best fishing and hunting in the South. Reelfoot Lake was created by the New Madrid earthquake in 1811, which lowered a block of land 22 miles long and seven miles wide. The Mississippi flooded the real estate, creating Tennessee's only large natural lake.

Known for its stump-studded shallows (so many that a creative soul invented reversing oar locks that allow you to row and face forward), Reelfoot is ideal fish habitat. Largemouth bass are the prime attraction. They're legal all year, although the limit is three and they must be longer than 15 inches. This is wonderful country to work worms, fish topwaters or race buzzbaits over lily pads. Flyfishers find great sport here with poppers at dusk. You won't find limits on crappies, bluegills or white bass, all fair game for flyfishermen, though spinfishers may have the advantage. Big catfish up to 50 pounds are definitely a baitcaster's game.

While this is a fishing book, it would be a shame not to mention waterfowl hunting on Reelfoot. It's an important stop on the Mississippi Flyway. Mallards are most plentiful, but virtually all duck species are represented. Geese are available too; blinds and pits are heated. Duck and goose seasons open in early December. Ducks close in mid-January and geese continue into March, when crappie fishing begins to get good again.

The Hamilton Resort is a down-home kind of place. Those who don't want to do their own cooking can eat at the restaurant on the property. Numerous packages are available and many include the use of boat and motor. Rates are unreasonably low: four nights and three days with a boat for $99 per person double occupancy.

Mansard Island Resort & Marina

Springville, Tennessee

It's summertime and the living's lazy at this rural resort on Kentucky Lake.

VITAL STATISTICS:

KEY SPECIES:
Largemouth bass; crappies; bluegills; catfish; sauger

Season:
All year

Accommodations:
CABINS, COTTAGES AND MOBILE HOMES
NUMBER OF GUEST ROOMS: 40
MAXIMUM NUMBER OF GUESTS: 175

Conference Groups: Yes

Meals: Housekeeping

Rates:
From $35 for 2 per day

Guides: $175 per day for 2

Gratuities: Client's discretion

Preferred Payment:
Major credit cards

Getting There:
Drive from Nashville or Memphis.

Other Activities:
Swimming, boating, water skiing, four-wheeling, hunting, antiquing, biking, tennis, golf.

Contact:
**J.D. Koenig
Mansard Island Resort & Marina, 60 Mansard Island Dr., Springville, TN 38256; 901/642-5590, fax 901/642-3120.**

WITH 2400 MILES of shoreline, 180-mile-long Kentucky Lake is full of structure that holds largemouth and, increasingly, smallmouth bass. About a third of the way down the lake, just across the Tennessee line, is a laid-back, home-style, affordable resort that offers accommodations and facilities that will suite a wide range of tastes and interests. And the fishing is good not five minutes from the marina.

The resort caters to anglers. Largemouths, the lake's premiere fish, run up to 10 pounds, but stringers of two- to three-pounders are more normal. Gravel points, creek-mouths, brushpiles, drowned timber and stumps, and other structure are all worth fishing. In spring, work the shallows when bass are bedding. Don't overlook weedy shore-lines. June is usually a top month for bass; worms, jig 'n pigs, crankbaits and buzzbaits all produce. Try points, channels of old river channels, and islands near the mouths of creeks. As the water heats, and the weather does get hot in west Tennessee, bass go deep. Fish them early and late. You may find topwater action at night. Come fall, they'll feed a little more aggressively, but the best fishing is generally in spring.

While bass is definitely the main event, don't pass up crappies from one to three pounds in the spring, bluegills (real treats on a flyrod, and great fun for kids), catfish and sauger, a cousin of the walleye that is prized table fare. Sauger fish best in winter.

Situated on the Sandy River arm of the lake amidst the trees, Mansard Island Resort offers everything from housekeeping town houses, cottages and house trailers, to a campground for recreational vehicles and tents. Along with a laundromat and a grocery and general store, you'll also find tennis, a swimming pool and a playground for kids. Fishing and pontoon boats can be rented from the full-service marina, which can accommodate boats up to 60 feet long. A launch ramp and covered slips are available. A number of guides work out of the marina, which also sells licenses and bait. You'll find restaurants in nearby Paris, Tennessee and Murray, Kentucky.

777 Ranch

H o n d o ,   T e x a s

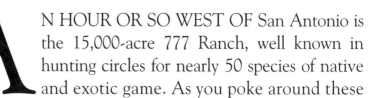

VITAL STATISTICS:

KEY SPECIES:
Largemouth bass; crappies; catfish

Season:
All year

Accommodations:
THREE RUSTIC LODGES
NUMBER OF GUEST ROOMS: 25
MAXIMUM NUMBER OF GUESTS: 50

Conference Groups: Yes

Meals: American plan

Rates:
From $200 per person per day, double occupancy

Guides: Included

Gratuities: $30 per person per day

Preferred Payment:
Major credit cards

Getting There:
Transfers from San Antonio's airport to the lodge are included.

Other Activities:
Golf, tennis, swimming, boating, bird watching, antiquing, wildlife photography, hunting.

Contact:
Kevin Christiansen
777 Ranch, Rt. 2, Box 777, Hondo, TX 78861; 210/426-3476, fax 210/426-4821, email 777ranch@ranch.com, website http://www. 777ranch.com

Where do largemouths look eland in the eye? In the ponds of this West Texas game ranch.

AN HOUR OR SO WEST OF San Antonio is the 15,000-acre 777 Ranch, well known in hunting circles for nearly 50 species of native and exotic game. As you poke around these hills, rolling with mesquite and acacia, you're liable to see eland or oryx and think you're in Africa. You're not, of course. And largemouth bass aren't all that prevalent there. But you will find them aplenty in the 30 ponds of the Triple Seven.

Ranging from ponds so small that you can chuck a stone across them to lakes of 100 acres or so, these waters hold largemouths averaging six to eight pounds. Florida-strain bass were planted here about 20 years ago, and the 777 has been practicing catch-and-release ever since. You'll fish for them from 16-foot Carolina skiffs pushed by electric trolling motors. The time of year doesn't make much difference in terms of catching bass on the ranch. But the tactics and lures will vary. Bassassasins and Slugos in pumpkinseed and chartreuse are effective when the wind has made the water a little dingy, as are white, yellow and chartreuse spinnerbaits. When the water's clear, darker colors perform better. In spring you'll do well with buzzbaits cast toward shore early and late in the day. In summer and fall, go deeper with Rat-L-Traps. Booking is by advance reservation only, and a week before you come, the ranch staff calls, confirms and tells you what plugs are hot. That's smart service! And the ranch maintains a fully stocked pro shop.

Cast-and-blast takes on a new meaning here. Big-game hunting is the bread and butter of this ranch. You'll find species from Africa, Europe and India, along with American whitetails and elk. Not to be overlooked are turkeys, quail, ducks, geese and sandhill cranes when in season. Fill your big-game tag and then, chill out with an afternoon of bassin' in one of the ponds. Or fish for crappies, catfish or perch.

Accommodations in the ranch's main California cedar lodge are as comfortable and well appointed as any of the country's first-rate motels: twin double beds, night tables with reading lights, private baths, phone and an alarm clock to get you up before the bass. Corporate groups of 10 or more can have exclusive use of small lodges at Twin Lakes and Sugar Lake. Food is good and stick-to-your-ribs solid: chicken-fried steak for dinner and eggs, biscuits and gravy for breakfast. A large pool and outdoor barbecue complete the facilities.

Lake Fork Lodge
Alba, Texas

VITAL STATISTICS:

KEY SPECIES:
Largemouth bass

Season:
All year

Accommodations:
LODGE WITH ROOMS AND SUITES
NUMBER OF GUEST ROOMS: 7
MAXIMUM NUMBER OF GUESTS: 24

Conference Groups: Yes

Meals: Bed and breakfast, dinners additional upon request

Rates:
From $85 to $160 for 2

Guides: $250 per day for 2 anglers

Gratuities: 15%

Preferred Payment:
American Express, MasterCard, Visa

Getting There:
Fly to Dallas/Ft. Worth, rent a car and drive to the lodge.

Other Activities:
Golf, swimming, boating, bird watching, antiquing, wildlife photography, skiing.

Contact:
Kyle Jones
Lake Fork Lodge, PO Box 160, Alba, TX 75410;
903/473-7236.

Some of the biggest bass in Texas come out of Lake Fork.

COUNT THEM: 19 of Texas' top 25 largemouths, including the state's 18-pound 3-ounce record, have come from Lake Fork Reservoir. This 28,000-acre impoundment 70 miles east of Dallas not only produces big fish, but lots of fish. Nearly 20 years ago, 800,000 Florida-strain largemouths were stocked in this lake, and like everything else in Texas, they've grown in a big way.

Lake Fork is not particularly deep, averaging between 12 and 18 feet except at the dam, and it offers a wide variety of structure. You'll find flooded timber, reefs, grass beds, abandoned road rights-of-way and stream channels, rocky points and some drop-offs. While the season is open year-round, the most productive months are March through May, October and November. Spawning generally occurs from mid-February to mid-March. Nightfishing during the height of summer is very effective. Try the popular Zara Spook or other topwater plugs. For general fishing, locals recommend a jig and crawl rig. While largemouths get most of the attention on this trophy lake, you might want to factor in a little fishing for crappies, which fish best in spring and late fall. And if you feel up to the task, try tussling with some big blue cats (five to 70 pounds) in early summer.

Motel/marinas and guide services are plentiful here. But if you're looking for something different, try Kyle and Debbie Jones' contemporary brick lakeside "Bass & Breakfast." Make that plural: You get two breakfasts, one before going fishing and another when you get back. Enjoy a whirlpool and relax in front of a VCR in your spacious guest room, some of which even have king-size beds. Dinners are not included in the price of the room, but they can be catered on special request. Or, at a local market, you can pick up steaks or chicken and charcoal them on one of several grills provided for just that purpose. In addition, Lake Fork Lodge has a private launch ramp and parking and slips for boats.

Inn at Narrow Passage

W o o d s t o c k , V i r g i n i a

Stay at Stonewall Jackson's headquarters while fishing for Shenandoah smallmouths.

VITAL STATISTICS:

KEY SPECIES:
Smallmouth bass

Season:
All year

Accommodations:
COUNTRY INN
NUMBER OF GUEST ROOMS:12
MAXIMUM NUMBER OF GUESTS: 30

Conference Groups: Yes

Meals: Bed and breakfast

Rates:
From $85 for 2 per day

Guides: $150 per day

Gratuities: $20 per day

Preferred Payment:
MasterCard, Visa

Getting There:
Drive west from Washington, D.C. on I-66, then south on I-81. About a 1 1/2-hour drive.

Other Activities:
Golf, tennis, canoeing, rafting, hiking, bird watching, antiquing, biking, wildlife photography, Civil War history.

Contact:
Ed Markel
Inn at Narrow Passage, PO Box 608, US Rt. 11 South, Woodstock, VA 22664; 540/459-8000, fax 540/459-8001, website http://www.inn book.com

THE SHENANDOAH'S NORTH FORK is an angler's dream. Rock ledges give way to bouldery gravel runs bordered by grassbeds. All you'll need is a 6-weight rod, a weight-forward floating line and a plastic box with a few streamers, poppers and big nymphs. Or use ultralight spinning gear. A five-foot rod, a little reel spooled with 4-pound-test line and a half dozen three-inch black-and-silver floating and diving crankbaits will keep you in smallmouths all day. If you've a mind to, pack along a couple crawdad imitations. Perhaps the best month on this river is October, when the big leaves on the sycamore trees get leathery along the edges. Float it in a canoe, or wade.

Public access to the river is plentiful. Just north of Woodstock, Route 665 turns east from U.S. 11 toward Green Mountain. In a couple of miles it joins Route 758 and crosses the North Fork below an old mill dam. The plunge pool at the dam holds fish, but the better fishing is downstream along the rocky shoals and ledges. Several state and county roads cross the river as it meanders down the valley. Each bridge has a parking pull-off.

One of these is a couple hundred yards from the Inn at Narrow Passage. Once Stonewall Jackson's headquarters, the log inn has been lovingly restored by Ed and Ellen Markel, who run it as a bed and breakfast. Choose from Jackson's room in the original inn that dates from 1740 or pick a newer room with a private door onto the front porch. The inn has 12 rooms, all with private baths. Breakfast is country and served in front of a stone fireplace. A jar of chocolate chip cookies sits on a sideboard in the main room.

For local patterns and advice on where to use them, drop in on smallmouth guru Harry Murray (540/984-4212) in his pharmacy turned tackleshop south on U.S. 11 in Edinburg. Murray is a gregarious guy whose flyfishing schools (two days for $275) for Shenandoah smallmouths are frequent and well attended. Murray guides as well. If you're a smallmouth fan, his fee of $150 per day is well worth it. And if the Civil War piques your curiosity, you're right in the heart of Stonewall Jackson's Valley Campaigns of 1862.

Shenandoah Lodge
L u r a y ,   V i r g i n i a

Overnight here, then fish for smallmouths and brookies in the shadows of the Blue Ridge.

VITAL STATISTICS:

KEY SPECIES:
Smallmouth bass; brook trout

Season:
March through October

Accommodations:
Log and stone lodge and cabins
Number of Guest Rooms: 6
Maximum Number of Guests: 12

Conference Groups: No

Meals: American plan

Rates:
$495 per person for 3 days

Guides: Included

Gratuities: $100

Preferred Payment:
Credit cards

Getting There:
About a 2-hour drive west of Washington, D.C. Call for specific directions.

Other Activities:
Golf, tennis, canoeing, whitewater rafting, swimming, boating, hiking, bird watching, antiquing, biking, wildlife photography, skiing.

Contact:
Charlie Walsh
Shenandoah Lodge, 100 Grand View Dr., Luray, VA 22835; 540/743-1920, email flyfish@ shentel.net

"OH SHENANDOAH, I love your water..." A corruption of the original tune, perhaps, but that's what anglers hum down here on the west flanks of Virginia's Blue Ridge. It's smallmouth bass country, popularized by flyfishing guru Harry Murray in Edinburg, and Gerald Almy's writings for *Sports Afield*. There's no doubt about it, the Shenandoah is one fine river. Actually it's two. The North Fork breaks off the main stem at Front Royal and drains the valley through which Interstate-81 runs. The south Fork is a continuation of the main stem. You can trace its course by following U.S. Route 340.

Anglers from Shenandoah Lodge generally fish the South Fork and a number of mountain creeks known for good populations of brook trout. Shenandoah smallmouths are rapacious. In April and May, they'll nail small spinnerbaits, plastic grubs, worms and floating-diving minnow plugs such as Rebels and Rapalas. Black and silver is always a good pattern. Don't overlook Mepps spinners: a No. 1 silver bucktail can be a killer. Ultralight is the way to go here. A four- or five-pounder will put a bend in your mind as well as your rod. In summer, poppers work at dusk. Fishing is best in September and October, as that's when the bigger fish become more aggressive. While spinfishers do well, the river was made for flyfishing. Use Clousers, Zonkers, Woolly Buggers, Strymphs in white, black or brown and, of course, poppers. Flies are big and you'll need at least a 5-weight rod to throw them effectively. Among the best water on the South Fork is the lodge's home stretch of riffled shallows and a run or two that harbor big bronzebacks and an errant trout or two.

Trout in the Shenandoah? That's right, and the five-pound rainbow that guide Steve Tenney pulled from the lodge's water is proof. Scores of trout streams drain into the South Fork. It stands to reason that rainbows and browns can live in the colder and better oxygenated sections of the river and run up small creeks to spawn. However, they are few and far between. In the main, trout fishing means angling in Shenandoah National Park with a fly for native brookies in the six- to 12-inch range.

Bass and trout anglers share the same dinner tables at Shenandoah Lodge, so conversation is apt to be lively. So is the menu: chilled gazpacho, roast Cornish game hens, vidalias and mushrooms in herb sauce. Of six guest rooms, two are in the main lodge and four in log cabins on the hillside. All have private baths. An Orvis dealer, the lodge has plenty of tackle. Fishing instruction is available.

Cheat Mountain Club

D u r b i n ,   W e s t   V i r g i n i a

Deep in the heart of West Virginia, Cheat Mountain is an intimate lodge with a mile and a half of private trout stream.

VITAL STATISTICS:

KEY SPECIES:
Brown trout;
smallmouth bass

Season:
All year

Accommodations:
RUSTIC COUNTRY INN
NUMBER OF GUEST ROOMS: 10
MAXIMUM NUMBER OF GUESTS: 26

Conference Groups: Yes

Meals: American plan

Rates:
From $80 per person per night,
double occupancy

Guides: $100 for 1 per day

Gratuities: 10% of guide fee

Preferred Payment:
MasterCard, Visa

Getting There:
Pittsburgh is the closest major
airport; rent a car and drive
from there, using the club's map
as your guide.

Other Activities:
Canoeing, hiking, bird watching,
whitewater rafting, skiing,
wildlife photography.

Contact:
Gladys Boehmer
Cheat Mountain Club,
PO Box 28, Durbin, WV
26264; 304/456-4627,
fax 304/456-3192.

MOST OF THE 20TH CENTURY seems to have bypassed this log hotel, a private retreat set on 187 acres in the midst of the Monongahela National Forest. Around it rise nine of West Virginia's highest mountains, while a mile and a half of the Shavers Fork of the Cheat River flows through its property and past the front porch. Owners of the hotel stock the river with 12- to 14-inch rainbows and only those who stay at the hotel may fish it, catch-and-release, of course. When it comes to accommodations and fishing, guests here are in for a treat on both counts.

The upper Shavers Fork is not big water, but rather riffles and runs with a stony bottom. Maples, beech and some spruce line its banks. Occasional undercut banks, heavy with grass, hang over the stream, sheltering browns, rainbows and a few brookies. The water warms in midsummer, sending trout into springholes or shady mouths of coldwater tributaries. The best time to fish this stream is in April, May and June, when the water is cool. Then you'll fish among blooming dogwoods and, later, laurel and rhododendron. In September and October, the river revives with autumn temperatures. This is the time for terrestrials. Fish the shadows, as that's where trout hold in this low, clear water. The lower part of the river, a 10-mile and half hour ride from the lodge, offers smallmouth bass fishing. Flip a bucktail Mepps or toss a Rebel Crawdad. Two- to three-pounders are frequently released, says Bill Murray of Mountain State Outfitters (304/925-5959), who guides in the area. If big trout consume your agenda, he'll probably recommend the West Fork of the Greenbrier River.

The Cheat Mountain Club is a day's drive from Atlanta, New York or Cleveland, and the trip is well worth it. At the end of the lane, you'll find that what this retreat lacks in modern amenities (only one room has a private bath, the others share as they did when Messrs. Ford, Edison and Firestone visited in 1918), it more than makes up for in pure, traditional warmth. Guest rooms are softly paneled. On the third floor, there's a special bunkroom for children. Downstairs, in the great room, handmade sofas and chairs are grouped in front of the fieldstone fireplace, and in corners just made for casual conversation or a stint with a good book. Candles and crystal complement china of the club's own pattern for full-course, family-style dinners that may feature Cornish hens or prime rib, topped off by apple pie.

Class VI River Runners

Lansing, West Virginia

For a thrill, try extreme smallmouth fishing deep in the New River Gorge.

VITAL STATISTICS:

KEY SPECIES:
Smallmouth bass; muskellunge

Season:
April through October

Accommodations:
CAMPING OR LODGING NEARBY
NUMBER OF GUEST ROOMS: N/A
MAXIMUM NUMBER OF GUESTS: N/A

Conference Groups: Yes

Meals: Included

Rates:
Day trips from $410 for 2; $800 for 2 for an overnight run

Guides: Included

Gratuities: Client's discretion

Preferred Payment:
Major credit cards

Getting There:
Charleston, West Virginia is the closest airport with commercial service. Rent a car, follow US 60 and Rt. 16S to Fayetteville, pick up US 19N, cross the New River Gorge Bridge, exit onto Ames Heights Road.

Other Activities:
Golf, rafting, hiking, bird watching, antiquing, biking, wildlife photography, rock climbing.

Contact:
Dave Arnold
Class VI River Runners, Ames Heights Rd., PO Box 78, Lansing, WV 25862; 800/252-7784, fax 304/574-4906.

YOUR FLOAT STARTS GENTLY enough, the light green water flowing lazily by the launch site. You climb into the raft and cinch tight the life vest. The raft moves easily with the current and you toss a crawdad crankbait here and there and pick up a smallmouth or two. But now there's a rushing sound, and the raft is buckling over waves. You stow the rod and hang on. Squirrel (that's what you're supposed to call him; his real name, Brian, seems out of place here), shouts "Get ready!" The raft stands on its bow, then tailwalks, and above it all Squirrel is screaming his head off: "Cast behind that boulder." You do and a bronzeback of a couple of pounds nails the plug; then you plunge into the next caldron of boiling white-water. This is extreme fishing.

The New River is a tailwater known for some of the highest quality smallmouth fishing in the country. However, even die-hard anglers would not take a boat into the gorge. Water there is dangerously rough for anything other than a reinforced raft. But you can fish from a raft, so why not? Day trips of six miles and longer overnight expeditions down the New are something of a specialty for Dave Arnold, a whitewater nut who owns Class VI River Runners. Class VI rafts have rigid floors with padded pedestal seats. Personal gear is stowed in dry bags. All you have to do is plug pockets behind the boulders and hang on!

Smallmouth fishing is best in May, June and August, while your best shot at muskies up to 45 inches comes in August and September.

You'll want to take your own tackle and camping gear. If you need to rent tents, pads or sleeping bags, you can from Class VI. Equipment for overnight treks—tents, sleeping bags, dry clothing, food—is carried in a supply raft. Day trippers will marvel at the gourmet lunch spread beside the river. Overnighters will welcome hors d'oeuvres and wine that precede dinner. If you'd rather have a hot shower at the end of the day, the staff at Class VI will make arrangements for your stay at one of more than a dozen hostelries ranging from the elegant Greenbrier at White Sulphur Springs, an hour and a half from the river, to bed and breakfasts or rustic cabins nearby.

THE MIDWEST

ARKANSAS, ILLINOIS, INDIANA, IOWA, KANSAS, MICHIGAN, MINNESOTA, MISSOURI, NEBRASKA, NORTH DAKOTA, OHIO, OKLAHOMA, SOUTH DAKOTA, WISCONSIN

IN KEEPING with the prairie populism that spreads like morning sun across the great plains, most who travel the Midwest to fish the many lakes and rivers put up in motels and eat in little restaurants where nothing is fancy and everything is good. Except for the well-known angling in the Great Lakes, this is a region where fisheries tend to be hidden jewels—spawning walleyes in the Missouri at Chamberlain, South Dakota, spring creek trout of Minnesota and Wisconsin's Driftless Area, steelhead and salmon in the cobble-bottom rivers of Michigan, smallmouths and pike in the Boundary Waters. Not to be overlooked are towns along the great rivers or marinas on big lakes where bass, crappies and catfish rule.

Lodges:

Arkansas
1 ANDERSON HOUSE INN
2 GASTON'S WHITE RIVER RESORT
3 PJ'S LODGE

Illinois
4 STARVED ROCK LODGE

Michigan
5 GATES AU SABLE LODGE
6 JOHNSON'S PERE MARQUETTE LODGE

Minnesota
7 ANGLE OUTPOST RESORT
8 BIRCH KNOLL RANCH
9 EAGLE RIDGE AT LUSTEN MOUNTAINS
10 GOLDEN EAGLE LODGE
11 JUDD'S RESORT
12 ROCKWOOD LODGE

Missouri
13 BIG CEDAR LODGE
14 TAYLORMADE RIVER TREKS
15 WIND RUSH FARMS

Ohio
16 GAYLES BED & BREAKFAST

Backcounry Publications,
The Countryman Press, Rt. 2, PO Box
748, Woodstock, VT 05091;
802/457-4826

FLY FISHING FOR TROUT IN MISSOURI
— Chuck & Sharon Tryon
Ozark Mountain Fly Fishers,
1 Johnson St., Rolla, MO 65401;
573/364-5509

Oklahoma

17 LAKE TEXOMA RESORT PARK

South Dakota

18 CEDAR SHORE RESORT

Wisconsin

19 JAMIESON HOUSE INN

20 SERENDIPITY FARM

References:

GREAT LAKES STEELHEAD GUIDE
— Mike Modrzynski
Frank Amato Publications, PO Box
82112, Portland, OR 97282;
503/653-8108

WISCONSIN & MINNESOTA
TROUT STREAMS
— Jim Humphrey & Bill Shogren
GREAT LAKES STEELHEAD:
A GUIDED TOUR FOR FLY-ANGLERS
MICHIGAN TROUT STREAMS — Bob
Linsenman & Steve Nevala

Resources:

ARKANSAS GAME AND
FISH COMMISSION,
Information Section, 2 Natural
Resources Dr., Little Rock, AR 72205;
501/223-6351, 800/364-4263/x6351,
website http://www.state.ar.us

ILLINOIS DEPARTMENT OF
NATURAL RESOURCES,
Lincoln Tower Plaza, 524 S. Second
St., Springfield, IL 62701-1787;
217/785-0075, website
http://dnr.state.il.us

References & Resources

INDIANA DIVISION OF
FISH AND WILDLIFE,
_402 W. Washington St., Rm W-273,
Indianapolis, IN 46204; 317/232-
4087, website http://www.ai.org/dnr_

IOWA DEPARTMENT OF
NATURAL RESOURCES,
_Wallace State Office Bldg., East Ninth
and Grand Ave., Des Moines, IA
50319-1220; 515/281-5145, website
http://www.state.ia.us/government/
dnr/index.html_

KANSAS DEPARTMENT OF
WILDLIFE AND PARKS,
_512 S.E. 25th Ave., Pratt, KS 67124;
316/672-5911, website
http://www.ink.org/
public/kdwp/_

MICHIGAN DEPARTMENT OF
NATURAL RESOURCES,
Fisheries Div.,
_Box 30446, Lansing, MI 48909;
517/373-1280, website
http://www.dnr.state.mi.us/www/fish_

MINNESOTA DEPARTMENT
OF NATURAL RESOURCES,
_500 Lafayette St., St. Paul, MN
55155; 612/296-6157, website
http://www.dnr.state.mn.us/_

MISSOURI DEPARTMENT
OF CONSERVATION,
_2901 W. Truman Blvd., PO Box 180,
Jefferson City, MO 65102-0180;
573/751-4115, website
http://www.state.mo.us/conservation/
welcome.html_

NEBRASKA GAME AND
PARKS COMMISSION,
_2200 N. 33rd, Lincoln, NE 68503;
402/471-0641, website
http://www.ngpc.state.ne.us_

NORTH DAKOTA STATE
GAME AND FISH DEPARTMENT,
_100 North Bismarck Expressway,
Bismarck, ND 58501; 701/328-6300,
website http://www.state.nd.us/gnf/_

OHIO DIVISION OF WILDLIFE,
_1840 Belcher Dr., Columbus, OH
43224-1329; 614/265-6300,
website http://www.dnr.state.
oh.us/odnr/wildlife/wildlife.html_

OKLAHOMA DEPARTMENT OF
WILDLIFE CONSERVATION,
_1801 N. Lincoln, Oklahoma City, OK
73105; 405/521-3721, website
http://www.state.ok.us/~odwc.fish.html_

SOUTH DAKOTA DEPARTMENT
OF GAME, FISH AND PARKS,
_Joe Foss Bldg., 523 E. Capitol, Pierre,
SD 57501-3182;
605/773-3485, website
http://www.state.sd.us/gfp/_

WISCONSIN DEPARTMENT OF
NATURAL RESOURCES,
_Bureau of Fisheries, PO Box 7921,
101 S. Webster St., Madison, WI
53707; 608/266-1877, website
http://www.dnr.state.wi.us_

_Fish a private spring creek for two-pound rainbows
while staying in the 150-year-old cabins of Wind Rush
Farms in Cook Station, Missouri. —_ page 100.

Anderson House Inn

Heber Springs, Arkansas

Fish for 30-pound brown trout in the river of records.

VITAL STATISTICS:

KEY SPECIES:
Brown, brook and rainbow trout; hybrid and smallmouth bass; walleyes

Season:
All year

Accommodations:
COUNTRY INN
NUMBER OF GUEST ROOMS: 16
MAXIMUM NUMBER OF GUESTS: 36

Conference Groups: Yes

Meals: Bed and breakfast

Rates:
From $78 per night for 2

Guides: $225 per day for 2

Gratuities: $25 to $50

Preferred Payment:
Major credit cards

Getting There:
Drive from Little Rock or Memphis (about 2 hours east).

Other Activities:
Golf, tennis, canoeing, rafting, swimming, boating, hiking, bird watching, antiquing, biking, wildlife photography, sailing, scuba.

Contact:
**Jim Hildebrand
Anderson House Inn, 201 E. Main St., Heber Springs, AR 72543-3116; 501/362-5266, fax 501/362-2326, email jhildebr@cswnet.com, website http://www. bbonline.com/AR/Anderson/Fishing.html**

ARKANSAS gets pretty laid back once you leave Little Rock and its environs. About an hour north is Heber Springs, a sleepy town about a mile from the Little Red River. The Little Red, along with the Norfolk and White rivers, completes Arkansas' trio of fine tailwater fisheries. However, unlike the White and Norfolk, the Little Red fishes more like a spring creek and less like a freestone stream.

Beds of long aquatic vegetation wave in the current. They're loaded with sow bugs, and browns in the Little Red thrive on them. A 14-incher stocked in April will be 16 inches in July. Trout grow fast and big. How big? In May 1992, Rip Collins landed a 40-pound 4-ounce brown that became the world record. That was no fluke. Other browns approaching 30 pounds have been taken from the Little Red.

Though saturated with fodder for grazing browns, the Little Red isn't easy to fish. Water weeds make presentation of nymphs difficult. Bill Combs, of The Ozark Angler (501/362-3597), an Orvis-endorsed outfitter near Heber Springs, claims that the only way to catch big browns on a fly is to perfect a dead-drift technique imitating the natural movement of the sow bugs. You can't swing a nymph or streamer here: too much grass. But no matter. It fishes well all year. In January and February, rainbows make spawning runs upstream toward the dam; then the browns do the same, from September through December. Summer brings good dry fly fishing. Most anglers will fish from rafts or driftboats, as wading access is limited and the water can rise in a hurry. If you prefer lake fishing, switch to hybrid bass, which feed on schooled shad in Greers Ferry Lake, above the dam, throughout the summer. Use binoculars to locate bass gorging on the shad, then run up in the boat, and cast white streamers for three- to six-pounders. When you hook up, the bass will race for bottom. Keeping the fish from reaching the submerged treetops is the only way to win the battle.

The Anderson House is a great place to stay whether you're fishing the lake or the river. Rockers line a front porch that stretches the length of the white-frame, green-shuttered country hotel, now a bed and breakfast. Your room will be one of 16, all with private baths, furnished with handmade quilts and regional antiques. Breakfasts are country hearty: egg casseroles, biscuits, cheese garlic grits, sausage gravy, fresh fruit. If you've taken an afternoon off from the fishing, you'll find lemonade or hot chocolate and cookies, compliments of the house.

Gaston's White River Resort

L a k e v i e w ,   A r k a n s a s

VITAL STATISTICS:

KEY SPECIES:
Brown and rainbow trout; smallmouth bass

Season:
All year

Accommodations:
COTTAGES
NUMBER OF GUEST ROOMS: 74
MAXIMUM NUMBER OF GUESTS: 250

Conference Groups: Yes
Meals: Full-service restaurant
Rates:
From $66 for 2 per night
Guides: $200 for 2 per day
Gratuities: $10 to $20
Preferred Payment:
MasterCard, Visa

Getting There:
Fly to Mountain Home, rent a car and drive 15 miles west to Lakeview.

Other Activities:
Golf, tennis, swimming, boating, hiking, bird watching, antiquing, wildlife photography.

Contact:
Jim Gaston
Gaston's White River Resort, 1 River Rd., Lakeview, AR 72642; 501/431-5202, 501/431-5216, email 73522,3605 @Compuserve.com, website http://www. gastons.com

Tailwater browns top 10 pounds at this Arkansas resort.

RESORT IS THE RIGHT WORD to describe Jim Gaston's place on the White River below Bull Shoals Dam. Seventy-four cottages (some with fireplaces and wood decks, all with private baths), sleeping from two to 10 guests, string along the river, flanking the main lodge with its river-view restaurant, bar, gift shop, tackleshop and game room. Behind the lodge, nestled in a copse of trees, is a pool and, nearby, tennis courts. Across the road from the cottages is a private landing field with a 3200-foot grass runway. This place gives a different meaning to the idea of roughing it at an Arkansas fish camp.

Despite the creature comforts, fishing is taken seriously here. With each cottage, you also get a 20-foot johnboat. Rent a 10-horse motor and you're in business for fishing this outstanding tailwater. The White River rises in Missouri and is impounded by Bull Shoals Dam. As is the case with most tailwaters, flows can fluctuate dangerously. If you're wading you'll want to move to the shallows as soon as you see the water begin to rise. But the releases from the dam are a constant 55°F. Even in the dog days of summer, the water warms less than 1°F per mile downstream from the dam.

That promotes an abundance of aquatic insects and crustaceans on which browns and rainbows feed. Browns of more than 10 pounds are frequent, rainbows run to five pounds or so. Fishing is generally good here year-round, but most trophy browns are taken in the dead of winter. From November 1 through January 31, from the base of the dam to the downstream boundary of Bull Shoals State Park, brown trout are strictly catch-and-release and may be taken only with artificial lures carrying a single barbless hook. Cress Bugs, Sulphurs and midges work well, as do

Woolly Buggers. Spinfishers will find spinners and imitation minnows effective where they are legal. And while you're at it, don't overlook the smallmouth bass. Another year-round fishery, the best months are March through May and September and October for bronzebacks up to seven pounds.

PJ's Lodge
Norfolk, Arkansas

*Stay at a California lodge along the White River,
where trophy browns and rainbows hit all winter.*

VITAL STATISTICS:

KEY SPECIES:
Brown, rainbow, brook and cutthroat trout

Season:
All year

Accommodations:
CALIFORNIA-STYLE LODGE
NUMBER OF GUEST ROOMS: 10
MAXIMUM NUMBER OF GUESTS: 20

Conference Groups: Yes

Meals: Bed and breakfast; dinners additional

Rates:
$75 for 2 per night

Guides: $175 for 1

Gratuities: 15%

Preferred Payment:
Cash or check

Getting There:
Fly to Mountain Home and rent a car, or have the lodge provide transportation for $10 each way.

Other Activities:
Canoeing, rafting, swimming, boating, bird watching, hiking, antiquing, biking, wildlife photography, caves, folk music, arts and crafts.

Contact:
Paul or Joyce Campbell PJ's Lodge, PO Box 61, Norfolk, AR 72658; 501/499-7500, email amcminn@southwind. net, website http:// www.kanweb.com/ arkansas/pi.html

THE WINNING COMBO at PJ's Lodge on the White River is a long, limber rod throwing a No. 2 weight-forward floating line with a 12-foot 6X leader. Use weighted nymphs, No. 16 and smaller, and cast with finesse. In November and December, spawning 10-pound browns and five-pound rainbows will wear you out. Rainbows spawning in winter? That's right, they're a little precocious, and the White and its North Fork are tailwater fisheries. They're good all year, but come into their prime when leaves turn russet and a chill braces the air.

While you'll find many that are smaller, 16- to 26-inch rainbows are caught and released each week. Browns in this part of the river have tipped the scales at 39 pounds. November through January are especially good for the rainbows, though they crank up again for traditional hatches from March through August. Browns peak from December through January and later in March and April. In addition, you can fish for brook trout and cutthroats year-round (trophy cutts up to 10 pounds have been landed in November through January). You may also want to test your flytackle against stripers from December through March or catch them on trolled baits year-round. Flyfishers prefer to wade and fish while baitfishers generally drift the river. Opportunities to freelance, that is fish without a guide, are legion, but it makes sense to use a guide for a couple of days to get the lay of the water.

Ozark trout lured Paul and Joyce Campbell from California to 50 acres at the end of a gravel road where they built their lodge overlooking the river. Wood, glass and open vistas give this 10-guest-room (private baths) hideaway a distinctly western flavor. Joyce, a native of Holland, has added lace tablecloths and touches of blue delft in the dining room. People come to PJ's to eat her cooking—roast Cornish game hens with grape sauce—as often as they come to fight White River trout. After dinner, wander out to the long front porch to plunk down in a lounge chair, prop your feet on the rail and think of the fish you'll catch on the morrow.

Starved Rock Lodge
U t i c a ,   I l l i n o i s

VITAL STATISTICS:

KEY SPECIES:
Sauger; walleyes; smallmouth and white bass

Season:
All year

Accommodations:
RUSTIC LODGE AND CABINS
NUMBER OF GUEST ROOMS: 72 in lodge; 22 in cabins
MAXIMUM NUMBER OF GUESTS: 280
Conference Groups: Yes
Meals: Restaurant
Rates:
From $56 for 2 per night
Guides: $220 for 2 per day
Gratuities: Client's discretion
Preferred Payment:
Major credit cards
Getting There:
Just east of the intersection of I-80 and I-39.
Other Activities:
Golf, tennis, canoeing, swimming, boating, hiking, bird watching, antiquing, biking, wildlife photography, cross-country skiing.

Contact:
Charlotte Wiesbrock Starved Rock Lodge, PO Box 570, Rts. 71 & 178, Utica, IL 61373; 815/ 667-4211, fax 815/667-4455, email srlodge @ivnet.com, website http://dnr.state.il.us/ parks/lodges/srsp.htm

Fish some of the best sauger and walleye water in the Midwest while staying at an historic lodge.

THE ILLINOIS RIVER at Starved Rock Lock and Dam is not known as big-fish water, though channel cats can go into the double digits. Some anglers come here for the cats, but those who know the secret come to Starved Rock for sauger. Sauger are similar to walleyes, but they are smaller, averaging a pound or two and carry round spots on the membranes between the dorsal spines. They can stand water with a heavier silt content than walleyes, and like their more popular cousins, prefer deep water. In fact walleyes like shallower water than sauger. In the Midwest, some of the best sauger waters are those below dams.

At Starved Rock, you'll find four times as many sauger as walleyes. Typical fish run between 14 and 18 inches. Walleyes tend to be a little larger, though not as plentiful. Best fishing is from April through June, and again from September through November. Fall fishing, because water levels are more stable, is more predictable. Anglers working jigs and minnows, minnows under slip bobbers and spinnerbaits should do well. Some anglers may be disappointed that they're catching sauger and not walleyes, but that only lasts until their first mouthful of broiled sauger filet.

Above the dam, the Illinois River takes on the character of still water. Fish the mouths of feeder creeks for smallmouth bass of 12 inches or so in the spring. Scrappy white bass, also called striped bass (which they're not), hit jigs and spinners with abandon in spring. Throughout summer, you'll find a profusion of panfish made for kids with light spinning tackle. Information, licenses and guides are available from Starved Rock Bait & Tackle (815/667-4862).

As you'd expect, anyplace with a name like Starved Rock has to have a bit of lore behind it. In the 1760s, members of the Illiniwek slew the noble Pontiac, chief of the Ottawas. In revenge, the Ottawas and their allies, the Potawatomi, surrounded a high bluff to which the Illiniwek had retreated, and starved them to death. Today, no one starves at this state park resort. The restaurant is open year-round and has something of a local reputation for fine fish. Guests stay in rooms in the lovely old hotel, built by the CCC in the 1930s, in nearby cabins or camp. Myriad hiking and horse trails weave through the bluffs, and a launching ramp is provided for boats.

Gates Au Sable Lodge

Grayling, Michigan

Fish a true blue-ribbon stream for big rainbows and browns.

IF THE EIGHT MILES of the Au Sable below Grayling is the Holy Water, then its church is the flyshop at Gates Au Sable Lodge, and its high priest is Rusty Gates. For more than a quarter of a century, he's guided anglers, tied patterns specific to the river and fought like a pit bull to ensure that development, pollution and politics do not upset the balance of this, one of the nation's premiere trout rivers. More than 150 miles of this river have been accorded "Blue Ribbon" status by the Michigan Department of Natural Resources, which does not make such designations lightly.

The grayling, sadly, are gone. But in their place are brookies in the headwaters of the main stem and its North and South branches, rainbows, and the hulking browns for which the river is held in such high regard. Browns of 24 inches are not uncommon, and those in the 16- to 18-inch class are plentiful. The river is famed for *hexagenia limbata.* "Overblown," says Gates, but he still enjoys drifting the river at night in his high-stern, low-freeboard, canoelike Au Sable River Boat and casting to slurping browns while the northern lights flash overhead. Hatches on the river are prolific from opening day in April well into the fall, when the wise angler takes along a 20-gauge for grouse. Au Sable ("sands" in French) is easily waded in most spots and access is readily available. Best fishing is from May through July. Numerous sections of this long river are governed by special regulations. Spinfishers as well as flyfishermen will enjoy themselves.

As for the lodge, 16 spacious rooms, efficiencies and a suite (all with private baths) face the river. So, too, does the dining room where Gates' wife, Julie, runs the restaurant and, according to Messrs. Meck and Hoover, authors of *Great Rivers and Great Hatches,* turns out the "best food in Crawford County." Gates operates one of the most complete shops in the Midwest and it is well stocked with flies proven on the river. Fish freelance or hire a guide and float the river.

VITAL STATISTICS:

KEY SPECIES:
Brown and rainbow trout

Season:
May through October

Accommodations:
MOTEL ROOMS
NUMBER OF GUEST ROOMS: 16
MAXIMUM NUMBER OF GUESTS: 36

Conference Groups: Yes
Meals: A la carte from on-site restaurant

Rates:
From $75 for 2 per night

Guides: $175 for 1 per day, $250 for 2

Gratuities: $25 to $50

Preferred Payment:
MasterCard, Visa

Getting There:
Traverse City has the closest commercial flights, or rent a car from there, pick up I-75 and head north to the Grayling exit, turn right on Rt. 72 and left on Stephan Bridge Road.

Other Activities:
Canoeing, swimming, hiking, bird watching, biking.

Contact:
Rusty Gates
Gates Au Sable Lodge,
471 Stephan Bridge Rd.,
Grayling, MI 49738;
517-348-8462, fax
517-348-2541, email
71542.1437@compu
serve.com

Johnson's Pere Marquette Lodge
B a l d w i n ,   M i c h i g a n

VITAL STATISTICS:

KEY SPECIES:
Brown and rainbow trout; salmon; steelhead

Season:
All year

Accommodations:
CEDAR LODGE AND RUSTIC CABINS
NUMBER OF GUEST ROOMS: 34
MAXIMUM NUMBER OF GUESTS: 70

Conference Groups: No

Meals: In Baldwin, 3 miles north

Rates:
From $39 per person per night

Guides: $225 for 2 per day

Gratuities: Client's discretion

Preferred Payment:
Discover, MasterCard, Visa

Getting There:
Drive north on US 131 from Grand Rapids, take US 10 west to Baldwin, and Rt. 37 south to Johnson's.

Other Activities:
Golf, canoeing, biking.

Contact:
Jim Johnson
Johnson's Pere Marquette Lodge,
Rt. 1, Box 1290,
Baldwin, MI 49304;
616/745-3972, fax 616/745-3830.

Browns, rainbows, salmon and steelhead thrive on this southernmost of Michigan's premiere streams.

ACCORDING TO BOB LINSENMAN and Steve Nevala, authors of _Michigan Trout Streams_, too many anglers concentrate on the Pere Marquette's glamour fish, salmon and steelhead, and give short shrift to "its everyday citizens, beautiful and healthy brown trout." Sure, everyone loves to see a nine-pound steelhead slam a Wiggler pattern, slash off 75 feet of line and somersault upstream. But browns are the mainstays of this river, and you can avoid the crowds by fishing where most others don't.

A good bet is the upper river between Rosa Road and Switzer Bridge. Resident browns predominate. Linsenman recommends attractors: Royal Wulffs, Adams and Rusty's Spinners; black and brown stonefly nymphs, Sizes 8 to 10; and terrestrials, especially small 'hoppers for those days when puffs of summer wind blow them onto the water and turn on trout like nothing else. From the Michigan Route 37 bridge west eight miles to Gleason's Landing is fly-only water. Many anglers float this section, nymphing for browns and rainbows. Others wade it, casting dries. When steelhead are in the stream, November to May, it may get crowded. Salmon run from August to October, with the end of the season being better than the beginning.

Orvis-endorsed Johnson's Lodge is on the flyfishing-only section of the river where it's crossed by Route 37 just below Baldwin. Built of cedar, with a rustic fieldstone fireplace and log stair banister, the main lodge has 10 rooms, each with a large whirlpool tub. Five fishing cabins, two cottages and two houses round out accommodations at Johnson's. The lodge has yet to add a restaurant, but several local eateries provide breakfasts, and many of the lodge's guests dine at the Big Star Lake Inn, known for its steaks and ribs, three miles up the road in Baldwin. Flies Only, a full-service tackleshop, supplies local patterns and plenty of information about stream conditions. You can arrange guides and floats here, as well as buy licenses.

Angle Outpost Resort

Angle Inlet, Minnesota

This is perhaps the best place to fish for trophy muskies.

VITAL STATISTICS:

KEY SPECIES:
Walleyes; muskellunge; smallmouth bass; northern pike

Season:
All year

Accommodations:
CABINS
NUMBER OF GUEST ROOMS: 30
MAXIMUM NUMBER OF GUESTS: 60 plus

Conference Groups: No

Meals: Various plans

Rates:
From $36 per night for 2

Guides: $155 per day for up to 3 anglers

Gratuities: Client's discretion

Preferred Payment:
Discover, MasterCard, Visa

Getting There:
Winnipeg is the closest airport with commercial flights.

Other Activities:
Swimming, boating, hiking, wildlife photography.

Contact:
Diane Edman
Angle Outpost Resort, Box 36, Angle Inlet, MN 56711; 800/441-5014, phone/fax 218/223-8101.

REMEMBER THIS TEASER from 7th grade geography: What's the northernmost spot in the contiguous United States? (Clue: It's frequently the coldest as well.) If you said "Lake of the Woods," you're right. Roughly 66 miles long and 52 wide, Lake of the Woods contains 14,000 or so islands. Adjacent to it is a chunk of U.S. mainland, the Red Lake Indian Reservation, also known as the Northwest Angle.

This is one of the finest freshwater fisheries in North America. Flattened and gouged by glaciers, the land is low and rocky. Boulders by the millions pave the shores of all the islands. Submerged reefs are everywhere. Some bays and backwaters are sandy, silt-bottomed and fringed with beds of reedy grass. The habitat is ideal for smallmouths, walleyes, pike and muskies. Bronzebacks are plentiful, though they seldom exceed two pounds. Fishing is best for them in July and August. Walleyes, also abundant, generally run in the two- to three-pound class, but may top seven. Action with them begins in mid-May and peaks in June and July. Northern pike average five to eight pounds, but bruisers of 20 pounds or more take spoons or spinners often enough to keep you on your toes. Your best chance for a trophy is just after ice-out in May. And if you're after muskellunge, you'll find lots of 15-pounders, and many between 20 and 30. Fish for them from July through September. Don't forget icefishing for walleyes and sauger.

Angle Outpost is one of the few full-service resorts serving anglers who want to fish Lake of the Woods. Numerous packages are available, from straight rental of one of 12 modern housekeeping cabins to a deluxe American plan that includes boat, motor and guide. The cabins are warm and homey, cheerfully decorated and scattered among the trees near the main lodge. Each has a fully equipped kitchen (coffee maker and microwave) and most feature fireplaces or wood stoves. In addition to the restaurant, you'll find a camp store that sells groceries as well as bait, tackle and gifts. You can launch or rent a boat at the marina.

Birch Knoll Ranch

L a n e s b o r o ,   M i n n e s o t a

Unspoiled and uncrowded, the Driftless Area can't be beat for small creek browns.

VITAL STATISTICS:

KEY SPECIES:
Brook and brown trout

Season:
April through October

Accommodations:
1900s VICTORIAN FARMHOUSE
NUMBER OF GUEST ROOMS: 3
MAXIMUM NUMBER OF GUESTS: 6

Conference Groups: No

Meals: Breakfast only

Rates:
From $55 per night for 2

Guides: From $150

Gratuities: 15%

Preferred Payment:
MasterCard, Visa

Getting There:
Fly to Minneapolis, Rochester or La Crosse, Wisconsin, rent a car and drive to the ranch.

Other Activities:
Canoeing, biking, hiking, bird watching, wildlife photography, antiquing.

Contact:
Duke Hust
Birch Knoll Ranch, 820 Old Crystal Bay Rd., Wayzata, MN 55391; 612/475-2054.

THIS MAY COME AS A SHOCK to anglers who fly east and west searching for the best trout fishing in the U.S., but southeastern Minnesota has more and better mileage of wild brown and brook trout water than most other states. How come? To some degree, it's an accident of geography and geology. The region escaped the heavy continental glaciation that filled most of the narrow valleys in the north-central part of the U.S. with sand and gravel. Known as the Driftless Area, valleys here are deep and often no more than a few hundred yards wide. Streams in these valleys originate in and are fed by limestone springs.

A second reason for this high-quality fishery can be found in partnership between landowners, the state's department of natural resources and the Win-Cres and Rochester chapters of Trout Unlimited. Since the 1960s they've been working together to abate silt and chemical pollution, to develop public easements along trout waters and to improve habitat. The result is a network of creeks that harbor healthy populations of brown and brook trout. Little of the water is posted.

Pressure is heaviest where the streams touch highways, but it's never overwhelming. And after walleye season opens, 99 percent of the state's anglers head for bigger rivers and lakes, leaving the streams to diehard trouters. The season opens in April and closes in October. Among the better streams are the South Fork of the Root River and tributaries such as Trout Run, Willow Creek and Rush Creek. Hatches are prolific. But a flybox containing Elk-Hair Caddis (No. 14 to 18), Blue-Winged Olives (No. 16 to 18), Adams (No. 14 to 18) and a stock of Gold-Ribbed Hare's Ears, Woolly Buggers and Pheasant Tail Nymphs will suffice. Guide Wayne Bartz (507/289-7312) can be helpful to first-time visitors.

A third reason for the high quality of the fishery is its relative isolation. Minneapolis, two hours north, is the closest major metroplex, though Rochester (Mayo Clinic) is only half an hour away. Lanesboro provides accommodations and restaurants. Among the most congenial hostelries for weary anglers is Birch Knoll Ranch, a bed and breakfast owned by Duke Hust, a Twin Cities trout activist. You and your friends will be the only ones at the house when you book it. Breakfast is a do-it-yourself affair: all the fixings for blueberry French toast and similar fare are delivered (with instructions) to the refrigerator each day. Cook when you want, which may be a tough decision, as the South Fork of the Root River flows through the farm, and its browns may be calling.

Eagle Ridge at Lusten Mountains

L u s t e n ,   M i n n e s o t a

Big 'bows and brookies feed after dark on little lakes near this stylish lodge.

VITAL STATISTICS:

KEY SPECIES:
Steelhead; chinook salmon; brown and rainbow trout

Season:
All year

Accommodations:
STUDIOS AND CONDOMINIUMS
NUMBER OF GUEST ROOMS: 75
MAXIMUM NUMBER OF GUESTS: 300

Conference Groups: Yes
Meals: Restaurant or use condo kitchen

Rates:
From $49 per person per day
Guides: $275 for 2 per day
Gratuities: $20

Preferred Payment:
MasterCard, Visa

Getting There:
Fly to Duluth, rent a car and drive to the resort.

Other Activities:
Skiing, golf, rafting, canoeing, swimming, boating, hiking, bird watching, biking, wildlife photography.

Contact:
Kristin Althaus
Eagle Ridge at Lusten Mountains, Box 106, Lusten, MN 55612; 800/360-7666, fax 218/663-7699, website http://www. lusten.com/eagleridge /index

THINK MINNESOTA and what pops into mind? Walleyes and *Grumpy Old Men*. That may be true in the state's endless prairies and forested plains, but when you hit the North Shore, you're talking trout, salmon and steelhead. It's as if somebody transplanted the best of coastal Maine to the Midwest, only the waves lapping the stony shore are fresh, not salt. You do have the impression of being on the ocean here; Superior is the world's largest freshwater lake. You're also in the mountains, or so it seems. Rocky headlands rise 300 feet above the lake and climb steadily to nearly twice that a few miles west of the beach. Myriad little streams, and some major ones, too, cut down through the highlands to the lake. Headwaters teem with native brook trout, the rivers are more brown trout water, and at the base of falls and impassable cataracts, you'll find steelhead and chinooks.

Flowing by the lodge is the Poplar River, a tannin-water brook trout stream. But better fishing is to be found in numerous lakes up in the hills, says Dave Brower, the congenial owner of Clearview Store (218/663-7476 or 349-0154), which has a complete stock of flies and related tackle. Brower and his guides prefer the lakes because fishing is better and easier than on the streams. Inland lakes, heavily stocked by Minnesota's Department of Natural Resources, produce healthy catches of 12- to 14-inch rainbows and brook trout. Best fishing is in early summer, from the opening of the season in mid-May to the end of June. September is also good. However, you could be in for a treat if you schedule your trip for late June or early July. These inland lakes see good hexagenia hatches and that means stellar fishing from dark until midnight. That's when rainbows of six or seven pounds and brookies up to five come out to feed. The North Shore steelhead and chinook fisheries are in decline as of this writing. While there is some fishing in the Arrowhead Brule, numbers of fish entering the river are falling off.

Located at one of the North Shore's finest ski complexes, Eagle Ridge offers a range of modern and well-appointed accommodations from studios with fireplaces, Jacuzzi, microwaves and refrigerators to one- to three-bedroom condominiums, many with fireplaces or Jacuzzi and all with complete kitchens. Nearby is the Superior National Golf Course and hundreds of miles of trails for hiking or biking.

Bass Pro's Big Cedar Lodge near Ridgedale, Missouri,
offers a range of luxurious accommodations for anglers
fishing Table Rock Lake. — page 98.

Golden Eagle Lodge

G r a n d   M a r a i s ,   M i n n e s o t a

VITAL STATISTICS:

KEY SPECIES:
Lake trout; northern pike; walleyes

Season:
All year

Accommodations:
HOUSEKEEPING CABINS
NUMBER OF GUEST ROOMS: 11
MAXIMUM NUMBER OF GUESTS: 66

Conference Groups: No

Meals: Cook for yourself

Rates:
From $89 for 2 per day

Guides: From $85 for 2 per day

Gratuities: $20 to $50

Preferred Payment:
Discover, MasterCard, Visa

Getting There:
Fly to Duluth, rent a car and enjoy the drive along Lake Superior to Grand Marais.

Other Activities:
Canoeing, swimming, hiking, bird watching, biking, berry picking, wildlife photography, cross-country skiing, camping.

Contact:
Dan Baumann
Golden Eagle Lodge, 325 Gunflint Trail, Grand Marais, MN 55604; 218/388-2203, fax 218/388-9417.

Fish for lakers, walleyes and pike at the gateway to the Boundary Waters Canoe Area.

FLOUR LAKE IS LIKE HUNDREDS along the watery border between Minnesota and Ontario. Shores are rocky. Boulders are strewn about the bottoms. Small, secret rivers, often caroming down tight, narrow channels, link one to the next. Rocky reefs rise underneath, but do not break the surface. Low ridges thick with pine and spruce separate the lakes, channeling any winds. Flour is small as these lakes go, only three miles long and not a mile at its widest spot. Though powerboats are allowed, this is canoeing water at its best.

That's the way to fish it. When ice leaves the lake in May, lake trout (up to 26 inches), walleyes in the three- to five-pound range and northern pike go on the feed. The trout are rapacious now. Large lake trout fall for crawlers and Rapalas cast from shore or fished from a boat. Use a canoe to troll the lake. Rest your rod on the gunnel with the grip cocked behind one leg and the butt section braced against the front of the other. Tie your paddle to the thwart with a thin, eight-foot line. When a fish hits the lure, you can drop the paddle without losing it overboard and grab the rod. June to September is best for smallmouths. They are not big here, going mostly two to three pounds, but they are plentiful. Cast spinners into the rocks at the water's edge. As temperatures climb, time your fishing to the early and late parts of the day. Walleyes become predatory at dusk, moving out of the depths and into shallower water. You'll also find perch, available year-round. The outflow of Flour Lake leads into the Boundary Waters Area, accessible only by canoe.

Golden Eagle Lodge is not massive by resort standards. Eleven cabins spread out from the lodge along Flour Lake. The cabins (with kitchenettes, fireplaces and private baths) can sleep two to six comfortably. The Golden Eagle provides meals for cross-country skiers and icefishermen, but during summer guests either cook in their cabins or avail themselves of the excellent chow at Trail Center Black Bear Bar and Lounge, three miles away.

Judd's Resort

B e n a ,   M i n n e s o t a

VITAL STATISTICS:

KEY SPECIES:
Walleyes; northern pike; perch

Season:
All year

Accommodations:
LAKESIDE ANGLING RESORT WITH GUEST CABINS
NUMBER OF GUEST ROOMS: 51
MAXIMUM NUMBER OF GUESTS: 150

Conference Groups: Yes
Meals: American plan
Rates:
From $70 per person per day
Guides: $200 for 2 for a full day
Gratuities: $20 to $40 per day
Preferred Payment:
Diner's Club, Discover, MasterCard
Getting There:
Fly to Bemiji and rent a car.
Other Activities:
Golf, canoeing, swimming, boating, hiking, bird watching, biking, wildlife photography, skiing, snowmobiling.

Contact:
Sharon Hunter
Judd's Resort, HCR 1 Box 35, Bena, MN 56626; 218/665-2216, fax 218/665-2237.

When the ice is in, the fishing's on for big walleyes on Winni.

AT JUDD'S RESORT, you won't hear much about flyfishing. What you'll hear is walleye-talk. That means one-eighth-ounce fireball jigs and minnows year-round. Come summer Judd's is walleye headquarters on Lake Winnibigoshish. Unlike Mille Lacs or some of the other famed Minnesota walleye waters, few other lodges and only a smattering of cabins are found on Winni's shores. That means fishing pressure is relatively light and walleyes have a chance to mature.

The best walleyes are taken in June and July, with six- to eight-pound fish being fairly common. That time of year also brings out anglers looking for northerns in the nine- to 15-pound range. Tackle is basic spinning gear and the fish hit Dardevles consistently. Most of the guests know the lake because they come back year after year. Among those is Gary Roach and his Mr. Walleye Team.

Fishing slows in the fall while everything freezes. But by the first of December, Judd's is pulling its angling houses out on the ice and anglers are lining up to catch buckets of yellow perch of up to a pound and a half. The action is nonstop, and anglers can possess up to 100 fish. This is where folks from Wisconsin and Iowa come to fill their freezers. Judd's will clean your catch at 20 cents per perch. That's the best deal in town. Winter also brings out the black shacks for anglers who like to spear northerns. Walleye fans take portable shelters on snowmobiles and prowl the lake looking for likely spots.

Food at Judd's is basic—steaks, ribs, chicken, fish (yours if you want)—and accommodations are comfortably utilitarian. Ten cabins overlook the lake and another 10 are spread under the oaks, pines and ash on a low bench near the main lodge. Two of the cabins are really full-size houses, ideal for families. Some of the cabins offer private baths with each bedroom. Others share. All have kitchenettes. No need to stock up on lures, bait or licenses. Along with a fleet of rental boats and motors, Judd's has everything you need in good supply.

Rockwood Lodge

Grand Marais, Minnesota

Fish the Gunflint Trail from canoes and see it as the Voyageurs did.

VITAL STATISTICS:

KEY SPECIES:
Lake, brook, splake and rainbow trout; walleyes; northern pike; smallmouths

Season:
May through September
Accommodations:
CABINS
NUMBER OF GUEST ROOMS: 9
MAXIMUM NUMBER OF GUESTS: 17
Conference Groups: Yes
Meals: American plan
Rates:
From $100 for 2 per day
Guides: $160 per day for 3
Gratuities: Client's discretion
Preferred Payment:
Discover, MasterCard, Visa
Getting There:
Drive from Duluth.
Other Activities:
Canoeing, swimming, boating, bird watching, biking, wildlife photography.

Contact:
Tim or Rick Austin
Rockwood Lodge, 625 Gunflint Trail, Grand Marais, MN 55604; 800/942-2922, fax 218/388-0155, email rockwood@boreal.org, website http://www. boreal.org/rockwood

IN THE BOUNDARY WATERS, the lakes, headlands and bogs merge with the sky and the loon's misty call summons a tranquility as enduring as the granite of the islands. The smallmouth fishing is superb, as is the angling for pike and trout. And they await your coming, silently, by canoe. The names of the lakes——Hungry Jack, Bearskin, Kiskadinna, Brule, Horseshoe...all long, dark with tannin, and fringed by spruce and pine, conjure up visions of Voyageurs with their freighter canoes laden with beaver pelts and trade goods. Though your canoes will be space-age synthetic, the waters are the same as are the narrow rivers and portages that join one lake to another.

Seven sporting species dominate these waters. When the season opens in mid-May, walleyes (one to three pounds), brook trout (one to three pounds), splake (one to three pounds, a brook trout/lake trout hybrid) and lake trout (two to eight pounds) will be ready for your lures. No need to go deep, as these fish find forage near the top of the water column in spring. Trolling is a good strategy now, as is casting from boat or shore. As summer warms, they will go deeper and you'll have to dredge or jig them up. In August and September, they move back into the shallows for a final feed before winter sets in.

Northern pike here go three to 10 pounds, and can exceed 20. They hit well all season. Flyfishermen will enjoy them best when they are shallow and can be sight-fished in May and early June. You'll find them in aquatic weeds in summer; anglers who use spoons and big spinners with spin or casting tackle have an advantage. In the height of summer, big rainbows can be taken from lakes and feeder streams. So can smallmouth bass.

Use Rockwood Lodge, a landmark on Poplar Lake on the original Gunflint Trail, as your entry into this timeless land. Built in the 1920s of pine logs the color of English toffee, the lodge is revered by those who know it for its eclectic and rustic decor, gingham tablecloths and barbecued pork ribs. Stuffed owls peer down from the massive fieldstone fireplace. Guests stay in comfortable cabins with private baths along the lake or on a nearby island. Rockwood also outfits parties for three- to seven-day canoe and fishing treks. Packages range from economical aluminum canoes to ultralight Kevlars for extended trips with many portages.

Big Cedar Lodge
R i d g e d a l e , M i s s o u r i

VITAL STATISTICS:

KEY SPECIES:
Largemouth and spotted bass; rainbow and brown trout

Season:
All year

Accommodations:
FROM HOTEL ROOMS TO SECLUDED COTTAGES AND CABINS
NUMBER OF GUEST ROOMS: About 150
MAXIMUM NUMBER OF GUESTS: 600 plus
Conference Groups: Yes
Meals: Various restaurants and meal plans

Rates:
From $79 for 2 per day
Guides:
DOGWOOD CANYON: $195 per person per day
TABLE ROCK LAKE: $215 for 2 per day
Gratuities: Client's discretion
Preferred Payment:
Major credit cards
Getting There:
Springfield/Branson Regional airport is the closest. Rent a car and drive from there.
Other Activities:
Golf, tennis, riding, hiking, swimming, bird watching, fitness center, kids' playground.

Contact:
Reservations
Big Cedar Lodge, 612 Devil's Pool Rd., Ridgedale, MO 65739; 417/335-2777, fax 417/335-2340, email bclrooms@cland.net, website http://www/ big-cedar.com

Here's the ultimate outdoor resort, with something for every taste and budget.

WHEN BASS PRO'S FOUNDER, John L. Morris, gets into something, he does it right. Outdoor World, his signature outdoor emporium in Springfield, Missouri, is the ultimate fantasyland for every angler. Hundreds of rods, reels, lines, lures, boats, motors—you'll find it all at Outdoor World, complemented by a 17,000-foot nature museum, a four-story waterfall and huge freshwater and saltwater aquariums.

So when Morris bought the defunct Devils Pool (guest) Ranch on Table Rock Lake, an hour south of Springfield, he planned to create the finest outdoor resort in the country. And he just may have done it. Big Cedar encompasses three lodges spread over 250 acres: Valley View and Spring View (in the elegantly rustic Adirondack tradition of great sporting hotels) and Falls Lodge, a plush non-smoking retreat and the newest of the trio. You can also pick from 13 log cabins, six with kitchens. Accommodations range from tastefully furnished hotel rooms to luxurious suites, decorated with mounts of game and fish, and equipped with Jacuzzis, fireplaces and other comforts. You'll find three restaurants at the resort offering everything from fresh muffins in the morning to late-night gourmet dining. Guest packages abound, as do activities for adults and children. There's even a fishing pond where kids can learn to fish.

Adult anglers can do some learning, too, on 43,000-acre Table Rock Lake, an impoundment on the White River. One of the first lakes to adopt a 15-inch limit on largemouths, Table Rock produces its share of good-size bass. The lake is relatively devoid of traditional structure. You'll find some flats in the upper end, but flooded timber and aquatic vegetation is minimal. Rocky bluffs line the shore. The best action is at creekmouths and their channels in winter. Then try crankbaits over spawning beds in spring; heavy spinnerbaits through deep schools of forage fish in summer; and back to the creeks in fall. You'll also find spotted bass near bluffs, and once in a while, pick up a smallmouth. Table Rock is very clear and fishing is a challenge.

Trout anglers might want to check out Morris' Dogwood Canyon Nature Park, 10,000 acres with a carefully manicured spring-fed trout stream stocked with rainbows up to eight pounds. There's no need to wade, and fishing is fully catch-and-release. Also nearby are the famed tailwaters of the White River, where browns and rainbows grow to record size. The area just below the dam is wadeable when the dam is not generating. One of the best ways to fish the White is to drift it in a johnboat.

Taylormade River Treks

Tecumseh, Missouri

Angling is without peer at this exclusive bed and breakfast.

THERE IS NO BETTER WATER in Missouri than the North Fork of the White River above Tecumseh. And on its bank is one of the finest small bed and breakfasts you'll ever check into. Chris and Shawn Taylor have turned Taylormade into a haven that is as well known as it is secluded. National figures from near and far slip into Taylormade, where they discover anonymity, seclusion and year-round fishing that is nothing short of superb.

It's no wonder that they find the North Fork of the White River sublime. The 13 miles downstream from Rainbow Spring, third largest spring in the state, has been designated trophy trout water and is the only major river in Missouri with a substantial population of wild rainbow trout. Some go seven pounds, but most average 19 inches. Browns, which may grow five pounds heavier, are stocked. While you'll find the usual mayflies and stoneflies, nymphs and streamers that imitate hellgrammites, crayfish and scuds will perform as well.

Taylor, an Alaska hand moved south, runs float trips using a low-sided MacKenzie made by Hyde and an 18-foot johnboat, a craft more in keeping with Missouri tradition. Floating and occasionally stopping to wade is the best way to fish the North Fork. Winter fishing may be better than summer, especially if you want to catch large 'bows and browns. Spring and summer feature dry fly action for trout, and don't overlook the smallmouths. Flyfishing schools and trips to the White and Red in Arkansas are also available.

The Taylors offer two rooms in the lower level of their log home, and what rooms they are. The first boasts a fireplace; rich oak paneling; decorations of antique rods, reels, flies and related equipage; a library of old fishing books and a bristle dart board. Off the room is a private bath. The second room is similarly appointed sans fireplace and private bath. When groups of four book Taylormade, the bath is shared.

Shawn and Chris are a flyfishing couple ("She was interested in me because of my flyfishing, not in spite of it," says Shawn). Though she'd rather be on the river, Chris handles kitchen chores turning out hearty and healthy meals including a cheese cake that is, according to Shawn, "reasonably good for you." The inn serves breakfast with the price of the room, and provides a streamside lunch if you're fishing with Shawn or one of his guides. Dinner is $12 per person.

VITAL STATISTICS:

KEY SPECIES:
Rainbow and brown trout; smallmouth bass

Season:
All year

Accommodations:
LOWER LEVEL OF LOG HOME
NUMBER OF GUEST ROOMS: 2
MAXIMUM NUMBER OF GUESTS: 4

Meals: Bed and breakfast with dinner on request

Conference Groups: No

Rates:
$60 for 2 per night

Guides: $225 for 2 per day

Gratuities: $25 to $50

Preferred Payment:
Cash or check

Getting There:
Fly to Springfield, Missouri, rent a car and drive to the inn.

Other Activities:
Canoeing, swimming, bird watching, antiquing, wildlife photography.

Contact:
Shawn or Chris Taylor
Taylormade River Treks,
HC-1, Box 1755,
Tecumseh, MO 65760;
417/284-3055.

[M I D W E S T]

Wind Rush Farms

C o o k   S t a t i o n ,   M i s s o u r i

Stay in a secluded retreat where you'll do your own cooking and fish two miles of private stream.

VITAL STATISTICS:

KEY SPECIES:
Rainbow trout

Season:
February 15 through
December 15
Accommodations:
LOG SUITES WITH KITCHENS
NUMBER OF GUEST ROOMS: 8
MAXIMUM NUMBER OF GUESTS: 16
Conference Groups: Yes
Meals: Cook for yourself
Rates:
$70 for 2 per night
Guides: $100 per day
Gratuities: $20 per day
Preferred Payment:
Cash or check
Getting There:
From St. Louis, drive south on
I-44 to St. James to Hwy. 68.
Take County NN to the farm.
About a 1 1/2-hour drive.
Other Activities:
Rafting, swimming, boating,
hiking, bird watching,
antiquing, wildlife photography.

Contact:
**Quint or Cicely Drennan
Wind Rush Farms, Rt. 2,
Box 34, Cook Station,
MO 65449; 573/743-
6555.**

QUINT AND CICELY DRENNAN didn't plan on creating a little fishing retreat when, a decade ago, they inherited 400 acres drained by a shallow stream. The two-mile-long creek, though spring-fed, was weed-choked and ravaged by cattle. You couldn't raise a bluegill, let alone a trout, in its languid water. That was a decade ago.

After the bequest, the Drennans began poking around the property. Quint had studied in New England and had fished the Battenkill and other Eastern streams. After that he had guided on Michigan's Upper Peninsula. The couple fished together and knew that a good trout stream starts with cold, limestone-rich water. That they had. All it took was a little engineering to resurrect Benton Creek with pools, gravelly runs, lots of cover and a variety of fish-holding structure. Today, the creek is a model trout stream, alive with Shasta-strain rainbows raised in a hatchery on the property. Limited natural propagation is occurring in the big springs that feed Benton. Fish between one and three pounds are standard fare, larger ones are not infrequent.

Later, the Drennans set to work on a pair of 1840s vintage log cabins, remodeling them into comfortable lodges with four suites apiece. Each suite has a log bedroom and modern bath, living room and kitchen. You'll do your own cooking here because Cook Station and nearby St. James aren't close to much besides antique shops, lots of outdoors and one of the Show-Me state's best trout fisheries, the headwaters of the Meremac. The Meremac gets crowded but Wind Rush Farms controls the number of anglers on its stretch of Benton Creek to preserve a sense of solitude. You'll hear quail calling on a spring morning, see deer and turkeys in the fields and find grouse drumming in the hardwoods. If you're between hatches, soothe your soul with a walk along the farm's self-guiding nature trails or a nap with feet propped up on the porch rail.

Gayles Bed & Breakfast

P u t - i n - B a y , O h i o

VITAL STATISTICS:

KEY SPECIES:
Walleyes; perch; smallmouth bass

Season:
All year

Accommodations:
FRAME HOUSE WITH COTTAGE
NUMBER OF GUEST ROOMS: 7
MAXIMUM NUMBER OF GUESTS: 14

Conference Groups: No

Meals: Bed and breakfast

Rates:
From $70 for 2 per day

Guides: $65 per person for icefishing; charterboats from $400 per day for 6

Gratuities: Client's discretion

Preferred Payment:
Cash or check

Getting There:
Summer: Take the ferry from Port Clinton or fly from Cleveland, Detroit or Toledo. Winter: Fly from Port Clinton.

Other Activities:
Walking, boating, swimming.

Contact:
Hank Polcyn
Gayles Bed & Breakfast, 85 Cessna Rd., PO Box 85, Put-in-Bay, OH 43456; 419/285-7181 (summer); 419/285-9010 (winter).

What could be finer than walleyes in winter and smallmouths in summer off this Lake Erie island?

THIRTY-FOUR BUCKS will buy you a round-trip ticket on a six-seat Piper Cherokee from Port Clinton, Ohio, near Sandusky to Put-in-Bay on South Bass Island. No matter what the season, Put-in-Bay is the center of one of the best walleye fisheries in Lake Erie, and anglers in the know stay at Gayles Bed & Breakfast. There they are stuffed with breakfasts so massive that few have room for lunch, and in winter, warm and snug in an icehouse, anglers have a tendency to doze rather than jig up walleyes and perch.

Among Put-in-Bay guides, you'll find Pat Chrysler (419/285-4631), who runs a pair of charterboats in summer and a string of ice shanties in winter. Though small, there's plenty of room in each shanty for two men, two holes, a fishfinder and a Thermos or two of hot coffee. If the action slows, Chrysler's four-wheeler parked outside can move the shanties to another spot in a jiffy. Walleyes, averaging 14 to 18 inches but once in a while reaching eight to 10 pounds, will be frozen for your trip home. Perch will be fileted for an on-the-ice fish fry. Jigging is the name of this January to mid-March game.

Come spring, Chrysler puts his 31- and 38-foot charterboats into the water, heads for the lee of the islands to escape the hard northwest winds and goes to work on walleyes with jig and minnow rigs. Later, in May and June, the smallmouth action heats up, first with minnows fished nearly on bottom and later with Berkeley Power Baits and Power Tubes (popular colors are motor oil and pumpkinseed). Soft crayfish also produce. The Ohio state record of 9 pounds 8 ounces came from these waters. When water temps hit 60°F, bass move onto spawning beds and flycast poppers and crankbaits fished with light spinning tackle generate explosive strikes. Average smallies run in the 15- to 17-inch range. Bass action moves deeper as summer progresses and then heats up again in fall. As the waters cool, walleyes form pre-spawn schools that can yield the biggest fish of the year.

Shaded by maples less than 100 yards from the lake, Gayles Bed & Breakfast is located in a 1900s vintage frame house. Three bedrooms have private baths, and the other two are fitted with lavatories but share showers. Also on the property is a two-bedroom cabin with bath. Decor is plain and simple. Killer breakfasts are apt to include French toast soaked overnight in a batter of milk, eggs, cornflakes and coconut. To this you can add bacon, sausage and eggs. Dinner is not served at the B&B, but guests walk next door to Terry's Skyway, reportedly the best restaurant on the island.

Lake Texoma Resort Park

Kingston, Oklahoma

VITAL STATISTICS:

KEY SPECIES:
Striped and smallmouth bass

Season:
All year

Accommodations:
HOTEL ROOMS AND LAKESIDE HOUSEKEEPING CABINS
NUMBER OF GUEST ROOMS: 167
MAXIMUM NUMBER OF GUESTS: 1000

Conference Groups: Yes
Meals: Restaurant
Rates:
From $38 per night for 2
Guides: $200 per day for 2 anglers
Gratuities: Client's discretion
Preferred Payment:
Major credit cards
Getting There:
!3 miles west of Durant on US 70.

Other Activities:
Golf, canoeing, tennis, swimming, hiking, bird watching, biking, wildlife photography, water skiing, horseback riding.

Contact:
Reservations
Lake Texoma Resort Park, PO Box 248, Kingston, OK 73439; 405/564-2311, fax 405/564-9322, website http://www.otrd.state.ok.us

At Texoma, small stripers and scrappy smallmouths will test your light tackle to the limit.

ONCE UPON A TIME Lake Texoma was the lake for striped bass. Stringers of four or five 15- to 20-pounders were not unusual, and 30-pounders hardly raised an eyebrow. Really big fish are few and far between these days on this 89,000-acre impoundment on the border between Texas and Oklahoma. But what the lake may lack in size, it makes up for in quantity. There's no sure thing, of course, yet here the odds favor your picking up a limit of 10 three- to five-pound fish.

According to guide Phil Jones (405/564-2037), April, May and June are the best months to fish for stripers on Texoma, and October and November are the second best months. In spring, especially when rains swell the lake and force it just above full pool, stripers move inshore. Fish shad-imitating crankbaits hard against the flooded brush. Topwaters can work too. As the season ages, stripers head for deeper water. Fishfinders will pinpoint schools anywhere from 20 to 40 feet deep. Hookups come from drifting live shad two feet below a barrel sinker. Sometimes, in the hot summer months, stripers will chase bait to the surface. You can see swarms of gulls in the air, and as you get close, a flotilla of anglers who have the same idea you do. If you're first on the scene, action can be fun, particularly if you're using light casting rigs spooled with 8-pound test. What caused the decline in the striper population? No one knows for sure. Texas A&M is conducting a study at the request of Texas and Oklahoma fish management agencies.

In the meanwhile, anglers will have to be content with smallmouth bass. Again for reasons that are not all together clear, the population of bronzebacks is skyrocketing. Four- and five-pounders are reasonably common, and at least once a season someone hauls out a behemoth that nudges the lake record 7-pound 13-ounce smallie. Fish rocky points with crawdad pattern crankbaits in spring.

With its full-service marina, comfortable hotel and spacious guest cabins scattered under the trees along the water, Lake Texoma State Resort is the place to stay when you're fishing the lake. In the hotel, you'll find standard rooms, terrace rooms with sundeck and cabanas with pool-side patios, sitting areas and wet bar. Two-bedroom cottages sleep four to eight and include kitchenette, and living area with fireplace. Similar amenities are found in one-bedroom "studio" cottages. The hotel restaurant offers delicious standard American cuisine.

Cedar Shore Resort

C h a m b e r l a i n ,   S o u t h   D a k o t a

*Springtime walleyes will hit almost
anything here, even a fly.*

SINCE WHEN IS A RADISSON a fishing lodge? Not all that often. But this one includes a marina on Lake Francis Case, which is walleye heaven come April and May. It's easy to find from the East: Just follow the parade of Lund boats pulled by 4x4s booming across I-90 from Minnesota, where fishing for these big-eyed denizens won't start until mid-May. Everyone is heading to Chamberlain, where the interstate crosses the Missouri. The river is impounded by Ft. Randall Dam, creating a 107-mile lake. Relatively shallow, the water warms early in the season, and that turns on the walleyes.

You'll catch them in their pre-spawn stage, when they've come up from the 30- to 40-foot depths where they've held semi-dormant all winter. Fish the rip-rap bank on the Chamberlain side, or along the approaches to the new bridge that carries I-90 over the river. Also try the rocky bank below St. Joseph's School. If the angling is too crowded, motor upstream to Crow Creek. The river belongs to those who fish from boats during the day. At night, small bonfires dot the shore, warming anglers who fish bait and wait. They're successful too. Early in spring, almost everyone fishes a jig and minnow, vertically. As the water warms to 40°F the walleyes move up onto the shoals. Crankbaits, stickbaits and spinnerbaits can all be effective now. Trolling is popular. And, as outlandish as it seems, now is the time when walleyes can be taken on a fly-rod. Use a 6 or 7 weight with six- or seven-foot 6-pound tippet to cast to the bank. Lefty's Deceivers in blue and white and green and white work well, as do Clousers. Fish are in the two-pound range, and a flyrod gets the most out of them.

At Cedar Shore's marina, you can rent a boat and motor or hook up with a guide. One of the best in the area is Jim Ristau (605/734-4240), who runs a fully equipped Skeeter out of the marina. For less than $200 per day, he'll provide everything you'll need. The Radisson was opened in 1994 and sits on a low bank above the Missouri. A full-service resort with an eye to the conference trade, here you'll also find a sporting clays course and easy access to the scenic Missouri Breaks.

Jamieson House Inn
P o y n e t t e ,   W i s c o n s i n

Combine 1890s charm with browns and brookies in the stream that flows right through town.

VITAL STATISTICS:

KEY SPECIES:
Brown and brook trout; bass; walleyes; sturgeon; northern pike

Season:
All year

Accommodations:
VICTORIAN MANSION
NUMBER OF GUEST ROOMS: 11
MAXIMUM NUMBER OF GUESTS: 30 plus

Conference Groups: Yes
Meals: Bed and breakfast, dinners available separately
Rates:
From $65 for 2 per night
Guides: $200 for 2 anglers
Gratuities: Client's discretion
Preferred Payment:
Cash or check
Getting There:
From I-94 take Rt. CS east to Poynette.
Other Activities:
Boating, hiking, bird watching, antiquing, biking, skiing.

Contact:
**Heidi Hutchinson
Jamieson House Inn, 407 N. Franklin St., Poynette, WI 53955; 608/635-4100, fax 608/635-2292.**

AN AURA of elegance surrounds Jamieson House in Poynette, a little town of 1500 a couple miles east of Interstate 94 about 30 miles north of Madison. Free from tourism along the four-lane, Poynette retains much of its 1890s charm. Yet by virtue of its proximity to the interstate, you can be on any one of half a dozen good trout streams in central Wisconsin, to say nothing of numerous nearby lakes and ponds in minutes. In these you'll find smallmouth bass, northern pike, sturgeon, walleyes and bluegills.

Troutfishers need look no farther than the center of Poynette to find angling. Rowan Creek cuts through town from east to west, eventually ducking under the interstate and flowing into Lake Wisconsin (good for walleyes and smallmouths), an impoundment of the Wisconsin River. Public access to Rowan Creek is ample. A mile of special regulation water runs east of town through property owned by the state's Department of Natural Resources. Access, of course, means other anglers, so odds are against having it to yourself. However, many who fish it are fair-weather fishers. When it's cloudy or drizzly it may be deserted. Brown and brook trout here hit the standard nymphs—Hare's Ears and Pheasant Tails—and the usual dries—Adams and Griffith's Gnats.

Other water in the area includes Rocky Run, particularly east of the Highway 51 bridge, the Mecan about 40 miles north near Richford and the Fox at Princeton. Also worth checking is the Black Earth, which follows U.S. 14 west of Madison, and Mount Vernon Creek just off U.S. 151 at Mt. Vernon. Humphrey and Shogren in *Wisconsin and Minnesota Trout Streams* call Mt. Vernon Creek a "jewel," known for hatches of spring creek mayflies and its "hex" hatch in June. Good-size browns can be caught from these clear waters. Ron Barefield (608/838-8756) guides anglers on streams and on Lake Wisconsin.

Jamieson House is a complex of three historic buildings—two brick Victorian mansions and a schoolhouse. Nine guest rooms are furnished with antiques and period reproductions. Most have sitting areas and queen beds. Two French country suites with cable television and whirlpools are located in the schoolhouse. Breakfast is served in the sunny conservatory, and at night Emily's Cafe offers elegant cuisine with a continental flare. Rooms have all the modern amenities. Breakfast, but not dinner, is included.

Serendipity Farm
Viroqua, Wisconsin

Stay at a working farm, and catch big browns in the pasture.

VITAL STATISTICS:

KEY SPECIES:
Brown trout

Season:
All year
Accommodations:
FARMHOUSE WITH COTTAGE
NUMBER OF GUEST ROOMS: 3 plus cottage
MAXIMUM NUMBER OF GUESTS: 12
Conference Groups: No
Meals: Bed and breakfast
Rates:
From $60 to $90 for 2 per day
Guides: $200 per day
Gratuities: Client's discretion
Preferred Payment:
Cash or check
Getting There:
LaCrosse, Wisconsin is the closest airport. Fly there, then rent a car and drive to the farm.
Other Activities:
Canoeing, hiking, bird watching, antiquing, biking, wildlife photography.

Contact:
Forrest or Suzanne Garret
Serendipity Farm, RR 3, Box 162, Viroqua, WI 54665; 608/637-7708.

DEEP IN THE DRIFTLESS AREA of southwestern Wisconsin are spring creeks and gentle rivers known for good brown trout fishing. The water is not deep nor is it big. But the trout are. Twenty-inchers are not unusual, and an average day can bring a dozen in the 12- to 14-inch range. Caddisfly, mayfly and stonefly dries all work, but bigger fish feed at dusk and beyond. Then Woolly Buggers and Muskrats, Size 6 or larger, will do the trick. Fishing runs from March through September, and it's mainly freelance. You don't need a guide, though the nearby town of Coon Valley, in the heart of Wisconsin's Coulee Region, is home to a couple of good ones. Try Dennis Graupe (608/452-3430) at Spring Creek Angler, an Orvis dealer.

Among the larger streams in the area is the West Fork of the Kickapoo River. Ample public access is available and farmers are frequently willing to grant permission to fish when asked. The Kickapoo has a strong regional reputation; anglers from Madison fish it regularly, and it's being discovered by those from Minneapolis and Chicago. But in comparison to water of similar caliber in the East and West, the river is virtually ignored. Recently the Wisconsin Department of Natural Resources and Trout Unlimited combined to add structure and rip-rap to stabilize the banks. As has proven to be the case in other streams in the region, the added cover should generate lots of big browns.

On a low bluff overlooking the river, Forrest and Suzanne Garret own and operate Serendipity Farm. Serendipity is one part bed and breakfast and three parts working farm...goats, pigs, chickens, geese and a few dairy cows. A rooster awakens anglers who want to fish early. Hearty breakfasts—eggs gathered that morning, sausage, homemade breads and jams—are the rule. Guests stay in three bedrooms in the Garret's house or in a cottage nearby. The cottage has a private bath: Guest rooms in the main house share.

It's best to stock up on flies or lures and buy your license before you head out to Viroqua. Incidentals can be found at the country store in Avalanche (where there's never been one), population 30, a mile up the road from the farm.

ROCKY MOUNTAINS

COLORADO, IDAHO, MONTANA, UTAH, WYOMING

FROM THE CRESTS and calderas of the soaring Rockies flow the Madison, Yellowstone, Bighorn, Green, North Platte, Henry's Fork and 100 other rivers, spring creeks and icewater lakes—the mother lode of modern flyfishing in America. Here is water as tough and technical as it gets, or as gentle and forgiving as a novice needs. Cutthroats, browns, rainbows, grayling and bull trout are regularly found here, as are pike and smallmouths in warmer waters. As diverse as the fishing, accommodations range from upscale flyfishing-only lodges to dude ranches to hotels and motels of modest price. At least once, every angler deserves a trip to the Rockies.

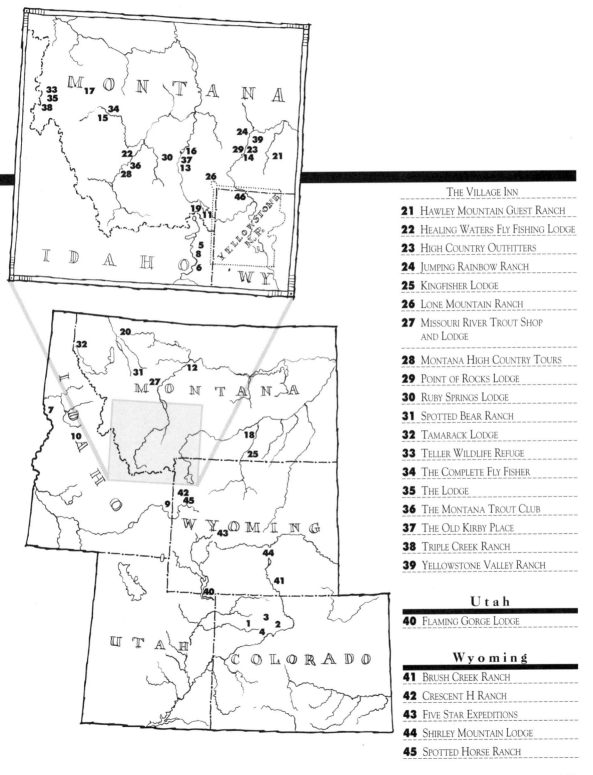

THE VILLAGE INN

References & Resources

References:

RIVER JOURNAL:
YELLOWSTONE NATIONAL PARK
— *Bruce Staples*
IDAHO FISHING GUIDE:
HOOK LINE & SINKER
— *Pete Simowsky*
Frank Amato Publications, PO Box
82112, Portland, OR 97282;
503/653-8108

THE ANGLER'S GUIDE TO MONTANA
— *Michael S. Sample*
Falcon Publishing Co., PO Box 1718,
Helena, MT 59624; 406/442-6597

THE COLORADO ANGLING GUIDE
THE MONTANA ANGLING GUIDE
THE WYOMING ANGLING GUIDE
— *Chuck Fothergill and Bob Sterling*
Stream Stalker Publishing Co., PO Box
238, Woody Creek, CO 81656;
970/923-4552

Resources:

COLORADO DIVISION OF WILDLIFE,
6060 Broadway, Denver, CO 80216;
303/291-7533, website
http://www.dnr.state.co.us

IDAHO FISH AND GAME DEPARTMENT,
PO Box 25, 600 S. Walnut St., Boise,
ID 83707; 208/334-3700,
800/544-8685, website
*http://www.state.id.us/fishgame/
fishgame.html*

MONTANA DEPARTMENT OF FISH,
WILDLIFE AND PARKS,
1420 E. 6th Ave., Helena, MT
59620; 406/444-2535, website
*http://travel.mt.gov/recadv/fishing/
fishing.html*

UTAH DIVISION OF
WILDLIFE RESOURCES,
1594 W. North Temple, Salt Lake City,
UT 84116; 801/538-4700, website
http://www.nr.state.ut.us/

WYOMING GAME AND FISH
COMMISSION,
5400 Bishop Blvd., Cheyenne, WY
82006; 307/777-4600, website
http://gf.state.wy.us

*Henry Kravis built Seven Lakes Lodge near Meeker,
Colorado, and improved three miles of the White River,
so others could enjoy the area's beauty.* — page 112.

Elk Creek Lodge

Meeker, Colorado

VITAL STATISTICS:

KEY SPECIES:
Brook, brown, cutthroat and rainbow trout

Season:
Late June to early October
Accommodations:
ANGLING RESORT AND CABINS
NUMBER OF GUEST ROOMS: 9
MAXIMUM NUMBER OF GUESTS: 16
Conference Groups: Yes
Meals: American plan
Rates:
From $2900 per person for 5 days and 6 nights, double occupancy
Guides: Included
Gratuities: 15% of package price
Preferred Payment:
Cash or check
Getting There:
Fly to Grand Junction, Colorado. You'll be met by a shuttle from the lodge.
Other Activities:
Golf, horseback riding, hiking, biking, bird watching.

Contact:
Chris Lockwood
Elk Creek Lodge, PO Box 130, 1111 County Rd. 54, Meeker, CO 81641; 970/878-5454 (summer); 970/878-5232 (winter); fax 970/878-5311 (all year), email elk@rmi.net

Try for brookies, browns, cutthroats and rainbows, while staying at one of the top lodges on everyone's list.

FIRST, ABOUT ELK CREEK: It's a modest, meandering stream that flows down from the Flat Top foothills and across the valley in front of the lodge before it joins the White River below. You can jump across Elk Creek if you need to, but most anglers aren't in that big of a hurry. The upper end is a technical—read that classic—small creek, dry fly fishery where casts should be precise. Lower down, the water opens up. All of the stream has been improved and your chances of landing the four-trout Colorado grand slam (brookies, browns, cutthroats, rainbows) are excellent.

The lodge's five-day fishing program is planned to give guests a shot at a variety of different water. The main stem of the White is traditional pool, riffle, pool water holding big 'bows, browns and cutthroats. The "Pot Hole" on the upper North Fork of the White is perfect water for fishing small caddis for rainbows and brook trout under the willows. Or try Dobbin's Water on the upper South Fork for 20-inch rainbows. Marvine Creek, about 15 minutes from the main lodge, is similar to Elk Creek, but a little wider. A day on Trapper's Lake fishing for wild cutthroats from handcrafted cedar boats is not to be missed. And if that's not enough entertainment, there's a fly out to the Green River for $150 additional per angler.

The season runs from late June through the first week or so of October. Early in the season, guests may contend with runoff. But by the second week in June, water levels are dropping and the fishing is picking up. A short but strong hatch of Green Drakes comes off in late July or early August, and with the first cutting of hay on the ranch in mid-August come the 'hoppers that provide action until late September. Then there's a hatch of big orange caddis, and the chance of snow. Local patterns, as well as other tackle, are available at this Orvis-endorsed lodge.

Accommodations at Elk Creek are first rate. Guests stay in nine cabins each with living rooms and private baths. Meals, complemented by fine wines, are truly gourmet...rack of lamb provencale, venison and so on. Special heart healthy and vegetarian diets are available on request. As part of the package, a guide is furnished for every two guests.

Elktrout Lodge
K r e m m l i n g ,   C o l o r a d o

The many small rivers, creeks and spring-fed ponds in the Elktrout area offer anglers a variety of good fishing.

VITAL STATISTICS:

KEY SPECIES:
Brown, cutthroat and rainbow trout

Season:
Mid-May through mid-October
Accommodations:
Rustic log lodge and cabins
Number of Guest Rooms: 11
Maximum Number of Guests: 22
Conference Groups: Yes
Meals: American plan
Rates:
Packages from $1300 per person for 3 days, double occupancy
Guides: Included
Gratuities: $50 per day
Preferred Payment:
MasterCard, Visa
Getting There:
Fly to Denver, rent a car and drive to the lodge.
Other Activities:
Golf, tennis, rafting, hiking, bird watching.

Contact:
Greg Cecil
Elktrout Lodge, PO Box 614, Kremmling, CO 80459; 970/724-3343, fax 970/724-9063, website http://www.elktrout.com

AMONG ESTABLISHED Rocky Mountain lodges, Elktrout has a well-deserved reputation for offering anglers a variety of good fishing. Spring-fed ponds on the ranch offer bellyboating and bank fishing for bruiser-size rainbows, cutthroats and browns. The Colorado and Blue are Elktrout's primary rivers, easily wadeable freestone water with gravel bottoms. The upper half of Troublesome Creek beats around boulders and crashes into plunge pools before settling down and meandering through a lower meadow section. And tucked away in fishmaster Greg Cecil's repertoire are a few tiny mountain brook trout creeks.

Not all of these waters fish well all of the time, but what waters do? Throughout Elktrout's five-month season, you can bet that two or more of the ranch's fisheries will be hot at a given time. Much depends on water levels and irrigation needs. If the Blue and Colorado are flowing between 250 and 400 cfs, angling will be quite good. Fish will not be big, generally in the 12- to 14-inch range, but they will be plentiful, and there's a reasonably good chance of playing a 16- to 18-inch fish.

More demanding is the lower Troublesome. Trout move up out of the Colorado into this small winding creek, as clear as mountain air. You can see 18- to 24-inch trout in this water; they, of course, can see you too. But a stealthy approach and precise casting can pay big dividends. Along with caddis and terrestrial imitations, Muddlers, particularly those heavily greased and skittered across the surface, can ignite savage strikes. And you really need to talk with Cecil about fishing "water boatman" beetles. When these beetles hatch under the clear blue skies of late August, they rise to the surface, spread their wings and paddle as if their lives depended on it for the grassy pond bank. Their lives do depend on it. Big trout gorge with abandon on these beetles.

At Elktrout, the fishing day begins around 8:30 a.m. with a trip to one of the lodge's dozen ponds. After lunch, you may fish one of the rivers. Dinner is around 6:30 p.m., and everybody stuffs themselves on charred rack of lamb, smoked prime rib or steak au poivre. You'll have a tendency to head for the porch, sit back, prop your feet on the rail and watch the sunset while others fish the evening rise. Don't give in to the temptation. Just a couple more hours on the river and then you can hit the sack. Orvis-endorsed, the lodge maintains a small but well-stocked tackleshop.

Little Grizzly Creek Ranch
Walden, Colorado

VITAL STATISTICS:

KEY SPECIES:
Brook, brown, cutthroat and rainbow trout

Season:
July through mid-September

Accommodations:
CONTEMPORARY LOG LODGE AND CABINS
NUMBER OF GUEST ROOMS: 8
MAXIMUM NUMBER OF GUESTS: 12

Conference Groups: Yes

Meals: American plan

Rates:
$290 per person per day, double occupancy

Guides: Included

Gratuities: About $100 for a 3-day stay

Preferred Payment:
Cash or check

Getting There:
Fly to Denver, rent a car and enjoy the 3-hour drive to the ranch.

Other Activities:
Trapshooting, hiking, archery, wildlife photography, bird watching.

Contact:
Doug Sysel
Little Grizzly Creek Ranch, 7113 N. Tatum, Paradise Valley, AZ 85253 (winter); 777 Country Road 1, Walden, CO 80480; 970/723-4209 (summer); 602/952-9732 (winter), website http://www.little-grizzly-creek.com

This is one place off the beaten path that you'll come back to time after time.

THE GRAVEL ROAD leads off the highway, grass growing between the twin tracks through the aspens. In summer, wildflowers grace the shoulders. In fall, the lane is framed in fluttering gold, a signal that the fishing is about done and that now is the time for elk. The woods give way to a high and spacious meadow, above which rise the mountains of the Rabbit Ear Range. Near the edge of the meadow rambles the red-roofed log ranch. Beyond the ranch, the land drops 400 feet to Little Grizzly Creek, headwater of the North Platte.

Never open to the public, Little Grizzly at the ranch is a small stream, one of those tight, shady marvels with riffles and pools that you can't fish from the bank. Get in and wade it. Cast close to the willows or work a fly through pockets. The browns, cutthroats, rainbows and brookies are not huge here, but you'll catch numbers of them in the 14-inch-plus range. In addition to the home waters, owner Doug Sysel takes guests to five private miles of Beaver Creek. Aptly named, this meandering meadow stream with its cut banks and beaver ponds is the favorite among Sysel's guests. Trout—browns, cutthroats, rainbows and brookies—average 12 to 16 inches and many are larger. Then there's Sysel's exclusive mileage on Roaring Fork, with its canyon and waterfalls and trout up to 16 inches, though bigger ones have been caught. All of these streams are relatively narrow, though the depths may surprise you. So if it's big water you want, and the challenge of seducing browns upwards of 24 inches, head for the North Platte and more private water. If you want really big browns, ask Sysel if he's up for a little nightfishing.

This ranch is a little different than most. You won't get the feeling that a guide is hovering over you. Instead, the guide will take you to the water you'd like to fish (and that's fishing best during your visit), give you flies, suggest tactics and then leave you to fish. If you want help, he'll be delighted to give you pointers. Sysel and wife Carol Mellen go all out to ensure that nonfishing spouses or those who fish a little have a chance to enhance their skills if they're interested or otherwise enjoy the wilderness or the pleasures of Steamboat Springs nearby.

Accommodations are superb. Guest rooms feature chinked log walls, hung with Native American weavings. Country quilts cover the beds. After fishing, you'll settle into plush leather couches and chairs, have a drink and chat with other couples before a five-course gourmet dinner. Fine wines complement the meal. And after dinner, as you linger by the fire, you know that this is a place you'll come back to.

Seven Lakes Lodge
M e e k e r ,   C o l o r a d o

VITAL STATISTICS:

KEY SPECIES:
Brook, cutthroat and rainbow trout

Season:
Mid-June through September

Accommodations:
MODERN STONE AND TIMBER LODGE
NUMBER OF GUEST ROOMS: 11
MAXIMUM NUMBER OF GUESTS: 22

Meals: American plan

Conference Groups: Yes

Rates:
$4600 per person for 5 nights and 6 days, double occupancy

Guides: Included

Gratuities: 15% of total package

Preferred Payment:
Major credit cards

Getting There:
Fly to Aspen or Grand Junction and the lodge van will meet you at no additional cost.

Other Activities:
Riding, sporting clays, hiking swimming, wildlife photography.

Contact:
Seven Lakes Lodge, Meeker, CO 81641; 970/878-4772, fax 970/878-3635 (summer); 970/878-3428, fax 970/878-5603 (winter).

The splendor of the Flat Tops Wilderness is complemented by Henry Kravis' new lodge.

BEFORE HENRY KRAVIS took the reins, Seven Lakes Lodge had been a modest place with a little mileage on a better than average trout stream. An angler and sportsman who does things in first-class fashion, he wanted to create the finest lodge in the West: Why? "I decided," he says, "to build Seven Lakes Lodge in my taste to share with others the incredible beauty of the Colorado Mountains and fabulous fishing on the White River." By all measures he's succeeded.

Take the White River. Seven Lakes bought and reconstructed three miles of it, adding 29 pools, homes for the deep-bellied rainbows and cutthroats that were stocked later. Average fish run between 18 and 20 inches, although 24-inch rainbows are common. If these guys seem too small, there's a bunch of 10-pounders in the lodge's lakes. And, of course, nothing says that while staying at Seven Lakes, you have to eschew other nearby trout waters. In the Flat Tops National Wilderness area are scores of small lakes, set like jewels amidst the mountains, and a few good-size ones like Trappers and Marvine lakes. Trappers Lake is accessible by vehicle, but even so it retains the pristine qualities associated with isolation: stunning vistas, superlative native cutthroats, and a litter-free environment. In the other lakes, many reachable only by horse or foot, you'll find rainbow, brook and cutthroat trout action. It's worth a day or two to explore these still-water fisheries. And a little time spent on the White below the lodge will offer yet another challenge, this one for smaller, though to large degree wild, stream trout.

Sprawling over 15,000 square feet, the main stone and timber lodge is as grand inside as the panoramas you see through countless picture windows. A giant rock fireplace commands the great room and attracts the attention of guests in the lounge and dining room. On sunny mornings and those clear evenings when alpenglow turns the mountains the color of a spawning brook trout's belly, what could be more delightful than having breakfast or dinner (gourmet with good wines, as you'd expect) on the large glass-enclosed porch. Eight guest suites are upstairs in the main lodge. A private, executive log cabin—a quick walk from the lodge—contains three bedrooms. Decor is haute couture in fascinating contrast to the bold natural materials of the lodge. Seven Lakes also includes an exercise center and spa, a sporting clays course designed by Michael Rose and riding stables. Full conference services and facilities are available.

Elk Creek Ranch
Island Park , Idaho

On the headwaters of Henry's Fork, this old-style ranch won't burn a hole in your billfold.

VITAL STATISTICS:

KEY SPECIES:
Brown, rainbow, brook and cutthroat trout

Season:
Late May through October
Accommodations:
RUSTIC LOG CABINS
NUMBER OF GUEST ROOMS: 8
MAXIMUM NUMBER OF GUESTS: 30
Conference Groups: Yes
Meals: American plan
Rates:
$70 per person per day, single occupancy
Guides: From $175 for 1 per day
Gratuities: 10%
Preferred Payment:
Cash, traveler's checks
Getting There:
Idaho Falls, Idaho, and West Yellowstone, Montana, are the closest commercial airports. Rent a car. You'll need it to fish Henry's Fork and nearby rivers.
Other Activities:
Boating, riding, hiking, bird watching, biking, wildlife photography.

Contact:
Gary Merrill
Elk Creek Ranch, PO Box 2, Island Park, ID 83429; 208/558-7404.

"ANGLERS WHO WANT TO CATCH a lot of fish are better off on the Madison," says Gary Merrill, who runs Elk Creek Ranch. "Henry's Fork can be tough." True. But the angler who wants a variety of river experiences will find them all on the Henry's Fork.

This fork of the Snake River is the big attraction in the caldera just south of the three-corner trout mecca centered at West Yellowstone, Montana. Plagued with low water and troubled by pollutants, Henry's Fork's sterling reputation took on a little tarnish in the early 90s. Still, rainbows upwards of 20 inches continued to ignore less-than-gracefully-presented dries on the Harriman Ranch stretch and artlessly fished nymphs in Box Canyon. Though water conditions have improved, Henry's Fork trout are as stubborn as ever.

To some degree, this is a classic tailwater. Flows are controlled by releases from Island Park Dam. In spring and fall, when downstream irrigation needs are minimal, the famed Box Canyon is wadeable. As canyons go, the Box isn't very deep, but boulders and deep holes and lots of good pocket water hold many large rainbows as well as cutthroats, browns and brookies.

After leaving the Box, the river broadens and slows, taking on the spring creek characteristics for which it is so highly regarded. Rapids end at aptly named Last Chance. Below that it flows silky and supine through the flat meadows of Harriman Ranch. Matching the hatch is essential if you're to take the 'bows here. Hatches are prolific from early Iron Blue Quills in March, through Green Drakes which draw anglers from around the world in late June, to tiny *Callibaetis* in September. At times the insects are so profuse that they look like lint on the water. The best strategy is to stalk working trout. Even while running full, the river here is easily wadeable. Below the ranch, the river picks up speed as the gradient steepens. Conditions are similar to the Box. Special regulations govern fishing on the Henry's Fork and you'll want to check on these at Mike Lawson's Henry's Fork Anglers (208/558-7525) in Last Chance. Lawson's shop is headquarters for the regulars who fish this river.

Up on the river's headwaters, you'll find Elk Creek Ranch and its private trout-filled lake. Comfortable and laid back in western tradition, Elk Creek puts its guests up in log cabins, each with private bath, living and bedrooms. Some have fireplaces. You'll eat in the rustic main lodge and while the fare isn't fancy, it's good. For a ranch in the heart of such prime fishing the price is certainly right.

Fish Creek Lodging

A s h t o n ,   I d a h o

VITAL STATISTICS:

KEY SPECIES:
Brown, cutthroat and rainbow trout

Season:
June through October
Accommodations:
LOG CABIN
NUMBER OF GUEST ROOMS: 2
MAXIMUM NUMBER OF GUESTS: 6
Conference Groups: No
Meals: Cook for yourself
Rates:
From $80 per day for 2
Guides: About $250 per day for 2
Gratuities: Client's discretion
Preferred Payment:
Cash or check
Getting There:
Idaho Falls has the closest airport. You'll want to rent a car and drive from there.
Other Activities:
Hiking, bird watching, biking, wildlife photography, skiing.

Contact:
Janet Keefer
Fish Creek Lodging,
Warm River, PO Box 833,
Ashton, ID 83420;
208/652-7566.

Stay in a special cabin, with access to an oft-overlooked section of the Henry's Fork.

ENRY'S FORK is a variety of different rivers. It originates in Henry's Lake, a float-tuber's paradise for rising brown trout. The thin outflow from the lake then joins the icy waters from Big Springs, where huge rainbows, browns and cutthroats fin in the boiling spring. After impoundment in Island Park Reservoir, the river emerges as a much-storied fishery. As a tailwater, it clatters through Box Canyon, slows and weaves through the Harriman Ranch (here resembling a spring creek), and picks up speed again below Osborne Bridge as it begins its descending run to Upper and Lower Mesa Falls.

The falls mark the edge of the caldera through which the upper river flows. Below the falls, Henry's Fork works its way through a deep valley that opens where the Warm River flows in from the east. As gradient diminishes, Henry's Fork becomes more like the cobble bottom sections of the Madison and the South Fork of the Snake. Long runs are punctuated by gravel riffles. Just below the U.S. Route 20 bridge north of Ashton, the river is again impounded. Above the lake, the fishing is good, but the lake itself is small. The tailwater below the dam holds huge rainbows, and the fishing can be outstanding.

Henry's Fork from the falls down through Ashton is much less heavily fished than the upper section. While hatches are not as prolific, they are still good. If you are staying in the Island Park area, you'll probably not drive down to the lower area to fish, but if you are lodged near Ashton, you'll be doing yourself a disservice if you forsake the lower Henry's Fork (and the Warm and Fall rivers nearby). All have excellent populations of browns and rainbows, with a few cutthroats. Flows are heavy in spring and summer, but tail off in the fall as irrigation needs lessen. The fishing is at its best then. Spinning and flyfishing are permitted, but regulations change so you'll want to check them out thoroughly when you buy your license.

Close to the confluence of the Warm River and Henry's Fork, about five miles below the falls, Janet Keefer rents out a private log guest cabin—Fish Creek Lodging— that offers all the conveniences of home, including a newly remodeled private bath. Use the cast-iron wood stove to steal the chill from cool evenings. Whip up your own gourmet dinner. Sleep deeply in comfortable beds, and if it rains, listen to it patter on the tin roof, then roll over and grab a few more winks. The fishing will keep.

Hell's Canyon Lodge
Lewiston, Idaho

Jetboats and choppers take you where the fish are.

VITAL STATISTICS:

KEY SPECIES:
Steelhead; rainbow trout; smallmouth bass

Season:
All year

Accommodations:
RESORT WITH NEARBY CABINS
NUMBER OF GUEST ROOMS: 10
MAXIMUM NUMBER OF GUESTS: 25

Conference Groups: Yes

Meals: American plan

Rates:
Numerous packages from $900 per person for 3 days and 2 nights, double occupancy

Guides: Included

Gratuities: $100 per week

Preferred Payment:
MasterCard, Visa

Getting There:
Guests fly to Lewiston and are ferried by jetboat up to the lodge. Helicopter service is also available at $175 per person.

Other Activities:
Golf, whitewater rafting, swimming, boating, helitours, hiking, bird watching, biking, skiing.

Contact:
Reed J. Taylor
Hell's Canyon Lodge, PO Box 576, Lewiston, ID 83501; 800/727-6190, fax 208/798-8929, email hclodge@valley-inter net.net

CRASHING THROUGH HELL'S CANYON, one of the deepest gorges in North America, the Snake River is none too tame as it races past this log lodge five miles upstream from the canyon's mouth. The fishery here is varied: steelhead up to 40 inches from mid-September through March; smallmouths of three to five pounds, sturgeon up to nine feet and five- to 15-pound catfish from May through September; and rainbows all year. Preferred tackle ranges from flyrods for trout and steelhead to heavy spinning and casting gear for cats and sturgeon.

The lodge will furnish all the tackle you'll need, with the exception of fly gear. In that case, bring your own. And if you won't have a chance to pick up a license on your way in, call the lodge before you come. Staff will get one for you and you'll reimburse them when you arrive. Fishing packages vary with angler interest and time of year. In most you'll ride a jetboat (and sometimes a chopper) to the waters where you'll fish. While guests may fish freelance, they are normally accompanied by a guide.

While fishing is central to the lodge's operation, it functions as a full-service river resort and specializes in combination helicopter tours and jetboat runs through Hell's Canyon. The white water below Hell's Canyon dam is awesome, and the lodge's steel boats are the safest way to run it. More adventurous guests ride the rapids in big rafts. Other boat/raft trips are available on the Salmon River (run the Eye of the Needle) and Granite Creek, with its Class IV and V rapids. After a day on the river, the hot tub on the deck is welcome indeed.

While the lodge caters to individuals, it specializes in groups and families. It's a favorite corporate retreat. Guests stay in one of 10 guest rooms with shared baths. Seven of the rooms are in the main lodge, the other three in cabins nearby. Meals—the 20-ounce rib eye steak, for instance—are stout, even by western standards. Hot lunches and picnics are provided on some of the excursions from the lodge.

Henry's Fork Lodge
Island Park, Idaho

VITAL STATISTICS:

KEY SPECIES:
Rainbow and brown trout

Season:
May through mid-October
Accommodations:
MODERN LOG LODGE
NUMBER OF GUEST ROOMS: 12
MAXIMUM NUMBER OF GUESTS: 24
Conference Groups: Yes
Meals: American plan
Rates:
From $1200 per person for 6-day week, double occupancy
Guides: From $300 for 2 anglers per day
Gratuities: 15% of lodge bill
Preferred Payment:
Discover, MasterCard
Getting There:
Fly to Idaho Falls, Idaho, or West Yellowstone, Montana, rent a car and drive to the lodge.
Other Activities:
Golf, tennis, rafting, hiking, antiquing, biking, wildlife photography, horseback riding, Yellowstone tours, bird hunting in the fall.

Contact:
Nelson Ishiyama
Henry's Fork Lodge, HC66 Box 600, Island Park, ID 83429; 208/558-7953, fax 208/558-7956 (summer); 465 California St., Room 800, San Francisco, CA 94104; 415/434-1657, fax 415/392-1268 (winter).

Represented By:
Kaufmann's Streamborn, 800/442-4359; Off the Beaten Path, 800/445-2995.

With awards for architecture and service, this lodge is as sophisticated as its namesake stream.

THANKS TO STABLE WATER FLOWS, the Henry's Fork is back. Catch the Green and Brown Drake and salmonfly hatches in the season's first weeks, move to terrestrials on the flat runs in the Railroad Ranch and nymphs in Box Canyon for midsummer, and wind up with small mayflies in fall. Rainbows, many larger than 20 inches, are plentiful but particular in this born-again wild-trout fishery.

Henry's Fork fishes as if it were three rivers: The upper section is classic freestone tailwater, the middle section at the ranch is a stream of cobbly bottom and sinuous weedbeds, and the lower section hastens over ledges and boulders on its way to the falls. When Island Park Dam is not releasing water, the Box Canyon is wadeable and big fish are plentiful. Although most anglers float the Box, Idaho law requires that you get out of the boat to fish. Some float the middle section as well, but fishing is better, and more fun, if you walk the bank and stalk rising trout. So it is also with the lower section, but floats have a larger appeal because you can cover more water.

Henry's Fork Anglers, Mike Lawson's congenial flyshop, is up the road in Last Chance. Get a cup of coffee, stand around the open fireplace, and talk hatches until the next one comes off. Then walk across the street and fish it. The surrounding national forest holds many ponds with various trout populations: brookies, browns, cutthroats and rainbows. Bellyboats are the order of the day. Over the continental divide is Yellowstone National Park, with all of its wonderful streams.

From the porch on Henry's Fork Lodge, you can see lunker rainbows rising in the river below. You can see them from the windows of your room (stylishly rustic with hand-hewn furniture, fireplaces, down comforters), and from the windows of the dining room (over salmon en croute or lamb with rosemary). You can see them but you can't watch them without pulling on your waders and clamoring down the bank to give them a try. Dinner will be held until the hatch is over. Named Fishing Lodge of the Year in 1995 by *Andrew Harper's Hideaway Report*, Henry's Fork Lodge hosts 24 guests in sophisticated style. The lodge buildings were nominated for a national architectural award, and wood-paneled interiors are complemented with antique furniture and Oriental rugs. Not only are there a variety of flyfishing schools (Mel Krieger, Joan Wulff for women only), but you'll enjoy after-dinner talks by naturalists, writers and historians as well.

The Lodge at Palisades Creek

Irwin, Idaho

VITAL STATISTICS:

KEY SPECIES:
Brown and cutthroat trout; cuttbows

Season:
Late May through November
Accommodations:
CABINS
NUMBER OF GUEST ROOMS: 7
MAXIMUM NUMBER OF GUESTS: 22
Conference Groups: Yes
Meals: American plan
Rates:
$2150 per person for 6 days and 7 nights, double occupancy
Guides: Included
Gratuities: $50 to $100 per day
Preferred Payment:
Cash or check
Getting There:
Idaho Falls is the closest airport. The lodge will arrange transportation for $50 each way. You may want to rent a car for side trips to Jackson, Wyoming.
Other Activities:
Golf, tennis, rafting, swimming, hiking, bird watching, biking, wildlife photography.

Contact:
Chip Kearns
The Lodge at Palisades Creek, PO Box 70, Irwin, ID 83428; 208/483-2222, fax 208/483-2227.

Indian summer is idyllic on the South Fork of the Snake.

THE SOUTH FORK of the Snake River ranks among America's best trout waters. Cutthroats, rainbows, cuttbows and browns cruise the cobbled bed of this cold, clear river. Float it in a MacKenzie driftboat or wade its banks; the South Fork below Calamity Dam in Idaho provides fly-fishermen and ultralight spinfishers with plenty of action. A tailwater, the South Fork runs high in summer when irrigation needs of potato farmers are at their peak. Then it begins to fall and the fishing picks up. Throughout summer you'll find extensive hatches of mayflies, stoneflies and caddisflies. 'Hoppers in late summer and early fall are particularly effective offerings. When no hatch is apparent, work black or olive Woolly Buggers and other weighted streamers and nymphs. Average fish go about two pounds, but browns in the five-pound range are not uncommon and bigger ones are taken each year. Cutthroats provide steady action throughout the season.

The Lodge at Palisades Creek is known for its guided all-day float trips from the fish-yielding riffles and runs below the dam on the upper section, to the canyon stretch noted for unparalleled activity during the salmonfly hatch in June. Don't overlook a visit to Henry's Bathtub or Brown Town below the canyon. Trout season opens on Memorial Day and closes on November 30. For sheer beauty (and good fish) Indian summer, the first week of October, is hard to beat. The lodge maintains a fully-stocked tackleshop.

Five rustic cabins, built of local lodgepole pine, and an A-frame chalet nestle in the cottonwoods along the bank of the river. Don't be fooled. This is rustic with style. You'll find all the modern amenities: attractive wood and twig furniture, plush double or queen-size beds, an overstuffed couch for lounging, a front porch for sitting and viewing the river and, of course, a private bath. Uphill from the cabins is the lodge proper, so thoroughly remodeled that no trace of its earlier existence as a fishing camp/general store/gas station remains. Breakfasts are served in a bright and sunny cafe or out on the patio. You can dine there too, or inside by the huge stone fireplace. Cuisine might be called California hearty: ample portions of fish, fowl or beef accompanied by appropriate wines.

Wapiti Meadow Ranch

C a s c a d e ,   I d a h o

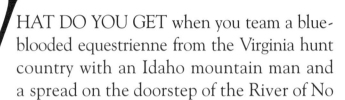
*Ride horses to high ponds or fly in and fish
a river that foiled a National Geographic expedition.*

VHAT DO YOU GET when you team a blue-blooded equestrienne from the Virginia hunt country with an Idaho mountain man and a spread on the doorstep of the River of No Return Wilderness? A lodge of heavy stone and log where the dinner service is china and crystal and silver and rooms are appointed with colonial antiques. East meets West at the Wapiti Meadow Ranch amidst split-rail fenced grasslands on the banks of Johnson Creek.

Wapiti Meadow is a dude ranch: Horse talk is taken seriously, and trail rides are de rigueur. But increasingly those treks are to high mountain lakes where fly and spin anglers do battle with native cutthroats. Overnight packtrips take guests deep into the wilderness to fish ponds that are only accessible by horse. Wild rivers abound in this terrain, so rugged that a 1935 National Geographic expedition to explore the deep canyon of Middle Fork of the Salmon River was forced to return without achieving its goal. Today, anglers fly a short 15-minute hop from the ranch to a strip on the Middle Fork for two days of fishing for cutthroats and rainbows at an overnight camp. Also nearby are the South Fork of the Salmon and Deadwood rivers. Cutthroats and rainbows here range from 12 to 20 inches, and bull trout—a subspecies of the dolly varden—can top 24 inches. The best fishing on flowing waters is after July 15, when spring meltwater has washed through the system and rivers have returned to clear summer levels. Still waters are fishable earlier, and the ranch's stocked pond provides trout for those of catch-and-eat persuasion. Orvis-endorsed, the ranch offers complimentary fly-tackle to guests booking fishing packages and rents spinning gear to those more conventionally inclined.

Scattered along the fringe of the South Meadow, four guest cabins reflect the history of the area: Ponderosa Bungalow, for the logging of its namesake pine; Lafe Cox's Cache, for a pioneer outfitter who helped explore the wilderness; Thunder Mountain Cabin, after Zane Grey's novel about gold miners; and The Rendezvous, a bow to those rugged hunters and trappers. All include two bedrooms (except Thunder Mountain, which has only one), a spacious sitting room, wood stove, kitchenette and private bath. An executive suite with sitting room, two bedrooms and bath is located in the main lodge. Candlelight dinners are elegant, with gourmet specialties.

VITAL STATISTICS:

KEY SPECIES:
Bull, cutthroat and rainbow trout; dolly varden

Season:
All year

Accommodations:
LOG CABINS
NUMBER OF GUEST ROOMS: 7
MAXIMUM NUMBER OF GUESTS: 14

Conference Groups: Yes

Meals: American plan

Rates:
From $1320 per person for 3 days

Guides: Included

Gratuities: 15% of package price added for staff; guides at client's discretion

Preferred Payment:
Cash or check

Getting There:
Best bet is to fly to Boise and rent a car, or shuttle in by private air charter—$90 per person one way.

Other Activities:
Hiking, horseback riding, whitewater rafting, biking, bird watching, skiing, wildlife photography.

Contact:
Diana Swift
Wapiti Meadow Ranch,
HC 72, Cascade, ID
83611; 208/633-3217,
fax 208/633-3219.

Bar N Ranch
West Yellowstone, Montana

VITAL STATISTICS:

KEY SPECIES:
Brown, cutthroat and rainbow trout

Season:
All year

Accommodations:
TRADITIONAL WESTERN LODGE
NUMBER OF GUEST ROOMS: 13
MAXIMUM NUMBER OF GUESTS: 35

Conference Groups: Yes
Meals: American plan
Rates:
From $75 per person per day, double occupancy
Guides: $250 for 2 per day
Gratuities: 15%
Preferred Payment:
MasterCard, Visa
Getting There:
West Yellowstone and Bozeman are closest airports. The lodge will pick you up free from West Yellowstone and charges additional fees from Bozeman.

Other Activities:
Golf, tennis, rafting, swimming, boating, bird watching, antiquing, biking, wildlife photography, skiing, snowmobiling, dog sledding, Yellowstone Park tours.

Contact:
James W. Kephart
Bar N Ranch, 3111 Targee Pass Hwy., West Yellowstone, MT 59758; 800/BIG SKYS, fax 406/646-7229; also 90441 N. Fifth St. # 201, Philadelphia, PA 19123; 215/440-0200, fax 215/440-8501.

Represented By:
Vanguard Travel, 215/563-2411.

Take seminars, earn tax-advantage credits and fish for golden-triangle trout at this long established lodge.

THE 640-ACRE BAR N RANCH has been in the Kephart family since 1908, and over the years it has occasionally hosted anglers, though for several years it was pretty much a family and friends affair. Four 10- to 15-acre ponds are on the property, all stocked with rainbow, brown and cutthroat trout. A few miles of the South Fork of the Madison flow through this rolling country; the ranch also borders Hebgen Lake.

The South Fork of the Madison is not the place for novice anglers. The stream is small, quite deep in places and cold all year. Clean gravel covers much of the bottom, making this a great spawning stream for rainbows and browns. While whitefish are looked upon with disfavor by most anglers, their presence is an indicator of high water quality. You'll also find some very big browns and rainbows. According to Bob Jacklyn, whose flyshop in nearby West Yellowstone is a must stop for any angler fishing the golden triangle, the South Fork is probably underfished. Good hatches of mayflies, caddis, Pale Morning Duns and Gray Drakes are prevalent from June 15, when the river opens, on into October. But the bad news is that the river's course is generally boggy and lined with willows. Accessing the stream can be challenging, and casting difficult.

If you're booked in to the Bar N, you'll want to fish the South Fork. But the ranch is within a few minutes of the main stem of the Madison as well as all the Yellowstone streams, Henry's Lake and the Henry's Fork. Anglers will do better on public sections of those waters than on the ranch. The two exceptions are the big ponds on the ranch and Hebgen Lake, where average trout run 16 to 21 inches.

Fishing is the mainstay of the Bar N Ranch, and it comes with a twist favored by tax-conscious doctors. Accredited and non-accredited seminars on tax issues, medical-legal updates and similar topics are available at additional cost. Non-docs can also take seminars from the ranch's video library.

By the time you read this, the ranch will have opened its new 8000-square-foot lodge with nine rooms, all with private baths, whirlpools, fireplaces and balconies. Owner Jim Kephart is decorating the lodge with works from his private collection of Western art (original Bierstadt and two Gary Carters). Furnishings will match. So will the meals. Steaks, turkey dinners and fried chicken with potatoes and vegetables feed hearty appetites sharpened by a day on stream or horseback.

Elk Creek Ranch, on the headwaters of Idaho's Henry's Fork,
provides guests with easy access to a wide variety
of fishing experiences. — page 113.

Designed to house seven anglers, Battle Creek features a special
flytying room, three bedrooms with baths plus stunning views
of the countryside. The fishing isn't too bad either. — page 121.

Battle Creek Lodge
Choteau, Montana

VITAL STATISTICS:

KEY SPECIES:
Brown, brook, cutthroat and rainbow trout

Season:
May through October
Accommodations:
LOG LODGE AND CABINS
NUMBER OF GUEST ROOMS: 5
MAXIMUM NUMBER OF GUESTS: 11
Conference Facilities: Yes
Meals: American plan
Rates:
From $1495 per person for 5 days and 4 nights, double occupancy
Guides: Included
Gratuities: $200
Preferred Payment:
MasterCard, Visa
Getting There:
Fly to Great Falls, Montana, and the lodge van will pick you up. Or you can rent a car and drive.
Other Activities:
Swimming, boating, hiking, bird watching, biking, wildlife photography.

Contact:
Jack Salmond
Battle Creek Lodge, Box 670, Choteau, MT 59422; 406/466-2815, fax 406/466-5510.

Fish for huge trout on a 40,000-acre spread with 22 miles of streams.

AT BATTLE CREEK, anglers are faced with a major dilemma each day. What will it be this morning? Fish the glacial lakes with the big Kamloops? The pond with the five-pound browns and brookies? The freestone stream with cuts up to three pounds? The choice is yours. So you stand on the front porch and sip your coffee and your eyes wander over what you can see of the 40,000-acre spread and you remember the 'bow that pulled your bellyboat around for a while last night before the tippet parted...he must have gone seven or eight pounds. It's back to that lake for you.

Eight lakes dot this high plains ranch where Libby Collins gained fame in the 1880s as the "Cattle Queen of Montana." (Remember Ronald Reagan and Barbara Stanwyck in the movie? Same title, but it wasn't filmed on the ranch.) Owner Jack Salmond has been expanding the fishery on the ranch since the early 1980s. Kamloops up to 28 inches cruise a pair of 25-acre ponds and browns and brookies up to five pounds reside in a second, slightly smaller pair. Four other ponds, one each for browns, brook trout and west slope cutthroats, and one for all three, are also under development. In addition, Salmond owns 22 miles of Deep Creek. Fish the pools and falls for cutthroats on the upper reaches, or go for rainbows, browns and brookies lower down. While the season runs from May 1 through September 15, the best fishing is in July when Green Drakes, damsels and caddis are hatching.

In 1995, Salmond and his wife, Myrtle, built a log lodge designed to hold a maximum of seven anglers. There's plenty of space to hang out, including a special flytying room. Each of the three bedrooms has a private bath and a view of stunning open country. Salmond is also remodeling some old ranch buildings into cabins. The 1886-vintage blacksmith shop now sleeps two, as does the old post office; another cabin currently under construction will have four bedrooms. Family-style meals are served on a wide pine table under an antler chandelier. When you push away from the table, your belt will be as tight as your lines to those big trout.

C-B Ranch

C a m e r o n ,   M o n t a n a

VITAL STATISTICS:

KEY SPECIES:
Brown, cutthroat and rainbow trout

Season:
Mid-June through early September

Accommodations:
CABINS
NUMBER OF GUEST ROOMS: 6
MAXIMUM NUMBER OF GUESTS: 18

Conference Groups: No

Meals: American plan

Rates:
From $185 per person per day, double occupancy

Guides: From $250 per day. Lodge will recommend.

Gratuities: 5% included in bill

Preferred Payment:
Cash or check

Getting There:
Fly to Bozeman or West Yellowstone. Rent a car, as you'll want it for off-ranch fishing and for sight-seeing. Follow directions provided by ranch.

Other Activities:
Golf, tennis, whitewater rafting, bird watching, wildlife photography, horseback riding.

Contact:
**Sandy Vander Lans
C-B Ranch, PO Box 148, Cameron, MT 59720; 888/723-3474, fax 619/723-1932 (winter).**

For a change, try riding your own horse to five miles of private fishing.

A MONG THE ABUNDANCE of guest ranches in the West are a few that are: 1) truly outstanding, and 2) provide really good fishing on their properties. C-B qualifies on both counts. First the fishing. Five miles of Indian Creek are open to guests. A brawling little freestone creek, you'll find rainbows and a few browns. Not big by western standards—a good fish is 16 inches—the fish hit dries best in July and August. A mile upstream from the ranch, the creek forks and provides more good water. But be warned, it is as clear as a mountain morning, and a stealthy approach to its pools and pockets is essential.

The C-B leases a small stretch of the Madison where O'Dell Creek comes in. Here are the browns, cutthroats and rainbows that made the West famous. C-B guests fish that section or arrange to float or wade under the care of one of a number of guides that the ranch recommends. Farther south on Highway 287 is the fork in the road that takes you to West Yellowstone or Island Park and Henry's Fork. What a choice!

Riding is big at the C-B and guests are given mounts for their stay. Pack a float tube, travel rod, flyvest and lunch; swing into the saddle and ride up into the Madison Mountains to an isolated pond. Fish all day and then amble back down, stopping to catch the evening hatch on Deep Creek.

Rates at the C-B are more than competitive. That's because the owner, angler and equestrian Cynthia Boomhower, is more interested in fishing than in financial return, says her son-in-law Chris Vander Lans who, with his wife Sandy, manages the ranch.

Accommodations are first class. Three pine cabins, each with two bedrooms, private bath and fireplace or Franklin stove, ring the foot of a hill. Guests take their meals in the main lodge, dining family-style on a range of old standbys—turkey, steak, lamb —with good Italian (bruschetta, gnocchi and meatballs with sauce) and Mexican for variety. Special diets can be accommodated.

Chico Hot Springs Lodge

Pray, Montana

VITAL STATISTICS:

KEY SPECIES:
Brown, cutthroat, rainbow and brook trout

Season:
All year

Accommodations:
RESORT
NUMBER OF GUEST ROOMS: 90
MAXIMUM NUMBER OF GUESTS: 175

Conference Groups: Yes

Meals: Not included

Rates:
From $39 to $84 per person per day, single occupancy

Guides: $275 additional

Gratuities: 15%

Preferred Payment:
American Express, Discover, MasterCard, Visa

Getting There:
Fly to Bozeman, Montana, and rent a car. You'll want one to sightsee and fish the streams in Yellowstone.

Other Activities:
Rafting, swimming, hiking, bird watching, biking, wildlife photography, cross-country skiing, dog sledding.

Contact:
Colin Davis
Chico Hot Springs Lodge, PO Drawer D, Pray, MT 59065; 406/333-4933, fax 406/333-4694.

Just north of Yellowstone is a wonderful old hotel with hot mineral springs, plus a catch-and-eat pond out back.

HALFWAY BETWEEN LIVINGSTON and Gardiner, Montana, is a rustic hostelry that's grown up around the turn-of-the-century lodge at Chico Hot Springs. Two miles from the Yellowstone River, the lodge is on the fringe of the Gallatin National Forest and is an easy drive from the renowned trout streams of Yellowstone National Park: the Gibbon, Firehole, Madison and others.

Lakes, big rivers and freestone and spring creeks abound in the park. Boats are required to fish the lakes, but the best angling is in flowing waters. To wade and fish those, a guide isn't needed (though for first-timers, booking a guide at $275 per day is a great way to learn new water). The lodge will arrange for guests to drift the Yellowstone for cutthroats, browns and rainbows in the two- to eight-pound class. And then there's the lodge's own pond, which is filled with brook trout. Though the season runs from May through October, meltwater swells the streams in the early part of the year. The fishing's best in September when Indian summer arrives and the mountains are at their loveliest.

Geothermal activity gave the lodge its birth in the early 1900s, and today guests can soak in 100°F water reputed to be therapeutic. Whether it actually is or not is moot: There's no doubt that a spell in the lodge's hot mineral pools soothes casting elbow and other angling maladies and puts one in a mellow disposition for dinner.

Open with smoked trout, served with cream cheese, lemon and tomato. Move on to a spinach salad. Choose from aged beef, Mediterranean chicken (a 10-ounce breast stuffed with herbs, roasted red bell peppers and goat cheese), Thai shrimp or a dozen other entrees. Hearty eaters may want to check out the buffalo steak.

Accommodations reflect the evolution of the resort. Guests in the main lodge stay in rooms of period decor and, in keeping with the era, share baths. More modern motel rooms as well as rustic cabins, houses and condominiums are also available.

[R O C K Y   M O U N T A I N S]

Craig Fellin's Big Hole River Outfitters
W i s e   R i v e r ,   M o n t a n a

VITAL STATISTICS:

KEY SPECIES:
Brown, cutthroat and rainbow trout; grayling

Season:
June through September

Accommodations:
LOG LODGE AND CABINS
NUMBER OF GUEST ROOMS: 6
MAXIMUM NUMBER OF GUESTS: 10

Conference Groups: Yes

Meals: American plan

Rates:
From $1895 per person per week, double occupancy

Guides: Included

Gratuities: $50 per boat per day

Preferred Payment:
MasterCard

Getting There:
Fly to Butte, Montana, and the lodge van will pick you up at no charge.

Other Activities:
Golf, hiking.

Contact:
Craig Fellin
Craig Fellin's Big Hole River Outfitters, Box 156, Wise River, MT 59762; 406/832-3252, fax 406/832-3252, email wsr3252@montana.com

Represented By:
Frontiers International, 800/245-1950; Off the Beaten Path, 800/445-2995.

Slow down, relax, catch fish and enjoy southwestern Montana.

SMALL AND INTIMATE is the best way to describe Craig Fellin's Big Hole River Outfitters on the Wise River. Booking only eight to 10 guests per week, Fellin and his guides help guests slow down, relax, catch fish and enjoy the southwestern Montana countryside. And what scenery it is. The main lodge and three spacious log guest cabins nestle up against a hillside timbered with lodgepole pine. The dining room, where the likes of baked eggs with asparagus spears greet you at breakfast, looks down a verdant valley toward the Pioneer Mountains. The Wise River is but a couple minute's walk away through the trees.

The Wise is a freestone stream that feeds the Big Hole. In front of the lodge is the home pool, where rainbows, cutthroats and a rare grayling will take dries or nymphs. You can wade the stream to your heart's content, but the main action here is floating the Big Hole. Guests typically will float two or three sections of this long river of diverse character. The upper river is too fast to be called a meadow stream, even though it flows through a large valley. Here you'll find brookies, cutthroats and grayling. Below the hamlet of Wise River, the Big Hole picks up steam, swirls around boulders and through deep pockets, and crashes between the walls of Maiden Rock Canyon. Fish here are bigger and tend to be more browns than rainbows. Below Glen, the river paces through braided channels, good brown trout water, on its way to the Jefferson at Twin Bridges.

The Beaverhead and Ruby rivers are within easy driving distance. And horseback trips to fish high mountain lakes with guide/outfitter Cliff Page are also available. The lodge maintains a small flyshop where you can stock up on the pattern du jour and purchase all those things you left at home. You can hear the river sing through the open window of your well and tastefully appointed log cabin. Dinners are gourmet: roasted garlic and brie soup, boneless pork chop grilled with nectarine salsa, ginger creme brulee.

Diamond J Ranch

Ennis, Montana

VITAL STATISTICS:

KEY SPECIES:
Brown, cutthroat and rainbow trout

Season:
June through October

Accommodations:
RUSTIC LOG CABINS
NUMBER OF GUEST ROOMS: 12
MAXIMUM NUMBER OF GUESTS: 35

Conference Groups: Yes

Meals: American plan

Rates:
$1150 per week

Guides: $275 for 2 per day

Gratuities: $40

Preferred Payment:
MasterCard, Visa

Getting There:
Gallatin, Montana has service by Delta and Northwest; rent a car at the airport, or arrange for the ranch van to pick you up ($60 per load each way).

Other Activities:
Tennis, whitewater rafting, hiking, bird watching, trap, skeet, sporting clays, horseback riding, bird hunting.

Contact:
Reservations
Diamond J Ranch, PO Box 577, Ennis, MT 59729; 406/682-4867, fax 406/682-4106.

A stay at the Diamond J is worthwhile if only to say that you've fished Jackass Creek.

TWELVE MILES EAST of Ennis is the well-known and highly regarded Diamond J Ranch. Owned by Peter and Jinny Combs since 1959, the ranch has earned a reputation for its outstanding service, rustic and comfortable cabins, excellent food and a range of activities that include riding, hiking, square dancing, bird hunting and flyfishing. Of special note are programs for children, including riding, games and storytelling in front of a blazing fire in the stone hearth; there are also special playing and dining facilities for children.

Jackass Creek flows through the ranch and offers fishing for rainbows. It is a little stream, but the angling can be quite challenging. Also on the ranch is a two-acre pond that's used during free flyfishing schools (every Monday afternoon). Other times on the pond, you can sharpen your casting or fish-playing skills. It's a nice place to practice before the main event. An Orvis-endorsed lodge, the Diamond J employs a fishmaster or guide to help guests find successful angling on the ranch. It also works closely with the Tackle Shop at Ennis to provide guide services for anglers interested in sampling the variety of trout water in this corner of the state.

Through Ennis flows the Madison, a stream where everyone can catch trout some of the time and some people can catch trout all of the time. With 52 miles of rather evenly graveled bottom from Quake Lake to Ennis, the Madison has a reputation of being fairly easy to wade and fish for rainbows, browns and cutthroats. Below Ennis Lake, the river drops into wild Bear Trap Canyon (Class III to V rapids), where fishing—particularly in the fall when water is low and cool—can be tremendous for browns up to five pounds. Fishing there isn't for the faint of heart. A 35-mile two-day float with an overnight in a log cabin on the river is a great way to survey the Madison. All the famous streams of Yellowstone—the Gibbon, Firehole and Madison—are worth a visit, even if you've been there and done that. And to the west are the Big Hole, Beaverhead and Jefferson. The Henry's Fork is just over the mountain in Idaho.

At the Diamond J, you'll sleep in spacious log cabins, each with private bath, fireplace and front porch. Meals with a southwestern flare are served in the main dining room. Fare is hearty as well as healthy; fish, fowl and occasionally pork and beef. Outdoor barbecues are a weekly feature, and breakfast trail rides are often held in the summer. Meals occur at regular times.

Double Arrow Resort

S e e l e y   L a k e ,   M o n t a n a

VITAL STATISTICS:

KEY SPECIES:
Brown and rainbow trout

Season:
All year

Accommodations:
Log cabins
Number of Guest Rooms: 30
Maximum Number of Guests: 70

Conference Groups: Yes

Meals: Restaurant

Rates:
From $65 for 2 per night

Guides: $270 for 2 anglers per day

Gratuities: $15

Preferred Payment:
Discover, MasterCard

Getting There:
Missoula is the closest airport. Rent a car and drive to the resort.

Other Activities:
Golf, tennis, rafting, swimming, boating, hiking, biking, wildlife photography, trail riding.

Contact:
Ed Bezanson
Double Arrow Resort, PO Box 747, Seeley Lake, MT 59868; 406/677-2777, fax 406/677-2922.

Try a family resort where the fishing is as serious as you want it to be.

GOLF OR FISHING? Fishing or golf? At this resort deep in the Seeley-Swan Valley surrounded by the Flathead National Forest, you don't have to make a choice. You can do both. Double Arrow Resort features a beautiful, challenging nine-hole course that winds through woods and around lakes with snow-capped mountains in the background. A little stream flows through it, and the stream is big enough to hold fish.

But that's not the primary attraction for anglers. The Blackfoot, about 20 miles south of the lodge, is one of Montana's great family rivers. Lest the wrong impression be given, the Blackfoot is good trout water. Rainbows are not persnickety; they'll take attractor patterns as well as flies that imitate hatches. Blue-Winged Olives are a good bet before runoff roils the river in May to mid-June. As water recedes, try various caddis imitations. Hopper patterns are particularly productive in fall. Browns are taken on occasion, and the angler who fishes nymphs or streamers in deep holes will likely encounter bull trout.

As a family river, the Blackfoot with its 30-mile recreation corridor is hard to beat. Flowing through mild canyons and meadows, it's a favorite with the genteel whitewater set. On weekends, armadas of canoes and rafts descend the river laden with bodies clad in bathing suits. If you and your family like congenial river floats, this is among the best. Later, when the recreational floaters have left the river, the trout come out of their hideouts and begin looking for dinner. Maybe that's why they're not to choosy about what they take. For a few hours in the twilight, you can fish this river with spin or flytackle in all the solitude that it lacks during the day.

The best fishing on the Blackfoot occurs in fall. The tourists have gone, terrestrials have turned on the trout and leaves on the trees are as yellow as lemons. The golf course is open until October 1, depending on weather, so if you want to get in a few holes on the side, book in mid-September. Virtually all of Double Arrow's accommodations are in cabins of peeled log, charmingly appointed with an eclectic mix of modern and period furniture. Brass beds boast cozy flowered comforters. Guests warm by the fire in the stone hearth on nights when the air is chilled, or lounge in the pool when it's warm. Cuisine, served in the restaurant, is continental gourmet, as pretty as it is delicious. Various meal plans are available.

Eagle Nest Lodge
Hardin, Montana

VITAL STATISTICS:

KEY SPECIES:
Brown and rainbow trout

Season:
April through October

Accommodations:
RUSTIC LOG LODGE
NUMBER OF GUEST ROOMS: 6
MAXIMUM NUMBER OF GUESTS: 12

Conference Groups: Yes
Meals: American plan
Rates:
$1700 per person for 4 days and 5 nights, double occupancy
Guides: Included
Gratuities: 10% to 15%
Preferred Payment:
Cash or check
Getting There:
Fly to Billings, rent a car and drive to the Bighorn Fly and Tackle Shop, where you will be met and escorted to the lodge.
Other Activities:
Boating, bird watching, wildlife photography, upland hunting.

Contact:
Keith Kelly
Eagle Nest Lodge, PO Box 509, Hardin, MT 59034; 406/665-3711, fax 406/665-3712, email eaglenest@mcn.net, website http://www. spav.com/progc/ eaglenest

Cast for browns and hunt pheasants or grouse at a lodge on Montana's most productive river.

LOFTY AND SOARING, the jagged peaks of the Bitterroot and Madison ranges dominate Bighorn country, drawing tourists who come to gaze at spectacular scenery that lifts the soul. They don't come to Bighorn country just for the scenery, though. No, many people come to the Bighorn to fish, and in the fall to hunt pheasants, partridge and grouse. Smart sportsmen time their arrivals for late September or early October, when big browns are on the spawn and birds are in the air.

With the closing of Yellowtail Dam in 1965, the Bighorn became a tailwater fishery. The first 13 miles below the dam—the stretch that fishes best—flows clear and reasonably cold year-round. Brown trout outnumber rainbows in sizes up to 22 inches. If you happen to hook a larger trout, odds are it will be a big 'bow. Rainbows tend to school up in tight pods at those junctions between riffles and deep, slow pools. Good guides will find those holding areas and fish them hard. While the river is open all year, fishing starts with the first hatches in March and continues into October. The flyfisherman should bring an assortment of midges, Blue-Winged Olives, Pale Morning Duns, tricos and caddis. Hoppers may produce in late summer and fall. However, don't forget a stock of standard nymphs: Gold-Ribbed Hare's Ears, Pheasant Tails, San Juan Worms, Scuds and Girdle Bugs. Woolly Buggers and Muddlers are effective too. Spinfishermen will find success with Mepps, Rooster Tails and Rapalas. Most anglers drift until they spot feeding fish or likely looking water, then pull ashore and wade. Neoprenes are required in spring and late fall.

You won't find verdant green farmlands here, rather acre upon acre of wheat stubble and grass along with the sage. It's prime pheasant country. Gunning for ringnecks gets under way in October after September's warm-up on grouse. Waterfowl seasons also overlap trout fishing. Bring an over/under and a few boxes of shells when you come. At Eagle Nest Lodge, Keith Kelly will have the pointers or setters ready.

Specializing in trout fishing with a nod to gunning in the fall, Eagle Nest is a first-rate sporting resort. Orvis-endorsed, the rich reddish log lodge provides guests with tastefully decorated rooms, all with private baths. Hungarian partridge and pheasants find their ways onto the menu, as do filet mignon and pork tenderloin. Located on the Bighorn, Eagle Nest is inside the Crow Reservation, and thus serves no alcohol. It's OK to bring your own.

Firehole Ranch
W e s t   Y e l l o w s t o n e ,   M o n t a n a

VITAL STATISTICS:

KEY SPECIES:
Brown and rainbow trout

Season:
May through October

Accommodations:
LOG CABINS
NUMBER OF GUEST ROOMS: 10
MAXIMUM NUMBER OF GUESTS: 20

Conference Groups: Yes

Meals: American plan

Rates:
From $450 for 2 per day

Guides: $275 for 2 per day

Gratuities: 15%

Preferred Payment:
Cash or check

Getting There:
West Yellowstone is served by Delta Airlines. Rent a car at the airport and drive from there.

Other Activities:
Canoeing, rafting, horseback riding, boating, hiking, bird watching, biking, wildlife photography, skiing.

Contact:
Stan Klassen
Firehole Ranch, Box 686, West Yellowstone, MT 59758; 406/646-7294, fax 406/646-4728, email firehole@sisna.com, website http://205.138. 107.3/jackson/firehole

For plush accommodations in the middle of Montana's finest fishing, look no further.

AMONG RANCHES IN THE WEST, there are those where anglers stay while they fish and those where they come to fish. The Firehole is in the latter category. It is an angling lodge first and foremost, though you'll find horseback riding as well. Since Dale Kinsella and Stan Klassen took over the operation (Kinsella is also the principal in The Lodge at Palisades Creek on the South Fork of the Snake), the Firehole has soared in popularity. Anglers book favorite weeks and cabins a year in advance, sometimes two.

Are fishing and accommodations really that good? Yes. The roster of waters within an easy drive of this lodge reads like a Who's Who of Western trout fisheries: the Madison, Gibbon, Firehole, Gallatin and Henry's Fork. You could stay here for years and never fish it all, and during the week while you are here, at least one of these rivers will offer the fishing of your dreams. Pick that which suits your mood: relax with a float on the prolific Madison. Fish the challenging Firehole among bubbling mudpots and fumaroles spewing steam (and keep an eye out for bison). Hike up to the falls on the Gibbon in early October and nymph for spawning browns holding in the plunge pool. Try 'hoppers in the meadows of the easily wadeable Gallatin. Or work dries for finicky rainbows on the Harriman Ranch section of the Henry's Fork. Snuggle into a float tube and cast to rising browns in Hebgen Lake, or ride horseback to Coffin Lake for mountain rainbows. Orvis-endorsed, the lodge includes a full-service tackleshop and a staff of accomplished guides.

Several miles down a one-lane gravel road, Firehole Lodge feels isolated, and that's the way guests want it. Ten luxurious, fully carpeted and tastefully decorated log cabins, each with stone fireplace, private bath and intimate sitting area, offer comfort without pretension. The dining room, with its huge stone fireplace, looks across the meadow to the lake. Pastries and omelettes are the normal bill of fare at breakfasts. Dinners, preceded by hors d'oeuvres and cocktails from the old mahogany bar, might feature a salad of organic greens with duck, pecans, raspberries and port vinaigrette, charbroiled tuna or braised red deer and a brown butter tart with blueberry sauce, all accompanied by Vivaldi or Mozart.

Glacier National Park
(Waterton-Glacier International Peace Park)
West Glacier, Montana

The stately Prince of Wales and five other historic hotels accommodate anglers willing to walk or ride for their trout.

VITAL STATISTICS:

KEY SPECIES:
Brook, cutthroat and lake trout; grayling

Season:
June through late September
Accommodations:
LODGES, MOTEL ROOMS AND COTTAGES
NUMBER OF GUEST ROOMS:
Varies per location
Conference Groups: Yes
Meals: Restaurants, some rooms with kitchens
Guides: $295 for 2 per day
Gratuities: 10% to 15% per angler
Preferred Payment:
Major credit cards
Getting There:
Fly to Kalispell, Montana, rent a car and drive to the park.
Other Activities:
Hiking, camping, boating, wildlife photography, bird watching.

Contact:
Reservations
Glacier Park Inc., 1850 N. Central Ave., Phoenix, AZ 85077; 602/207-6000.

SOARING AND JAGGED PEAKS, picked sharp by the alpine glaciers that gouged long finger lakes in the foothills below, provision this park which spans the U.S./Canada boarder with some of the most spectacular scenery in North America. You'll see active glaciers, dozens of tiny lakes tinted blue as the azure sky and scores of cataracts tumbling down steep slopes. Water is plentiful and you'd think that it holds lots of fish.

But unlike Yellowstone National Park, where fishing is among the dominant pastimes, angling at Waterton/Glacier is strictly an adjunct to sightseeing, hiking and camping. Years ago, park officials discontinued the stocking of Glacier's streams and lakes. The reason: Introduced species competed and hybridized with native fish, threatening the survival of the latter. An extremely short growing season and limited nutrients also conspire against Glacier's opportunity to produce large numbers of fish.

Randy Gayner (800/521-7238), who operates a guide service in the Glacier area, confirms that fishing in the park is indeed a bonus. The best fishing is in high alpine lakes such as the Quartz Lake trio. Cutthroat and bull trout in the 10- to 14-inch range readily strike spinners and flies cast from shore. There's one caveat: A two- to three-mile hike in precedes the fishing. But that's the case with most of the park's better waters. You may catch brookies, rainbows and grayling along with a few cutthroats. Lake trout reside in the parks larger and deeper lakes, and trolling just after ice-out is the most effective strategy. The North and Middle Forks of the Flathead River make up much of the western boundary of the park. Floats in driftboats result in catches of cutthroats of 10 to 15 inches and rainbows that are a little larger. Fish fly or spinning gear. Generally speaking, the park's fishing season runs from the third Saturday in May through November 30. However, Lake McDonald is open for lake trout fishing from April 1 to December 31. The best time to fish streams in the park is from mid-July after springmelt has passed into September. Check park regulations before wetting a line.

Lodging as exquisite as the scenery is available through six historic hotels and inns operated as concessions by Glacier Parks, Inc.

THE PRINCE OF WALES. Centered high on a bluff looking down Waterton

continued on page 130

Lake, the Prince of Wales hotel is a regal as its namesake, Prince Edward. Opened in 1927, this hotel maintains an air of British, yet rustic, gentility. Take tea in the lobby and dine on the best of English fare in Garden Court. Should sightseeing and angling pale, there's golf and tennis. Eighty-one rooms from $175 for two per night.

MANY GLACIER HOTEL. Built in 1914 and 1915 on the shore of Swiftcurrent Lake, the hotel is best known for its stunning views of Grinnel Point and Mt. Hinkel, prime habitat for mountain goats, bighorn sheep and bear. Reminiscent of Swiss mountain resorts (flags of Swiss Cantons decorate the dining room), with 208 rooms, this is the largest hotel in the park. From $91 per person per night, single occupancy.

SWIFTCURRENT MOTOR INN. A mile from the hotel at the base of Mt. Hinkel is this complex of 26 cabins (shared baths) and 62 modern hotel rooms. Meals are served in the coffee shop. Cabins without baths from $29 per person per night, single occupancy; inn rooms from $65 per person per night, single occupancy.

LAKE MCDONALD LODGE. Once John Lewis' grand hunting retreat, these accommodations date from 1913 and reflect the height of early Western elegance. The main lodge, motor inn and cottages combine to offer 100 rooms. A restaurant and coffee shop round out the complex. From $64 for small cottage rooms to $113 for rooms in the main lodge.

THE VILLAGE INN. On the opposite end of Lake McDonald is this small motel that contains 36 rooms, 12 of which have kitchens. View the lake from the window of your room or wade its chilly waters from the beach below. From $80 per person per night, single occupancy.

THE RISING SUN MOTOR INN. Near the east entrance to the park and close to St. Mary Lake, you'll find three motel buildings with a total of 72 rooms and 36 cottage rooms. Views of "The Land of Shining Mountain" are stunning. From $64 per night per person, single occupancy.

Hawley Mountain Guest Ranch
McLeod, Montana

Fish for trout in these untrammeled waters deep in the Beartooths.

VITAL STATISTICS:

KEY SPECIES:
Brook, cutthroat and rainbow trout

Season:
May through November

Accommodations:
Dude ranch with cabins
Number of Guest Rooms: 7
Maximum Number of Guests: 24

Conference Groups: Yes

Meals: American plan

Rates:
From $1292 per person for 4 days, double occupancy

Guides: Included

Gratuities: 15% of room charge

Preferred Payment:
Cash or personal or traveler's checks

Getting There:
Fly to Bozeman or Billings, Montana. Rent a car, as you may want one for off-ranch fishing or sight-seeing. Or arrange for a representative of the ranch to meet you ($150 additional per vehicle).

Other Activities:
Hunting, hiking, tubing on the river, bird watching, 4x4 trips, float trips, wildlife photography.

Contact:
Ellen Marshall
Hawley Mountain Guest Ranch, PO Box 4, McLeod, MT 59052; 406/932-5791 (summer); 510/523-4053, fax 510/523-5188 (winter).

DRIVING SOUTH OUT OF BIG TIMBER on Highway 298, you'll pass the Road Kill Cafe. This is a fair-to-middlin' watering hole on the Boulder, and the site of such esoterica as a reading of *Cowgirl Poetry and Prose*. On your way up to the Hawley Mountain Ranch, check out the Road Kill's evening schedule, and then beat it on up the road, past where the pavement ends, to the ranch.

Deep in the Absaroka-Beartooth Wilderness, the ranch is headquarters for fishing the upper Boulder River. Scenic doesn't begin to describe vistas along the river. Segments of *A River Runs Through It* were filmed here. The river is less that 40 feet wide at the ranch, difficult to wade because of its slippery namesake, but relatively easily fished. Here you'll find cutthroats and rainbows in the one- to four-pound class, and farther up toward the headwaters, brookies of a pound or so.

While the more productive fishing runs from July through October, the best months are August and September. Throughout, nymphs are the flies of choice, though caddis come off in fair profusion after May, and 'hoppers appear in August. Sculpin patterns work well on bigger fish. Ultralight anglers should consider Panther Martins, Rooster Tails and Mepps; check stream regulations regarding number of hooks.

Fishing on the Boulder is strictly catch-and-release. For folks who prefer otherwise, the ranch will cook trout caught in its private stocked pond. In addition it offers guests basic meals built around steaks, fried chicken and lasagna. The main lodge has four guest rooms with stunning views from private balconies, and three nearby cabins, scattered under the pines, boast living rooms, bedrooms and sleeping lofts. All have private baths.

While fishing is the core of the Hawley Mountain's business, it is a dude ranch and guests may have a horse for the duration of their stay if they wish. The horses know the way to high mountain ponds. One other note from manager Ellen Marshall: "We offer no TV, no radio, no fax and your cellular phones won't work." This is truly a place to get away from it all.

Healing Waters Fly Fishing Lodge
Twin Bridges, Montana

VITAL STATISTICS:

KEY SPECIES:
Brown, cutthroat and rainbow trout

Season:
All year

Accommodations:
STONE HOUSE AND CABINS
NUMBER OF GUEST ROOMS: 5
MAXIMUM NUMBER OF GUESTS: 10

Conference Groups: Yes

Meals: American plan

Rates:
From $395 per person per day, double occupancy (minimum 3-day stay)

Guides: Included

Gratuities: $30 to $50 per day

Preferred Payment:
MasterCard, Visa

Getting There:
Fly to Butte, Montana, and rent a car; or the lodge will provide round-trip transportation for $100 additional.

Other Activities:
Golf, canoeing, rafting, boating, hiking, bird watching, antiquing, biking, wildlife photography.

Contact:
**Greg or Janet Lilly
Healing Waters Fly Fishing Lodge,
270 Tyke St., Twin Bridges, MT 59754;
406/684-5960.**

Try a refreshing change from typical log lodges, in the heart of Montana's best trout country.

GREG AND JANET LILLY wrestled with this question: What should they call their new lodge? In a previous existence it had been known as "Healing Waters." They love the lodge and the name struck a resonate chord within both. But, was that too "new-age" for anglers? They surmise that angling for trout restores the spirit and perhaps the soul. Not an unreasonable supposition, particularly when alpenglow turns the Tobacco Root Mountains rosy and browns rise to a late caddis hatch.

Healing Waters is an ideal home base for fishing southwest Montana. Just upstream from Twin Bridges is where the Ruby meets the Beaverhead. A few miles downstream from town, the Big Hole comes in from the west and helps form the Jefferson. The most popular area on the Big Hole—between Divide and Glen—is an easy drive from the lodge, as is the Ruby. Much of the lower Ruby is private and access can be a problem, and turbidity in midsummer can limit fishing. Early in the season, though, and in late August and September, the Ruby can be very productive for rainbows on its upper sections and browns down below. At times, the Jefferson is greater than the sum of its parts. With a riffle and pool personality, the river is almost tranquil in comparison to its sources. The upper section has a reputation for fishing as well as the Madison and isn't nearly as crowded. If you're willing to fish nymphs and streamers for bigger fish, consider the beginning or end of the season.

A welcome diversion from typical angling retreats of lodgepole pine, Healing Waters is a charming stone and shingle, prairie-style house. Deep eves shade windows on the main house with one guest room and on four matching and adjacent guest cabins. Queen-size beds and private baths are standard in all rooms. Meals are family-style and dinners feature filet mignon and twice baked potatoes or pastas. The town of Twin Bridges is an angler's kind of place. Twin Bridges Trout Shop supplies flies and tackle, and the town is home to the R.L. Winston Rod Company.

High Country Outfitters
P r a y ,   M o n t a n a

Stay with friends on 40 private acres with a prime trout stream and pond.

VITAL STATISTICS:

KEY SPECIES:
Brown, cutthroat and rainbow trout

Season:
May through October

Accommodations:
LOG GUEST CABIN
NUMBER OF GUEST ROOMS: 1
MAXIMUM NUMBER OF GUESTS: 4

Conference Groups: No

Meals: American plan

Rates:
$3140 for 2 for 5 nights and 4 days

Guides: Included

Gratuities: Client's discretion

Preferred Payment:
Cash or check

Getting There:
Bozeman has the closest airport. Transfers to the lodge are $170 round trip.

Other Activities:
Hiking, bird watching, wildlife photography.

Contact:
**Chip Rizzotto
High Country Outfitters,
158 Bridger Hollow Rd.,
Pray, MT 59065;
406/333-4763.**

IMAGINE AN INTIMATE CABIN. Hudson Bay blankets warm log beds. Daily baskets of fresh fruit and flowers grace rustic wood furniture. Books on angling fill the library, a tier's bench awaits and rods of every description grace the wall. Across the breezeway, Francine Rizzotto is at work in the kitchen. She does not wear a toque, though her culinary creations might suggest that she does. Spicy corn salsa may accent the lamb; the salmon may be gingered. Meanwhile Chip—husband, chief guide and major domo—plots the next day's fishing.

The Rizzottos cater to one party of up to four anglers at a time. Frequently, though, their guests are a couple who rent the single cabin for the five-night minimum with four days of guided fishing. It is as if you have these wonderful friends with a fabulous place—40 acres of solitude with trout stream and pond adjoining the Absaroka Beartooth Wilderness. You are their guests for a week, and they won't let you lift a finger to help. Your job is to soak up the scenery and fish the streams of Paradise Valley.

That means the Yellowstone and its tributaries. The Yellowstone is the longest free-flowing river in the U.S. And it is wild. A heavy rainstorm high in the mountains may raise and discolor the river. Ice and spring flows are continually rearranging pools and runs. What you fished so well last year might not be there this year. Spring melt swells the river from May through June, and in normal years, the water becomes optimal by mid-July. Despite frequent flooding, the river supports prolific hatches (caddis and salmonfly) and extensive populations of cutthroats, rainbows, browns and whitefish. Cutthroats and browns predominate in the upper river from Gardiner south to Livingston. Fish are not huge—12 to 14 inches are normal—but they are plentiful. The most popular way to fish the river is to float it, and Rizzotto runs a MacKenzie driftboat for that purpose.

In addition to the Yellowstone, Rizzotto guides anglers on the spring creeks on the DePuy and O'Hair ranches, arranges horseback pack-in trips to the buffalo meadows of Slough and Pebble creeks and offers float-tube adventures on high-mountain lakes for big cutthroats. Increasing in popularity are "Not for men only" flyfishing schools, where women and men in groups from two to four can enjoy three days of personal on-stream instruction.

Jumping Rainbow Ranch

L i v i n g s t o n ,   M o n t a n a

VITAL STATISTICS:

KEY SPECIES:
Brown, cutthroat and rainbow trout

Season:
April through October

Accommodations:
Log Lodge and 2 cabins
Number of Guest Rooms: 9
Maximum Number of Guests: 20

Conference Groups: Yes

Meals: American plan available

Rates:
From $100 for 2 per day

Guides: $275 for 2 anglers per day

Gratuities: 15%

Preferred Payment:
Cash or check

Getting There:
Fly to Bozeman, rent a car and drive to the ranch.

Other Activities:
Horseback riding, hiking, bird watching, antiquing, wildlife photography.

Contact:
Charles Lakovitch Jumping Rainbow Ranch, 110 Jumping Rainbow Rd., Livingston, MT 59047; 406/222-5425, fax 406/222-5508.

Represented By:
Off the Beaten Path, 800/445-2995.

Six ponds, a spring creek and the Yellowstone in your front yard: Who could ask for more?

ASK ANYONE TO NAME two trout streams in the Rocky Mountains and one will surely be the Yellowstone. Famed it is, and it can be crowded, but there's plenty of water to fish and a variety of times to fish it. You'll run into anglers thick as 'hoppers blown out of a hayfield if you set your sights on working the Yellowstone in August. The water is low, hatches are good and everybody is on vacation.

High runoff dissuades some anglers from trying the Yellowstone from June to mid-July. On the other hand, that's when the salmonfly hatch begins down low at Livingston and begins to work its way upstream. If the water isn't too high, casting to the banks with big dries or nymphs or black spinners can produce. In late April, well before runoff begins, a massive but short-lived hatch of caddis will cover the river. In May, the caddis are in full force. In September, after tourists go home, hatches continue, but streamers fished deep will draw attention from big browns. Fall, with aspens and cottonwood colored yellow, a little nip in the morning air and the sun on the back of your vest at midday, is a glorious time to be in Paradise Valley.

Charles Lakovitch thinks so, too. But he's prejudiced. He and Galen Ibes own the Jumping Rainbow Ranch, on 300 acres that border a mile of the Yellowstone in the vicinity of Armstrong and Nelson spring creeks. Armstrong, perhaps better known by names of the ranches through which it flows—O'Hair and DePuy—is across the river. Nelson's is upstream. On the ranch itself are six stocked ponds, and a section of challenging spring creek flows through the property. From there, you can arrange to float the Yellowstone, take a pack trip to lakes high in the Absaroka Wilderness or explore the great streams of the north end of Yellowstone National Park, particularly Slough Creek.

Accommodations at the Jumping Rainbow are uncluttered and new. Furniture is made of log, floors are wood and trophies hang high on the walls. Double or queen-size beds are the order of the day in the guest rooms, each of which has a private bath. A full-time chef turns out good meals served family-style on the long pine table. A number of meal plans are available. And the Jumping Rainbow rents out a pair of guest cabins that include fully-equipped kitchens. After dinner guests sit in front of the main lodge's stone hearth where a fire will be roaring when it's chilly. Or they may walk down to the river and listen to trout rising under the stars.

Kingfisher Lodge

Ft. Smith, Montana

Lots of angling lodges have flytying tables, but here there's one in every room.

VITAL STATISTICS:

KEY SPECIES:
Brown and rainbow trout

Season:
All year

Accommodations:
Log motel
Number of Guest Rooms: 7
Maximum Number of Guests: 14

Conference Groups: Yes

Meals: Bed and breakfast

Rates:
$55 per person per night, single or double

Guides: $225 for 1 per day

Gratuities: $45 per day

Preferred Payment:
Cash or check

Getting There:
The closest airport is Billings, Montana. Rent a car or a representative of the lodge will pick you up for $100 each way.

Other Activities:
Custer National Monument, birding, biking, hiking, wildlife photography.

Contact:
George Kelly
Bighorn Country
Outfitters, Box 7524, Ft.
Smith, MT 57035;
406/666-2326.

SINCE 1981, WHEN THE BIGHORN was reopened for fishing after a seven-year closure, George Kelly has been serving anglers through his Bighorn River Outfitters. He also operates Kingfisher Lodge, a motel-style bed and breakfast with a difference. Each room contains a fold-down flytier's table, as well as a pair of double beds, private bath with shower and a refrigerator. Two of the rooms are handicapped accessible. Across the road is a renovated farmhouse with a kitchen for guests who want to cook their own dinners. Otherwise, eat at the diner in Ft. Smith. It's open long after the evening's last hatch.

Kingfisher Lodge is half a mile from the Bighorn River. Listen to what Fothergill and Sterling (in *The Montana Angling Guide*) say about the Bighorn: "If you should happen to receive an invitation to fish the Bighorn River and if it should happen to be your very first fishing trip ever, you may want to decline the offer on the grounds that you will undoubtedly be spoiled on trout fishing before you barely get started!" The river is that good. It rises in Wyoming and flows north through the Bighorn Mountains until impounded by Yellowtail Dam just south of Ft. Smith. From there to Hardin, 42 miles north, the Bighorn is one long tailwater rich in carbonates and aquatic life. The first 13 miles of the Bighorn below the dam are the best. While the water is seldom discolored by runoff, flows will range from 1200 to 9000 cfs in years with a heavy snowpack. On average, the river flows between 4000 and 5000 cfs in the peak of June and July's runoff and then drops back to ideal levels of 3000 cfs or so.

This section of the river has two to three times as many trout per mile than other premiere streams in Montana. Fish tend to be in the 14- to 18-inch range with more than a few exceeding 20 inches. Among larger fish, rainbows seem to be more prevalent than browns. Hook into a 'bow that's 22 inches or more, and you'll really be glad that your reel's loaded with 100 yards of backing. Take a pair of rods: an 8 1/2-foot 4 weight and a nine-foot 7 weight are ideal. Fish nymphs early in the season and dries toward fall. The flyshop at the lodge stocks the most effective patterns, sells licenses and rents equipment if you need it. The river is open to fishing year-round, with the best angling from March into November.

A romantic retreat, Triple Creek Ranch in Darby, Montana,
is one of those places where fishing, food and accommodations
earn top marks from everyone. — page 150.

Lone Mountain Ranch

Big Sky, Montana

VITAL STATISTICS:

KEY SPECIES:
Brown, cutthroat and rainbow trout

Season:
June through October 14; December through April 15

Accommodations:
Lodge and rustic log cabins
Number of Guest Rooms: 6 rooms, 24 cabins
Maximum Number of Guests: 90

Conference Groups: Yes

Meals: American plan

Rates:
From $3050 per week for 2

Guides: From $240 per day for 2

Gratuities: Included in guide fee for ranch guests

Preferred Payment:
Discover, MasterCard, Visa

Getting There:
Bozeman is the closest airport; transfers are provided without charge by the ranch.

Other Activities:
Horseback riding, golf, tennis, rafting, swimming, boating, hiking, bird watching, biking, wildlife photography, skiing.

Contact:
**Nancy Norlander
Lone Mountain Ranch,
PO Box 160069, Big Sky,
MT 59716; 800/514-
4644, fax 406/995-4670,
email lmr@lone
mountainranch.com,
website http://www.
lonemountainranch.com**

The headquarters for fishing the Gallatin offers a variety of enticing packages.

WHEN CHET HUNTLEY said "Good night, David" for the last time, he packed his duds and headed back to Big Sky, the resort community he sired. Big Sky is located on the Gallatin River, which is a quite different piece of water from the creek that drains Divide Lake upstream in Yellowstone National Park. Fothergill and Sterling in *The Montana Angler* divided the river into four sections: from the park to Big Sky—a fairly easily fished stretch punctuated by a canyon in the middle; Big Sky to the mouth of Gallatin River Canyon—perhaps the most diverse and interesting section; canyon to East Gallatin River—agricultural interests pump this section nearly dry in summer; and from the East Gallatin to the Missouri—an idyllic float, particularly in autumn when spawning browns move up from the Missouri.

Lone Mountain Ranch, about 4.5 miles from the Gallatin, is a headquarters for fishing the river. The season begins June 1. Runoff is still high in the river, so guides concentrate on spring creeks and waters where flow is controlled by dams. In July you can catch the tail end of the salmonfly hatch as well as mayflies, caddis and stones. This is the time when the upper Gallatin above Taylor Creek comes into its own. Hoppers begin to make up trout diets in August and casting to grassy banks with either fly or spinner may provoke strikes from rainbows, browns or cutthroats in the 12- to 16-inch class. In September, browns are spawning and succumb to streamers, Baetis and tricos on cloudy days. This is the best time for a trophy fish. The lodge closes for six weeks on October 15, opening again on December 1 to serve the skiing crowd. Smart skiers will pack a 6- or 7-weight system, waders and shoes, and nymph open water for trophy rainbows and browns.

Scattered on a bench in the pines, 24 log cabins—pine log furniture, carpeted floors, private baths, wood stoves or fireplaces—host two to nine guests. Just under the brow of the ridge sits the main lodge with six luxuriously appointed guest rooms. Nearby is a third lodge, also of log, that contains a ranch shop that sells Orvis tackle, a watering hole known as the saloon and a very good restaurant. You'll dine by candlelight on fresh fish or fowl or heavy steaks. A well-stocked cellar complements dinner. Packages vary depending on the guests' desires. Float trips, flyfishing schools, treks and packtrips; you can find them all at Lone Mountain.

Missouri River Trout Shop and Lodge

C r a i g ,   M o n t a n a

VITAL STATISTICS:

KEY SPECIES:
Brown and rainbow trout

Season:
April through October

Accommodations:
ROOMS, HOUSEKEEPING CABINS AND EFFICIENCY
NUMBER OF GUEST ROOMS: 8 plus 2 riverfront cabins
MAXIMUM NUMBER OF GUESTS: 25

Conference Groups: No
Meals: Breakfast with rooms, restaurant

Rates:
$50 per night for 2
Guides: $290 per day for 2 anglers
Gratuities: $50
Preferred Payment:
Major credit cards

Getting There:
Fly to Great Falls, rent a car and drive to the lodge.

Other Activities:
Swimming, boating, bird watching.

Contact:
Jerry Lappier
Missouri River Trout Shop and Lodge, 110 Bridge St., Craig, MT 59648 (summer); 127 Box Canyon Lane, Cascade, MT 59421 (winter); 800/337-8528, fax 406/235-4077, email troutshop@mcn.net, website http://www.mcn.net/~troutshop (winter).

Represented By:
Off the Beaten Path, 800/445-2995.

You can fish the blue-ribbon Missouri while other streams are still under the weather.

I**F YOU'RE EAGER** to get the jump on Western fishing in spring, or don't want to hang it up after the leaves fall, think about the Missouri River between Helena and Great Falls. A tailwater after it flows out of Holter Dam, it fishes quite well for rainbows in the 17-inch range in early May before meltwater swells the river. And from mid-October to mid-November, when the famous streams in the mountains of southwest Montana are threatened by heavy snow, the Missouri remains accessible. This is truly one of America's blue-ribbon trout rivers, and headquarters for fishing it is Jerry Lappier's trout shop, cafe and lodge in Craig, just off Interstate 15.

With more than 5300 trout per mile and 80 percent of those larger than 10 inches, the 10-mile section between Craig and Holter Dam is a prolific, flat-water dry fly fishery. Midge clusters and Blue-Winged Olives produce in April and May. Melt swells the river from mid-May to mid-June, but as it begins to go down, hatches of caddis appear and continue into fall. You'll find Pale Morning Duns as well. In July it's tricos in the morning, Pale Morning Duns in the afternoon and caddis for two hours before dark. August is problematic. A tremendous hatch of *Pseudocloen*, called the Green Curse by locals, blankets the river. At times it seems as if every square inch is covered, and trout are rising everywhere. You can barely distinguish your fly from the thousands of naturals. Fish a parachute pattern with a tiny nymph as a trailing fly and keep at it. In fall, when the curse leaves the river, small Baetis hatch and No. 18 Blue-Winged Olives can be effective, as can 'hoppers with a little bead-head nymph as a trailing fly.

Casts should be precise here, and longish leaders of 5X to 6X are generally required. A nine-foot 5 weight is a good all-around choice for a rod, though a nine-foot 4 might be better, depending upon your casting skills. Rods should have a fairly soft action, and you should school yourself to wait a one-count before tightening on the fish, or you'll either pull the fly away or break it off.

Accommodations vary at the lodge. You'll find seven rooms with two beds each that share three baths. Breakfast is included with the price of these rooms. A studio apartment with kitchen facilities and private bath is upstairs over the flyshop. Two modern cabins for four to six guests are nearby, down on the river. These feature two bedrooms each, private baths, full kitchens and living rooms. There's a hot tub in between. And, of course, the best restaurant in Craig is the cafe at the trout shop.

Montana High Country Tours
Dillon, Montana

VITAL STATISTICS:

KEY SPECIES:
Brown, cutthroat and rainbow trout; grayling

Season:
All year

Accommodations:
Log lodge and cabins
Number of Guest Rooms: 6
Maximum Number of Guests: 12

Conference Groups: No

Meals: American plan

Rates:
$75 per angler per day

Guides: $300 for 2 per day

Gratuities: 10%

Preferred Payment:
MasterCard, Visa

Getting There:
Fly to Butte and rent a car or the lodge will collect you for $75 round trip.

Other Activities:
Swimming, boating, hiking, bird watching, biking, wildlife photography, skiing, horseback riding, hunting.

Contact:
Russ Kipp
Montana High Country Tours, 1036 E. Reeder St., Dillon, MT 59725; 406/683-4920.

Represented By:
Off the Beaten Path, 800/445-2995.

A native of these parts shares his secrets with those who find their way to Grasshopper Valley.

RUSS KIPP GREW UP in southwest Montana and knows its rivers and lakes well. For 18 years he's been guiding on the Beaverhead, Big Hole and Ruby rivers, as well as on Clark Canyon Reservoir and little Grasshopper Creek. From his location near Dillon, he's in position to put his clients over fish no matter what the weather conditions.

The bane of western flyfishing is high runoff from June into July. However, Clark Canyon Dam moderates the heavy flow, providing stable and relatively clear conditions in the Beaverhead above Grasshopper Creek. Water is of constant temperature and rainbows and browns (up to six pounds) thrive. The bad news is that the river is so narrow that you can almost cast across it, so swift, deep and heavily brushed on its banks that wading is less than fun, and frequently dangerous. That's why Kipp usually floats this section, and anglers cast tight against the willows to provoke strikes from the trout that hold there. Fishing this requires not so much finesse as accuracy and power. Tippets in spring should be in the 20-pound range—more suitable for snook than rainbows. Trout aren't bothered by these hawsers and they'll come in handy when you want to retrieve an errant cast into the willows.

A second source of behemoth trout is 6000-acre Clark Canyon Lake itself. Fish from float tubes or rafts. Rainbows top seven pounds and browns, though fewer, can break into double digits. Prime time is right after ice-out, and trolling spinning lures is the preferred tactic. As water warms, fish go deeper, but the mouth of Red Rock River will continue to provide action on both dry and wet flies into fall.

Grasshopper Creek is one of those feast-or-famine streams. After heavy rains it silts terribly and irrigation can draw the creek down to a trickle. But sections of the Grasshopper can fish well. If they don't, Kipp keeps a few high mountain lakes in reserve. Here you'll find cutthroats and rainbows that aren't huge, but the scenery alone is worth the pack in.

Located in the upper Grasshopper Valley, the lodge of taffy-colored log framed by pine and spruce boasts a stone fireplace, gleaming board floors and easy chairs upholstered in floral patterns, adding a touch of brightness. You'll find digital TV, an indoor Jacuzzi, and wonderful country cooking: steak and potatoes and chicken and rice, with vegetables and homemade desserts. Guests stay in bedrooms in the lodge or in two cabins. Three rooms have private baths.

Point of Rocks Lodge
E m i g r a n t ,   M o n t a n a

VITAL STATISTICS:

KEY SPECIES:
Brown, cutthroat and rainbow trout

Season:
Mid-June through October

Accommodations:
RUSTIC CABINS
NUMBER OF GUEST ROOMS: 8
MAXIMUM NUMBER OF GUESTS: 30

Conference Groups: No

Meals: American plan or bed and breakfast

Rates:
From $60 per person per night

Guides: $260 per day for 2 anglers

Gratuities: 10% to 20%

Preferred Payment:
Major credit cards

Getting There:
Fly to Bozeman, rent a car and drive to the lodge.

Other Activities:
Horseback riding, hunting, rafting, swimming, hiking, bird watching.

Contact:
Max Chase
**Point of Rocks Lodge,
2017 US 89 South,
Emigrant, MT 59027;
406/333-4361, fax
406/848-7222.**

Anglers on a budget (and those who aren't) will like the four-miles-plus of the Yellowstone at this lodge.

ROUGHLY 20 MILES NORTH of the entrance to Yellowstone National Park, Point of Rocks Lodge is an ideal choice for anglers who want to spend some time on the park's waters and avail themselves of the Yellowstone as well. The lodge, a working ranch, owns property along more than four miles of the Yellowstone, right off U.S. 89, the main route from Livingston to the park. Access to the lodge is a piece of cake.

From the park border north to Corwin Springs, the Yellowstone brawls through boulders and races down turbulent riffles, smoothing (but seldom) in occasional pools. It is easy to identify holding water for cutthroats, and some browns, in this section, but it is difficult to float. Next comes a short stretch of relatively easy water, but then banks constrict and the river plunges into Yankee Jim Canyon. Class III rapids make this a very questionable float. The river in the canyon is accessible by trails and fishing from the bank can be productive. After exiting the canyon, the river is still narrow and fast until reaching Point of Rocks, where it begins to broaden and slow.

Guests at the lodge have it all. Above the ranch is fast pocket and pool water, below it's more riffles and runs. By this point on the Yellowstone, brown trout have become dominant, and they are big. A leviathan of 23-plus pounds was once pulled from a pool behind the ranch, which each year yields a four-pounder or two. Caddis and salmonfly hatches are particularly good on this section, but the best chance of landing a trophy brown comes after September 15. Big streamers and nymphs can really pay off.

When it comes to fishing, ranch owner Max Chase enjoys catching big browns in the fall above all else. But he's equally content guiding clients who want to fish Nelson and Armstrong spring creeks downstream, or heading for the park to fish Slough Creek above Gardiner for its cutthroats. An easy drive from the ranch will carry guests into the headwaters of the Gallatin and Gibbon; a bit farther opens up the Firehole and upper Madison. Unlike many guest ranches that cater to anglers, you need not hire a guide when you stay at Point of Rocks.

Accommodations at Point of Rocks are comfortable but not all tricked up. Cabins sleep between two and four each and have private baths. Anglers can opt for a bed and breakfast plan and take advantage of good restaurants elsewhere in Paradise Valley, or go for a full meal plan that includes breakfast, lunch and dinner.

Ruby Springs Lodge
Alder, Montana

At Ruby Springs, you'll have seven miles of private access to grasshopper heaven.

VITAL STATISTICS:

KEY SPECIES:
Brown trout

Season:
May through mid-October

Accommodations:
MODERN RANCH
NUMBER OF GUEST ROOMS: 6
MAXIMUM NUMBER OF GUESTS: 12

Conference Groups: Yes

Meals: American plan

Rates:
From $385 per day to $2165 for 6 nights and 5 days per person, double occupancy

Guides: Included

Gratuities: $20 per rod per day

Preferred Payment:
MasterCard, Visa

Getting There:
Fly to Butte or Bozeman, Montana, and rent a car. Or the ranch van will pick you up for $35 per person.

Other Activities:
Golf, tennis, canoeing, whitewater rafting, swimming, boating, hiking, bird watching, biking, wildlife photography.

Contact:
Paul or Jeanne Moseley
Ruby Springs Lodge, PO Box 119, Alder, MT 59710; 800/278-7829, fax 406/842-5806.

Represented By:
Off the Beaten Path, 800/445-2995.

I F YOU ARE LOOKING FOR a less well known and less heavily fished river in Montana, try the Ruby. It's west across the mountains from the Madison. Together with the Beaverhead, it joins the Big Hole to form the Jefferson below Twin Bridges. Innkeepers Paul and Jeanne Moseley own and lease seven miles of private access to the Ruby. Within a few minutes are a number of lakes and ponds. And if this isn't enough, take State 287 across the Gravelly Range to Ennis and the Madison. An hour or so later you're in West Yellowstone.

The lower Ruby is a tailwater fishery: small, brushy, cobbly bottomed and meandering through open meadows. It fishes well in May and early June, before sediment-laden meltwater spills over the dam. Later, in August and September, it has a reputation for resembling a spring creek. Above the dam, the story is a little different. Meltwater discolors the creek in June, but by mid-July it's fishing fine. Fish caddis in May. Pale Morning Duns in July and tricos in August also draw strikes, but it's the 'hoppers in mid-July through late September that turn on the browns like nothing else. While you're in the area, check out Clear Creek, a tributary to the Ruby. When the Ruby warms in late summer, Clear Creek's cool spring waters, deep and shaded by a tangle of willows, attract big browns of up to 22 inches that feed on 'hoppers.

While anglers normally fish with Ruby Springs' guides (included in the basic package), they may freelance if they wish. Float trips are possible farther down, but the name of the game here is stalking fish from the meadow and planning your approach. An eight-foot 4-weight rod is ideal for these waters.

Rustic elegance is one way to describe Ruby Springs' accommodations. Six cabins sleeping two each feature river rock fireplaces, distressed pine furniture and private baths. After fishing, have a cocktail in the River Room that overlooks the home pool. You'll see fish rising. If you can't stand it, grab one of the rods by the door and make a cast or two. But beware. Other guests may save you no dinner (grilled salmon drizzled with pesto cream, roasted garlic potatoes, fresh asparagus tips and Kahlua cheesecake). Breakfasts are grand. Forget the boxed lunch, you won't need it.

Spotted Bear Ranch

K a l i s p e l l ,   M o n t a n a

VITAL STATISTICS:

KEY SPECIES:
Cutthroat trout

Season:
June 15 through September 15

Accommodations:
RUSTIC LOG CABINS
NUMBER OF GUEST ROOMS: 10
MAXIMUM NUMBER OF GUESTS: 20

Conference Groups: Yes

Meals: American plan

Rates:
From $995 per person for 3
days; $1995 for 5-day wilderness pack and float trip

Guides: Included

Gratuities: $30 to $50 per day

Preferred Payment:
MasterCard, Visa

Getting There:
Fly to Kalispell, Montana and
rent a car, or the ranch will provide transfers for $60 round
trip.

Other Activities:
Swimming, hiking.

Contact:
Kirk Gentry
Spotted Bear Ranch,
2863 Foothill Rd.,
Kalispell, MT 59901;
406/755-7337.

Take a five-day horse and float trip for native cutthroats on the secluded South Fork of the Flathead.

NO DOUBT ABOUT IT, many of Montana's premiere trout rivers become crowded after spring melt recedes in mid to late June. Fortunately, trout are plentiful and most anglers find success. You'll find trout, mainly cutthroat and bull trout (a variant of dolly varden), on the Spotted Bear and nearby South Fork of the Flathead. Anglers will be few, as the Spotted Bear is well off the beaten path and the South Fork is isolated.

No roads parallel the upper reaches of the South Fork of the Flathead, only a trail for hikers and horseback riders. No towns discharge effluent and no agricultural interests siphon off the flow. The only thing upstream is water clear as mountain air. It caroms through narrow canyons, streams across gravel flats, races through runs shaded by heavy stands of lodgepole and ponderosa pine, and placidly glides through wildflower meadows. Native cutthroats in the one- to two-pound range are abundant and not very selective. Bull trout to four pounds are rare, but are occasionally taken by anglers fishing deep pools with hardware.

Saddle up at the Spotted Bear Ranch for a five-day pack and float on the South Fork of the Flathead. You'll ride for two days upriver, stopping in the evening to fish sections that virtually never see flies. With gear loaded in inflatables, you'll then drift back downstream, pulling ashore when you feel like it. Thirty-fish days are not uncommon. Elk, deer and mountain goats will watch your progress.

Spotted Bear also offers shorter floats on the South Fork and Spotted Bear rivers. You can float a different section, below the upper wilderness area, each day and return to your rustic log cabin in the stand of pines each night. Each cabin contains two bedrooms, a fireplace, private bath and central heat. Daily maid service is provided. You'll find the main lodge on a bluff with a stunning view of the South Fork. Club chairs surround an open fire pit and game mounts decorate the walls. Meals are family-style, and on Wednesday nights the barbecued ribs are not to be missed. And while you're there, talk to owner Kirk Gentry about guided hunts for deer and elk in the fall.

Tamarack Lodge

Troy, Montana

A pristine wild river and graceful log lodge await you off the beaten path in Montana.

VITAL STATISTICS:

KEY SPECIES:
Bull, cutthroat and brook trout

Season:
Late June through October

Accommodations:
RUSTIC LOG LODGE
NUMBER OF GUEST ROOMS: 9
MAXIMUM NUMBER OF GUESTS: 22

Conference Groups: Yes

Meals: American plan or bed and breakfast

Rates:
All packages are custom. Typical: $2875 for 2 for 6 nights and 5 days of guided fishing

Guides: $275 for 2 per day

Gratuities: Client's discretion

Preferred Payment:
Major credit cards

Getting There:
Fly to Kalispell, Montana or Spokane, Washington, rent a car and enjoy the drive. A shuttle from the lodge is available at additional cost.

Other Activities:
Hiking, bird hunting, sporting clays, horseback riding, wildlife photography.

Contact:
**Judy or Bill McAfee
Tamarack Lodge, 32855
South Fork Dr., Troy, MT
59935; 406/295-4880,
fax 406/295-1022, email
tamarack@libby.org,
website http://libby.
org/tamarack**

Represented By:
Off the Beaten Path, 800/445-2995.

IF IT'S TROUT AND TRANQUILITY you're seeking, you'll find it on the Yaak in the northwestern corner of Montana. Here you're a world away from the state's better-known streams—the Madison, Big Horn, Missouri— and the anglers that flock to them every summer.

The Yaak might be divided into two sections, the seven-mile stretch below the falls and the longer section above it. The lower section is contained in a deep canyon with limited access. But its waters contain large trout, especially dolly varden-like bull trout, that move up from the Kootenai. Some anglers hike trails down into the canyon, others approach it from the bridge at Yaak River or the campground below the falls. While the fishing is good, it has yet to be discovered. The upper section of the Yaak is smaller, more easily accessible, and populated with brook, cutthroat, rainbow and bull trout.

Guests at Tamarack enjoy the solitude of the Yaak as much as they like floats on the Kootenai. It would be hard for two rivers in the same area to be more different. The Yaak is wild and pristine. The Kootenai is a tailwater where not only levels fluctuate widely—from 4000 to 24,000 cfs, depending on generating requirements—but temperatures do, too. Releases from Libby Dam are drawn from various thermal strata within the lake. Why? So that fish schooled up at any given level will not be sucked into the turbines. Fish and aquatic life in the river adapt to the erratic flows, though it takes them a few days to adjust. Wading can be dangerous, as water may rise four feet during a discharge. The best and safest way to fish for the river's rainbow and bull trout is via driftboat, working banks or boulders with nymphs and, when there's a hatch on, mayflies and caddis-imitating dries. Fluctuations in temperature and velocity have made these trout finicky. Precise casts are a must. Anglers will also enjoy float tubing alpine lakes for cutthroats.

Judy and Bill McAfee stumbled onto the Yaak in the mid-1970s and have been in the outfitting business since 1980. Their lodge, yellowed pine logs capped with a green metal roof, includes eight guest rooms with private baths and a dorm room with six double beds for single anglers. Focal point of the great room is a huge stone fireplace built by McAfee (he was a New York mason in an earlier incarnation). The kitchen turns out scrumptious family-style meals. And an on-site shop offers flies, tackle and last-minute miscellanea.

Teller Wildlife Refuge

C o r v a l l i s , M o n t a n a

VITAL STATISTICS:

KEY SPECIES:
Brown and rainbow trout

Season:
All year

Accommodations:
PRIVATE FARMHOUSES
NUMBER OF GUEST ROOMS: 11
MAXIMUM NUMBER OF GUESTS: 20
Conference Facilities: Yes
Meals: American plan or kitchens
Rates:
From $180 per person per day, double occupancy (3-night minimum stay)
Guides: $290 for 2 per day
Gratuities: $20 per rod
Preferred Payment:
Cash or check
Getting There:
Fly to Missoula. For $50 round trip, the lodge will provide transportation to and from the airport.
Other Activities:
Biking, bird watching, hiking, skiing, wildlife photography.

Contact:
Mary Stone
Teller Wildlife Refuge,
1292 Chaffin Rd.,
Corvallis, MT 59828;
800/343-3707.

Rent your own 1870s farmhouse and fish four miles of the blue-ribbon Bitterroot.

A FEW MILES DOWNSTREAM from Hamilton, a town of 3000, and the largest in the Bitterroot Valley, is the 1300-acre Teller Wildlife Refuge. Through the refuge flows four miles of the Bitterroot River, an 85-mile-long blue-ribbon trout stream that shares its name with Montana's state flower. Here the river resembles a braided stream. Loose cobbles constitute the streambed, and springmelt and occasional floods shift the bars and pools somewhat and occasionally collapse undercut banks.

For all of that, this section is productive. You'll find browns, rainbows and cutthroats. Fishing begins in March with nymphs and big streamers, takes a pause from late May to mid-June when the melt rolls through and then continues in earnest with caddis in June and July and 'hopper patterns in August and September. Local anglers rely on a pair of caddis patterns: the Ugly Rudamus and Madam X, for reasons unknown. Also flowing through the refuge is an unnamed spring creek where browns and rainbows up to 20 inches are a fairly regular occurrence. Anglers who arrive in mid-October should pack an over-and-under shotgun and go after pheasants as well as trout.

Situated in the middle of the valley, the refuge is a fine base for fishing the upper Bitterroot, smaller water to be sure, but fed by a number of spring and freestone creeks. The lower end of the river warms as it slows and holds populations of largemouths and pike. Fish for these in the slack backwaters.

A project of Otto Teller, past president and founding member of Trout Unlimited and the Trout and Salmon Foundation, the refuge is a private nonprofit initiative to protect agricultural land from subdivision. The refuge is among the first of its kind in Montana and a model for similar initiatives in other states. Seasonal wildlife populations contain white-tailed deer, occasional moose and elk, beavers, foxes, geese, ducks, owls and more than 200 other bird species.

On the refuge are three houses, two of which—Teller Lodge and Slack House—operate as full-service lodges. Meals are not served at the third, Burrough's house. The refuge also houses guests in two cabins and a small house 14 miles upstream, halfway between Hamilton and Darby. These contain kitchen facilities where you can prepare your own meals. Teller and Slack, with wrap-around screened porches, are gracious farmhouses that date from the 1870s. The refuge only books one party into each house or set of cabins at a time. Minimum party size is two and minimum stay is three nights.

The Complete Fly Fisher

W i s e   R i v e r ,   M o n t a n a

VITAL STATISTICS:

KEY SPECIES:
Brook, brown and cutthroat trout

Season:
May through October

Accommodations:
MODERN ANGLING INN
NUMBER OF GUEST ROOMS: 12
MAXIMUM NUMBER OF GUESTS: 14

Conference Groups: Yes

Meals: American plan

Rates:
From $2250 per person for 6 nights and 5 days of fishing, double occupancy

Guides: Included

Gratuities: $40 to $60 per boat

Preferred Payment:
Cash or check

Getting There:
Fly to Butte and the lodge van will meet you at no additional charge.

Other Activities:
Whitewater rafting, hiking, bird watching, biking, wildlife photography, horseback eco and nature tours.

Contact:
David or Stuart Decker
The Complete Fly Fisher,
PO Box 127, Highway 43,
Wise River, MT 59762;
406/832-3175, fax
406/832-3176, email
comfly@montana.com

Represented By:
Angler Adventures, 800/628-1447.

Book at this premiere lodge in the Rockies, and you'll learn a few things about angling and yourself.

TWO THINGS MAKE THIS LODGE different from most. Here the guiding philosophy goes beyond providing guests with a first-class experience, though when it comes to angling and accommodations, The Complete Fly Fisher has few peers. The lodge exists to help every guest learn more about flyfishing—casting, fly selection, river reading, fish playing; about some of the environmental issues affecting wild trout in the Big Hole watershed; and as a kind of subconscious theme, the way we all relate to others and our daily surroundings. Don't worry, you won't find any in-your-face environmental evangelism or preservationist proselytizing. What will happen is that guides will help you improve your fishing. You'll fish the rivers, and you'll talk about the fishing. And you'll come away with new skills and maybe a few new understandings.

The Big Hole rises on the eastern flank of the Bitterroot Mountains and flows about 125 miles to Twin Bridges, where it joins the Beaverhead to form the Jefferson. Once down from the high peaks, it courses through the Big Hole Basin, a deep valley surrounded by mountains, before plunging into a set of canyons and cuts below Dickey Bridge where the water is swift and fishing, water permitting, can be awesome. Below, the river races out of the canyon at Melrose and canters on toward Twin Bridges. The upper reaches contain brook and cutthroat trout. The only significant population of Montana grayling, remnants of arctic stock left over from the last glacial advance, are found in the river's upper sections. "Their numbers are dwindling," co-owner Stuart Decker says. "We'll pull the boat over to watch them feed, but otherwise we leave them alone." The population of rainbows, many in the 14- to 18-inch range, increases in the canyon, and the lower section belongs to brown trout. Dry fly fishing is at its peak in July and early August. During a week at the lodge, many guests sample the Wise, Beaverhead and Ruby nearby.

Nestled behind a screen of cottonwoods, The Complete Fly Fisher fronts on the Big Hole. Low and long, yet open and airy, natural wood and big glass windows help the lodge blend into its surroundings. Dinner on some nights when the hatch is great may not be served until 10:00 p.m. Breakfast is at your convenience. Lunches too. You have a choice of accommodations from two rooms in the lodge, rooms in five cabins near the lodge, or Spring Creek Cabin, a cottage with two bedrooms a mile from the lodge. All rooms have private baths and one is handicapped accessible.

The Lodge

H a m i l t o n ,   M o n t a n a

VITAL STATISTICS:

KEY SPECIES:
Brown, cutthroat and rainbow trout

Season:
Mid-March through October

Accommodations:
LODGE
NUMBER OF GUEST ROOMS: 3
MAXIMUM NUMBER OF GUESTS: 6

Conference Groups: Yes

Meals: Breakfast and dinner

Rates:
From $675 per person for 4 nights, double occupancy

Guides: $275 per day for 2 anglers (includes lunch)

Gratuities: $20 to $50

Getting There:
Fly to Missoula, rent a car and drive to the lodge.

Preferred Payment:
Cash or check

Other Activities:
Hiking, wildlife photography, skiing.

Contact:
John Talia
The Lodge, PO Box 302, Hamilton, MT 59840-0302; 406/363-4661, fax 406/363-6964.

Represented By:
Off the Beaten Path, 800/445-2995.

You won't encounter other anglers as you fish for big browns and rainbows here.

WHEN YOU THINK OF MONTANA, the big names come to mind: Madison, Yellowstone, Big Hole. Don't forget the Bitterroot. Flowing north into Missoula, the Bitterroot has western-slope cutthroats, rainbows and browns. The cutthroats and 'bows sometime produce a hybrid that "eats like a cutthroat and fights like a rainbow," says John Talia, co-owner of The Lodge. Rainbows here tend to be bright, silvery fish, lacking the colors of their cousins farther east. Speculation is that they may be more than nominally related to steelhead.

The Lodge, in a two-mile-wide valley, is right on the river. Mountains rise 7000 feet above the valley floor. This, too, adds to the fishing. Pale March sun sparks the Skwala hatch, a stonefly, which turns on the browns. Yet the sun isn't high enough or the air warm enough to melt the snow in the mountains. From mid-March to late April, the river fishes very well. If you want a big brown on a dry, this is the best time to do it. Dress warmly.

You can spend a week wading and fishing the Bitterroot in front of the lodge and never cover it all; or you can float the river. In either case you'll come off the river at the door to your room. Soak in the hot tub and take a nap before dinner. Yours will be one of three guest rooms, all with private baths and beds with thick down comforters. Evening meals—butterflied leg of lamb, carne asada with chili rellenos, grilled salmon—are frequently held in the boardroom, which offers stunning views of the Bitterroot Mountains and the river. For the inspired, a tier's bench is in the corner. For the less compulsive, sofas before the fireplace in the great room can be very inviting. You make your own breakfasts from a fully stocked larder.

Seldom will you encounter other anglers. The lodge is a mile and a quarter beyond paved road and four or five miles from public river access. With no more than five other guests per week, The Lodge is private indeed. Most guests hire guides (not included in the room rate) to float the river. Some drive over the mountains to fish the name brand streams. Others are content to stay in this bit of primitive heaven.

The Montana Trout Club-
Diamond O Ranch

Twin Bridges, Montana

*Corporate groups can have exclusive use
of this private trout club for a few weeks every year.*

VITAL STATISTICS:

KEY SPECIES:
Brown and rainbow trout

Season:
May 15 through July 5;
August 28 through mid-October
Accommodations:
RANCH HOUSES OF LOG AND FRAME
NUMBER OF GUEST ROOMS: 3 in
main house, 8 in ranch houses
nearby
MAXIMUM NUMBER OF GUESTS: 22
Conference Groups: Yes
Meals: American plan
Rates:
$425 per person per day
Guides: Included
Gratuities: $20 to $30 per
person
Preferred Payment:
American Express, MasterCard,
Visa
Getting There:
Fly to Butte or Bozeman and
the lodge will provide airport
pick up and drop off; or use the
private airstrip.
Other Activities:
Riding, hiking, bird watching,
wildlife photography.

Contact:
Greg Lilly
**The Montana Trout Club,
PO Box 411, Twin
Bridges, MT 59754;
406/683-5960.**

LOOKING FOR A FIRST-CLASS summer or fall fishing retreat for a corporate confab? Then book the Montana Trout Club on the Diamond O Ranch exclusively for your group. With 6000 acres, 11 combined miles of the lower Beaverhead and Albers Slough, and a stocked pond, there's plenty of fishing to go with the 11 guest rooms. Prior to 1997 the club had been operated as a traditional angling lodge. But owner David Ondaatje, president of Winston Rod, wanted to reserve the middle weeks of summer—July 6 through August 27—for family and friends. That left the beginning and ends of Montana's trout seasons, generally the best times to fish, open for groups of anglers.

In June the salmonfly hatch, particularly on the upper section of the river, is very good. In September, anglers will catch the final weeks of 'hoppers and then will do well with wets, nymphs and streamers. According to Greg Lilly, who manages fishing at the ranch, the lower Beaverhead has fewer fish per mile than the upper section above Barrett's diversion, but they tend to be bigger—in the 18- to 20-inch range. Albers Slough has its share of big fish. You'll work for them with nymphs and streamers.

Albers Slough is always a wild card and fishing the lower Beaverhead should be considered a bonus to the real business at hand: the Big Hole. One of Montana's premiere rivers, the Big Hole meets the Beaverhead at Twin Bridges. Also in the immediate vicinity are the Ruby and Wise rivers, both good streams. Groups staying at The Montana Trout Club will select the best water of the day and fish it, two anglers per guide. They may float or wade as fishing dictates.

The Montana Trout Club books only one group at a time. Each will have full run of the main house and the recently remodeled ranch houses nearby, where large bedrooms are plushly furnished in elegant country style with easy chairs, pine tables and antique quilts. A long wooden table, suitable for board meetings but more enjoyable for gourmet dinners of Montana steak and salmon, stretches the length of the richly paneled dining room, hung with 19th century paintings. The living room is not log, but open, airy and sunny.

The Old Kirby Place

C a m e r o n ,   M o n t a n a

VITAL STATISTICS:

KEY SPECIES:
Brown and rainbow trout

Season:
May through November

Accommodations:
TRADITIONAL LOG CABIN
NUMBER OF GUEST ROOMS: 4
MAXIMUM NUMBER OF GUESTS: 10

Conference Facilities: Yes

Meals: American plan

Rates:
$150 per day or $1000 per week per person

Guides: $250 for 2 per day

Gratuities: $20

Preferred Payment:
American Express, Visa

Getting There:
Fly to Bozeman or West Yellowstone, rent a car and drive to the lodge.

Other Activities:
Golf, rafting, hiking, bird watching, antiquing, biking, wildlife photography.

Contact:
Walter Kannon
The Old Kirby Place,
West Fork Bridge,
Cameron, MT 59720;
406/682-4194.

Stay at a traditional log lodge on the most interesting stretch of the Madison.

MODERN LOG LODGES of peeled pine with cathedral windows of California style are almost de rigueur when it comes to Western trout hostelries. That's why it's so nice to find a log lodge that Jim Bridger might have found comfortably familiar. Built of hand-squared dovetail jointed logs, weathered and dark brown, with a front porch that wraps around the side, this two-story lodge resembles log houses more typically found in the hills of West Virginia. Behind the lodge is a two-room cabin in the same style. Each of the two rooms in the lodge and the two rooms in the cabin have private baths. Dinner and breakfast are served on a long table of pumpkin pine in the lodge's great room. Lunch is on the stream.

Set in a copse of trees, The Old Kirby Place fronts on the Madison River. Fothergill and Sterling describe the Madison as a "one tire skid mark" of consistent width and depth pretty much from Quake Lake south 80 miles to its mouth at Three Forks. For most of its run, the Madison's bottom is flat and pools are seldom more than six feet deep. Among the exceptions is the mileage from below Quake Lake to the mouth of the West Yellowstone. Here the Madison holds more pools, a nice contrast to the rest of the river, which has been described as "the world's longest riffle." The Old Kirby Place sits at the downstream end of the pool water.

That gives its anglers certain advantages. The character of the river above the lodge contains more classic water for fishing dry flies morning and evenings. The upper river, too, holds more rainbows than browns, though they may not be as large. Yet downstream from the lodge, at the head of the riffles, trout have less time to inspect an offering and seem to feel the need to nail a fly before it's gone. This relative lack of selectivity has given the Madison a rep as a good beginner's river. Anglers using ultra-light tackle can have a ball with gold-bladed Mepps and Panther Martins. While the Madison is catch-and-release, anglers staying at The Old Kirby Place who want to catch-and-eat can fill their frying pans in the West Fork of the Madison just downstream. You can also catch dinner in the lodge's stocked pond. One final note about the fishing: the famous streams near the western edge of Yellowstone Park—the Gibbon, Firehole and Henry's Fork—are only an hour from The Kirby Place. Rates do not include guide fees. A couple days of guided fishing will introduce you to the river, then you can fish it on your own for the rest of the week.

The Complete Fly Fisher at Wise River, Montana, rolls angling, hospitality and a little ecology into a comfortable yet stimulating stay on the Big Hole. — page 145.

Jim Bridger might have felt comfortable sitting on the porch of the Old Kirby Place at Cameron, Montana, on the Madison. — page 148.

Triple Creek Ranch

D a r b y ,   M o n t a n a

Romance and angling join hands at this plush retreat high in the Bitterroot Mountains.

VITAL STATISTICS:

KEY SPECIES:
Bull, brown, cutthroat and rainbow trout

Season:
All year

Accommodations:
LOG CABINS
NUMBER OF GUEST ROOMS: 8 cabins of 1 to 3 bedrooms
MAXIMUM NUMBER OF GUESTS: 21 couples or 28 singles

Conference Groups: Yes
Meals: American plan
Rates:
From $475 per couple per night
Guides: $275 for 2 anglers per day
Gratuities: $25 to $30
Preferred Payment:
Major credit cards
Getting There:
Fly to Missoula, rent a car and drive to the ranch.
Other Activities:
Horseback riding, golf, tennis, rafting, swimming, hiking, bird watching, antiquing, biking, wildlife photography, snowmobiling.

Contact:
Dana Monroe
Triple Creek Ranch, 5551 West Fork Stage Rd., Darby, MT 59829; 406/821-4600, fax 406/ 821-4666, email info@ triplecreekranch.com, website http://www. triplecreekranch.com

Represented By:
Relais & Chateaux, 212/856-0115.

I F "POSH" DIDN'T HAVE nautical roots, it would be perfect to describe this 250-acre mountain hideaway high in the Bitterroots. You'll find Triple Creek on everyone's (*Travel & Leisure, Conde Nast Traveler, Forbes, Southern Living,* to name a few) list of best lodges. Not only are the 18 cabins delightfully appointed; the cuisine, elegant (pheasant au poivre) yet not effete; and atmosphere utterly relaxing for couples and singles alike; but here is a place where you can do whatever you want. And if it's fishing for rainbows, browns and cutthroats, you couldn't find a better retreat.

The road to Triple Creek follows the West Fork of the Bitterroot River. This is very comfortable water to wade and fish. Between 40 and 50 feet wide and with a fairly even cobble bottom, this river holds cutthroat, rainbow, brook and bull trout (one of dolly varden's close cousins). The lower section can be floated in spring. At Conner, the West Fork joins the East Fork to form the main stem of the Bitterroot. Not as pristine as the West Fork, the East Fork above Sula holds wild brook trout, some bull trout, and small rainbows and cutthroats. Below the junction, cutthroats, rainbows and browns predominate. You'll find traditional riffles, runs and pools, undercut banks and pockets, all those lies which hold trout. Fothergill and Sterling advise working undercut banks very carefully in summer. Streamers out in the current produce better in fall.

The Bitterroot sheds its load of spring melt in mid-June, earlier than many of the other blue-ribbon streams in southwestern Montana. And it's not as quick to cloud as others. But if for some reason it doesn't suit, you've only to cross into Idaho to fish the Selway and Salmon rivers, head east through Chief Joseph Pass to strike the Big Hole at Wise, or arrange with a guide to fish any number of alpine lakes near the lodge.

Triple Creek pampers its guests like few other places. Each room contains a fully stocked wet bar. Chips and salsa and fresh fruits and homemade cookies still warm from the oven appear in your room as if by magic. Fireplaces are standard. There are virtually no extra charges for on-site activities. Accommodations range from small one-room log cabins to luxury cabins with steam showers and hot tubs to El Capitan, with its cathedral-ceilinged living room and two bedrooms, each with private bath. While the ranch will provide transfers from Missoula airport ($200 round trip per vehicle), you'll want to rent a car to get to the fishing.

Yellowstone Valley Ranch
Livingston, Montana

Try the Montana Sampler from this lodge in Paradise Valley.

VITAL STATISTICS:

KEY SPECIES:
Brown, cutthroat and rainbow trout

Season:
May through October
Accommodations:
MODERN LODGE WITH 5 GUEST CABINS
NUMBER OF GUEST ROOMS: 10
MAXIMUM NUMBER OF GUESTS: 20
Conference Groups: No
Meals: American plan
Rates:
From $1995 per person for 6 days and 5 nights, double occupancy
Guides: Included
Gratuities: $25 to $50 per day (for 2 rods)
Preferred Payment:
MasterCard, Visa
Getting There:
Fly to Bozeman. You can arrange to be picked up by a representative of the lodge, but you'll want a rental car for exploring.
Other Activities:
Rafting, swimming, hiking, horseback riding, nature tours.

Contact:
Nancy Boisvert
Yellowstone Valley Ranch, 3840 US Hwy. 89 South, Livingston, MT 59047; 406/333-4787 (summer); 422 S. Main St., Livingston, MT 59047; 800/626-3526, fax 406/585-3526 (winter).

Represented By:
Destinations, 800/626-3526.

THE YELLOWSTONE SLIDES BY the cabin on the bank. The tips of the Absarokas glow with the last of the day's sun. Your rod rests on pegs and your waders are drying. The day has been good and tomorrow promises more of the same. You started early, before breakfast, with a Woolly Bugger in the river below the cabin. Why not? You worked out a little line, cast once, then twice, feeling the line power the rod. Across and down, you drifted the black wet fly. And then there was a fish. No slashing strike. It was just there, the way cutthroats are sometimes. Nice to go to breakfast the first day at a new lodge with your hands smelling faintly of fish.

If you haven't fished this area before, Yellowstone Valley Ranch's "Montana Sampler" is an offer not to be bypassed. About 14 miles south of Livingston, the ranch is an ideal jumping-off point for exploring Paradise Valley. The legendary Armstrong and Nelson's spring creeks are 10 minutes down the road from the ranch. Counterpoint to the rocky Yellowstone, these spring creeks are slow affairs lush with weedbeds, hatches and trout that feed thereon. DuPuy and O'Hair ranches control access to Armstrong. Rod fees are charged, and reservations must be made well in advance. In addition, the north gate to Yellowstone National Park is an hour south. Head for the lower Gardner, Gibbon and upper Madison. No trip to Yellowstone is complete without a stop at Muleshoe Bend on the Firehole—fumaroles blow off steam and mudpots percolate as you fish in this geyser basin just north of Old Faithful. If you haven't done it before, a quick trip to these park waters is certainly worth it. You'll find a favorite or two that you'll dream about when you get home. In addition, another must is a float trip on the Yellowstone through Paradise Valley. Depending on water conditions, your guide will suggest a run that will put you into cutthroats, browns or rainbows.

As you'd suspect, Yellowstone Valley Lodge is first class in all aspects. Rooms, two to a cabin, are spacious, comfortably furnished and offer views of the river. Meals are truly outstanding: rack of lamb with broiled herbed potatoes, grilled tuna with wasabi, herbavorian pasta. Dine on the terrace and watch dusk swallow the mountains.

Flaming Gorge Lodge

D u t c h   J o h n ,   U t a h

VITAL STATISTICS:

KEY SPECIES:
Brown, rainbow and lake trout

Season:
All year

Accommodations:
MOTEL AND CONDOS
NUMBER OF GUEST ROOMS: 45
MAXIMUM NUMBER OF GUESTS: 200

Meals: Full-service restaurant

Conference Groups: Yes

Rates:
Rooms from $52; condos $92 per person per day, single occupancy

Guides: From $150 wading for a half-day, $300 for full-day float for 2

Gratuities: 15%

Preferred Payment:
Major credit cards

Getting There:
The lodge is 7 hours north of Denver, 3 1/2 hours from Salt Lake City.

Other Activities:
Canoeing, whitewater rafting, swimming, boating, hiking, bird watching, biking, wildlife photography, water skiing.

Contact:
Herald Egbert
Flaming Gorge Lodge,
155 Greendale (US 191),
Dutch John, UT 84023;
801/889-3773, fax
801/889-3788, email
greenriverherald@
union-tel.com

Float the Green River Canyon for
20-inch browns, cutthroats and rainbows.

LOCATED FOUR MILES from Flaming Gorge Dam, this large lodge puts anglers in the catbird seat for fishing either the lake (three miles away) for monster trout or the wild and scenic Green River, one of the top 10 trout rivers in the U.S. Cedar Springs Marina, near the dam, provides guides and rental boats to fish Flaming Gorge Lake, home of the state-record brown (33 pounds 10 ounces), rainbow (26 pounds 20 ounces), Mackinaw lake trout (51 pounds 8 ounces) and Kokanee salmon (5 pounds 5 ounces). Trolling is the name of the game here. You need to go deep for the lake's trout—downriggers or longlines—and the best months are June, July and August. Rainbows hit all year long, as do browns. Salmon tend to tail off in August when they begin their spawn.

While some of the guests at the lodge troll the lake, most focus on the Green River, a classic tailwater fishery. Water comes out of the dam at 56°F. The upper section courses through Green River Canyon with pocket water, long pools, riffles and rapids. The river is extremely clear in this stretch, and you can see trout lying on the bottom of pools that are 15 feet deep. On a float through the canyon, you'll catch rainbows, cutthroats and browns. Best fishing is from April through October. Try scuds, cranefly larvae and midges early in the season; fish cicada, caddis imitations and terrestrials in midsummer, and wrap up with Blue-Winged Olives, nymphs and Woolly Buggers in fall. Floating is best early and late. Wet wading, where access is available, can be productive and enjoyable in July and August. At the lodge, you'll find a full-service tackleshop and guide service. A full-day guided floatfishing trip for fly or spin anglers with lunch is about $300.

The lodge offers motel rooms and condos on a daily or weekly basis. Condos include one queen, one single and a hide-a-bed, and a fully equipped kitchen. Motel rooms are furnished with a pair of twin beds with a roll-away available on request. Some are handicapped accessible. Meals are served in the main dining room.

Brush Creek Ranch
Saratoga, Wyoming

VITAL STATISTICS:

KEY SPECIES:
Brook, brown, cutthroat and rainbow trout

Season:
All year
Accommodations:
LOG RANCH AND CABINS
NUMBER OF GUEST ROOMS: 11
MAXIMUM NUMBER OF GUESTS: 22
Conference Groups: Yes
Meals: American plan
Rates:
From $145 per person per night, double occupancy
Guides: $300 per day for 2
Gratuities: 15% to 25% of fee
Preferred Payment:
Cash or check
Getting There:
Fly to Laramie and rent a car or Brush Creek will provide round-trip transfers for $150 per party.
Other Activities:
Riding, hiking, bird watching, biking, wildlife photography, skiing, dog sledding, snowmobiling.

Contact:
Kinta or Gib Blumenthal
Brush Creek Ranch, Star Route 10, Saratoga, WY 82331; 800/726-2499, fax 307/327-5384.

On three miles of trout stream near the upper North Platte, this lodge dates from the 1900s.

BORDERING ON THE Medicine Bow National Forest in the Snowy Mountains, the 6000-acre Brush Creek Ranch slopes down from the steep shoulders of the mountains to broad meadows of sage. Coming down from the mountains as well is icy cold Brush Creek, three miles of which cuts across the ranch.

Brush Creek fishes best in fall. Its browns are on the spawn then and so, too, are its brookies. Browns range up to 18 inches; the brook trout, 10 inches or so. You'll also find rainbows and cutthroats in the 12- to 14-inch range. The entire length of Brush Creek is fishable, but its name is no lie. Portions are thick with stunted cottonwoods and willows (and these, naturally, hold the better trout), but much of the creek is open. Angling can be a challenge, but taking a 20-inch brown on a No. 18 Caddis does have its rewards. Much less challenging, but fun, is the casting pond. Here's a perfect place to introduce children to flyfishing, the only method allowed on the ranch.

After leaving the ranch, Brush Creek rushes on to its junction with the North Platte at the One Bar Eleven Ranch. The North Platte is the premiere trout stream in southeast Wyoming. It rises in Colorado, and from the Wyoming state line, after runoff is complete, the river is a favorite float down to Saratoga. Populated mainly with rainbows and browns, some ranging up to four pounds but with most smaller, the river fishes well in summer and fall. Also of interest is the nearby Encampment River with its browns and rainbows and occasional brook trout. Though limited public access exists on both rivers, better fishing is found on private waters. Great Rocky Mountain Outfitters, Orvis-endorsed as is the ranch, leases several stretches of the upper North Platte and Encampment Rivers. Another of their favorite stretches is the Miracle Mile below Seminoe Dam, where five-pound browns are not uncommon.

If you time your trip right, you can help Gib Blumenthal and his hands move cattle on the ranch. You'll stay in the lodge, which dates from the early 1900s. Exposed logs grace some of the guest rooms in the main lodge and outlying cottages. Furnishings are definitely Western—bedsteads of log and quilts in cowboy motifs—but they're understated and tasteful in comparison to typical dude ranches. Read and relax before the stone fireplace in the library. At Brush Creek, everybody—staff and guests included—gathers for family-style dinners: prime rib, chicken, baked salmon. Afterwards, go for a walk, or settle into a rocking chair on the wide front porch.

Crescent H Ranch
W i l s o n ,   W y o m i n g

VITAL STATISTICS:

KEY SPECIES:
Brown, cutthroat and rainbow trout

Season:
All year

Accommodations:
RUSTIC CABINS
NUMBER OF GUEST ROOMS: 10
MAXIMUM NUMBER OF GUESTS: 25

Conference Groups: Yes

Meals: American plan

Rates:
From $2400 per person per week, double occupancy

Guides: $275 per day

Gratuities: 15%

Preferred Payment:
Cash or check

Getting There:
Fly to Jackson and rent a car. You'll want one to tour this fabulous country.

Other Activities:
Riding, golf, tennis, whitewater rafting, swimming, hiking, biking.

Contact:
Tamara Fox
Crescent H Ranch, PO Box 347, Wilson, WY 83014; 307/733-3674, fax 307/733-8475.

Slip into the old West at this ranch at the base of the Teton Mountains.

ONLY A STONE'S THROW from Jackson, at the Crescent H Ranch you'll slip into the old West of the 1920s as easily as putting on a flannel shirt. With 1500 acres rising gently from the Snake River, the ranch is highly regarded for its relaxed atmosphere, which is what folks come here to do. Wildflowers poke up through the meadows that surround the weathered log lodge. Tongues of pine, fingered with aspen that yellows in the fall, edge the grasslands through which flow Fish Creek and a number of smaller spring creeks, all rainbow water.

For most anglers, the main attraction at this Orvis-endorsed lodge is the nearby Snake and its tributaries—especially the 10-mile stretch from the south entrance of Yellowstone National Park to Jackson Lake. Narrow, this section of the river is wadeable and much of it is relatively unaccessible from roads. South of Jackson Lake, the Snake is big, braided and best fished from a driftboat. Cutthroats make up more than 90 percent of the fish in this stretch of river. Spin and flyfishers will enjoy frequent hookups, with a good fish running about 16 inches.

Less than 10 miles north of Jackson, the highway crosses the Gros Ventre River, a freestone river with good pocket water, pools and riffles. The lower section of the Gros Ventre fluctuates with irrigation. Above Lower Slide Lake, the flow is more normal. Cutthroats in the eight- to 12-inch range populate these lightly fished waters. A third, especially challenging option is Flat Creek on the northern edge of Jackson. This is a special-regulation stream that meanders through the National Elk Refuge. Most successful anglers here crawl on their hands and knees to reach the grassy bank and pray that an errant gust doesn't blow their dry flies astray. The reward: cutthroats up to 14 inches. Below Jackson the Snake cuts through a canyon, floatable in the fall, down to Palisades Reservoir on the Idaho border.

The Crescent H is an ideal headquarters for fishing these waters, and it's close enough to the Henry's Fork over the mountains in Idaho, the Green River, and the Lewis and Firehole in Yellowstone to make daytrips feasible. When you get back to the lodge, you'll change your duds in your private rustic pine cabin and wander over to the main house. Chat with guests around the wagon wheel coffee tables or rest in an elk-horn rocker by one of the two huge stone fireplaces. Dinner might be a hearty Western barbecue or venison tenderloin with sun-dried fruit sauce, gratin potatoes, broccoli and yellow squash.

Five Star Expeditions

L a n d e r ,   W y o m i n g

VITAL STATISTICS:

KEY SPECIES:
Brown and cutthroat trout

Season:
April through November

Accommodations:
VARIES WITH LOCATION FROM RESORTS TO TENTS
NUMBER OF GUEST ROOMS: Varies
MAXIMUM NUMBER OF GUESTS: 6 to 8

Conference Groups: No
Meals: Included in lodge packages

Rates:
From $635 per person for 2 days and 3 nights, double occupancy
Guides: Included
Gratuities: 6% to 10%
Preferred Payment:
American Express, MasterCard, Visa

Getting There:
Laramie is the closest airport; rent a car there or Beattie will provide pick-up service for you and your party for $100 each way.

Other Activities:
Canoeing, rafting, swimming, boating, hiking, bird watching, wildlife photography, biking, golf.

Contact:
Ed Beattie
Five Star Expeditions, PO Box 582, 431 Main St., Lander, WY 82520; 307/332-3197, fax 307/332-3198.

Here you'll find good fishing on a variety of western rivers, with good lodging nearby.

WHEN ED BEATTIE STARTED guiding 20 years ago, he worked one river. At times, fishing was great. Other times, it wasn't. The quality of the fishing varies with the hatches, and generally, but not always, follows a calendar. Beattie found he had to diversify or die, and now he has identified six or seven rivers and the periods when he thinks they fish best. He organizes trips to fish those rivers, in some cases providing accommodations and in others, pointing clients toward good and reasonable lodging and restaurants.

Beattie has a passion for the upper North Platte, rated as Wyoming's premiere trout stream. From conifer-capped canyon rims to high desert, the river offers 120 miles of classic western big river fishing. The window here is 20 days: June 20 through July 10. Fishing big nymphs and streamers, skilled anglers will land 20 to 50 trout, generally browns, per day. The best way to fish the river is to float it and camp on its banks. A supply raft precedes anglers in their driftboat, and by the time they reach the campsite, tents are up, the fire's going, and if you're lucky, fresh pie is baking in a Dutch oven. A riverside libation is the precursor to steaks or chops grilled over the coals. Before and after the float, guests overnight at Platt's Rustic Mountain Lodge, the 6000-square-foot home of big-game hunter Ron Platt. Four guest rooms share three baths. The lodge also hosts Beattie's anglers who fish the upper North Platte, but who like showers and clean sheets every night. Meals are sturdy: roast beef and turkey with all the fixings.

From the end of July through August, 'hoppers draw Beattie and his clients to the Upper Green and its browns and to New Fork River, a challenging stream for big brown trout. For river anglers, Pinedale, Wyoming is headquarters and at night, after the fishing's done, you'll find them at McGregor's Pub swapping lies with other guides and their sports. Lodging is in local motels. Across the border in Idaho, the South Fork of the Snake has periods when the fishing's great: salmonfly hatch (July 1 through 25), 'hoppers (August 10 through September 20), and for spawning browns of 10-pounds-plus (October 20 through November 30). The South Fork Lodge and Restaurant provides creature comforts, especially welcome in November's driving sleet and snow. Among other favorite hotspots: August for cutthroats on the Snake at Jackson Hole (motels in Jackson or Spring Creek Resort if you're flush), and March through April and November through December on the upper Big Horn (motels and restaurants in Thermopolis).

Shirley Mountain Lodge

M i l l s ,   W y o m i n g

Enjoy the solitude of southeastern Wyoming at a lodge with 30 ponds stocked with trout.

VITAL STATISTICS:

KEY SPECIES:
Brook, brown, cutthroat and rainbow trout

Season:
June through September

Accommodations:
MODERN WOOD AND GLASS LODGE
NUMBER OF GUEST ROOMS: 5
MAXIMUM NUMBER OF GUESTS: 10

Conference Groups: Yes

Meals: American plan

Rates:
$450 per angler per day

Guides: Included

Gratuities: Client's discretion

Preferred Payment:
Cash or check

Getting There:
Casper, Wyoming, is the closest airport; rent a car there or the lodge van will pick you up at no additional charge.

Other Activities:
Hunting, boating, hiking, bird watching, biking, wildlife photography.

Contact:
Steve Steinle
Shirley Mountain Lodge, PO Box 2850, Mills, WY 82644; 307/235-0899, fax 307/265-7633 (summer); 1563 Kelly, Casper, WY 82609; 307/266-1470 (winter).

THIS INTIMATE WESTERN LODGE hosts no more than 10 guests at a time on a big ranch. Just how big is big? Well, the Shirley Mountains are roughly 41 miles long, and the ranch sprawls over most of them. It's one of the largest chunks of private real estate in the country, and its private trout fishery is one of the best.

When he bought the ranch in 1981, Clayton Williams set out to create habitat that would produce trout. While this country is an arid land of sage and grass, numerous springs breech the surface. Williams has harnessed their waters in a series of 10-acre ponds that step like stairs down gullies on the sides of the mountains. Cold and clear and undisturbed by cattle, these ponds, all 30 of them, hold trout. You'll find browns and cutthroats up to five pounds, rainbows and cuttbows (rainbow/cutthroat hybrids) to eight and brookies to three. Angling is easy. Fish from float tubes or walk the shore. Fish larger than 20 inches are frequent. It's not unusual to net half a dozen or more in an afternoon. For variety try the riffles, runs and pools of the ranch's small spring-fed creeks. The size of these trout will surprise you.

Less than an hour from the ranch is the "Miracle Mile" of the North Platte, which some argue is Wyoming's best trout river. The mileage runs from Seminoe Reservoir down to Pathfinder Reservoir, a distance of six miles. Spawning browns and rainbows run up from Pathfinder and many remain in the tailwater. This is a popular stretch. Even so, fishing is quite good during the season. Small mayflies and midges perform below Seminoe Dam; and larger dries, streamers like the Woolly Bugger and big nymphs take trout up to five pounds. Shirley Mountain, an Orvis-endorsed lodge, will provide guided trips on this water as well.

Located in the foothills, the 2000-square-foot modern California-style lodge contains five guest rooms (one with private bath). Breakfast and dinner are served family-style and cuisine is substantial Western fare: steaks, chops, and, of course, trout. Sofas and easy chairs invite guests to gather in front of the living room's big stone fireplace. Other times, you'll lounge on the expansive deck, inhaling the perfume of barbecuing steaks on the charcoal grill, while watching elk, deer and antelope graze in the pastures below. Think about coming back in the fall with a rifle for a record bull.

Spotted Horse Ranch

Jackson   Hole,   Wyoming

VITAL STATISTICS:

KEY SPECIES:
Cutthroat, rainbow and brown trout

Season:
All year
Accommodations:
MAIN LODGE AND LOG CABINS
NUMBER OF GUEST ROOMS: 11
MAXIMUM NUMBER OF GUESTS: 43
Conference Groups: Yes
Meals: American plan
Rates:
$174 per person per day,
double occupancy
Guides: $250 for 2 anglers
per day
Gratuities: $25 to $50
Preferred Payment:
MasterCard, Visa
Getting There:
Fly to Jackson Hole.
Other Activities:
Horseback riding, hiking, bird
watching, swimming, golf,
tennis, antiquing, skiing,
whitewater rafting.

Contact:
Clare Berger
Spotted Horse Ranch,
Star Rt. 43, Jackson
Hole, WY 83002;
800/528-2084, fax
307/733-3712.

The rivers south of Jackson Hole are rich with cutthroats, and they're easy to reach from the Spotted Horse.

SOME 16 MILES SOUTH of Jackson in Hoback Canyon is an elegant little ranch, steeped in the traditions of Rocky Mountain fishing. A 46-acre spread, it owns more than a mile of private water on the Hoback River, which is a stone's throw from the Snake and not more than a hour from the Salt and upper Green rivers.

The Hoback earns a modest rating from Fothergill and Sterling in their comprehensive *The Wyoming Angling Guide* because it is apt to color excessively with runoff from rains. Primarily a cutthroat river, its fish tend to be a bit smaller than those downstream in the Snake below Hoback Junction, where the two rivers meet. In the ranch's mileage, you can expect cutts in the 12- to 14-inch class, though fish up to 22 inches have been taken. The ranch's chief guide, Ben Peterson, prefers to ferry anglers over to the upper Green, a 45-minute ride through the scenic Gros Ventre Range. The headwaters of the Green are primarily rainbow and brown trout water, and fish reasonably well once the spring melt has flushed through by mid-July. Peterson uses rubber rafts with casting chairs for his all-day floats ("Less prone to mishap," he says). Fish average about 14 inches, but it's not uncommon for a three-pounder to hit your fly or spinner. Equidistant from the ranch is the Salt River, which flows north out of the mountain range of the same name and joins Palisades Reservoir just east of the Wyoming/Idaho line. Like the Hoback, this is principally a cutthroat river except that spawning browns move into the stream in August. Not to be forgotten, of course, is the Snake and its indigenous fine-spotted cutthroats averaging 14 inches. Floats on the section below Hoback Junction offer grand scenery as well as top-notch angling.

When you return from fishing, a cane-bottom rocker awaits on the deck of the lodge overlooking the Hoback. Sit back, watch the eagles and listen to the wind in the lodgepole pine and the river below you. Dinners, simple and scrumptious featuring staples such as steak and turkey and Mexican entrees, leave you little room for anything more. You'll walk in the evening chill back to your log cabin, furnished with all amenities including, of course, private bath. All activities of the ranch except float trips are included in the American plan fee. And while the ranch will provide transfers from Jackson airport for $30 each way, you may want to rent a car to poke around in the Grand Teton or Yellowstone National parks, or to slip over to Idaho for a day on the South Fork of the Snake below Palisades Dam.

Yellowstone Park Hotels

Y e l l o w s t o n e   N a t i o n a l   P a r k ,   W y o m i n g

Stay in the middle of America's finest Western fisheries, at prices everyone can afford.

VITAL STATISTICS:

KEY SPECIES:
Brook, brown, cutthroat and rainbow trout

Accommodation:
VARIES WITH EACH LODGE; SEE TEXT.

Guides:
Available throughout the park, the managers of each of Yellowstone's hotels can provide names and phone numbers of those familiar with the waters in the vicinity. Expect to pay between $250 and $300 per day for two. Tips should average 15%.

Weather:
Snows come early to the high caldera that is the floor of the park. You can expect temporary closures of all roads after October 1. And as of November 1, all roads within the park are closed, with the exception of the road between Mammoth and Cooke City. Again regulations for travel and fishing within the park vary from season to season. If you plan a late- or early-season expedition, check with the park in advance.

Other Activities:
In addition to its wonderful and varied fishing, Yellowstone teems with deer, elk, sheep, bear, antelope, bison, moose and mudpots along with geysers. Here, in every season, the wilderness is on display. The park service and concessionaires have developed a number of interpretive activities from instructional multi-media pre-

YELLOWSTONE'S CALDERA is more than a place of awesome grandeur. For anglers, it is the mother lode of American trout fishing. Count its famous streams: Falls, Firehole, Gallatin, Gardner, Gibbon, Lamar, Lewis, Madison, Slough Creek, Snake and the Yellowstone itself. Don't forget Shoshone and Yellowstone lakes. West Yellowstone is the mecca. Paradise Valley, just what it says. Yellowstone's 2.2-million acres provide more angling opportunities than any other national park in the U.S.

And unlike most national parks, Yellowstone boasts a wealth of fine old hotels, each with its own ambiance and personality. At rates that are reasonable in comparison to those charged by facilities on the fringes of the park, one can stay the night, eat well, and fish to heart's content. The current concessionaire operating the hotels is AmFac Parks and Resorts of Aurora, Colorado. Reservations at any of the Yellowstone hotels may be made by calling 307/344-7311. Seasons may vary slightly at each.

CANYON LODGE & CABINS. Canyon Village is in the center of the park, where the Yellowstone River breaks off to the northwest and enters the Grand Canyon of the Yellowstone. From the falls down to Inspiration Point, the river is closed to fishing, but below, for anglers willing to hike 1500 feet down to its waters, the river offers excellent cutthroat fishing. 609 rooms, restaurant, $48 to $93.

GRANT VILLAGE. Near West Thumb, Grant is on Yellowstone Lake, home of pure-strain cutthroat trout. Covering 150 square miles, the lake is more than 300 feet deep in spots. Use of motors is restricted in some sections of the lake. Fishing is often very good near shore and in feeder creeks. Float-tube and wading anglers can do as well as boaters. Check regulations carefully: Streams open later than the lake. 300 rooms, restaurant, marina, $68 to $84.

LAKE LODGE AND LAKE YELLOWSTONE HOTEL AND CABINS. Just west of the outlet and on Yellowstone in Lake Village, you'll find extensive accommodations close to the first fishable section of the Yellowstone River, beginning a mile downstream from the lake. Yellowstone cutthroats of 16 to 18 inches are the prime attraction: wading—dicey at times—is the best way to fish it. As with elsewhere in the park, things change. Check regulations before wetting a line. Lake Lodge—186 rooms, restaurant, $43 to $84; Lake Yellowstone Hotel and Cabins—194 rooms, 102 cabins, restaurant, $63 to $342.

MAMMOTH HOT SPRINGS HOTEL. Fans of massive 1890s military-post architecture will love Mammoth Hot Springs, headquarters for the park. While it receives some pressure, the Gardner River below Osprey Falls holds nice browns that migrate up from the Yellowstone River in fall. You'll also find cutthroats here. 96 rooms in the hotel, 126 in cabins, restaurant, $34 to $226.

OLD FAITHFUL. Here are three large lodges and adjacent cabins: the Inn; the Lodge Cabins; and Snow Lodge & Cabins. Of massive logs with its towering interior, the Inn is the park's signature hotel. Nearby is Snow Lodge & Cabins, and a little beyond, Lodge Cabins. All three are convenient to the Firehole, Gibbon and upper Madison. In the heat of summer try Iron Spring and Sentinel creeks, cool havens for hot Firehole browns. Inn: 325 rooms, restaurant, $47 to $289; Lodge Cabins, 132 (85 with private bath), $22 to $38; Snow Lodge & Cabins: 31 lodge, 34 cabins (some with private bath), $47 to $84.

ROOSEVELT LODGE. The road from Cooke City at the northwest entrance to the park follows Soda Butte Creek to its junction with the Lamar River. Both are good fisheries. The Lamar has nice populations of cutthroats and rainbows. When the Lamar muddies, the Soda Butte is often clear, though fish average only 10 inches. At Tower, the Yellowstone flows out of its Grand Canyon, through relatively gentle terrain, and then into the Black Canyon of the Yellowstone. Fishing is quite good, but once in the canyon, the river becomes difficult to wade. Slough Creek, another fine stream known for cutthroats and less fishing pressure than most streams in the park, can be reached by the road to Slough Creek Campground, north of the Tower-Cooke City Road. 80 rooms (17 with private baths), restaurant, $24 to $63.

sentations in visitor centers to horseback rides to fairly arduous hikes to see flora, fauna and fascinating geology. In addition, particularly in the Mammoth area, special waters are set aside for children to fish, one more way that the park service is committed to propagating the species.

Contact:
AmFac Parks and Resorts, PO Box 165, Yellowstone National Park, WY 82190; 307/344-7901, 307/344-7311 (reservations), fax 307/344-7456.

THE WEST

ARIZONA, CALIFORNIA, NEVADA,
NEW MEXICO, OREGON, WASHINGTON

W RAPPING around the southern tip of the Rockies and swinging up the Pacific Coast, these states offer their own brands of fishing, from clear and cold streams high in the Sierras, to California's spring creeks, to winding rivers draining lush northwest forests. Salmonoids dominate—silvers and chinooks along the coast, browns, rainbows and cutthroats in the uplands. In southern California, there are trophy bass to be caught in lakes Casitas and Castaic north of Los Angles and in the ponds around San Diego. Don't forget stripers running the Golden Gate, while in Oregon and Washington the smallmouth fishing is superb. Lodges run the gamut from ranches to cedar and glass affairs on points overlooking the surf.

Lodges:

Arizona
1 LEE'S FERRY LODGE

California
2 ARCULARIUS RANCH
3 CLEARWATER HOUSE ON HAT CREEK
4 HAT CREEK HOUSE
5 HENDERSON SPRINGS
6 OAKRIDGE INN
7 SORENSEN'S RESORT
8 THE SEA RANCH LODGE

New Mexico
9 BLACKFIRE FLYFISHING GUEST RANCH
10 RIZUTO'S SAN JUAN RIVER LODGE
11 STEP BACK INN
12 THE LODGE AT CHAMA

Oregon
13 C&J LODGE
14 GRANDE RONDE LODGE
15 LONESOME DUCK
16 MORRISON'S ROGUE RIVER LODGE
17 STEAMBOAT INN
18 THE BIG K GUEST RANCH
19 WILLIAMSON RIVER CLUB AT CRYSTALWOOD LODGE
20 YAMSI RANCH

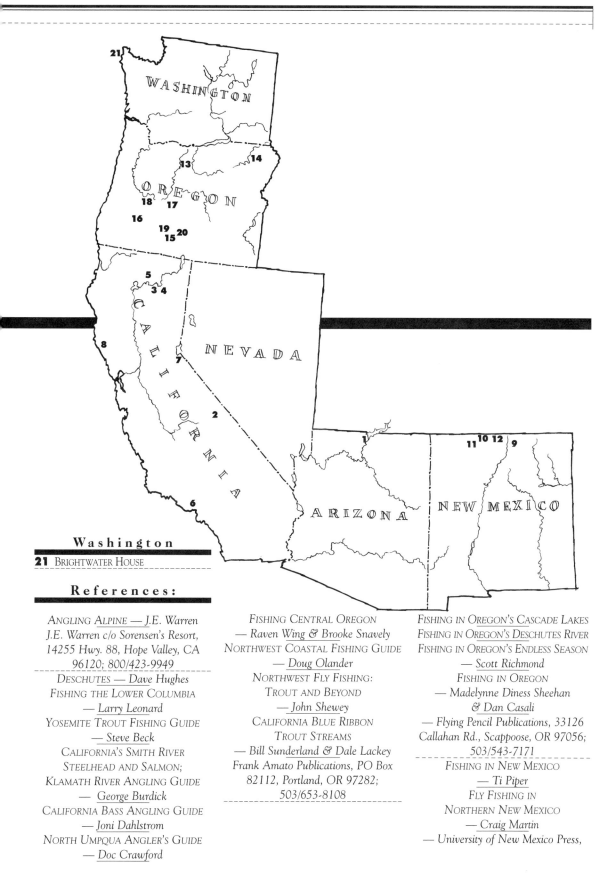

WASHINGTON

OREGON

CALIFORNIA

NEVADA

ARIZONA

NEW MEXICO

Washington

21 BRIGHTWATER HOUSE

References:

ANGLING ALPINE — J.E. Warren
J.E. Warren c/o Sorensen's Resort,
14255 Hwy. 88, Hope Valley, CA
96120; 800/423-9949

DESCHUTES — Dave Hughes
FISHING THE LOWER COLUMBIA
— Larry Leonard
YOSEMITE TROUT FISHING GUIDE
— Steve Beck
CALIFORNIA'S SMITH RIVER
STEELHEAD AND SALMON;
KLAMATH RIVER ANGLING GUIDE
— George Burdick
CALIFORNIA BASS ANGLING GUIDE
— Joni Dahlstrom
NORTH UMPQUA ANGLER'S GUIDE
— Doc Crawford

FISHING CENTRAL OREGON
— Raven Wing & Brooke Snavely
NORTHWEST COASTAL FISHING GUIDE
— Doug Olander
NORTHWEST FLY FISHING:
TROUT AND BEYOND
— John Shewey
CALIFORNIA BLUE RIBBON
TROUT STREAMS
— Bill Sunderland & Dale Lackey
Frank Amato Publications, PO Box
82112, Portland, OR 97282;
503/653-8108

FISHING IN OREGON'S CASCADE LAKES
FISHING IN OREGON'S DESCHUTES RIVER
FISHING IN OREGON'S ENDLESS SEASON
— Scott Richmond
FISHING IN OREGON
— Madelynne Diness Sheehan
& Dan Casali
— Flying Pencil Publications, 33126
Callahan Rd., Scappoose, OR 97056;
503/543-7171
FISHING IN NEW MEXICO
— Ti Piper
FLY FISHING IN
NORTHERN NEW MEXICO
— Craig Martin
— University of New Mexico Press,

Arcularius Ranch in California's Mammoth Lakes area contains
five-plus miles of the Owens River, a blue-ribbon trout stream. — page 164.

Lee's Ferry Lodge at Vermilion Cliffs, Arizona, is the jump-off
point for anglers fishing the Colorado below Glen Canyon Dam. — page 163.

References & Resources

1720 Lomas Blvd. N.E., Albuquerque, NM 87131-1591; 505/277-7564

Resources:

ARIZONA GAME AND FISH DEPARTMENT, 2222 W. Greenway Rd., Phoenix, AZ 85023; 602/942-3000, website *http://www.state.az.us/gf/*

CALIFORNIA DEPARTMENT OF FISH & GAME, Inland Fisheries Div., PO Box 944209, Sacramento, CA 94244; 916/653-7664, website *http://www.dfg.ca.gov/*

NEW MEXICO DEPARTMENT OF GAME AND FISH, PO Box 25112, Santa Fe, NM 87504; 505/827-7901, website *http://www.gmfsh.state.nm.us*

NEVADA DEPARTMENT OF CONSERVATION AND NATURAL RESOURCES, PO Box 10678, Reno, NV 89520; 702/688-1500, website *http://www.state.nv.us*

OREGON DEPARTMENT OF FISH AND WILDLIFE, Fish Div., Box 59, Portland, OR 97207; 503/872-5252, website *http://www.dfw.state.or.us/*

WASHINGTON DEPARTMENT OF FISH AND WILDLIFE, 600 North Capitol Way, Olympia, WA 98501-1091; 360/902-2200, website *http://www.wa.gov/wdfw/*

Lee's Ferry Lodge
Vermilion Cliffs, Arizona

Eagles soar over the head of the Grand Canyon, where the Colorado tailwater holds big trout.

VITAL STATISTICS:

KEY SPECIES:
Rainbow trout

Season:
All year

Accommodations:
CABINS
NUMBER OF GUEST ROOMS: 11
MAXIMUM NUMBER OF GUESTS: 32

Conference Groups: Yes

Meals: Breakfast, lunch and dinner additional

Rates:
$53 per night for 2

Guides: $275 per day for 2 from Lee's Ferry Anglers

Gratuities: 10%

Preferred Payment:
MasterCard, Visa

Getting There:
Page, Arizona has the closest commercial airport, but check fares to Las Vegas and Flagstaff.

Other Activities:
Hiking, bird watching, biking, wildlife photography.

Contact:
Maggie Sacher
Lee's Ferry Lodge,
Vermilion Cliffs HC67-Box 1, Marble Canyon, AZ 86036; 520/355-2231.

THE COLORADO RIVER, from the base of Glen Canyon Dam to the gate of the Grand Canyon, is one of the finest tailwater fisheries in the West. It is also among the most scenic. Eagles soar between cliffs of rugged red sandstone rising 1000 feet above the river. Vegetation is sparse, but the river is cold and green. Since the closing of the dam in 1963 and their stocking in 1964, rainbow trout have thrived in the upper river. Water temperature is constant; the flow, relatively constant. A simulated flood release in 1996 was designed to flush sediment from the river channel, and similar releases are contemplated every seven to 10 years. However, the flood's impact on the trout fishery was minimal, and the river will continue to produce massive amounts of aquatic insects and crustaceans on which the rainbows feed.

Average fish here are 16 to 19 inches and two and three pounds. Bigger rainbows are frequent enough to make fly and spinfishers want reels with good drags. During the winter spawn period, from November through February, egg patterns and small attractors work well. There is also some action on wet and dry midges. The spawn concludes as March warms into May, and that's when dry fly anglers will enjoy casting to fish working on midges, and spin and nymph fishers will find success working riffles and runs. Hot days and warm nights of high summer tend to increase fish activity in riffles, where nymph imitations can be productive. The same pattern continues into early fall, when the spawn begins again.

Most anglers staying at the lodge engage a guide from Lee's Ferry Anglers (800/962-9755) next door. You'll boat upstream to the dam in a 20-foot shallow-draft skiff, and start working riffles, runs and pools on your way down. You'll wade and fish from the boat, depending on conditions. This is catch-and-release fishing, as the river here is managed as a trophy trout fishery.

Lee's Ferry Lodge began operation in 1929, the year of the stock market crash. Built of stone and hand-hewn timbers, flat-roofed, with flower boxes and outdoor chairs of bright blue, it looks like the set for an early Western movie. Guest rooms (all with private baths), however, are modern and can accommodate up to six good friends. Your door opens onto a path to the garden patio. A full-service restaurant offers breakfast, lunch and dinner.

Arcularius Ranch
Mammoth Lakes, California

Torn between a skiing or fishing vacation? Here you can do both.

VITAL STATISTICS:

KEY SPECIES:
Brown and rainbow trout

Season:
Late April through October

Accommodations:
HOUSEKEEPING CABINS
NUMBER OF GUEST ROOMS: 11
MAXIMUM NUMBER OF GUESTS: 65

Conference Groups: No

Meals: Cook for yourself or eat in nearby Mammoth Lakes

Rates:
From $120 per person per night, double occupancy

Guides: From $200 per day

Gratuities: Client's discretion

Preferred Payment:
Cash or check

Getting There:
Mammoth Lakes Airport has regular commercial service.

Other Activities:
Hiking, skiing.

Contact:
**Bill or Diane Nichols
Arcularius Ranch, Rt. 1,
Box 230, Mammoth
Lakes, CA 93546;
619/648-7807 (sum-
mer); PO Box 1658,
Minden, NV 89423;
702/782-7428 (winter).**

THROUGH ARCULARIUS RANCH flows five and a half miles of the Owens River, one of California's few spring creeks. Water levels, even early in the year, are fairly consistent from the end of April through October, when the ranch closes for the winter. Essentially, the Owens resembles a steelhead stream. In spring, rainbows move up the river from Crowley Lake, 12 miles downstream, to spawn. A second wave of rainbows, a fall-spawning variety developed at the nearby Hot Creek Hatchery, begins to move up in September. Along with them come brown trout. Spawners can reach 25 inches and weigh in the neighborhood of six pounds. During the summer the Owens is filled with juvenile trout, both rainbows and browns. Most are in the 12- to 14-inch range, but bigger fish are frequent.

Through May and into June, big nymphs and streamers cast hard against the banks will produce good-size fish. The same tactics work in fall. You'll also find typical mayfly hatches from the end of April through October. The river is known for excellent caddis activity that starts in June, and 'hoppers in August through September. The upper section of the river on the Arcularius property resembles a classic spring creek, but on the lower section it takes on more of a freestone persona. The keys to successful fishing on both stretches are precise casts, drag-free floats, light tippets and stealth. Grassy banks border the stream for most of its length, so an approach on hands and knees is less likely to spook big fish. Wading is prohibited except to cross the river. Barbless hooks are required. While fishing the Owens, you'll want to test nearby Hot Creek's .9 miles of public water, known for its big and finicky trout.

Operated by the Arcularius family as a working and fishing ranch since 1919, the operation has quite a following of clients, some of whom have been coming for generations. Reservations are best made well in advance. Eleven serviceable log cabins range in size from two to four bedrooms. All include fully equipped kitchens and private baths. Some have screened porches. On the ranch you'll find a country store, stocked with essential groceries and a wide selection of dry and wet flies. For parties that lack culinary expertise or motivation, a number of good restaurants can be found in the nearby ski and resort town of Mammoth Lakes. In fact a number of families book into the ranch and combine skiing with fishing in May and early June.

Clearwater House on Hat Creek
Cassel, California

VITAL STATISTICS:

KEY SPECIES:
Brown and rainbow trout

Season:
May 1 through November 15
Accommodations:
1920S STUCCO FARMHOUSE
NUMBER OF GUEST ROOMS: 7
MAXIMUM NUMBER OF GUESTS: 14
Conference Groups: Yes
Meals: Bed and breakfast or American plan
Rates:
$150 per person per night (American plan)
Guides: $250 for 2 per day
Gratuities: $50
Preferred Payment:
MasterCard, Visa
Getting There:
Drive from Redding or Sacramento.
Other Activities:
Golf, tennis, swimming, hiking, bird watching, biking, wildlife photography.

Contact:
Dick Galland
Clearwater House on Hat Creek, PO Box 90, Cassel, CA 96016; 916/335-5500 (summer); 310 Sunset Way, Muir Beach, CA 94965; 415/381-1173, fax 415/383-9136 (winter); email d1trout@aol.com, website www.clearwater trout.com

If trout went to school, this is where they'd go to learn about flyfishing.

DICK GALLAND of Clearwater House offers a course, Mastering the Art of Fly Fishing, for those who stay at Clearwater House. You won't master flyfishing in this four-day series of demonstrations, video-taped practice, fishing and more practice. But don't feel bad. Nobody ever masters flyfishing; some just get better at it than others. Mastering the Art...will prepare you to fish freestone streams, spring creeks and still waters. After the course, if you practice, you'll make short casts with reasonable accuracy, read the water reasonably well, select flies with more than a good hunch and tie them to your tippet so they'll stay on. And you'll probably catch trout. And if this new-found confidence piques your interest, Galland has other courses: Big Trout Tactics (nymph and streamer fishing with long distance casting); Casting and Sight Nymphing Weekends (gain that extra 10 feet with accuracy and learn drag-free drift); The Guide School (required preparation for incipient midlife crises); and The Master Angler (five days that will turn you into a topflight flyfisher).

Experiential learning at its finest, Clearwater courses use Hat Creek, one of northern California's premiere spring creeks known for extensive caddis hatches, as its lab. You may also fish the Pit, with its wildly beautiful and challenging canyon below Lake Britton; the McCloud for big rainbows and browns; Fall River, where large rainbows inhale tricos; and the Sacramento River. Stillwater anglers will enjoy float-tube fishing on Baum, Eastman, Manzanita and McCumber lakes. You can take part with up to four other anglers in Directed Fishing Clinics, where instruction is tuned to specific waters, or you can simply come and fish with or without a guide. With a season that runs from May 1 through November 15, you can fish spring, when rainbows begin to feed voraciously, through fall, when aspens turn golden and browns go on the spawn.

Clearwater House is a light-gray stucco farmstead on the bank of Hat Creek. A sunny porch is draped with waders and rods. Inside this quaint and gracious home, oriental rugs carpet polished hardwood floors. Antiques and period furniture appoint the living room dominated, not by its fireplace, but by a huge window and the woods beyond. Spacious guest rooms boast queen, twin or king-size beds, all are served by private baths. Dinners (shrimp pasta with green curry, sea bass with tomatillo relish) are accompanied by good wines and served on a round table under open beams. Orvis-endorsed, Clearwater offers a range of packages from bed and breakfast to full American plan with guided fishing.

Hat Creek House
C a s s e l ,   C a l i f o r n i a

**VITAL
STATISTICS:**

KEY SPECIES:
**Brown and rainbow
trout**

Season:
May through early November
Accommodations:
RANCH HOUSE
NUMBER OF GUEST ROOMS: 4
MAXIMUM NUMBER OF GUESTS: 8
Conference Groups: No
Meals: American plan
Rates:
From $185 per person per day,
single occupancy
Guides: $200 per day for 1 or
2 anglers
Gratuities: 10%
Preferred Payment:
MasterCard, Visa
Getting There
Fly to Redding, California, rent
a car and drive to the lodge.
Other Activities:
Biking, bird watching, hiking,
wildlife photography.

Contact:
**Duane Milleman
Hat Creek House, 18101
Doty Rd., Cassel, CA
96016; 916/335-5270 or
916/222-3555.**

*Put your tackle to the test on trout of
truly gigantic proportions.*

SOME LODGES FEEL LIKE LODGES, others feel
like home. So it is with this unpretentious white
farmhouse with four bedrooms tucked away in the
woods on a private half-mile of Hat Creek. The creek,
an improved meadow stream of long pools, weedbeds, undercut banks and little riffles,
winds right behind the house. In some sections, alders overhang the water; in others,
it flows through open flats. Both make for challenging fishing. And the fish, which can
run up to 15 pounds, are of trophy caliber. While the season runs from April through
November, the best fishing occurs in May, June and October.

Behind the lodge and next to the barn is one of two cold-water ponds. The
smaller teems with 12- to 15-inch rainbows. It's an idyllic place to work the kinks out
of your casts. The larger pond is stocked with serious fish of up to 20 pounds. These
monster 'bows and browns will run you down to backing in nothing flat. Want to learn
how to handle big fish on light tackle? Use a float tube and go wrestle these Jurassic
trout. Then fish the stream. Use of a guide on the ranch is optional.

The number of guests at this working ranch is limited to eight. All four bedrooms
have private baths. Breakfasts are hearty buffets and dinners are served family-style.
Heart healthy, MSG/salt free and vegetarian diets can be accommodated with
advanced notice. Dinners—lazy, laid-back family-style affairs—are timed to not inter-
fere with evening hatches. Afterwards, retire to the living room or go to the tier's bench
to work out a pattern for the next day's fishing.

Along with the stream and lakes on the ranch, The Fly Shop (800/669-3474) in
Redding also manages several miles of private streams and a number of lakes, and provides guides for clients who want to explore the best of northern California's trout
waters. You'll need a car to reach the ranch. On the way stop at The Fly Shop for
licenses and local patterns. And while in the vicinity, explore Lassen Volcanic National
Park, an hour or so south of the ranch.

Henderson Springs

B i g   B e n d ,   C a l i f o r n i a

VITAL STATISTICS:

KEY SPECIES:
Brown and rainbow trout

Season:
March through November
Accommodations:
MODERN YET RUSTIC ANGLING LODGE
NUMBER OF GUEST ROOMS: 7
MAXIMUM NUMBER OF GUESTS: 12
Conference Groups: Yes
Meals: American plan
Rates:
$185 per person per day, single occupancy
Guides: From $150 for 1 angler per half day
Gratuities: 10%
Preferred Payment:
MasterCard, Visa
Getting There:
Fly to Redding, a van from the lodge will pick you up.
Other Activities:
Bird watching, hiking, wildlife photography, ropes course.

Contact:
Mark Henderson
Henderson Springs, PO Box 220, Big Bend, CA 96011; 916/337-6917, fax 916/337-6257.

Represented By:
The Fly Shop, 800/669-3474.

Three lakes keep you busy with big rainbows and browns.

THREE LAKES, ranging from seven to 20 acres and separated by heavy forests of pines and oaks, are within a half-mile of Henderson Springs and the main attraction of this 500-acre ranch. Floating peat islands that drift slowly in the spring-fed currents, the mats are rich with aquatic life. Big browns and rainbows up to 10 pounds cruise the dark green shade underneath them, feeding when the opportunity arises, or when they're presented with an offer that's too good to pass up. If nothing's hatching, work Woolly Buggers or bead-head nymphs on a medium sinking line. Sometimes a bit of split-shot is needed to get the fly down fast, though casting with such combinations is cumbersome. Fishing is from pontoon boats or float tubes—no other watercraft allowed.

In addition to improving the lakes, owner Mark Henderson has created a half-mile spring creek behind the ranch house. It flows from one of the lakes to the Pit River, and 1997 is the first year it is open to fishing. Stocked with rainbows and browns, it should be a great addition to the angling lineup at the ranch. Here, most guests do not use guides, though they are available, as is flyfishing instruction. It's best to pick up licenses and tackle before you arrive. Strictly catch-and-release, barbless hook and flyfishing only, April, May and October are the best months in a season that runs March through November.

Framed by towering peaks on three sides, the lodge itself is massive, and tastefully marries local log architecture with lots of glass. Its five bedrooms and three baths, two living rooms, and a huge deck provide inspiring vistas of the creek, rolling hills and the mountains beyond. Breakfast and dinner are served family-style; heart healthy and vegetarian meals are available, and meals are timed to miss major hatches. Anglers are sent out with boxed lunches. In addition to the main lodge, the ranch includes a housekeeping cottage with a single bedroom, sleeping loft for four and fully equipped kitchen. Henderson Springs also features a ropes course for personal and professional growth through team building, meeting facilities for corporate retreats and numerous trails for hiking and jogging.

Oakridge Inn
Oak View, California

VITAL STATISTICS:

KEY SPECIES:
Largemouth bass

Season:
All year
Accommodations:
MOTEL ROOMS
NUMBER OF GUEST ROOMS: 33
MAXIMUM NUMBER OF GUESTS: 125
Conference Groups: Yes
Meals: Nearby restaurants
Rates:
From $45 per night, single occupancy
Guides: $300 per day for 2
Gratuities: Client's discretion
Preferred Payment:
Major credit cards
Getting There:
Fly to Los Angeles, rent a car and drive to the inn.
Other Activities:
Golf, tennis, canoeing, kayaking, swimming, hiking, bird watching, antiquing, biking.

Contact:
Vijay Patel
Oakridge Inn, 780 N. Ventura Ave., PO Box 1560, Oak View, CA 93022; 805/649-4018, fax 805/649-4436.

This is the motel where the pros stay when they come to fish famed Lake Casitas.

ON EVERYONE'S LIST of top bass lakes in the U.S. is 2700-acre Lake Casitas, 70 miles north of Los Angeles in the Ojai Valley. Anglers from all over the world travel to fish this lake where average bass run eight to 10 pounds. Bass tipping the scale in the teens are almost an everyday occurrence for anglers who know what they're doing. However, the uninitiated will find this lake tough. It doesn't fish like the bass lakes on television. Forget about working the banks. Big bass hang over midlake structure: reefs and ridges, flooded roadbeds and stream channels and submerged timber.

Small and clear, Casitas gets unbelievable pressure. The bass, Florida-strain largemouths, have seen it all, and guides like John Shull (805/649-1108) have developed special techniques that increase chances of success. Primary foods for these behemoths are shad and rainbow trout, which were stocked by the state as a kind of put-and-take fishery. A 10-pound bass that's looking for dinner will inhale an eight-inch trout like a teenager wolfing down a Big Mac. Most effective are Castaic Lures or the AC plugs that look like swimming trout. At times, you'll see a bass chasing rainbows and with the right lead, you can cast and provoke a strike. In February and March, bass will feed on crawdads fished with little or no weight on a No. 4 hook. Pros use 12-pound-test Triple Fish camo line, which they believe leads to increased strikes. Fishing is generally good through September, but then it slacks off.

Serious anglers who come to fish Casitas stay at Vijay Patel's Oakridge Inn. Only five minutes from the lake, this motel was recently refurbished from top to bottom. You'll find comfortable rooms, some with kitchenettes and most with microwaves and refrigerators. Cable TV brings you the sports channel. Dock your bassboat in the well-lighted lot and charge depleted batteries with outlets provided for that purpose. Half a dozen good restaurants are within walking distance.

Sorensen's Resort

H o p e   V a l l e y ,   C a l i f o r n i a

VITAL STATISTICS:

KEY SPECIES:
Golden, brook, brown, Mackinaw, Lahontan cutthroat, Kamloops and Paiute rainbow trout

Season:
All year

Accommodations:
HOUSEKEEPING CABINS
NUMBER OF GUEST ROOMS: 30
MAXIMUM NUMBER OF GUESTS: 100

Conference Groups: Yes

Meals: Three bed and breakfast cabins, others are cook for yourself

Rates:
From $70 for 2 per night

Guides: $50 first hour, $20 per hour thereafter

Gratuities: Client's discretion

Preferred Payment:
Major credit cards

Getting There:
Fly to Reno, Nevada, rent a car and drive to Sorensen's.

Other Activities:
Swimming, hiking, bird watching, biking, wildlife photography, skiing, special activities for families.

Contact:
John or Patty Brissenden, Sorensen's Resort, 14255 Hwy. 88, Hope Valley, CA 96120; 800/423-9949.

High in a gentle valley in the Sierra Nevada are equal measures of tranquility and trout.

SURROUNDED BY THE MOUNTAINS south of Lake Tahoe and an hour or so from Reno, Sorensen's Resort should be a ski center, and indeed it is. Hope Valley provides marvelous cross-country trails, and Sorensen's quaint log cabins offer wood stoves to warm frozen fingers and toes. Come spring and fall, anglers sit and rock in front of the stoves, feet toasting on the hearth. They're in from fishing the West Fork of the Carson River, a mile of which flows through the resort, or from one of a number of small lakes and ponds nearby.

At the resort, the West Fork is stocked with rainbows averaging 18 inches. You'll also find a naturally propagating population of brook trout up to 12 inches plus. Browns run in the 18- to 20-inch range, and attempts are under way to establish Lahontan cutthroats. The river is not wide, 20 feet in many places, and features riffles, pocket water, plunge pools and deep holes. In late April and early May, it runs high with meltwater, making wading somewhat of a challenge. Yet anglers score well using sinking-tip lines and weighted nymphs or sculpin patterns.

Later, from the end of May into October, standard dries and wets produce consistently. Flyboxes should contain mosquitoes, While Millers and Hendricksons as well as Hare's Ears and Prince nymphs. The ideal rod is an eight-foot six-inch 4 weight, according to Judy Warren, who runs Horse Feathers Fly Fishing School at the resort. In September, grasshoppers play an important role in trout diets, and October brings caddis. Fish West Fork headwaters for brook trout or a number of the ponds for cutthroats, Mackinaw (lake trout) and at least three species of rainbows: golden, Paiute and Kamloops. Rimmed with stately Jeffrey pines and fringed with mock peach, the ponds are float-tube water that can also be fished from shore or boat.

Horse Feathers is not the usual flyfishing school where everyone lines up and flails away. Instead, Warren acts as coach and mentor with individuals, families and children. She also provides flytying courses at the lodge. Her book, *Angling Alpine,* is a good guide to trouting in the region.

Sorensen's is fairly modest in size as resorts go—only 30 cabins and a main lodge. Dotted under the pines, each cabin has a theme—from the festive St. Nick's, once part of a Santa's village, to the old-world Norway House, carved in the manner of a 13th-century Norwegian cottage. All are cozy, offer private baths and many have kitchenettes. Three function as bed and breakfasts.

The Sea Ranch Lodge

T h e   S e a   R a n c h ,   C a l i f o r n i a

VITAL STATISTICS:

KEY SPECIES:
Steelhead

Season:
All year

Accommodations:
LODGE WITH VACATION HOME RENTALS
NUMBER OF GUEST ROOMS: 20
MAXIMUM NUMBER OF GUESTS: 29

Conference Groups: Yes

Meals: A la carte

Rates:
From $125 for 1 per night; plus
$15 for each additional person

Guides: $175 per day

Gratuities: Client's discretion

Preferred Payment:
MasterCard, Visa

Getting There:
About 2 hours north of San
Francisco on Rt. 1.

Other Activities:
Golf, hiking, bird watching,
biking, wildlife photography,
whale watching.

Contact:
Rosemary McGinnis
The Sea Ranch Lodge, PO
Box 44, The Sea Ranch,
CA 95497; 800/732-
7262, fax 707/785-2917,
email searanch@
mcn.org, website
http://www.
searanchvillage.com

Steelhead run in a hidden gem of a river
that joins the Pacific near this isolated resort.

THERE IS, on the northern coast of Sonoma County, a charming resort whose weathered buildings crouch on a rocky finger that projects into the Pacific pounding below. Nothing, save its golf course and vacation homes, is nearby. Except, that is, for the tiny steelhead stream that blooms in winter when runoff breaches the bar at its mouth. You won't find this stream in many guidebooks or on large-scale maps. It's only six miles long and most of it is not accessible by road. What there is of it is narrow, like a necklace spread beneath the redwoods. Its name is the Gualala River.

Seldom wider than 50 feet and not deeper than six, the riverbottom is gravelly and easily waded. Steelhead averaging six to eight pounds enter the river when the bar washes out sometime between Thanksgiving and the first week of December. The fish flow into the river and move through the deeper cuts. It is good fishing then, but it gets better as the season progresses. Since the river is short, steelhead finish their spawn early, and begin moving back downriver in late January and February. Jeff Leopold (707/436-7277), who fishes the river, believes that post-spawn steelhead are more aggressive than those that are moving upstream. Still, good anglers catch and release only one steelhead per day on average, maybe two. Like all who fish for these sea-running rainbows, Leopold has had days when he's released 18 fish. He's also gone 15 days without a hookup. Heavy rains will discolor the river, but it clears in two or three days and that's when the fishing is best. While spinning is legal, flyfishing is the preferred method. A nine-foot 7-weight rod, sink-tip line and 4X tippet will deliver a No. 8 purple Boss or flame Comet down where the steelies lie. The first three or four miles of the river fish best; the easiest access is to drive to Annapolis and walk in. Fishing here tails off in March when tides seal the rivermouth. From The Sea Ranch, you can also fish the Garcia, 30 miles north, or the Russian, an hour or so south.

The Gualala is an intimate river, complemented by The Sea Ranch Lodge. The sound of the surf soothes in an elegantly modern atmosphere in which telephones and TVs are purposely absent. Rooms are bright and airy even when fog shrouds the coast, and the fire on the hearth in the main lodge feels so good. Pause for refreshment in the solarium overlooking the ocean, or play a little golf along the coast. Organic herbs and vegetables complement fresh salmon in tastefully prepared and presented California cuisine served in the lodge's restaurant, Points.

Blackfire Flyfishing Guest Ranch

Angel Fire, New Mexico

Book a house and private lake on this working ranch, then catch five-pound trout until your arms are weak.

VITAL STATISTICS:

KEY SPECIES:
Brown, cutthroat and rainbow trout

Season:
June through October

Accommodations:
GUEST HOUSE
NUMBER OF GUEST ROOMS: 3
MAXIMUM NUMBER OF GUESTS: 12

Conference Groups: Yes

Meals: American plan

Rates:
From $125 per person per day, double occupancy (minimum 2-day stay)

Guides: From $150 per person per day

Gratuities: 20%

Preferred Payment:
Cash or check

Getting There:
One hour southeast of Taos. Fly to Albuquerque, rent a car. About a 3-hour drive. Lodge provides specific directions.

Other Activities:
Hunting, nature walks, bird watching, self-guided auto tours, golf, tennis, rafting, wildlife photography.

Contact:
Mickey or Maggie Greenwood Blackfire Flyfishing Guest Ranch, PO Box 981, Angel Fire, NM 87710; 505/377-6870, fax 505/377-3807.

THE DREAM IS IN ALL OF US: a house with a private lake loaded with leviathan browns, rainbows and cutthroats. How big? Well, the rainbows generally range between four and eight pounds, the cutts and browns, two to five pounds. The ranch season opens in June and continues through October, with June through August providing the best action. While trout will hammer dries on occasion, most of the lake's denizens fall to streamers and nymphs. Fish a 5 weight with a sink-tip line from float tube, canoe or shore, your choice. Around the lake are stands of pine and hills that roll upward to mountains in the distance. There's nothing else, except for bald and golden eagles and maybe an elk, to keep you company. For as little as $750 apiece you and a buddy can have the lake and its lodge to yourselves for a week. Blackfire books only one party at a time.

If fishing the lake pales, and everyone gets tired of five-pound 'bows running deep into the backing, a short drive will take you to the Red River, Rio Grande or Cimarron. These rivers and several smaller streams drain the Sangre de Cristo Mountains. Runoff inhibits fishing until mid-June, but it picks up after that, peaking in early fall. A guide isn't necessary to fish the lake, but you may want one if you plan on exploring other water in the area. You also may want to check out the lodge's flyfishing schools.

Located on a 133-acre working ranch, the lodge is a modern three-bedroom home with two baths that can accommodate a maximum of 12 anglers. Dinners have a Southwestern flair...chicken fajitas or blue corn, red chili enchiladas and breakfasts are simple and good...homemade blueberry coffeecake and fresh fruit. MSG/salt free, vegetarian and heart healthy diets are available on request.

"Half-pound" steelhead on light rods are the rage at Morrison's
Rogue River Lodge near Merlin, Oregon, but their nickname belies
the power of these young steelies that average 15 inches. — page 179.

Cottages is a misnomer for the three fine guest houses
of Lonesome Duck on the Williamson River at Chiloquin, Oregon.
Big rainbows are the fish of choice here. — page 178.

Rizuto's San Juan River Lodge

Navajo Dam, New Mexico

This is a year-round fishery where rainbows average 17 inches and you'll hook 20 or more a day.

VITAL STATISTICS:

KEY SPECIES:
Rainbow trout

Season:
All year

Accommodations:
MOTEL CABINS
NUMBER OF GUEST ROOMS: 8
MAXIMUM NUMBER OF GUESTS: 16

Conference Groups: No

Meals: Restaurants nearby

Rates:
$75 for 2 per night

Guides: $250 for 2 per day

Gratuities: $20 per angler

Preferred Payment:
Major credit cards

Getting There:
Farmington, New Mexico, and Durango, Colorado, are the closest airports; rent a car or, if you book a 3-night/2-day package, Rizuto or one of his staff will provide transportation.

Other Activities:
Sight-seeing, hiking, bird watching.

Contact:
Peggy Harrell
Rizuto's San Juan River Lodge, PO Box 6309, 1796 Hwy. 173, Navajo Dam, NM 87419; 505/632-3893, fax 505/632-8798, email flyreel@aol.com

Represented By:
Marriott's Flyfishing Store, 714/525-1827.

THERE'S NO OFF-SEASON at this lodge a mile south of the quality water on the San Juan in northwest New Mexico. Sure, in winter the temperature drops and skies turn gray, and it may even snow. But the water comes out of the dam at a consistent 42°F. By the time it reaches the midpoint of the 3 1/2-mile-long no-kill/flies-only stretch, the flow has warmed only to the mid-50s. Cold days in winter stay below freezing, but they are as rare as fishless days on the river. Normally the midday temperature hovers in the 40s and 50s, and sunny days in the 60s are common. No wonder snowbirds from the frozen North beat it to the San Juan when sleet rattles on their windowpanes.

Then there's the matter of the fish. They are big, with the average rainbow between 16 and 18 inches. According to Chuck Rizuto, who guides, runs a flyshop and operates a little lodge for anglers, "everybody will hook at least one 20-inch fish a day." Bigger fish are possible. It's also possible that you'll break off your first few fish. These guys like their flies small (No. 18 to 22) in the main, and their tippets fine (5X to 6X). Rods should be long, limber and light. Not only are the fish of good size, but they readily take artificials. Baetis duns and midge clusters produce consistently on top. Under the surface, use the San Juan Worm. In an average float of the quality water stretch, anglers will hook 20 to 40 fish. Below, in the next 13 miles where bait and spinfishing is legal, the number of hookups will be about half that (still not bad). Clearly the highest concentrations of fish are closer to the dam. And the closer to the dam, the greater the percentage of rainbows to browns.

Good, basic accommodations await you at this lodge. Two cabins each contain four motel-like rooms with private baths and daily maid service. Meals are available in nearby restaurants. Rizuto's flyshop is at hand. Prices for guided floats and wading trips are reasonable. And the river fishes well all year long. What more could you want?

Step Back Inn
A z t e c ,   N e w   M e x i c o

If you don't catch a trout, the trip is free.

VITAL STATISTICS:

KEY SPECIES:
Rainbow trout

Season:
All year

Accommodations:
HOTEL
NUMBER OF GUEST ROOMS: 40
MAXIMUM NUMBER OF GUESTS: 80

Conference Groups: Yes

Meals: Restaurant in hotel

Rates:
From $58 per night for 2

Guides: $265 for float trip
for 2

Gratuities: Client's discretion

Preferred Payment:
Major credit cards

Getting There:
Durango, Colorado, and
Farmington, New Mexico, are
the closest airports. Rent a car
at either airport and then drive
to the inn.

Other Activities:
Golf, tennis, swimming, boating,
hiking, bird watching,
antiquing, biking, wildlife
photography.

Contact:
Karen Rapp
Step Back Inn, 103 W.
Aztec Blvd., Aztec, NM
87410; 505/334-1200,
fax 505/334-9858.

SOFT-SPOKEN TROUT GUIDE Jerry Freeman makes his clients two promises. Catch a fish bigger than the shop record, and the trip's on him. "Sure," you say, "big deal." And then there's his second pledge: You don't catch trout, the trip is free. Are we paying attention now?

Freeman (970/385-4665) is talking about the San Juan, a world-class tailwater for eight-plus miles below Navajo Dam. Cold and consistent, except when it's a bit higher in June, the river holds some of the finest rainbows in the West. Fish of 18 to 20 inches are commonplace. When they reach 22 to 26 inches, things begin to get interesting. A smattering of 28s and 29s are landed each year, and in 1996 two 30-inchers tied the shop record. Generally, the smaller the fly, the bigger the fish: Blue-Winged Olives in Sizes 18 to 20, midges in 24, 26 and 28 (he uses a 2X magnifier to tie them on), midge pupae in the 20s, larva in Size 18. San Juan Worms, Size 16, are about as large as Freeman goes.

Except, that is, for a few magic days in early July when black carpenter ants swarm. You never know when it will happen, but when it does, the fish go bonkers. You'll throw a No. 6 Black Ant dressed to float high. You can skate it across the water, and a big old rainbow will chase it like a beagle after a rabbit. Nine-foot rods are the order of the day on the San Juan, and anglers seldom need anything heavier than a No. 4 or 5. The softness of the lighter rods tends to protect the 5X and 6X tippets required for fishing all but the Black Ants.

Freeman floats the river and occasionally pulls ashore so anglers can work wadeable water where fish are rising. Algae on the round river rocks is very slippery, and felt soles are a necessity. So, too, is a belt at the top of your waders. The river is open, so there's no problem with backcasts. Wind is rarely a problem either. If the tailwater fishing pales for one reason or another, try the high mountain creeks above Durango, or the small tailwater at Dolores Dam. Freeman and his guides supply all the flies you'll need, and tippets too, when you fish with them.

You'll want to stay at Tweeti Blancett's Step Back Inn in Aztec, a 20-minute drive from the dam. Of deep blue-gray wood, with a full-length front porch, the inn projects the motif of an old West Main Street hotel. Each of the rooms is named for a locally prominent pioneer, the famous and infamous alike. With turn-of-the-century ambience, rooms also contain all key modern amenities. Guests awaken to the smell of freshly perked coffee. Breakfast and dinner are available in the restaurant downstairs.

The Lodge at Chama
Chama, New Mexico

The consummate guest ranch in northern New Mexico offers fine fishing as well.

VITAL STATISTICS:

KEY SPECIES:
Rainbow, cutthroat, brown and brook trout

Season:
All year

Accommodations:
MOUNTAIN RANCH
NUMBER OF GUEST ROOMS: 11
MAXIMUM NUMBER OF GUESTS: 22

Conference Groups: Yes

Meals: American plan

Rates:
$375 per person per day

Guides: Included

Gratuities: Client's discretion

Preferred Payment:
Major credit cards

Getting There:
Albuquerque, New Mexico is the closest commercial airport. Rent a car and drive. The ranch also has a strip for private planes.

Other Activities:
Hiking, bird watching, wildlife photography, horseback riding, sporting clays, hunting.

Contact:
Frank Simms
The Lodge at Chama, PO Box 127, Chama, NM 87520; 505/756-2133, fax 505/756-2519.

HIGH IN THE SOUTHERN Rocky Mountains, a bit south of the Colorado border, is the tiny town of Chama. Nearby, you'll find excellent fishing in Rio Chama and Rio Brazos, and a wonderful ranch retreat—owned by the Jicarilla Apache Tribe—with outstanding fishing of its own. On 32,000 acres overlooking the tawny and verdant Chama Valley, the 13,500-square-foot Lodge at Chama has been named both Fishing and Hunting Lodge of the Year and Best Sporting Resort by *Andrew Harper's Hideaway Report*.

Anglers will find varied water. On the ranch are numerous lakes and ponds stocked with browns, brookies, cutthroats and rainbows. The rainbows are the heavyweights, tipping the scales at 10 to 12 pounds. Cutthroats follow in the four- to five-pound range, with brookies and browns running two pounds or more. A private fishery, no licenses are required here, and anglers may use spinning as well as flytackle as long as lures have single barbless hooks. Some of the ponds are designated catch-and-release water, but from others anglers may keep up to four fish per day.

The Rio Chama flows right through town and has ample public water. Stocked rainbows predominate, and there are some self-sustaining browns. The tailwaters below Heron Dam and El Vado Reservoir provide some action, with big browns below El Vado being the better alternative. Guides from the lodge also float anglers down the San Juan below Navajo Dam. The San Juan is one of the four or five top tailwaters in the U. S., and a chance to fish it for rainbows that consistently exceed 18 inches must not be missed.

But if it's wild trout that you want, ask your guide about fishing the Rio Brazos. A tumbling and swift freestone stream, seldom wider than 30 feet, the Rio Brazos chases down through narrow canyons and surges through brushy meadows. The angling is challenging, but the results are worth it. The population of brown trout of 18 inches or more is sizeable, though the fish are wary. Much of the stream is controlled by private interests, but access is possible with permission.

After a day's fishing, try a round of sporting clays, then chill out in the sauna and whirlpool, fix a drink and slump into one of the plush leather couches under the heavy timbered ceiling in front of the huge stone fireplace. Heads of western game adorn the walls. Meals are both hearty and gourmet and feature traditional steaks and roasts as well as buffalo, trout and fowl often prepared with New Mexican flare.

C&J Lodge

M a u p i n ,   O r e g o n

A B&B with wild red-side trout and steelhead down in the Deschutes Canyon: Who could ask for more?

VITAL STATISTICS:

KEY SPECIES:
Steelhead; red-sided trout

Season:
All year

Accommodations:
FRAME BED AND BREAKFAST
NUMBER OF GUEST ROOMS: 11
MAXIMUM NUMBER OF GUESTS: 30

Conference Groups: Yes

Meals: Several packages

Rates:
From $65 for 2 per night

Guides: $375 for 2 per day

Gratuities: Client's discretion

Preferred Payment:
Major credit cards

Getting There:
Fly to Portland, rent a car and drive to the lodge.

Other Activities:
Bird watching, biking, whitewater rafting, sporting clays, pheasant hunting.

Contact:
Carrol or Judy White
C&J Lodge, 304
Bakeoven Rd., PO Box
130, Maupin, OR 97037;
800/395-3903, fax
541/395-2494, email
cnjlodge@aol.com

ASK ANYONE TO TELL YOU the name of the best steelhead river in Oregon and odds are they'll start talking about the Deschutes. Ask them the name of a riverfront place to stay while you fish it, and they'll likely scratch their heads. Here's one: the C&J Lodge on the river at Maupin. C&J's is better known for its succulent beef, chicken and pork barbecue than it is as a bed and breakfast that serves a filling breakfast buffet by the river on summer mornings. You can fish before breakfast, or have breakfast early or late, depending on your fishing schedule.

One hundred miles long, the lower Deschutes is different than other western rivers. You can float it. You can fish it. But you can't fish it from anything that floats. Instituted in the 1940s as a safety measure, the rule now ensures that much of the river never sees a fly. Why? The lower section of the river is more than 100 yards wide, the current is heavy and it's too deep to wade. "Divide the river into quarters," advises guide John Smeraglio of the Deschutes Canyon Fly Shop (541/395-2565). "Fish the quarter nearest you." Often, at dawn, fish are holding under the junipers and aspens along the bank. "You'll never need to wet your knees," says Smeraglio.

Steelhead and "red-sides" constitute the primary sport species in the river, though there are also brown and bull trout. Starting by the end of July and running into December, steelhead of both wild and stocked persuasion use the river. Fish with clipped adipose fins (behind the dorsal) may be and should be kept. While the state stocks these fish to satisfy those who like to catch-and-eat, it's not interested in diluting the wild gene pool with hatchery strains. Wild fish run smaller (four to six pounds) than stocked fish (six to nine pounds). Red-sides are a cross between cutthroat and rainbow. Fast growing (four to five inches a year), red-sides fight more fiercely than their length (12 to 16 inches) or weight (average one to two pounds) would suggest. To fish them, use both dries—midges, little Blue-Winged Olives, Pale Morning Duns and Pale Evening Duns, Salmonflies and Golden Stoneflies—and wets. Bring a 7- or 8-weight system, which will work well for steelhead too.

Attractive, with the false front characteristic of the Old West, C&J Lodge provides rooms with private baths. Some rooms overlook the river. All are comfortably furnished and served by private baths. During steelhead season, breakfast fixings are delivered the night before to anglers' rooms because they like to head for the stream by 5:00 a.m., and not even the cook is working that early.

Grande Ronde Lodge
LeGrande, Oregon

Hidden away in the Blue Mountains is a little lodge on a river that runs heavy with steelhead.

ABOUT A QUARTER of the size of the Deschutes, the Grande Ronde River rises in the Wallowa/Whitman National Forest on the flanks of the Blue Mountains in northeastern Oregon. It flows a jagged course toward the Snake just north of the border with Washington. Located on the lower leg of the river between Bogan's and Troy is Grande Ronde Lodge, from which John Ecklund's Little Creek Outfitters runs a number of fishing excursions for steelhead, smallmouths and rainbows.

STEELHEAD: A mixture of wild and stocked steelhead run in the Grande Ronde. One of the best introductions to fishing for these finicky sea-run rainbows is through six-day schools featuring Bill McMillan, author of *Dry Line Steelhead.* The curriculum covers topwater steelheading (dry fly, skated fly, walking flies) as well as wet fly presentations. Morning instruction on the first two days is followed by fishing on the lodge's half mile of river. On the last two days, you'll spend all your time streamside with McMillan and your guide. Tuition: $1850 per angler

SMALLMOUTH BASS: When it comes to aggressive warmwater species, smallmouth bass top everyone's list. Little Creek Outfitters guides for smallmouths on the river from June through September. You might also want to check out their four- and five-day float/camp trips on the John Day. Smallies were introduced there in 1971 and they've taken hold in a big way. Anglers frequently have 100-fish days. While most are less than two pounds, occasionally a five-pounder will surprise you. The price: from $1100 per person for a four-day trip.

RAINBOW TROUT: You'll find rainbows in the 14-inch range in the water near the lodge during summer. As with smallmouths, Little Creek runs guided floats on the Grande Ronde where you may encounter bull trout (char) as well. Fish the hatches in the morning and muddlers and leeches after midday. From $1375 per person for a five-day trip.

THE LODGE: Built in 1981, the full-timbered lodge with open beam ceilings combines creature comforts with traditional western ambience. Sit on the back porch and view the river and its canyon beyond. Your room may be upstairs in the main lodge or one of four in the three-bath cedar guest house on a bench 100 feet above the river. Prime ribs, pasta and seafood will greet you when you walk down the hill for dinner. And should you need tackle, you'll find it in the shop next to the lodge.

Lonesome Duck

Chiloquin, Oregon

VITAL STATISTICS:

KEY SPECIES:
Rainbow trout

Season:
End of May through October

Accommodations:
TWO LOG HOMES
NUMBER OF GUEST ROOMS: 6
MAXIMUM NUMBER OF GUESTS: 22

Conference Facilities: Yes

Meals: Cook for yourself or arrange for catering at $35 per person per day

Rates:
From $150 for 2 per night (minimum 2-night stay)

Guides: $240 for 2 per day

Gratuities: Client's discretion

Preferred Payment:
MasterCard, Visa

Getting There:
Fly to Klamath Falls or land private planes at Chiloquin Airport. You will be met by a representative of Lonesome Duck.

Other Activities:
Boating, hiking, bird watching, antiquing, biking, wildlife photography, skiing.

Contact:
Steve Hilbert
Lonesome Duck, PO Box 8164, Incline Village, NV 89452; 800/367-2540.

At times the Williamson fishes like a big spring creek.

WILLIAMSON RIVER RAINBOWS are known for their size. Three- to four-pounders are not rare, fish in the teens are almost frequent enough to be expected and once in a while someone nets a monster of 20 pounds. It happens. How come so big? Upper Klamath Lake, into which the Williamson flows, is like an ocean to these rainbows. They behave more like steelhead and run up the Williamson and Wood rivers when the lake becomes too warm in summer.

Biologists believe that low acidity, high levels of nitrogen and phosphorus and the resultant massive burst of algae and plankton creates a huge population of aquatic and other insects on which the 'bows gorge. Life's great for theses rainbows until there's a cloudy spell. When algae and plankton die and decompose, the pH rockets to ammonialike levels and the fish head for fresher water, which means up the Williamson or into a springhole.

Others liken the Williamson to a big spring creek with prolific hatches: Blue-Winged Olives, Pale Morning Duns, salmonflies, hexagenia, hordes of Gray Drakes. Then there are the tricos and caddis. Heard enough? But it isn't easy. Big trout are selective.

Steve Hilbert knew all this when he built the Lonesome Duck, a little resort of log housekeeping cabins nestled under the pines. Actually, they're not exactly cabins. The Arrowhead Cottage boasts two bedrooms, single bath, dining room, living room, fireplace, kitchen and front porch where you can watch the river roll by. Rivers Edge and Eagle's Nest are larger, having additional sleeping lofts and baths. Eagle's Nest is a non-smoking cabin and the view from the front porch across a pond to the mountains is stunning. Bring your own food or arrange for the Hilberts to provide meals in your dining room.

Lonesome Duck owns a mile and a half of the Williamson. The runs are deep with massive rock structure. Fish big Woolly Buggers or leeches or, in the evening, when the wind dies, work a hexagenia pattern over the weedbeds. You won't have to worry about setting the hook. The rainbows do it for you. Boats to fish the river are available at the lodge and licenses and tackle can be found at Williamson River Anglers. If you want, Hilbert will recommend a guide or you're welcome to fish freelance.

Morrison's Rogue River Lodge

Merlin, Oregon

Fight a steelhead "half-pounder" on a light rod and don't be surprised if it goes 12 pounds.

VITAL STATISTICS:

KEY SPECIES:
Steelhead; salmon

Season:
May through November
Accommodations:
LOG LODGE AND COTTAGES
NUMBER OF GUEST ROOMS: 13
MAXIMUM NUMBER OF GUESTS: 34
Conference Groups: Yes
Meals: American plan
Rates:
Packages from $75 per person per day
Guides: $225 per day for 2 anglers
Gratuities: $25 to $50
Preferred Payment:
Discover, MasterCard, Visa
Getting There:
The closest airport is Medford-Rogue Valley; rent a car there and drive to the lodge.
Other Activities:
Tennis, whitewater rafting swimming, hiking, bird watching.

Contact:
Michelle Hanten
Morrison's Rogue River Lodge, 8500 Galice Rd., Merlin, OR 97532; 800/826-1963, fax 541/476-4953.

ONCE ONE OF ZANE GREY'S favorite rivers, the Rogue became one of the most popular steelhead rivers in the West. Intense fishing pressure as well as logging took their tolls, and the Rogue slipped from the ranks of fashionable angling destinations. Despite this, a small and loyal cadre of knowledgeable anglers makes its way to Morrison's each fall to fish for "half-pounders"—steelhead of 12 to 18 inches that weigh two pounds or so, fight like alley cats and run like lightning. They enter Morrison's waters in mid to late September. Traditional steelheading demands heavy rods, 8s or 9s, but these fireballs are made for 5 weights. Just make sure your reel has at least 100 yards of backing. Morrison's will ferry you to good runs via jetboat, or you may engage a guide and float the river.

While you're there, you may want to fish for mature steelhead as well. They run in the lodge's waters in late September, reaching full stride in October before tailing off in mid-November when Morrison's closes for the winter. You may also encounter the fall run of chinooks and cohos. Most times salmon are only taken on lures or bait, but not always. If you're working light gear for half-pounders and one of these big guys slams your fly, you're in for a treat or heartbreak and maybe both. Chinooks also run the Rogue from mid-May through June. The upper river can provide good summer trout fishing, particularly during the June salmonfly hatch. And a little travel will put you on the Wood, Williamson or Umpqua for trout in the height of summer.

Situated next to a heavily pined hillside, the red roof of Morrison's has been a beacon for anglers since it was opened as a fishing lodge in 1946. The lodge wears its age with grace and gentility. Four homey guest rooms are in the main log lodge and nine others are in cottages with fireplaces. The restaurant is renowned for gourmet regional cuisine (poached salmon with blanc sauce) and a good cellar of imported as well as California and Northwest vintages. And at this Orvis-endorsed lodge, you'll find a complete flyshop that rents and sells whatever you need.

Steamboat Inn

S t e a m b o a t ,   O r e g o n

VITAL STATISTICS:

KEY SPECIES:
Steelhead

Season:
March through December
Accommodations:
CABINS WITH ALL AMENITIES
NUMBER OF GUEST ROOMS: 19
MAXIMUM NUMBER OF GUESTS: 64
Conference Groups: Yes
Meals: Meals additional
Rates:
From $125 for 2
Guides: From $175 per day
for one angler
Gratuities: 15%
Preferred Payment:
MasterCard, Visa
Getting There:
Eugene, Oregon is the closest
commercial airport. Rent a car
there and drive to the lodge.
Other Activities:
Rafting, swimming, hiking,
biking.

Contact:
Jim Van Loan
Steamboat Inn, 42705 N.
Umpqua Hwy.,
Steamboat, OR 97447-
9703; 800/840-8825, fax
541/498-2411.

Represented By:
John Eustice & Assoc., 800/288-
0886.

Fish the last of Zane Grey's rivers from a lodge established for steelheading anglers.

ZANE GREY, AMERICA'S most prolific writer of westerns, loved two rivers best. The Delaware River between New York and Pennsylvania was his first love. There he wrote the first of many fishing stories and the novel, *Riders of the Purple Sage*, that brought him his first fame. A generation later, Grey was renowned worldwide for his westerns and his prowess with rod and reel, and to fish summer steelhead, he came to the North Fork of the Umpqua. Here, in 1937, he suffered the stroke that led to his death in 1939. It was his last river, and he treasured it.

From Rock Creek 31 miles upstream to Soda Springs Dam, the North Umpqua is flyfishing-only water. Spinfishers can be successful by using a clear plastic bubble as weight to cast traditional flies. In the main, this is large water with deep runs and pools. (Umpqua means thundering waters in the language of the Yoncalla Indians). At places the channel is narrow and the constricted river is swift, brawling, and difficult and sometimes dangerous to wade. Steelheading is permitted year-round, but the better fishing occurs from July through October. Doc Crawford, in his useful and informative *North Umpqua Angler's Guide*, reports that the river generally fishes best from dawn until the sun has been on the water for two hours. A 7-weight system will suffice, though an 8 may provide anglers with a bit more brawn and power for pitching big flies into the wind. Early in the season when the water is cold and heavy, larger, brighter patterns such as the No. 2 Poodle Dog work well. As water warms and lowers, artificials should become smaller and darker.

Among the best locales for picking up info is during dinner at the Steamboat Inn. This place is as much a part of the lore of the Umpqua as Grey's exploits. A relic of the old North Umpqua Lodge, the inn's wide sugar-pine table has hosted fishermen for more than 60 years. On the table today you'll find the superb regional cuisine of co-owner Sharon Van Loan and her colleague Pat Lee (also an outstanding steelhead guide). Opening in the library with an aperitif and hors d'oeuvres, the meal moves to the dining room for entrees of fish, fowl, beef or lamb accompanied by local vegetables and fruits and Oregon wines. As it was when the table was new, dinner is only served after the day's last light has left the river. A range of accommodations is available: eight pine-paneled streamside cabins, five modern cottages in the woods with soaking tubs, fireplaces, lofts and mini-kitchens; two luxurious and romantic river suites and a quartet of three-bedroom homes.

The Big K Guest Ranch

Elkton, Oregon

Smallmouth is spoken here, with a few steelhead on the side.

VITAL STATISTICS:

KEY SPECIES:
Smallmouth bass; steelhead; sturgeon

Season:
All year

Accommodations:
RESORT
NUMBER OF GUEST ROOMS: 20
MAXIMUM NUMBER OF GUESTS: 80

Meals: American plan

Conference Groups: Yes

Rates:
From $195 for 2 per day

Guides: From $200 per day for 1

Gratuities: $20 per day

Preferred Payment:
Discover, MasterCard, Visa

Getting There:
Fly to Eugene and rent a car or arrange in advance for lodge shuttle at $50.

Other Activities:
Birding, biking, hunting, sporting clays, wildlife photography.

Contact:
Kathie Williamson
The Big K Guest Ranch,
20029 Highway 138 W.,
Elkton, OR 97436;
800/390-2445.

ON THE SWEEPING LOOP of the middle Umpqua, emerald green in the summer sun, smallmouth, not steelhead, is the game. White and chartreuse spinner and buzzbaits, cast hard against the bank in deep shadows of towering firs, provoke strikes from bass that frequently top five pounds. Flyrodders will find that Woolly Buggers work just as well. The midsection of the Umpqua, south of Elkton, may have the greatest population of record-size smallmouth of any stream in Oregon, according to that state's Department of Fish and Wildlife.

Yet, while smallmouth reign, don't be deceived. Steelhead run from December to March and 25-inch fish are not uncommon. If that doesn't strike your fancy, try shad and chinooks in May. Sturgeon are legal all year and have been caught upwards of 70 pounds. And September brings more chinooks up the river.

Though driftboats are the most popular conveyance for anglers, much of the water near the ranch is wadeable. And though fly is the tackle of choice for all but sturgeon, spinfishermen do well. The middle Umpqua is good-size water and The Big K, a 2500-acre working ranch that's been in the Kesterson family for decades, fronts on 10 miles of it. The ranch employs a staff of guides, but guests may freelance if they wish. Boxed lunches are available for anglers out on the water all day.

Twenty log guest cabins climb the gentle hill behind the main lodge that overlooks the river. All rooms have private baths, and all are handicapped accessible. Dinners feature hearty cuts of beef and lamb as well as quail, duck and salmon. Guests wanting an after-dinner smoke will do so outside, as the lodge and cabins are smoke free.

If you're fishing in the fall, think about taking a firearm. The Big K guides for elk, deer and turkey. Ducks, geese and grouse round out your options.

The Nordic cabins at Sorensen's Resort in
Hope Valley, California, house anglers who fish the
West Fork of the Carson and nap in the hammocks
between hatches. — page 169.

Williamson River Club at Crystalwood Lodge

Fort Klamath, Oregon

Fish for trophy browns and rainbows while staying at a remodeled, first-rate ranch homestead.

VITAL STATISTICS:

KEY SPECIES:
Brown and rainbow trout

Season:
May through November
Accommodations:
REMODELED FAMILY RANCH
NUMBER OF GUEST ROOMS: 7
MAXIMUM NUMBER OF GUESTS: 14
Conference Groups: Yes
Meals: American plan
Rates:
From $195 per person per day,
$1365 per week, single
occupancy
Guides: $290 for 2 per day
Gratuities: $30 per day
Preferred Payment:
MasterCard, Visa
Getting There:
Medford (75 minutes away) and
Klamath Falls (45 minutes)
both have commercial flights.
The ranch van will provide
transportation for $200 round
trip.
Other Activities:
Golf, canoeing, whitewater
rafting, boating, hiking, bird
watching, biking, wildlife
photography.

Contact:
Rich McIntyre
Williamson River Club,
PO Box 469, Fort
Klamath, OR 97626;
541/381-2322, fax
541/381-2328.

Represented By:
Angler Adventures, 800/628-
1447; Frontiers International,
800/245-1950; Tightline
Services, 401/625-1936.

WHEN RICH MCINTYRE SET OUT to establish the Williamson River Club as a private anglers' club similar to the old, tradition-steeped establishments of the Northeast, he failed to take into consideration that the Eastern clubs were all located in relatively close proximity to major urban centers. His error, if one can call it that, is a boon for traveling anglers the world over. Now there's an absolutely first-class angling establishment in the heart of some of the finest water in the Northwest. The club is located on and fishes 130-acre Crystalwood Ranch and a second ranch of 230 acres nearby. Here you'll find a number of spring creeks and ponds managed for trophy rainbows and steelhead. A short walk from the lodge puts you into fish of memorable proportions.

That's just part of the attraction. Within a few minutes' drive are the Wood and Williamson rivers. The Wood, a trophy spring creek, holds resident populations of browns in the five- to six-pound category. You'll also find two races of migratory rainbows, reportedly a unique strain with genetic links to the steelhead that spawned in these waters before dams were built downstream. Fish here are huge for the lower 48; 15-pounders are taken every year. Similar but larger than the Wood, the Williamson River holds a resident population of rainbows and hosts two migratory strains. Fish range between three and 12 pounds. With significant populations of aquatic insects, both the Wood and the Williamson are fertile rivers. The best time to fish them is in July (trico and a hexagenia hatch) and in August and September, when 'hoppers dot the surface and big rainbows are there to feed on them.

Crystalwood Lodge began its life as the homestead on the ranch. Over the years it's seen several renovations, the most recent at the hands of Rich and wife, Karen Greene. You'll find seven bedrooms with private baths. Dinners are elegant: fine wines, crystal and china. Rates are for lodging and meals. Guests may fish without a guide if they wish, but most hire one from the staff employed by the ranch.

Yamsi Ranch
Chiloquin, Oregon

VITAL STATISTICS:

KEY SPECIES:
Rainbow and brook trout

Season:
May through October

Accommodations:
LODGE AND CABINS
NUMBER OF GUEST ROOMS: 7
MAXIMUM NUMBER OF GUESTS: 12

Conference Groups: Yes

Meals: American plan

Rates:
$200 per person per day (minimum 3-day stay)

Guides: $125 per day for 2 anglers

Gratuities: $20 per day per angler

Preferred Payment:
Cash or check

Getting There:
Fly to Klamath Falls, rent a car and drive to the ranch.

Other Activities:
Hiking, bird watching, wildlife photography.

Contact:
Gerda Hyde
Yamsi Ranch, Box 371, Chiloquin, OR 97624; 541/783-2403.

Represented By:
Kaufmann's Streamborn, 800/442-4359.

Fishing is an integral element of this holistically managed ranch.

WITH THE HEADWATERS of the Williamson River flowing through its 5000 acres, Yamsi Ranch, a working spread, controls some of the best trout fishing in south-central Oregon. When it comes to hospitality, this laid-back holistic cattle and trout ranch does itself and its guests proud. Everything has its place and is part of a natural progression of life at Yamsi. Owner Gerda Hyde doesn't want angling (flyfishing and catch-and-release only) left to the vagaries of chance, however, so she also has a 300-acre man-made lake, stocked with rainbow and brook trout, about 15 miles from the ranch.

The lake is for fans of bellyboating. But most will enjoy the serpentine ranch water that meanders through the meadows over beds of pumice. Rainbow and brook trout, once stocked but now wild, feed on a rich diet of aquatic insects and crustacea. Hatches are prolific. Hexagenia, isonychia and Black Drakes come off often, as do esoteric mayflies indigenous to the Williamson and nearby streams. Don't forget caddis and, later in the season, terrestrials. Five miles downstream from the ranch, the Williamson matures. Wild rainbows and brookies up to 20 inches abound. There's some debate about whether the lower Williamson supports a significant resident population of big trout. A few argue that those in the river system come up from Upper Klamath Lake. And it's true that when the lake warms in summer, big rainbows move up into the cooler Williamson. In addition to the Williamson, the nearby Wood River offers good angling.

Utterly charming, the twin-chimneyed quarried rock lodge is nestled amongst trees and mature flowering shrubs. Seven rustic bedrooms, five in the main lodge and two in cottages (all with shared baths; electricity is only available when the ranch's generators are on), are comfortable. And conversation around the dinner table will be as eclectic as Hyde's meals, served ranch-style with no menu. Here is a place to kick back, catch a few fish either with a guide or on your own, and watch deer, antelope and elk roam the meadows. At night you'll go to sleep to the chorus of coyotes.

Brightwater House
Forks, Washington

Innkeeper Richard Chesmore fishes 200 days a year in his own backyard!

VITAL STATISTICS:

KEY SPECIES:
Steelhead; chinook, sockeye and silver salmon; cutthroat trout

Season:
All year

Accommodations:
CONTEMPORARY WOOD RANCH
NUMBER OF GUEST ROOMS: 3
MAXIMUM NUMBER OF GUESTS: 6

Conference Groups: No
Meals: Breakfast only
Rates:
From $65 per night for 2
Guides: About $235 per day
Gratuities: Client's discretion
Preferred Payment:
MasterCard, Visa
Getting There:
Fly to Fairchild Airport in Port Angeles, Washington, rent a car and drive to the inn.
Other Activities:
Canoeing, rafting, swimming, boating, hiking, bird watching, biking, wildlife photography.

Contact:
Richard Chesmore Brightwater House, 440 Brightwater Dr., PO Box 1222, Forks, WA 98331; 360/374-5453.

THE SOL DUC RIVER is one of those rivers that slides off the flanks of the Olympic Mountains, pushing for the Pacific. It is an unusual river in a number of ways. In June and July, sockeye salmon spawn in it and in Lake Pleasant near its headwaters. Three distinct runs keep the river in steelhead all year. And if year-round steelheading isn't enough, you'll find fall and spring runs of chinook and silvers in July. Naturally, cutthroats up to 24 inches follow the salmon.

Steelhead are the premiere species. In October, hatchery stock begins to work its way upstream. In mid-January, native spawners enter the system. These are the biggest, some reaching more than 20 pounds. As that run passes, a final surge of slightly smaller (six- to 15-pound fish) enters in late May and remains through September, when the cycle begins again. Despite their prevalence, they are not easily caught. The Sol Duc is not a big stream and it is easily waded. But seldom is there room for long backcasts. (Spinfishing is permitted on much of the river, but Brightwater House caters to flyfishers.) Rollcasting is a refined art here. That complicates matters because as water levels fall in summer, steelhead get spooky. "You have to fish for them by stealth," says innkeeper Richard Chesmore.

Here is a man who, like B'rer Rabbit, fell into the brier patch. No one in his right mind wants to operate a country inn. After spotting the place in a real estate ad, Richard and wife Beth looked it over and snapped it up. "Our deck is a double-haul from the river," he almost chortles, before going on to say that he spends at least part of 200 days every year on the river. The Chesmores live in a contemporary wooden house and rent three upstairs rooms to guests. One is a small suite with a private bath; the other two share a bath. Breakfast is the only meal of the day—quiche and fritattas—but custom gourmet dinners are available with advance notice from the Miller Tree Inn nearby. With 60 acres and 3500 feet on the Sol Duc, there's ample water to fish. Some approach it solo but many hire guides such as Bob Pigott (360/327-2554) or Michael Struznik (360/374-9345). Tackle and flies can be found at the Manuel Bernardo's Quality Flyfish Shop (360/452-5942).

ALASKA

YOU MIGHT have time to read Jack London or Robert Service in this land of salmon and perpetual twilight, but don't count on it. You'll be busy with five species of salmon: kings, chums, sockeyes, pinks and silvers; rainbows so big and plentiful that they boggle the imagination; dolly varden; and in the southern panhandle, steelhead and sea-run cutthroats. And for those who like to haul fish up from the deep, halibut await your pleasure. The Iliamna region of the headwaters of Bristol Bay is thick with lodges boasting services ranging from housekeeping cabins and unguided fishing to daily flyouts. The fishing there is the best in the state. But for a change of pace (and fewer anglers), take a look at Kodiak and Afognak islands or the wilderness in Alaska's southeast tail.

Lodges:

1. AFOGNAK WILDERNESS LODGE
2. ALAGNAK LODGE
3. ALASKA RAINBOW LODGE
4. ALASKA WILDERNESS PENINSULA SAFARI CAMP
5. ANGLER'S ALIBI
6. ANGLER'S PARADISE LODGES:
   GROSVENOR LODGE
   KULIK LODGE
7. ANIAK RIVER LODGE
8. BARANOF WILDERNESS LODGE
9. BOARDWALK WILDERNESS LODGE
10. BRISTOL BAY LODGE
11. CHELATNA LAKE LODGE
12. CHRIS GOLL'S RAINBOW RIVER LODGE
13. CLASSIC ALASKA CHARTERS
14. COPPER RIVER FLY FISHING LODGE
15. CREEKSIDE INN
16. CRYSTAL CREEK LODGE
17. DEER CREEK COTTAGES
18. ENCHANTED LAKE LODGE
19. FISHING UNLIMITED LODGE
20. GOODNEWS RIVER LODGE
21. ILIASKA LODGE
22. ISLAND POINT LODGE
23. KATMAI LODGE
24. KING KO INN
25. KODIAK ISLAND RIVER CAMPS
26. LIONS DEN WILDERNESS LODGE
27. MIKE CUSACK'S KING SALMON LODGE

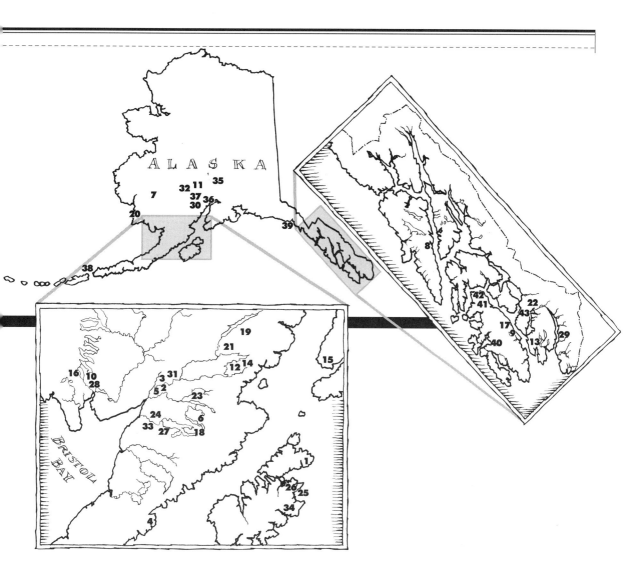

References:

THE ANGLER'S GUIDE TO ALASKA
— *Evan and Margaret Swenson*
Falcon Publishing Co.,
PO Box 1718, Helena, MT 59624;
406/442-6597

ROADSIDE GUIDE TO
FLY FISHING ALASKA
FLIES FOR ALASKA
FLY FISHING ALASKA
— *Anthony J. Route*
Johnson Books, 1870 S. 57th Court,
Boulder, CO 80301;
800/258-5830

HOW TO CATCH ALASKA'S
TROPHY SPORTFISH
THE ALASKA ANGLER'S HANDBOOK
FISH ALASKA ON $15 A DAY
CHRIS BATIN'S 20 GREAT ALASKA
FISHING ADVENTURES
— *Christopher M. Batin*
Alaska Angler Publications
PO Box 83550, Fairbanks, AK 99708;
907/455-8000

Resources:

ALASKA DEPARTMENT OF FISH AND
GAME
Div. of Sport Fishing, PO Box 25526,
Juneau, AK 99802-5526; 907/465-
4180, website
http://www.state.ak.us/local/akpages/FI
SH.GAME/adfghome.htm

At Afognak Wilderness Lodge, anglers fish for Pacific salmon,
rainbow trout and halibut while staying at a plush,
owner-built lodge. Seal Bay, Alaska. — page 189.

The Goodnews River Lodge
is a permanent tent camp where anglers
can fish for Pacific salmon or rainbows. Jetboats run them
up- or downriver to the best fishing. — page 209.

Afognak Wilderness Lodge
Seal Bay

A pioneer husband and wife team runs an elegant family-style lodge on Afognak Island.

VITAL STATISTICS:

KEY SPECIES:
Silver, king, pink and sockeye salmon; rainbow trout; halibut

Season:
All year

Accommodations:
LOG CABINS
NUMBER OF GUEST ROOMS: 6
MAXIMUM NUMBER OF GUESTS: 12

Conference Groups: Yes

Meals: American plan

Rates:
$3150 per person per week

Guides: Included

Gratuities: $20 to $50 per day

Preferred Payment:
MasterCard, Visa

Getting There:
Fly to Kodiak, take a floatplane to Seal Bay. About $200 per person round trip.

Other Activities:
Hunting (bear, deer, elk), swimming, boating, bird watching, hiking, wildlife photography, kayaking, waterskiing.

Contact:
Shannon Randall Afognak Wilderness Lodge, Seal Bay, AK 99697; 907/486-6442, fax 907/486-2217.

ALASKA HAS MANY DELIGHTFUL fishing lodges, but none more surprising or casually elegant than Roy and Shannon Randall's Afognak Wilderness Lodge on Seal Bay. A variety of careers lured Randall west from his native Kentucky hills and eventually to Hollywood, where he paid the rent by writing scripts. In 1961, at 28, Roy heard there was still land to be homesteaded in Alaska, and so he camped his way north. At the time, Alaska paid a bounty on seals and a small market existed for fur. He became a sealer, and by hand built a 12x16-foot cabin on the loneliest and most beautiful place he could find. The lonesome part didn't last long. In Kodiak for supplies, he met Shannon, took a liking to her, and invited her to go sealing. She went and stayed, she the skiff man and he the shooter. And when the Marine Mammals Act of 1972 put them out of business, they thought they'd build a guest lodge.

With chainsaws, a pair of homemade calipers and an old hand winch and boom pole, they put up the main lodge building and, later, three two-bedroom cabins with private baths overlooking Seal Bay. In the main lodge, spiral log stairs climb to the second story, which the Randalls have occupied since the cabins were built. Meals...you won't know the meaning of hearty until Shannon feeds you a breakfast of sourdough pancakes, eggs and halibut fingers. At Afognak, everyone—family and guests—eats together, at a long spruce table with stumps for chairs.

Low and brooding, Afognak Island lacks the big rivers of its sibling Kodiak Island, 30 miles across Marmot Straits. Instead, scores of clear streams drain the island's low mountains and the boggy lakes in between. Each of these streams is a magnet for spawning salmon. First come the sockeyes, from June 10 to the middle of July. They're followed by pinks that run through the end of August. Silvers hit full stride from August 1 through September 15. You'll find rainbows up to 20 inches all summer. Because the streams are small and generally shallow, the salmon are accessible not only to you, but to brown bears as well. When fishing the salmon runs, Randall carries a .375 H&H for insurance.

If you prefer to fish the salt, the lodge's fleet of cabin cruisers and Makos can take you trolling for king salmon (up to 40 pounds) or put you to work lifting halibut of up to 300 pounds from the ocean floor. Seals and sea lions abound, as do sub-arctic birds and eagles.

Alagnak Lodge
A l a g n a k   R i v e r

Stay at a comfortable, basic lodge, and fish for salmon, rainbows and grayling in any weather.

VITAL STATISTICS:

KEY SPECIES:
King, silver, sockeye, chum and pink salmon; rainbow trout; grayling

Season:
June through September
Accommodations:
2-STORY WOODEN LODGE
NUMBER OF GUEST ROOMS: 9
MAXIMUM NUMBER OF GUESTS: 21
Conference Groups: Yes
Meals: American plan
Rates:
From $1880 per person for 3 days and 4 nights
Guides: Included
Gratuities: $15 to $20 per day per guest
Preferred Payment:
Cash or check
Getting There:
Fly to King Salmon and take a floatplane to the lodge at no additional expense.
Other Activities:
Bird watching, wildlife photography.

Contact:
**Vin Roccanova
Alagnak Lodge,
4117 Hillcrest Way,
Sacramento, CA 95821;
800/877-9903, fax
916/487-1322.**

Represented By:
High Country Fly Fishers, 801/298-3895.

ALAGNAK LODGE sits on a rise 45 feet above the Alagnak River near the upper end of its tidal zone. There it catches every breeze. Boardwalks, connecting outbuildings to the main lodge where guests stay, keep the mosquitoes down. "When you walk on the tundra," says Vin Roccanova, owner of the lodge, "you'll scare up a cloud of mosquitoes that'll follow you everywhere."

Without ever setting foot on terra infirma, you can get to the 18-foot skiffs docked at the base of the hill. A crank of the outboard will take you and your guide out onto the river. Seven or eight miles upstream is the boundary of Katmai National Park. A few miles beyond you'll find the braided zone (four miles of channels and little islands with good flyfishing water when fish are running), and another 20 minutes will bring you to some of the best rainbow and grayling water on the Alagnak. The river carries all five species of Pacific salmon: kings (20 to 60 pounds) from late June through August, silvers (eight to 17 pounds) from late July into September, sockeyes (four to nine pounds) from mid-June through mid-July, chums (eight to 17 pounds) and pinks (two to eight pounds) from mid-July through late August. Rainbows up to 10 pounds and grayling to four run from the second week in June through September. The best time to be there is in early June when rainbows are ravenous or in September when they are gorging on salmon spawn.

Most fishing is done from boats captained by guides. If, after dinner, you haven't fished your fill, borrow a boat and fish the pools in front of the lodge. Fly outs to remote waters are available at additional cost, normally about $200 per person for groups of four to six. The lodge also offers a variety of packages, some of which include fly outs on alternating days. And when rain and fog socks in the camp, you'll still have the Alagnak and its tributaries.

Roccanova is a back to basics kind of guy and so is his lodge, a two-story frame house. Guest rooms with two to four beds each have wash-up sinks, and those on the first floor have hot water. Showers are shared. Everyone gathers around the dining-room table for steaks, prime rib and salmon. You'll find no surcharges on your bill for booze, baits, lures or preparing your catch for the trip home. All you pay is the fee, your license (bought in King Salmon), and a tip for the guide and the cook.

Alaska Rainbow Lodge

King Salmon

Fly or float to big rainbows and salmon in the Iliamna area.

VITAL STATISTICS:

KEY SPECIES:
Rainbow and lake trout; king, sockeye, chum, pink and silver salmon; dolly varden; arctic char; grayling; northern pike

Season:
June through September

Accommodations:
RIVERFRONT LODGE
NUMBER OF GUEST ROOMS: 6
MAXIMUM NUMBER OF GUESTS: 12

Conference Groups: Yes

Meals: American plan

Rates:
$4850 per person per week. Float trips $1995 per person, double occupancy

Guides: Included

Gratuities: 5% to 7% of package

Preferred Payment:
Cash or check

Getting There:
Fly to King Salmon, take a floatplane to the lodge at no charge.

Other Activities:
Bird hunting, wildlife photography.

Contact:
Ron Hayes
Alaska Rainbow Lodge, PO Box 10459, Ft. Worth, TX 76114; 817/236-1002, fax 817/236-1696 (winter); PO Box 39, King Salmon, AK 99613; 800/451-6198, fax 817/236-1696 (summer).

RON HAYES BELIEVES that the Iliamna area of Bristol Bay has the best sportfishing in Alaska. He's biased, of course. All lodge owners are. Still, Iliamna is the only designated trophy trout region in Alaska, and rainbows that run the rivers and tributaries of this, Alaska's largest lake, are the stuff of dreams. Four- and five-pound fish are everyday affairs, and double digit 'bows are landed often enough to be expected. In this corner of the 49th state, you can take your choice of dozens of close by lakes and rivers. Finding water where rainbows are running is not a problem, but getting there can be.

That's where Hayes comes in. A bush pilot with more than 25,000 hours in the air, he's flown floatplanes into a good bit of backcountry. Daily fly outs from his lodge on the Kvichak River will put you where the species you want to catch is most likely to strike flies or lures. Kings average between 22 and 28 pounds and run between the middle of June and the end of July. Sockeyes enter the system in the fourth week of June and fish well through July. Chums of two to eight pounds come in during the first week of July and are followed by pinks. Chum fishing fades in early August, but that's when eight- to 12-pound silvers show up. They'll hang around all fall. In the first three weeks of June, you can fish for trophy rainbows, kings and sockeyes. In the last three weeks of August, silvers and trophy rainbows overlap. And, all during the season, you'll find arctic char, dolly varden, arctic grayling, northern pike and lake trout.

Fly outs are not the only way to reach great fishing. From mid-June through September 1, Hayes also stages river float trips. If you want an up close and personal experience in the Alaskan bush, this is the way to do it. You and three other anglers, and your guide and his helper, ride big inflatables, casting from fishing chairs. If a pool looks good, you'll stop and wade. As evening rolls around, you'll find a campsite, put up tents, then go out and catch dinner. If you opt for a float trip, you'll need to supply all your own fishing gear, clothing, libations and a sleeping bag.

The lodge stretches along a bank on the river. It's a family-style place. Help yourself to the bar and hors d'oeuvres, kick back in an overstuffed chair and swap stories with the other 11 anglers in camp. Dinner (seafood, steaks, chops) will be served at 7:30 p.m. Afterwards, you can fish for grayling and rainbows rising in front of the lodge, tie flies for the morning or hit the sack. Bedrooms and one cabin, all with private baths, sleep two each and are dressed up with plush carpeting and period-style furniture.

Alaska Wilderness Peninsula Safari Camp

N e a r   C h i g i n a g a k   B a y

Go to this remote tent camp where luxury reigns and the salmon and char fishing is hot and heavy.

VITAL STATISTICS:

KEY SPECIES:
Chum, pink and silver salmon; dolly varden; arctic char; halibut

Season:
July 20 through September 30
Accommodations:
WEATHERPORT AND EUREKA TENTS
NUMBER OF GUEST ROOMS: 5
MAXIMUM NUMBER OF GUESTS: 10
Conference Groups: Yes
Meals: American plan
Rates:
$3200 per person per week
Guides: Included
Gratuities: $150 per angler per week
Preferred Payment:
Cash or check
Getting There:
Fly to King Salmon and catch the charter to the camp ($300 additional).
Other Activities:
Wildlife photography, bird watching.

Contact:
J.W. Smith
Alaska Wilderness Peninsula Safari Camp, c/o Rod &Gun Resources Inc., Rt. 3, Box 465, Killeen, TX 76542; 800/211-4753, fax 512/ 556-2367, email rodgun resources@n-link.com, website http://www. rodgunresources.com

THIS ONE YOU WON'T FIND on the map for two reasons: The river that feeds the bay has no name, and J.W. Smith, who runs it with his wife, is a little reluctant to pinpoint its location. The last thing a truly remote Alaska lodge needs is the world beating a path to its salmon. But you can find the general vicinity of the camp if you look northwest of the Trinity Islands off the southern tip of Kodiak. The camp rises on a spit that projects into a bay at the mouth of one of the rivers draining the eastern slopes of Mt. Chiginagak. That bay, and the river that feeds it, provides sportfishing different from most in Alaska.

The bay is long and shallow. Eight- to 10-foot tides fill it to the mouth of the river. For those few hours each day, schools of salmon—mainly chums, pinks and silvers—roam widely. But when the tide falls, the salmon are compressed into river channels cut in the cobble and sand bottom of the bay. In spots at full ebb, you can walk across the bay without getting your knees wet. Salmon are concentrated and in easy range of fly-rodders. Early in the season, from July 20 through August 20, you'll fish for chums up to 20 pounds and pinks to eight. Silvers from 12 to 20 pounds come in late August and stay until the camp closes at the end of September.

When tides flood the bay, Smith, guests and guides clamber into 18-foot inflatable catamarans and run up rivers to fish for arctic char and dolly varden that average three-pounds-plus. Flies of choice include Sculpins, Muddlers and Spuddlers, with the best rod being a 5 weight. Sometimes, when the wind is right, you'll sight-cast to schooling pinks and chums from the beach. And for a bit of relief, you'll take boats out to haul in a few halibut for dinner. During the day you and two partners will fish with a guide. After dinner, if you've still got the bug, walk down to the bay and have a go.

Though Peninsula is best described as a tent camp, put away those old images from Boy Scout days. Sturdy camouflage Weatherports shelter a stainless-steel commercial kitchen and dining room, bath and drying room for wet gear. Gourmet meals feature twin entrees—salmon and New York strip steak or halibut and Jamaican jerked chicken—accompanied by good wines and homemade desserts. Guests sleep on comfortable single beds in two-person, 12-foot-square Eureka "bombproof" tents. At this first-class operation, maid service is provided daily.

Angler's Alibi
King Salmon

VITAL STATISTICS:

KEY SPECIES:
King, sockeye, silver, chum and pink salmon; rainbow trout; arctic char; grayling; northern pike

Season:
June 1 through August 20

Accommodations:
TENT CAMP
NUMBER OF GUEST ROOMS: 3
MAXIMUM NUMBER OF GUESTS: 9

Conference Groups: No

Meals: American plan

Rates:
$2875 per person per week

Guides: Included

Gratuities: $230 week

Preferred Payment:
Cash or check

Getting There:
Fly to Anchorage and take a connecting flight to King Salmon. Angler's Alibi provides floatplane service to the camp.

Other Activities:
Bird watching, wildlife photography.

Contact:
Karl Storath
Angler's Alibi, PO Box 271, King Salmon, AK 99613; 907/439-4234 (June through August); 6105 Poplar Beach, Romulus, NY 14541; 607/869-9397, fax 607/869-9656 (September through May).

Represented By:
Frontiers International, 800/245-1950.

Get a grand slam on salmon at this high-class tent camp on the Alagnak.

RIVERS DRAINING INTO BRISTOL BAY are among the most productive in Alaska. A few miles up from the mouth of one of the best rivers, the Alagnak, Angler's Alibi operates a tent camp lodge where fishermen stay in Weatherports: high, green-roofed 16x12-foot tents with screen doors, heaters and carpeted floors. Two or three anglers share each of three tents, and they dine—Cornish game hens, prime rib and salmon—in a jumbo 16x25-foot Weatherport. A log bathhouse has hot showers, welcome after a day's fishing, and laundry facilities.

The Alagnak drains Nonvianuk Lake in the watershed just south of Iliamna Lake. The five Alaskan salmon—kings, sockeyes, silvers, chums and pinks—use the river along with rainbows, arctic char, grayling and pike. The last week in June and the first week in July is choice for kings and sockeyes. Kings normally run better than 30 pounds, and fish from 45 to 50 pounds are common. Sockeyes in the 7- to 14-pound range provide good sport on flyrods or medium-weight spinning gear. Chums start running in the second week of July. The last week in that month is the best time to hit a salmon grand slam...all five species in one week. By then, silvers have entered the river and the first pinks have shown up as well.

At Angler's Alibi, the Alagnak is tidal and salmon are invariably bright. It's easy to fish incoming tides whenever they occur. They carry fish right past the camp, and the river here is shallow enough to wade. If you tire of salmon, you can run up the Alagnak in one of the camp's power boats to water where rainbows of three to five pounds, char, grayling and pike are found. The camp also offers fly outs ($175 to $275 additional cost) to nearby Katmai National Park, where rainbows up to 10 pounds can be caught, especially in August. No more than nine anglers are in camp at any time and they are assisted by three guides. Angler's Alibi also provides tackle, although it's normally better to bring your own.

[A L A S K A]

Angler's Paradise Lodges
Grosvenor and Kulik
Katmai National Park Area

Take your pick of a pair of fine retreats
for salmon, char and rainbow trout.

VITAL STATISTICS:

KEY SPECIES:
Rainbow and lake trout; sockeye salmon; arctic char; northern pike

Season:
June through September

Accommodations:
GUEST CABINS
NUMBER OF GUEST ROOMS/GUESTS:
GROSVENOR: 3/6
KULIK: 12/28

Conference Groups: Yes

Meals: American plan

Rates:
GROSVENOR: From $1625 per person for 3 days and 3 nights
KULIK: From $1700 per person for 3 days and 3 nights

Guides: Included

Gratuities: 15% of package

Preferred Payment:
American Express, MasterCard, Visa

Getting There:
Fly to Anchorage, then Angler's Paradise provides air transportation to lodges.

Other Activities:
Boating, hiking, bird watching, wildlife photography, flight seeing.

Contact:
Kip Minnery
Angler's Paradise Lodges, 4550 Aircraft Dr., Anchorage, AK 99502; 800/544-0551, fax 907/243-0649.

Represented By:
Will work with you or any qualified travel agent.

T HESE TWO LODGES are operated by Katmailand, Inc. out of Anchorage. While the accommodations and locations differ, the fishing programs are similar. At Kulik, you'll fish the lake and river of the same name; the river is one of southwestern Alaska's best for rainbows. The water is clear, the bottom consists of gravel, and the wading is easy. In its upper reaches the Kulik River is relatively small. Rainbows peak in June, taper off slightly in July then come on strong in August and September. Fish are big—in the five-pound-plus range—and the latter part of the season is when to get them. On Kulik and nearby Nonvianuk lakes, you'll catch lake trout, sockeyes, char and pike. The sockeyes run in June and early July.

At Grosvenor Lake, trout, char and sockeyes run through the narrows adjacent to the lodge. Two rivers feeding the lake hold the largest concentrations of spawning sockeyes in the Naknek drainage. You'll reach these and smaller streams by jetboat. Should catching and releasing trout and salmon wear thin (you can keep a few salmon to take home), you may want to cast spoons, spinnerbaits or flies for northern pike.

With 12 spruce cabins accented by forest-green porches and all with private baths, Kulik is the flagship lodge. Close to the cabins is the main lodge, also of spruce. Comfortable easy chairs and a sofa face the huge stone fireplace that dominates one wall. Family-style meals of fresh seafood, as well as cuts of beef, are served on long pine tables. One corner of the room is devoted to complimentary libations and another attractive grouping of chairs offers views of the lake. Grosvenor, a bit more rustic, is ideal for a group of fishing friends. Three cabins share a bathhouse. The lodge is smaller, but as comfortable. You'll have dinner overlooking the lake, and the menu here is similar to Kulik's.

All fishing packages include licenses and use of rods and reels and waders if needed. Angler's Paradise also has boats cached on many lakes and rivers within a 100-mile radius of the lodges. Fly outs to fish all five species of salmon and trout in isolated waters are available at $275 per person. In addition, you may want to check out their week-long guided and unguided float trips on the Alagnak.

Aniak River Lodge

Aniak

At a lodge off Alaska's beaten path, salmon are taken seriously and mosquitoes aren't.

VITAL STATISTICS:

KEY SPECIES:
King, chum, sockeye, coho and pink salmon; rainbow trout; grayling

Season:
Mid-June through September 1
Accommodations:
Log lodge and cabin
Number of Guest Rooms: 5
Maximum Number of Guests: 10
Conference Groups: Yes
Meals: American plan
Rates:
From $1750 per person for 5 days and 5 nights, double occupancy
Guides: Included
Gratuities: Client's discretion
Preferred Payment:
Cash or check
Getting There:
Aniak has regular air service; the lodge van will pick you up.
Other Activities:
Bird watching, wildlife photography.

Contact:
Lee Brooks
Aniak River Lodge, PO Box 29138, Bellingham, WA 98228-1138; 800/747-8403 (winter); PO Box 64, Aniak, AK 99557; 907/675-4333 (summer).

FIRST, THE BAD NEWS. "In June, until they begin to die off in July, the mosquitoes are as big as hummingbirds," says Lee Brooks, honcho of Aniak River Lodge. He's the first lodge operator to admit that. But if you're playing king salmon averaging 25 pounds apiece, and you're catching 10 to 15 a day, you're going to be too whipped to scratch. So slather more bug dope onto the brim of your hat and the bandanna around your neck, and keep fishing.

The Aniak is off the beaten path. About 320 miles due west of Anchorage, it's far removed from the Bristol Bay area and the crowds of anglers who flock there each season. You and the eight or nine other anglers in camp will have this place pretty much to yourselves. Walk out the front door, rig your rod and wade out into the Aniak, a 60-foot-wide river that fills up with king (July), coho (August) and chum (July) salmon, with sockeyes and pinks mixed in. Spinfishers can take 50 cohos a day throwing seven-eighth-ounce Pixies. Fly anglers will only catch a third as many. But hey, just how many times a day do you want to run that downstream foot race with a silver? Don't worry about busting your tackle. If you do you can buy more from the lodge.

Rainbows play well here, too. Brooks will put you and a couple of other anglers in a boat and the guide will run up to the Salmon River. (It's only 20 feet wide, but it's called a river just the same.) In June, rainbows there average four pounds, but by the end of August they're up to six or seven. A real glutton for punishment might plan a trip for kings and rainbows in the second or third week of June. Light-tackle anglers would do well to schedule their forays in August when they can tussle with cohos and 'bows. You may pick up a few grayling then as well.

The lodge is in the tundra. In the main lodge are four rooms with bunks and a shared bath. A log cabin nearby has two rooms that share a bath. Meals are straightforward: turkey, ham, shrimp or salmon for dinner; bacon, egg and pancake breakfasts; and fish cooked on the shore for lunch. Anglers wanting a true wilderness experience can talk Brooks into an outpost adventure at no extra charge. He'll load a boat with camping gear and food and off you'll go with a guide for three days, roughing it in the bush. You fish. The guide makes camp, cooks and keeps the bears away.

Baranof Wilderness Lodge
Sitka

Jump off from this little white house into the wild fishery around Baranof Island.

VITAL STATISTICS:

KEY SPECIES:
King, chum, sockeye, silver and pink salmon; halibut; dolly varden; cutthroat trout

Season:
June through September

Accommodations:
CABINS, MAIN LODGE AND OUTPOST CAMP
NUMBER OF GUEST ROOMS: 7
MAXIMUM NUMBER OF GUESTS:
MAIN LODGE: 12
KELP BAY: 6

Conference Groups: Yes
Meals: American plan
Rates:
From $1085 per person for 3 days and 2 nights
Guides: Included
Gratuities: $100 per week
Preferred Payment:
American Express

Getting There:
Fly to Sitka, where a bush flight will transfer you to the lodge at no additional charge.

Other Activities:
Whale watching, canoeing, boating, bird watching, wildlife photography, seminars.

Contact:
Mike Trotter
Baranof Wilderness Lodge, PO Box 2187, Sitka, AK 99835; 907/752-0154 (summer); PO Box 42, Norden, CA 95724; 916/582-8132 (winter).

Represented By:
Fishabout, 800/409-2000; Hunters & Anglers, 214/363-2525.

NARROW TIDAL PASSAGES, secluded deepwater bays and rivers that roll down out of thickly forested islands are the stuff of southeastern Alaska, the panhandle that probes toward the lower 48 but doesn't quite make it. Russian Alaska, it was explored but never settled by merchants of the Czar. They came for whales and fur. You, too, will see whales, but from a seat in an Avon inflatable skipping across the bay en route to waters where salmon are stacked up waiting to move onto spawning grounds.

Baranof Lodge is 20 miles by air from Sitka on Warm Springs Bay off the sheltered Chatham Passage. Salmon run the passage: kings (20 to 50 pounds) from May through July, chums (nine to 17 pounds) and sockeyes (five to eight pounds) in July and August. Later in July silvers (eight to 15 pounds) and pinks (two to five pounds) come in. Pinks phase out in September, but the silvers hang on into October. You'll fish salt water (halibut are a bonus), and freshwater streams where salmon spawn. In other streams and ponds on Baranof and nearby islands you'll find rainbows, dolly varden and cutthroats. Saltwater gear is provided; bring your own spinning or flytackle for the strictly catch-and-release freshwater species.

The lodge is a charming little white frame house set on the grassy shore. Tucked back under the tall pines are four cozy paneled cabins with private baths and front porches overlooking the water. Dinners revolve around local seafood and feature herbs and vegetables from the garden. An extensive list of fine wines complements dinner. After dinner soak in the hot tub or mineral springs, much as the Tlingit Indians did centuries ago.

Mike Trotter, who owns the lodge, also runs expeditions to Kelp Bay, a tent camp that's a short flight from Sitka, and week-long float trips on The Chosen (late July through late August) and Tikchik (mid-July) rivers in the Bristol Bay watershed. Accommodations are tents with bunks, but you'll find hot showers, gourmet food, great wines and outstanding fishing.

In addition to fishing, Baranof Island Lodge also hosts the University of Southeast Alaska Elderhostel during the first week in June, seminars for lawyers (18 MCLE credits) addressing trial and pre-trial skills with experienced attorneys, and wildlife photography with John Henrickson, whose work has appeared in *National Geographic* and *Audubon*.

Boardwalk Wilderness Lodge

Thorne Bay

VITAL STATISTICS:

KEY SPECIES:
Steelhead; king and coho salmon; halibut

Season:
April through September

Accommodations:
RUSTIC LOG LODGE
NUMBER OF GUEST ROOMS: 8
MAXIMUM NUMBER OF GUESTS: 16

Conference Groups: Yes

Meals: American plan

Rates:
Packages from $2360 per person for 3 days and 3 nights

Guides: Included

Gratuities: $25 per angler per day

Preferred Payment:
MasterCard, Visa

Getting There:
Fly to Ketchikan, take floatplane to lodge (shuttle is included in package prices).

Other Activities:
Canoeing, rafting, boating, hiking, bird watching, whale watching, wildlife photography, cave exploration.

Contact:
**Doug Ibbetson
Boardwalk Wilderness Lodge, PO Box 19121, Thorne Bay, AK 99919; 907-828-3918, fax 907-828-3367, website http://www.boardwalk-lodge.com**

Fish steelhead in streams seldom visited by other anglers.

YOU HEAR IT ALL OVER. On the Miramichi, they tell you that Atlantic salmon is the fish of 1000 casts. In Florida, it's the permit. British Columbia, steelhead. For those who haven't risen above the mean, this Olympic timbered lodge on Prince of Wales Island where the Thorne River dumps into Thorne Bay offers a great opportunity to rectify the situation in a hurry.

April, May and June are the prime steelhead months on Prince of Wales, the third largest island in the U. S. Eighty-five of the island's rivers have been documented as steelhead streams. Early in the season, it's reasonable to assume hookups with two to four steelhead per day. Though the island is 135 miles long and 45 miles wide, mountains provide its backbone and watersheds tend to be modest in size. That means plenty of small rivers that are relatively easily fished. About a dozen, including the Karta, have runs of both spring and fall steelhead. Rivers on the island also hold cutthroats, and virtually all see salmon runs.

Your guide from the lodge will help you select your species for the day from among 23 different waters that lodge guests fish on a regular basis. Fish steelhead in the morning when you're fresh, then board one of the lodge's cabin cruisers to go deep for halibut, ling cod, salmon or rockfish. Mooching—drifting a strip of herring for kings on medium-weight tackle—is pure fun. You stand by the rail, working the bait up and down, when suddenly your rod does a little tango and dives for bottom. Kings run in the 30- to 40-pound-plus range, and you'll find them in rivers as well as the inshore waters. Best king fishing is in June. Cohos show up in July and stay through September; the end of the run offers better fishing.

An Orvis-endorsed lodge, Boardwalk Wilderness is top rated by its guests. This hand-built lodge of stripped and notched spruce logs, with porches and balconies and deep overhanging eves, blends well with the verdant hillside where it sits by Thorne Bay. Inside are cozy, hand-hewn log walls complemented by antiques and reproductions from a variety of periods. Lounge in the cathedral-ceilinged great room, feet pointed toward the glowing wood stove. It'll be hard to lever yourself up for the short walk through the arched door into the dining room, where dinner of shrimp, halibut or Cornish hen awaits. Half of the guest rooms are upstairs in the main lodge and half are in a new lodge nearby. After dinner, watch Sitka deer from the hot tub on the deck.

Bristol Bay Lodge

Dillingham

Daily fly outs to remote rainbow and salmon streams bring anglers success at this well-established lodge.

VITAL STATISTICS:

KEY SPECIES:
Rainbow trout; king, chum, silver, pink and sockeye salmon; arctic char; grayling

Season:
June through September

Accommodations:
LODGE ROOMS AND CABINS
NUMBER OF GUEST ROOMS: 17
MAXIMUM NUMBER OF GUESTS: 24

Conference Groups: No

Meals: American plan

Rates:
$4700 per person per week (Sunday to Friday)

Guides: Included

Gratuities: 8% to 10% of package

Preferred Payment:
Cash or check

Getting There:
Fly to Dillingham (Air Alaska does a round trip on a 737 every Saturday), and a representative of the lodge will pick you up.

Other Activities:
Hiking, bird watching.

Contact:
Ron McMillan
Bristol Bay Lodge, 2422 Hunter Rd., Ellensburg, WA 98926; 509/964-2094, fax 509/964-2269 (winter); Box 1509, Dillingham, AK 99576; 907/842-2500, fax 907/842-2599 (summer).

LOCATED 40 AIR MILES NORTH of Dillingham on Lake Aleknagik, Bristol Bay Lodge is in the center of some of the best trout, salmon and char water in southwestern Alaska. Since 1973, Bristol Bay Lodge has been putting anglers over trophy fish from their comfortable and well-appointed headquarters overlooking the lake. Daily fly outs are the order of the day. Within a short hop via Bristol Bay's fleet of three six-passenger Beavers and a three-passenger Cessna are the fertile waters of the Wood, TikChik, Nusagak, Togiak and Goodnews rivers. On each, the lodge has stashed boats with outboard jet or prop motors. In addition, Bristol Bay maintains several spike camps. In these you'll find comfortable tents with wooden floors and heaters and a dining/eating tent. Only four anglers are in camp at a time and their needs are looked after by a cook and a guide. If weather grounds the aircraft, fish the Agulawak River and Youth, Icy and Sunshine creeks, all trophy trout streams accessible by boat from the main lodge.

Fishing begins in June with early rainbows, char and grayling, and for these, angling stays good through August. King and chum salmon, also known as dog salmon, enter the river systems in June. Generally speaking the sockeyes and pinks (every other year) arrive at the end of June and early July, and silvers show up in August. Kings up to 50 pounds and sockeyes fish best in the last week of June and the first two weeks of July. Prime time for pinks is late July and early August. Silvers hit their peak after the first week in August. Spinfishermen will want to bring light and medium-weight systems, matching reels with 6- and 10-pound-test lines and a variety of spinners and spoons. Two systems are required for flyfishers as well: an 8 1/2-foot for a 6 weight, and a 9- or 10-foot for a 7 or 8 weight. Black and olive Woolly Buggers are the most versatile flies. The lodge has a well-stocked shop with lures, flies and other tackle.

Glowing warm and mellow from rich spruce paneling, each of the lodge's spacious guest rooms is handsomely turned out with a queen or two double beds, upholstered chairs and tables accented with brass lamps. Baths are private. Three cabins for families or special groups boast living rooms, bedrooms and baths. Picture windows in the main lodge bring views of the lake and mountains beyond into the comfortable living room and dining room, where scrumptious meals of steak, prime rib and seafood are served. The food is as special as the surroundings.

Chelatna Lake Lodge
Chelatna Lake

VITAL STATISTICS:

KEY SPECIES:
King, sockeye, silver, pink and chum salmon; rainbow and lake trout; grayling; northern pike

Season:
June through early September

Accommodations:
CABINS ON LAKE
NUMBER OF GUEST ROOMS: 8
MAXIMUM NUMBER OF GUESTS: 16

Conference Groups: No

Meals: American plan

Rates:
From $2090 per person for 3 nights, double occupancy

Guides: Included

Gratuities: 10% of package

Preferred Payment:
MasterCard, Visa

Getting There:
Fly to Anchorage, taxi to lodge office on Float Plane Drive, air shuttle to lodge at no additional expense.

Other Activities:
Canoeing, rafting, boating, hiking, bird watching, bear viewing, flight seeing, wildlife photography.

Contact:
**Duke Bertke
Chelatna Lake Lodge,
3941 Float Plane Dr.,
Anchorage, AK 99502;
800/999-0785, fax
907/248-5791.**

Spinning or flyfishing, take your choice. The salmon don't care.

DUKE AND BECKIE BERTKE'S Chelatna Lake Lodge is located on the southern boundary of Denali National Park. It sits up on a little rise overlooking four cedar guest chalets, the lake and the Alaska Range beyond. Four aircraft and 16 boats are tied to the dock, ready to take you off after the five salmon, rainbows, grayling, lake trout or northern pike, whatever is your pleasure.

Duke or one of his pilots will fly you to remote rivers and lakes, or you can arrange a float down Lake Creek for 'bows or grayling. You can also troll Chelatna for lake trout or cast for pike. The best fishing is in the rivers and streams that feed the lake and the best month is July. If you want to go for 25- to 60-pound kings, arrive before the 10th. After the 15th, silvers and sockeye are legal. Lake trout and grayling also reach their peaks in July. Bring spinning and/or flyfishing gear, whichever you prefer. The salmon hit spoons (Pixies and Dardevles), while the trout and grayling go after lures and spinners (Mepps, Rooster Tails and so on). The lodge employs a full staff of guides, obtains licenses for guests and rents and sells tackle if you need it.

In addition to the fishing, most guests spend a little time flying over Denali and observing grizzlies, moose and Dall sheep. A bear-viewing platform is located a few minutes' walk from the main chalet. And most guests find themselves up to their necks in the wood-fired hot tub at the edge of the lake. That's after the fishing and before dinner of grilled salmon with lime and ginger sauce with jasmine rice or halibut grenobloise with fettuccine. The chef can accommodate a variety of diet restrictions including heart healthy, vegetarian and MSG/salt free. After dinner and lingering over a cordial in the twilight, it's off to bed in one of the chalets. Each contains two bedrooms and private baths.

Chris Goll's Rainbow River Lodge

Iliamna

VITAL STATISTICS:

KEY SPECIES:
Rainbow trout; king, silver, red, pink and chum salmon; arctic char; grayling; northern pike; steelhead

Season:
June through September

Accommodations:
RUSTIC CABINS
NUMBER OF GUEST ROOMS: 6
MAXIMUM NUMBER OF GUESTS: 12

Conference Groups: Yes

Meals: American plan

Rates:
From $3300 per guest per week, double occupancy

Guides: Included

Gratuities: 5% to 10% of package

Preferred Payment:
MasterCard, Visa

Getting There:
Fly to King Salmon. You will be met and flown to the lodge.

Other Activities:
Rafting, boating, hiking, bird watching, wildlife photography.

Contact:
**Chris Goll
Chris Goll's Rainbow River Lodge, PO Box 330, Iliamna, AK 99606; phone/fax 907/571-1210 (summer); 4127 Raspberry Rd., Anchorage, AK 99502; 907/243-7894, fax 907/248-1726 (winter).**

Represented By:
Frontiers International, 800/245-1950; Destinations, 800/626-3526; Bob Marriott's Fly Shop, 800/535-6633; The Fly Shop, 800/699-3474.

Here a novice can fish like a pro, and a pro may land a lifetime trophy.

THE COPPER RIVER in the Iliamna district of Alaska is like many other rivers that feed the great lake. Rainbows grow to mythical size. Salmon run in swarms and grayling approach double-digit dimensions. But for all of this, the Copper River is different. It is slow enough to permit the accumulation of small gravel and pockets of fine-grained sediment that insects need to hatch. While you may find a few small caddis on other rivers in the watershed, on the Copper you'll find mayflies and stoneflies as well. If you're torn between fishing for huge rainbows on one hand and fishing with dry flies on the other, this 18-mile bit of heaven is for you, because here, you can do both.

Such fishing can be awesome. Rainbows of eight to 10 pounds are netted frequently enough to be called "common." Thirty- to 40-fish days are not infrequent. There are no "best" months here. It's all better than good from June through September. Those are also the prime months for arctic char up to 12 pounds; grayling, two to five pounds; all five species of salmon (king, silver, red, pink and chum), five to 50 pounds and northern pike in case you long for excitement. In August and September, when the rainbows are bigger because they've been eating like pigs since the salmon started spawning, you're liable to encounter steelhead up to 15 pounds.

As the river seems to impart its namesake color to its fish, it infects those who fish it as well. Wading is not difficult. Casts need not be of tournament winning length. Sometimes the trout are so hungry they'll race another fish to a bit of feathers, floss and steel in the water. A novice can feel like a pro here; and an experienced angler will have chance after chance to learn how to play and release huge fish on reasonably light tackle. Take a 5/6 and an 8. Choose reels with good drags. The Copper is restricted to fly-fishing, but spinfishers will find ample opportunity to tackle kings or troll for huge lake trout. Fly outs to other waters are also available.

Owner Chris Goll received the Conservationist of the Year award in 1980 from the National Wildlife Federation for his work on the Copper River. His guests toss him kudos for the quality of the lodge. It is immaculate, with snug and secluded cabins of cedar, all with private baths. Meals of near gourmet quality are served in the contemporary, cathedral-ceilinged log lodge. Floor-to-ceiling windows, 36 feet high, provide a stunning view of Pike Lake. At night, as you work your way under the covers, the call of the loons will lull you to sleep.

Classic Alaska Charters
Ketchikan

VITAL STATISTICS:

KEY SPECIES:
King, silver, pink and chum salmon; halibut; ling cod; rockfish

Season:
All year

Accommodations:
MOTOR YACHT
NUMBER OF GUEST ROOMS: 2
MAXIMUM NUMBER OF GUESTS: 6

Conference Groups: No

Meals: American plan

Rates:
From $1050 per person for 3 days and 2 nights (3-person minimum)

Guides: Included

Gratuities: Client's discretion

Preferred Payment:
Cash or check

Getting There:
Fly to Ketchican where a staff member will meet your plane.

Other Activities:
Touring, whale and other marine mammal watching, bird watching.

Contact:
**Capt. Robert Scherer
Classic Alaska Charters,
PO Box 6117, Ketchikan,
AK 99901; 907/225-0608.**

*Be the captain of your
own floating fishing lodge.*

WHO SAID THAT A FISHING LODGE has to have a foundation and four walls? Rob Scherer, skipper of the *Saltery "C,"* figured that if anglers could fish from a boat, eat on a boat and sleep on a boat, then a boat could be a lodge. Makes sense. And it gets better: You're the admiral. Scherer will tell you what's hot, then you pick the species and how you want to fish for them. Halibut, yelloweye, ling cod, king, silver, pink and chum salmon, black rockfish, cutthroats...the choice is yours. Salmon are generally best from late May through late September. Fish the salt from April through October.

Jig deep water—180 to more than 420 feet—for big halibut with lures weighing 16 to 32 ounces. Fights with fish can last an hour or more. Use medium-weight (20- to 40-pound-test line) tackle and vertical jig for cod, halibut and some salmon. If light tackle is your bag, fish massive schools of rockfish and yelloweye over pinnacles, reefs and kelp beds. You can also troll and drift for salmon and halibut. Run up the spectacular channels of the Misty Fjords National Wilderness Channel or the deep cuts in Revillagigedo Island. Put ashore at the mouths of clear, unnamed rivers teeming with salmon on the spawn. You'll see no other anglers.

Sometimes it just pays to laze on the boat...in the midst of a pod of killer whales or hundreds of jumping dolphin. Prowl ice caves in remnants of glaciers. Drift below a 1000-foot waterfall. Watch fishing brown bears and eagles. No roads penetrate southeastern Alaska from the mainland. The only way to explore it is by boat, and Scherer, guiding in these waters since 1984, knows the area well.

The *Saltery "C"* is a 40-foot motor yacht with two heads. It sleeps six, four in the forward cabin and two in the dinette. Meals are prepared from that day's catch—halibut, cod, salmon, dungeness crab and shrimp. Breakfasts open with homemade cinnamon rolls and coffee on deck, and then things get serious. Fish from the stern cockpit, and later, grill your catch. Not, as they say, a rough life.

Copper River Fly Fishing Lodge
Iliamna

An intimate lodge is tucked in the spruce at the edge of a river where rainbows grow to 20 pounds.

VITAL STATISTICS:

KEY SPECIES:
Rainbow trout; sockeye salmon; grayling; char

Season:
June through October

Accommodations:
CABINS
NUMBER OF GUEST ROOMS: 4
MAXIMUM NUMBER OF GUESTS: 8

Meals: American plan

Conference Groups: No

Rates:
$2750 per person per week

Guides: Included

Gratuities: 10%

Preferred Payment:
Cash or check

Getting There:
Fly to Iliamna, Alaska and meet the shuttle to the lodge (no charge).

Other Activities:
Bird watching, wildlife photography.

Contact:
**Jeff or Pat Vermillion
Copper River Fly Fishing
Lodge, PO Box PVY,
Iliamna, AK 99606;
907/571-1464 (summer); 411 S 3rd St.,
Livingston, MT 59047;
406/222-0624 (winter).**

MORE THAN 100 MILES LONG and 1000 feet deep in places, Iliamna is Alaska's largest lake. From Bristol Bay, salmon run up the Kvichak and enter Iliamna, where they disperse to the watersheds of their birth. Among those rivers is the Copper, which drains the flanks of the Aleutian Range. Steep, brawling, but tiny at its headwaters, the Copper broadens and slows as it enters the lowlands south of the lake. Its bottom is gravel and the current fairly fast, an ideal incubator for eggs of salmon and rainbows, and a marvelous fishery for those who come to angle. Neither wide nor particularly deep, the river is easily waded. And the lodge uses skiffs pushed by jet outboards to race you each morning to the best fishing.

And what fishing it is. In 1975, the state of Alaska restricted the Copper to fly-fishing only, and in 1989 mandated it a catch-and-release fishery for wild trout. In the Copper, rainbows grow fat on salmon spawn. Average summer fish run from three to five pounds. Trophy summer trout reach eight pounds or more. But in fall, as they gorge on salmon eggs, the rainbows will average twice their summer weight and a lunker will tip the scale at 20 pounds. Fight that on your 5 weight! Summer also sees a splendid run of four- to 12-pound sockeyes. To catch them you'll want to be in camp between the Fourth of July and the first week of August. For big rainbows, forget about salmon and come in September. For variety, you'll also catch grayling and arctic char. Bring 5- and 8-weight systems. Two anglers share a guide.

Rustic and hand-built of spruce log, the lodge sits on a little backwater of the Copper half a mile from its mouth on the south shore of Iliamna Lake. The lodge prefers to book small groups (no larger than six) of flyfishermen who know one another. Accommodations are in cabins adjacent to the lodge. Baths are shared. Wonderful meals: garlic-roasted pork tenderloin, mashed potatoes, salads, chocolate mousse are served family-style. No fly outs here; you'll spend your time fishing.

Creekside Inn
Ninilchik

VITAL STATISTICS:

KEY SPECIES:
King, sockeye, silver, chum and pink salmon; rainbow trout; dolly varden; halibut

Season:
All year

Accommodations:
LODGE
NUMBER OF GUEST ROOMS: 17
MAXIMUM NUMBER OF GUESTS: 44

Conference Groups: No

Meals: Breakfast and lunch, dinner on your own

Rates:
From $965 per person for 3 days and 4 nights, double occupancy

Guides: Included

Gratuities: Client's discretion

Preferred Payment:
Cash or check

Getting There:
Fly to Anchorage, rent a car and drive to the inn. About a 4-hour drive.

Other Activities:
Golf, tennis, boating, hiking, bird watching, wildlife photography, skiing.

Contact:
Bill Avarell
Creekside Inn, PO Box 39236, Ninilchik, AK 99639; 907/567-7333, fax 907/336-2211, email kadtec@js-net.com

Bargain base for the best fishing on the Kenai Peninsula.

THE KENAI PENINSULA, separated from most of Alaska by Cook Inlet, is a well-known destination for salmon, rainbows and halibut. The Creekside Inn at Ninilchik offers all three. It's near the mouth of Deep Creek, which has runs of all five species of salmon...sockeye, kings, silvers, chums and pinks. The river also hosts rainbows and dolly varden. Fish with fly or spinning tackle. Bill Avarell owns the inn and Kenai Peninsula Charters, which provides guides for stream fishing, driftfishing on the Kenai and Kasilof rivers, saltwater excursions for halibut and salmon and fly outs to remote waters for salmon and trout. Avarell will see that you go where you want.

The season opens with halibut in April. At the start of May the first run of kings moves up the peninsula from Anchor Point and reaches Deep Creek a week or so later. By the middle of the month they've entered Deep Creek and begun migrating up past the inn. Building steadily, numbers increase until fishing reaches its prime in mid-June. A second run of kings enters the creek in early July. The farther up the inlet, the later the peak fishing.

Deep Creek isn't known as a sockeye stream, though they begin running in late June and pinks show up at the end of July. Silvers, plentiful in Deep Creek, make their appearance near the first week of August, and September through mid-October brings the best runs. Don't forget the pinks, which debut in late July. While the Kasilof River, 19 miles to the north, and the Kenai, a dozen miles farther, are bigger rivers and floatable, Deep Creek will surprise you.

You can fly to the town of Kenai, about 45 minutes from the inn, but the better option is to rent a car and drive down the peninsula from Anchorage, 190 miles north. You'll travel through the Kenai National Refuge, pass the inspiring Portage Glacier, and chance seeing moose, caribou, bears and eagles. And you'll cross scores of rivers and streams. The trick is not to stop to fish. The inn is unpretentious, comfortable and offers budget accommodations. All but three of the 17 guest rooms have private baths. Packages include breakfast and a packed lunch; dinner is on your own.

Floating the Karluk for kings of 50 pounds or
steelhead is a favorite for guests
at Kodiak Island River Camps,
headquartered in Kodiak. — page 214.

Fly and spin anglers rub shoulders at
Northwoods Lodge near Skwentna, as they
fish for salmon and rainbow trout in the
Yenta and Sustina rivers. — page 222.

Crystal Creek Lodge
L a k e   N u n a v a u g a l u k

*Helicopter to where
you want to fish.*

**VITAL
STATISTICS:**

KEY SPECIES:
King and sockeye
salmon; rainbow trout;
arctic char; dolly varden;
grayling

Season:
June through September
Accommodations:
MODERN WOOD LODGE
NUMBER OF GUEST ROOMS: 13
MAXIMUM NUMBER OF GUESTS: 22
Conference Groups: Yes
Meals: American plan
Rates:
$4950 per person per week,
double occupancy
Guides: Included
Gratuities: 5% to 15% of
package price
Preferred Payment:
Cash or check
Getting There:
Fly to Dillingham, Alaska and
the van from the lodge will
meet you.
Other Activities:
Bird watching, hiking, wildlife
photography.

Contact:
**Dan Michels
Crystal Creek Lodge,
Box 92170, Anchorage,
AK 99509-2170;
907/245-1945, fax
907/245-1946, website
http://www.crystal
creeklodge.com**

THE BEAVERS, those great workhorses of the outback, line up along the dock, their navy and blue markings streamlined in the morning sun. On their tails flies the Crystal Creek emblem: floatplane over salmon. North and east of Dillingham by about 25 miles, Crystal Creek lodge is home base for a fleet of four Beavers and a Sikorsky S-55 helicopter that ferry anglers daily to the best fishing in the Bristol Bay area. You'll fly into remote sites and land where the lodge has cached jetboats to take you to the best wading stretches or to fish deeper waters. You may fish the Goodnews River system to the west or Katmai off to the east. The lodge also owns exclusive use permits for Togiak National Wildlife Refuge and holds exclusive access to a number of rivers leased from the Yup'ik Eskimos.

Among the waters you'll fish is the Agulawak River. In Alaska, you'll find two Agulawak Rivers. One of them is famous, the other unknown. Crystal Creek fishes the latter: a gravel-bottom stream that provides outstanding spawning habitat for sockeyes. The river fills with them in July and from later that month through August, this is an outstanding fishery for rainbows, char, sea-run dolly varden and grayling that move into the river to feed on eggs of spawning sockeyes. If you've set your sights on a trophy rainbow or grayling, try fishing Oxbow Creek. Resembling a meadow creek with few streamside or underwater obstructions, Oxbow's biggest rainbow topped 34 inches. Average fish are two feet long. Grayling exceed four pounds. Only 50 feet at its widest, this is an easy wading and easy casting creek. It's hard to imagine a river only 100 feet wide, but that's the story of another fine water, the North. After July 10, it receives a late run of king salmon; easy to wade, it may be the best place to catch a king on a flyrod.

The low modern wooden lodge fits comfortably among a few spruce on a little bay of the lake. A fire on the stone hearth invites you to sink into a plush leather couch and relax. In this paneled living room, a completely equipped bench allows three anglers at a time to tie new patterns for next morning's fishing. Guest rooms are comfortable motel-style with private baths, and the lodge boasts a whirlpool as well. Meals here are as good as the fishing. Salmon and prawns steamed in parchment paper, lamb persillade and veal piccata top a menu that ends with diet-busting desserts.

[A L A S K A]

Deer Creek Cottages

T h o r n e   B a y

Take a do-it-yourself vacation complete with boat, motor, salmon and steelhead.

VITAL STATISTICS:

KEY SPECIES:
Steelhead; silver, king and chum salmon; cod; halibut

Season:
All year

Accommodations:
HOUSEKEEPING COTTAGES
NUMBER OF GUEST ROOMS: 5
MAXIMUM NUMBER OF GUESTS: 10

Conference Groups: No

Meals: Cook for yourself

Rates:
$3000 for 4 per week; $3600 for 6 per week

Guides: $300 per day in fresh water; $500 per day in salt water

Gratuities: Client's discretion

Preferred Payment:
MasterCard, Visa

Getting There:
Fly to Ketchikan and then to Thorne Bay on Taquan Airlines for an additional $120 per person round trip

Other Activities:
Hunting, boating, hiking, bird watching, wildlife photography.

Contact:
Steve Scheldt
Deer Creek Cottages, PO Box 19475, Thorne Bay, AK 99919; 907/828-3393, fax 907/828-3438.

BUDGET FISHING VACATIONS in Alaska are not easily found. Accommodations can be less than inviting or the fishing modest. But Steve Scheldt has come up with an idea that makes a lot of sense. He's built two modern cottages, one with two bedrooms, the other with three; equipped them with kitchens, as well as charcoal grills and smokers; and added a 19-foot skiff and motor for your use. Provisions are available in Thorne Bay. You and three or five pals, depending on cottage size, will each ante-up $750 per week. Armed with charts, maps, boat and a van, you can set off to fish the rivers on Prince of Wales Island or the sheltered salt water around it.

Prince of Wales Island lies just off the mainland of southeast Alaska. It is accessible by ferry from Juneau and points south and is traversed by a system of roads, of sorts. Mountainous with deep, fiord-like inlets, the island is drained by scores of small rivers and streams. From January through May, and again in November and December, steelhead move into 85 of the rivers and larger streams. Depending on the size of the water, spinning gear or flyrods are favored tackle, but it's all catch-and-release. Steelheading is best in April and May (and the climate is more hospitable). You'll also find silvers in the streams.

Bigger action occurs in the salt waters of the Inside Passage. King salmon from 12 to 60 pounds arrive in December, with June and July traditionally the best months. Silvers start their runs in June, and the fishing peaks from in late summer and early fall. Chums also make an appearance and are best in July. Best months for deep jigging for halibut (25 to 300 pounds) are July through September. You can also catch cod and yelloweye rockfish.

As do-it-yourself camps go, this one has all the right pieces. If you book in, your group might consider hiring a guide for a day or two ($300 for fresh water, $500 for salt) to pick up a little local intelligence before heading out on your own.

Enchanted Lake Lodge
King Salmon

This luxurious lodge is located in the heart of trophy rainbow country.

VITAL STATISTICS:

KEY SPECIES:
Rainbow trout; king, sockeye, pink and coho salmon; grayling; arctic char; northern pike

Season:
June through early October

Accommodations:
CEDAR CABINS
NUMBER OF GUEST ROOMS: 7
MAXIMUM NUMBER OF GUESTS: 14

Conference Groups: Yes

Meals: American plan

Rates:
$5200 per week

Guides: Included

Gratuities: $300 per week

Preferred Payment:
Cash or check

Getting There:
Fly to King Salmon, where you'll be met and flown to the lodge.

Other Activities:
Wildlife photography.

Contact:
Dick Matthews
Enchanted Lake Lodge, 3222 W. Lake Sammamish Way SE, Bellevue, WA 98008; 206/643-2172 (winter); PO Box 97, King Salmon, AK 99507; 907/246-6878, email ell@aol.com (summer).

SURROUNDED BY KATMAI National Park, Enchanted Lake Lodge may be the ultimate in wilderness luxury. You're awakened with a fresh pot of coffee or tea. After a sumptuous breakfast you and your guide board Beavers and fly from the base on Nonvianuk Lake to your choice of salmon, rainbow, grayling, arctic char or northern pike fishing in the Bristol Bay area.

The season begins in June when rainbows gang up to feed on eggs of spring spawning salmon and salmon smolts from the year before. Kings enter the system this month and provide steady action for anglers who want to go toe to toe with a 50-pound fish. July brings the sockeyes, those hard-fighting red salmon that are great on the grill. They take wet flies readily, but that's the end of the easy part. Once hooked, they'll strip your backing in nothing flat, tailwalking all the way. In August the streams fill with pink, coho and chum salmon. Of inelegant name, chums try to get even by busting your tackle. September may be the best month on Nonvianuk and the nearby Kulik. The salmon spawn hits its high point, then the big rainbows—up to 15 pounds—leave the lake and head for the riffles to gorge on salmon eggs.

Dick Matthews, pilot and owner of Enchanted Lake, suggests that guests take 5/6- and 8-weight systems. While a weight-forward, floating line is standard, you may find use for a second spool loaded with a sink tip. One hundred yards of 20-pound backing is essential, and reels should have good drags as well as rims that can be palmed. Among standard flies, bring Royal Wulffs, Elk-Hair Caddis, Humpies and Adams in No. 14 to 18; leeches and sculpins (Woolly Buggers and Rabbit Fur Leeches, No. 4 to 8); and a variety of nymphs including Hare's Ears, Pheasant Tails and Princes, Sizes 12 to 18. Bring egg patterns if you wish, but the lodge stocks patterns that Matthews and sons Mike and Steve have found productive over the years.

While the resort revolves around fishing, you'll remember the food too. For lunch, the guide bakes fish you caught that morning, pulls fresh vegetables, fruits and homemade cookies from the cooler and serves it with a properly chilled white wine or imported beer. A nap restores the soul before afternoon fishing and the flight back to the lodge. A few minutes in the sauna readies you for cocktails and hors d'oeuvres preceding a gourmet dinner as you watch trout and salmon in the lodge's 350-gallon aquarium. Afterwards, you walk back to your cozy cedar cabin, one of seven near the main lodge, and contemplate tomorrow's angling.

[A L A S K A]

Fishing Unlimited Lodge
Port Alsworth

VITAL STATISTICS:

KEY SPECIES:
Rainbow and lake trout; king, chum, silver and pink salmon; arctic char; grayling; northern pike

Season:
June through mid-October

Accommodations:
MODERN WOOD LODGES AND CABINS
NUMBER OF GUEST ROOMS: 9
MAXIMUM NUMBER OF GUESTS: 18

Conference Groups: No

Meals: American plan

Rates:
$5000 per person per week

Guides: Included

Gratuities: $350 to $500 per person per week

Preferred Payment:
Cash or check

Getting There:
Fly to Anchorage. An aircraft will shuttle you to the lodge.

Other Activities:
Hiking, wildlife photography.

Contact:
**Lorane Owsichek
Fishing Unlimited Lodge,
PO Box 190301,
Anchorage, AK 99519;
907/243-5899, fax
907/243-2472.**

From this first-class lodge, daily fly outs take you anywhere the fish are biting.

WHEN YOU THINK OF rainbow trout and Alaska, Lake Iliamna comes immediately to mind. Its tributaries provide outstanding angling for rainbows in the double-digit weight class. One of Iliamna's larger tributaries is the Newhalen River, which drains Lake Clark. Clark is nearly 70 miles long and very narrow. It's fed by half a dozen medium-size rivers, all prime rainbow and salmon waters. Less well known in the lower 48 than Iliamna, the lake and its supporting streams are frequent destinations for fly-out camps in the area.

Located on Lake Clark near Port Alsworth, Fishing Unlimited's home waters can produce well. If they're not, the lodge has a fleet of Cessna 206 floatplanes that transport anglers to isolated rivers where fish are running. Here, your pilot is your guide. Each day you'll fly to a different river to fish for rainbows, salmon, grayling and char. The plane and pilot stay with you. If the fishing slows, you pack up and fly elsewhere. Or, if flying is not for you, you can choose from a number of one-day float trips, or opt to fish from one of the lodge's jet or conventional motorboats.

The first two weeks of June and the last week of August through the first week of October will give you your best shot at trophy rainbows of six to eight pounds and up. Kings run from mid-June through mid-July. Reds and chums start in the second week of June with reds tapering off a week earlier than chums in late July. Silvers come in the first week of August and remain through October, and pinks make a cameo appearance from late July through mid-August. Char, grayling, lake trout and northern pike are available all season. Anglers generally book in for a week—Friday to Friday—but half-week packages may be available. Packages include flights from Anchorage to Fishing Unlimited, licenses and stamps, and processing of salmon for your trip home.

Tucked in an isolated cove, Fishing Unlimited's two modern wood and glass lodges offer stunning views of Tanalian Peak, where Dall sheep are often sighted. Guests stay in spacious, attractive cedar cabins, scattered under the trees, with private baths. Wooden boardwalks connect the cabins to the lodges, where you'll find a sauna and hot tub, lounges with fireplaces and the dining room. The cuisine is excellent: When you return from a day's fishing, a plate of hors d'ouevres is waiting in your freshly cleaned cabin. After unwinding, feast on dungeness crab, New York steak, game hens and all the fixings in the dining room.

Goodnews River Lodge
Goodnews Bay

This plush and permanent tent camp is for anglers who want to go one-on-one with the river and its salmon.

VITAL STATISTICS:

KEY SPECIES:
King and silver salmon;
rainbow trout; dolly
varden

Season:
Late June through
mid-September
Accommodations:
WEATHERPORT TENTS
NUMBER OF GUEST ROOMS: 9
MAXIMUM NUMBER OF GUESTS: 18
Conference Groups: No
Meals: American plan
Rates:
$3550 per person per week,
double occupancy
Guides: Included
Gratuities: $200 per week
Preferred Payment:
Cash or check
Getting There:
Fly to Goodnews Bay, Alaska,
and take a jetboat to the lodge.
Other Activities:
Hiking.

Contact:
Frank Byerly
Goodnews River Lodge,
Alaska River Safaris,
Anchorage, AK 99508;
800/274-8371, fax
907/338-5356 (winter);
PO Box 11, Goodnews
Bay, AK 99589;
907/967-8526, fax
907/338-5356 (summer).

Represented By:
Frontiers International,
800/249-1950; The Fly Shop,
800/669-3474; Sport Fishing
Alaska, 907/344-8674.

BRISTOL BAY GETS ALL THE press when it comes to exceptional runs of salmon and the rainbows that precede and follow them. Farther north, around capes Pierce and Newenham, is Goodnews Bay and the river that feeds it. Runs of king and particularly silver salmon in this drainage are astounding. The other three salmon species—sockeyes, pinks and chums—play supporting roles. Rainbows open the show in June and bring down the curtain in late August, and dolly varden constitute the chorus in the second and third acts.

Because this is a valley watershed that is not fed by streams washing down from the steep slopes of high mountains, the Goodnews doesn't discolor and flood as heavily as do some other streams in southeast Alaska. Water can be high in spring, but it's quite fishable when the lodge opens in the last week of June, and it normally stays that way through the end of the season in the second week of September. Smaller than many rivers in the area and with numerous pools, runs and riffles, the Goodnews is less than 50 yards wide. The gravel bottom makes for easy wading.

Guests, never more than 18 at a time, ride jetboats as far as 15 or 20 miles to select fishing sites favored by owner Ron Hyde and his guides. But you don't have to go far from the lodge if you don't want to. When the silvers (12 to 20 pounds) are running in August and early September, the pool just downstream and around the bend can produce 50 fish a day for good anglers. In fact, silvers are so plentiful in this system that they force rainbows into the backseat. Yet every day big rainbows hit flies fished for silvers, and once in a while anglers connect with huge 'bows of 15 to 20 pounds. Kings are fewer than the silvers, but they make up for it in size, averaging between 35 and 50 pounds. Relatively free of obstructions, the Goodnews is a great place to fight kings on a fly.

Standing on a high bank, the lodge's two-man Weatherport tents line the river. Each is heated and has a private bathroom with a hot shower, electricity, and even a front porch. Anglers bed down on comfortable cots. Meals here are either meat and potatoes affairs or fish prepared with a slight Bahamian flare. The head chef is from the Florida Keys and staffs Papa Joe's, one of the best restaurants on Islamorada, during the winter.

Iliaska Lodge
Iliamna

On the shore of the lake that gave Alaskan rainbows their fame, you'll find more than fishing.

VITAL STATISTICS:

KEY SPECIES:
Rainbow and lake trout; king, sockeye, pink, chum and silver salmon; grayling; arctic char

Season:
June through September

Accommodations:
RUSTIC LAKESIDE LODGE
NUMBER OF GUEST ROOMS: 6
MAXIMUM NUMBER OF GUESTS: 12

Conference Groups: Yes

Meals: American plan

Rates:
Packages from $2350 per person for 3 days

Guides: Included

Gratuities Client's discretion

Preferred Payment:
Cash or check

Getting There:
Fly to Anchorage, and on to Iliamna by ERA Aviation.

Other Activities:
Hiking, bird watching, wildlife photography.

Contact:
Ted Gerken
Iliaska Lodge, 6160 Fairpoint Dr., Anchorage, AK 99507; 907/337-9844 (winter); PO Box 228, Iliamna, AK 99606; email agerken@alaska.net (summer).

Represented By:
Frontiers International, 800/245-1950; John Eustice & Assoc., 800/288-0886.

ILIAMNA IS THE MOTHER LODE of Alaskan rainbows. The largest freshwater lake in the state, it's also a way station for more than 5 million trout that spawn in its tributaries yearly. From Bristol Bay they come up the Kvichak into the lake. There they hang, for a while, until their imprinted genes drive them to the waters of their birth.

The five salmon—kings, sockeyes, pinks, chums, silvers—each run in their season through the waters fished by Iliaska Lodge. So, too, do char, grayling, lake trout and rainbows. The lodge focuses on trophy rainbows and char, but it does not ignore the salmon. Quite the contrary. Using the lodge's fleet of two Cessna 206s and a meticulously maintained DeHaviland Beaver, you will fly out daily with a guide to fish rivers or lakes where the bite is on. If there are rainbows feeding on top water anywhere in reasonable range of the aircraft, a pilot will fly you and your guide there. If they aren't hitting, the guide will likely know that too and suggest something else. The region offers virtually every kind of water, from plunge pools beneath waterfalls, to bouldery pocket water, to long gravel slicks and runs. Most is wadeable, but no matter. The floatplane will put down next to one of Gerken's cached boats with motor. You'll be able to work the fish wherever you find them.

Roofed with tin and grayed by the weather, Iliaska Lodge looks more like it belongs on the Maine coast. It sits on a tundra point, open to winds off the lake. After you've returned from a day's fishing and showered, you'll wander into the living room for the pre-dinner "Liar's Hour." Here you're bound to catch a whopper even if you didn't on the stream. Meanwhile, the kitchen crew is putting the finishing touches on an exquisite dinner. Afterwards, owner Ted Gerken taps a glass and lays out plans for the next day. In that lovely lingering Alaskan twilight, you may want to stretch your legs and take a walk on the town's only road before retiring. Rooms are simply furnished, brightened with colorful curtains and spreads on twin beds.

Island Point Lodge

Kupreanof Island

*Fish 18 hours a day for salmon
and halibut at this self-guided lodge.*

VITAL STATISTICS:

KEY SPECIES:
King, sockeye, chum, pink and silver salmon; halibut; steelhead; arctic char; cutthroat; cod

Season:
May through September
Accommodations:
LOG CABINS
NUMBER OF GUEST ROOMS: 7
MAXIMUM NUMBER OF GUESTS: 18
Conference Groups: No
Meals: American plan
Rates:
$1325 per person, 2 in a boat;
$1220 per person, 4 in a boat,
double occupancy
Guides: $200 per day
Gratuities: 5% of package
Preferred Payment:
Cash or traveler's check
Getting There:
Fly to Seattle, overnight, then catch the Air Alaska flight to Petersburg the next morning.
Other Activities:
Hiking, bird watching.

Contact:
**Frank Stelmach
Island Point Lodge,
Kupreanof Island,
Petersburg, AK 99833;
800/352-4522 (summer);
10 Olde Stonebridge
Path, Westborough, MA
01581; 800/352-4522,
fax 508/366-5941
(winter).**

LOCATED IN THE SOUTHERN panhandle of the 49th state, Island Point Lodge offers anglers a week of self-guided salmon, halibut and trout fishing for a price that's hard to beat. Here's what you get: five and a half days of fishing, use of an Alaskan Lund side-console boat equipped with main (48 horsepower) and trolling outboards, bait, gas, three meals a day and a bunk. The digs aren't fancy—wood-sided cabins or rooms in the main lodge proper, with shower and toilets in the rear of the lodge and power that goes off between 10:00 p.m. and midnight—but you can fish to your heart's content.

Summer dawns break between 3:00 and 4:00 a.m. and twilight fades at 11:00 p.m. Many Island Point anglers get in three or four hours of fishing (often the best time) before breakfast. Lunches are of the do-it-yourself brown bag variety, which you'll probably wolf down out in the boat. Naturally, you can fish after dinner, served in the lodge dining room.

You'll arrive at the lodge on Saturday after a short van and boat trip from Petersburg. After orientation by the staff, you're on your own until you return home the following Friday. Depending on which species are running, staff will show you good locations on the nautical chart (and how to read one if you don't know), load your bait cooler with frozen herring and point you in the right direction. You'll find all five salmon running in the Wrangell Narrows: kings (20 to 30 pounds) from May through July; sockeyes (five to seven pounds) in July; chums (eight to 20 pounds) in July and August; pinks (three to six pounds) in July and August, and silvers (eight to 18 pounds) in August and September. Rivers flowing into the Narrows and adjacent straits hold steelhead in April and May and char and cutthroats from June through September. Cod and halibut are available throughout the season.

Bring your own fishing gear, including a fairly stiff rod and a medium-heavy reel loaded with 25-pound-test line. Slip a lightweight spinning system into your duffel for char and cutthroats. Flyfishers will be happy with an 8- or 9-weight system and a 5 weight for trout. This is definitely a catch-and-keep operation. Load your gear into two coolers. Pack along a duffel bag. You'll fill the coolers with filets, and stuff your baggage into the duffel for your trip home. Don't forget a box of heavy-duty freezer bags in which to pack your fish and duct tape to seal the coolers.

Katmai Lodge
King Salmon

VITAL STATISTICS:

KEY SPECIES:
Rainbow trout; king, sockeye, chum, pink and silver salmon; grayling

Season:
June through October

Accommodations:
Rustic wooden cabins
Number of Guest Rooms: 40
Maximum Number of Guests: 86

Conference Groups: Yes

Meals: American plan

Rates:
Several packages from $2100 per person for 3 nights

Guides: Included

Gratuities: $15 to $20 per rod per day

Preferred Payment:
MasterCard, Visa

Getting There:
Packages vary from King Salmon.

Other Activities:
Hiking, bird watching, wildlife photography, flytying.

Contact:
Tony Sarp
Katmai Lodge, 2825 90th St. SE, Everett, WA 98208; 206/337-0326, fax 206/337-0335, email katmai@accessone.com, website http://www. katmai.com

Rainbows grow to legendary proportions, and this established lodge is your hookup.

IF EVER WATER WAS MEANT for rainbows, it's the Alagnak River below Nonvianuk Lake in the Bristol Bay area. It's a classic braided river, with a gravel bottom that is ideal for spawning. The runs flow into pools that shallow out into channels that divide among islands where rainbows hide beneath cutbanks. The river also draws wave after wave of spawning salmon: kings and sockeyes in late June, chums in early July and pinks later that month, then silvers in August. All this means food for rainbows, to say nothing of considerable caddis action.

The curtain rises when smolt—salmon that have grown beyond the parr stage—begin to move down the Alagnak to Bristol Bay and salt water. Rainbows shake off winter lethargy and the rigors of their own spawning, charge the flashing fingerlings and follow them into the sea. The smolt run ends in early summer, the rainbows begin to return to the rivers and "mousing" is the fun way to catch them.

Voles are lemming-like rodents that live in the grasses by the streams. It isn't an urge to leap into the sea that makes voles trout bait. The fact is that a percentage of voles are clumsy and fall in. Rainbows, especially those upwards of 20 inches, want the greatest return on every chomp of their jaws. If it's about an inch long and hairy and casts an oval shadow, a 'bow is likely to slam it, especially if it lands with a splat next to an undercut bank. Forget finesse here. Drive the mouse imitation forward so it lands where you want, flip a quick mend in the line, work it so it thrashes on the surface like it's swimming for dear life and steel yourself against striking too soon. Use the steelhead technique of working the fly with a loop of line between your rod hand and reel. When the fish strikes, slip the line. The fish will turn and your odds of a secure hookup are instantly increased.

July is salmon time on the Alagnak and angling for them overshadows rainbows. In a week, you can pick up all five species on a flyrod. When the sun begins to drop in the sky along with temperatures, spawn from salmon reaches critical mass, turning on the rainbows. Egg patterns are killers.

Larger than most, Katmai Lodge can host more than 80 anglers a week. But don't let size be of too much concern. This full-service operation employs upwards of 20 guides and operates a fleet of more than 25 jetboats to ferry anglers to remote waters. You'll fish in a party of four with a guide who'll grill salmon or burgers streamside while you're fighting fish. A post-fishing sauna may relax you for the hearty dinner buffet.

King Ko Inn
King Salmon

Get Alaskan salmon, trout and grayling
at a do-it-yourself lodge for less than $300 per day.

VITAL STATISTICS:

KEY SPECIES:
King, chum, red and silver salmon; rainbow trout; grayling

Season:
April through October
Accommodations:
HOUSEKEEPING EFFICIENCIES
NUMBER OF GUEST ROOMS: 18
MAXIMUM NUMBER OF GUESTS: 50
Conference Groups: Yes
Meals: Eat in restaurant or cook for yourself
Rates:
$170 for 2 per day
Guides: $190 for 1 per day
Gratuities: Client's discretion
Preferred Payment:
Major credit cards
Getting There:
Fly to King Salmon.
Other Activities:
Canoeing, rafting, boating, bird watching, wildlife photography.

Contact:
**Matt Norman or
Biz Smith,
King Ko Inn, 3340 Arctic
Blvd., #203, Anchorage,
AK 99503; 907/562-
0648, fax 907/563-7238
(winter); PO Box 346,
King Salmon, AK 99613;
907/246-3377, fax
907/246-3357 (summer); website http://
www.alaska.net/nkingko**

THERE'S NO DOUBT that the Bristol Bay area of Alaska is the heart of that state's trophy salmon and rainbow fishery. It's the jumping-off place for Iliamna and the Kvichak, Alagnak and Nonvianuk, and scores of other lakes and rivers where millions of salmon spawn. Everybody who fishes this region flies to King Salmon and transfers to a Beaver, Otter or Cessna for a flight into the bush. Yet King Salmon itself offers guest accommodations, among them the King Ko Inn.

In 1943, shortly after the U.S. Army Air Corps established a base on the flats near the Naknek River, the King Ko Inn opened its doors. A fire in 1993 burned the original structure and in its place a new King Ko has emerged. Each of nine modern cabins contains two efficiencies complete with kitchenette and private bath. Adjacent is the main lodge with restaurant and bar featuring live entertainment. Units may be rented with American plan or without meals.

Fishing arrangements here differ from those at most lodges in the region. Owners Matt Norman and Biz Smith employ no guides and own no plane or boats. They'll refer you to guides who frequently lodge their parties in the inn. Guests often book a day or two with a knowledgeable local guide and then rent a boat ($125 per day) and drift or troll the Naknek River freelance for kings. In the general vicinity of the lodge you'll find four species of salmon. Kings, up to 60 pounds, are best in June and July; chums (four to 20 pounds) and reds (four to 15 pounds) in July; and silvers (four to 15 pounds) in August. Grayling in the two- to three-pound range open the season in May and rainbows (two to 10-pounds-plus) bring it to a close in September and October.

Think of the King Ko Inn as do-it-yourself Alaska. If you don't need fancy and are willing to do your own cooking, you can enjoy guided fishing for less than $300 per person per day excluding your flight to King Salmon. And, of course, fly outs to more exotic waters can be arranged for additional fees.

Kodiak Island River Camps

K o d i a k   I s l a n d

You have four options for silver salmon on this, Alaska's Emerald Isle.

VITAL STATISTICS:

KEY SPECIES:
Silver and king salmon; steelhead

Season:
June through October

Accommodations:
GUEST ROOMS, CABINS AND TENTS
NUMBER OF GUEST ROOMS: Depends on trip
MAXIMUM NUMBER OF GUESTS: 4 to 6

Conference Groups: No

Meals: American plan

Rates:
ROAD SYSTEM: $1295
AFOGNAK CAMP: $1595
KARLUK FLOATS: $2495;
all per person per week, double occupancy

Gratuities: Client's discretion

Preferred Payment:
Cash or check

Getting There:
Fly to Kodiak and you'll be met by a representative of the camps.

Other Activities:
Hiking, bird watching, wildlife photography.

Contact:
Dan Busch
Kodiak Island River
Camps, Box 1162,
Kodiak, AK 99615;
907/496-5310.

Represented By:
Kaufmann's Streamborn,
800/442-4359.

SEPARATED FROM THE MAINLAND by the Shelikof Strait, Kodiak is warmed by the Japanese Current. Moisture-laden winds condense on its low mountains. The northeast third of Kodiak is heavily forested with Sitka spruce; to the southeast vegetation is stunted and the landscape looks like a tufted carpet of kelly green. Kodiak is known as Alaska's Emerald Isle. It's also known for good populations of migrating salmon and steelhead.

Since 1989, Dan Busch has been guiding anglers out of his home base in Kodiak. Home base is a two-room (private baths) bed and breakfast on the outskirts of this quaint town. From his headquarters Busch runs four, week-long fishing programs:

PAUL'S LAKE CAMP on Afognak: Fly to Afognak Island, about half an hour by air from Kodiak, to an island camp on this mile-long lake. The river connecting the lake to Paul's Bay is only a few hundred yards long. From the second week in August through the middle of September, silver salmon run up the channel into the lake, heading for Laura and Gretchen lakes upstream. Four anglers fish from inflatables or float tubes or wade the lake, river or tidal shore under the eye of a guide. Accommodations are utilitarian—three unheated cabins—but the dining and kitchen cabin is warmed by its gas stove and oven.

KARLUK FLOAT for king salmon: After flying into the Karluk, you, a guide and up to three other anglers will drift down the Karluk for six days camping and fishing where the fishing is best. You'll sleep on a cot in a pop-up tent and eat hearty in the stove-equipped cook tent.

KARLUK FOR STEELHEAD: Not a replay of the above, on this trip anglers fly into a different section of the river where Koniag, Inc., a cooperative of native associations, maintains four cabins that sleep up to six in bunk beds. They're warm and dry and when steelhead are running in the last two weeks of October, who cares about anything else?

KODIAK ROAD SYSTEM: In August and the first two weeks of September, silvers show up in many of the rivers along Kodiak's 100-mile-plus road system. Guests stay at Dan's B&B and drive out daily to the American, Olds or other rivers. Anglers booking this trip can also fly out to a remote river or lake at no extra charge. You'll stay in the B&B and eat dinners prepared by Busch's wife.

Lions Den Wilderness Lodge
Port Lions

This all-weather lodge is a jumping-off point for float trips for kings and steelies.

VITAL STATISTICS:

KEY SPECIES:
Sockeye, silver, king and pink salmon; steelhead; halibut

Season:
May through December

Accommodations:
LODGE
NUMBER OF GUEST ROOMS: 6
MAXIMUM NUMBER OF GUESTS: 12

Conference Groups: Yes

Meals: American plan

Rates:
From $1600 per person for 3 days and 4 nights, single occupancy

Guides: Included

Gratuities: Client's discretion

Preferred Payment:
Cash or check

Getting There:
Fly from Anchorage to Kodiak, taxi and boat or floatplane depending on weather at no additional charge.

Other Activities:
Hiking, hunting, bird watching, wildlife photography, kayaking.

Contact:
Kevin Adkins
Lions Den Wilderness Lodge, PO Box 29, Port Lions, AK 99550; 907/454-2301.

IF THERE'S ONE BUGABOO ABOUT FISHING Kodiak Island, it's the weather. Clear and sunny one minute, in the next you can be enveloped in thick fog. That's one reason why Lions Den Wilderness Lodge is so popular. No matter what the weather, you can get there. It's a short boat ride around the north end of Kodiak Island into Port Lions and Settler's Cove on Kizhuyak Bay. The lodge is on the bay at the east end of the tiny village. If you're socked in, just walk up the street and fish a little nameless river for sockeyes in June and silvers in July. Or you can slip into a sea kayak and catch them in the bay in front of the lodge.

That, of course, isn't the main event. The Lions Den is really a jumping-off point for float trips on the Karluk for kings in June and steelhead when scrub alders and cottonwoods yellow up in the fall. Equally popular is the short run across Marmot Bay to Afognak Island and its namesake river for sockeyes and early pinks in July. Halibut are plentiful on the north side of Whale Island, a 20-minute boat trip from the lodge.

The four-day/four-night fly-out package includes your choice of two fly-out trips to rivers in the region or an overnight float trip on the Karluk. Go for the float. Operator Kevin Adkins takes four to six guests who drift the river, famous for kings but also heavy with late-summer silvers and sockeyes, and spend the night at a tent camp at the midway point.

Tent camp is a bit of a misnomer, as the tents are erected on plywood platforms and heated with stoves. One provides sleeping accommodations for guests. Activity centers around the other, equipped with a full-size cook stove and oven. No canned food here. Everything's flown in fresh, including Katy Adkins' homemade pastries. Dining family-style in the kitchen tent is a cozy end to the day, especially if you've been fighting steelhead in the chill of October.

The main lodge includes six guest rooms with private baths and Katy's cooking, which can be heart healthy, MSG/salt free or vegetarian if need be. And, of course, there's lots of fresh bread and homemade desserts.

Mike Cusack's King Salmon Lodge
N a k n e k   R i v e r

VITAL STATISTICS:

KEY SPECIES:
King, silver, coho, sockeye and pink salmon; rainbow trout; dolly varden; grayling

Season:
June through mid-October
Accommodations:
RIVERFRONT LODGE
NUMBER OF GUEST ROOMS: 22
MAXIMUM NUMBER OF GUESTS: 34
Conference Groups: Yes
Meals: American plan
Rates:
$5800 per week, single occupancy
Guides: Included
Gratuities: $300 to $400 per week
Preferred Payment:
Major credit cards
Getting There:
Fly to King Salmon and the lodge van will meet you.
Other Activities:
Boating, hiking, wildlife photography.

Contact:
**Don Meahan
Mike Cusack's King Salmon Lodge, 3340 Providence Dr., Suite 555, Anchorage, AK 99508; 907/277-3033, fax 907/563-7929.**

Represented By:
Alaska's Inside Passage Resorts, 800/350-3474.

If American lodges were rated, this would earn five stars.

HERE, ON A REALLY PRIME RIVER feeding Bristol Bay, is one of the finest angling lodges in the country. Its strategic location on the Naknek River provides anglers with access to the hottest rainbow and salmon fishing in southwest Alaska. The Wild Trout Management Area around Iliamna Lake is but a short hop, as are the bounteous waters of Katmai National Park. No wonder this lodge attracts such folks as Bob Hope, Norman Schwarzkopf, Chuck Yeager, Olivia Newton-John, Tom Weiskopf and John Riggins.

It's a toss-up just which is the biggest attraction. All five species of Pacific salmon migrate up the Naknek. Kings up to 50-pounds-plus arrive in mid-June and complete their run by August. Sockeyes from four to 12 pounds play a short but intense engagement from late June to mid-July. If you want to test your skills against the biggest and scrappiest members of the salmon clan, book the first week in July. And speaking of duos, what about rainbows averaging six pounds and silver salmon of eight to 16 pounds? If you hit them in early September, as the rainbows gorge on salmon eggs, you will have truly been there and done it all. Fans of wispy spinning and flyrods will love the grayling and dolly varden fishing. Angling is via boat, wading, floatplane or whatever works. Often two anglers share a guide, but sometimes you may fish one-on-one. If you don't have the tackle you think you'll need, don't worry. King Salmon Lodge will supply everything, not just flies or lures, but rods, reels, waders, you name it.

Anglers who book late in the year might work in a little cast-and-blast. Ptarmigan, grouselike fowl of northern climes, open in mid-August, about the time that rainbows and silver salmon reach their peaks. Starting in September duck season also overlaps with the height of rainbows and silvers. King Salmon Lodge has a kennel of pointers and champion black Labs. You may want to bring your own 20- or 12-gauge.

Quality service isn't just a slogan at King Salmon Lodge, it's a way of life. Owner Mike Cusack grew up here, at his mother's "cabin on the river." As second-generation lodgekeepers, Mike and family know what appeals and what does not. Guest rooms (private baths) are country comfy but informal, homey, and not the least overdone. Along with fine regional cuisine, you'll enjoy the weekly pig roast. In a corner of the sunken dining room is a concert grand piano. Imagine Beethoven and twilight over the Naknek River, or someone riffing out a little jazz as you relax with an after-dinner libation, complimentary, of course, around the circular stone fireplace.

Mission Lodges

Anchorage

A splendid lodge and two tent camps
put salmon and trout in reach of any angler.

VITAL STATISTICS:

KEY SPECIES:
King, sockeye, silver, chum and pink salmon; rainbow trout; arctic char; grayling

Season:
June through September

Accommodations:
MISSION LODGE: Modern California-style lodge
ALASKA WEST: Wood-floor tents
ALASKA KINGFISHERS: Tent camps
NUMBER OF GUEST ROOMS/GUESTS:
MISSION LODGE: 20/20
ALASKA WEST: 9/18
ALASKA KINGFISHERS: 4/8

Conference Groups: Yes

Meals: American plan

Rates:
MISSION LODGE: $4750
ALASKA WEST: $3450
ALASKA KINGFISHER: $2650;
all per person per week

Guides: Included

Gratuities: 10% of total bill

Preferred Payment:
MasterCard, Visa

Getting There:
MISSION LODGE AND KINGFISHERS: Fly to Dillingham
ALASKA WEST: Fly to Quinhagak

Other Activities:
Bird watching, wildlife photography, hiking.

Contact:
Dennis Gearhart or Mike Sanders, Mission Lodges/ Kingfishers, 111201 SE Eighth, Suite 100, Bellevue, WA 98004; 800/819-0750, fax 206/452-9351 (winter). Alaska West, 200 W. 34th, Suite 1170, Anchorage, AK 99503; 800/344-3628, fax 907/563-9787 (winter).

DALE DE PRIEST, Dennis Gearhart and Mike Sanders have teamed up to provide a trio of angling lodges that make the most of salmon, rainbow, grayling and char in the Bristol Bay area. From upscale wilderness tent camps to the almost-elegant timber resort north of Dillingham on the Aleknagik River, the trio offers anglers a range of opportunities that will suit varying interests and wallets.

MISSION LODGE: Daily fly outs ferry anglers to hot fishing on the numerous rivers and lakes in the Nushagak Basin. All five species of Pacific salmon—kings, sockeyes, silvers, chums and pinks—spawn in these waters. Rainbows, dolly varden, arctic char and grayling are thick in specific locales known to the pilots and guides. Beginning with kings and rainbows in June, angling winds up with trophy rainbows in fall. You'll fish from aluminum skiffs or wade as conditions and fish dictate. The long, many-gabled two-story lodge with ample windows offers spectacular views of the river and the bush, teeming with wildlife. Inside, the carpeted interior with free standing fireplace and modern furnishings has a distinctly California feel. Each guest enjoys a private and cheerful room with thick comforters on double beds (no bunks here). Rooms with queen-size beds are available for couples. With the exception of two rooms, baths are shared. Steak, seafood and prime rib are on the menu at dinners served family-style.

ALASKA WEST: Nine wood-floored tents outfitted with heaters and beds with linens, a drying tent for wet waders and gear, a dining tent with a tying bench and a tent with hot showers make up accommodations on the Kanetok River, which flows into Kuskokwim Bay at Quinhagak. Salmon, trout, char and grayling are found here with July and August the better months for rainbows of five-pounds-plus. Flyfishing for kings in the 50-pound-plus range and tossing Polliwogs (big pink deer-hair poppers) for silvers are the prime sports. Two anglers and their guide set off every morning in an 18-foot boat. And at night, after dinner, you can fish in front of the camp until dark, if you've got the stamina.

ALASKA KINGFISHERS: If monster king salmon feed your dreams, then this eight-angler tent camp on the Nushagak River may be for you. With similar accommodations to Alaska West, the camp boasts 22-foot big river sleds pushed by 60-horse motors with 9.9-horse trolling motors. The camp is only open for a few weeks during the height of runs of king and chum salmon.

Misty Fjords Lodge
B o c a   d e   Q u a d r a

Five mountain streams meet here among
narrow fingers of the sea named Misty Fjords.

VITAL STATISTICS:

KEY SPECIES:
King, coho, pink, chum and sockeye salmon; steelhead; cutthroat trout

Season:
June through September

Accommodations:
Cedar and pine lodge
Number of Guest Rooms: 6
Maximum Number of Guests: 12

Conference Groups: No

Meals: American plan

Rates:
$2265 per person for 4 nights and 3 days, double occupancy

Guides: Included

Gratuities: $30 for guide, $15 for wait staff

Preferred Payment:
Major credit cards

Getting There:
Fly to Ketchikan and meet the floatplane pilot who will fly you to the lodge (included).

Other Activities:
Canoeing, boating, hiking, bird watching, wildlife photography, flight seeing.

Contact:
Luis Martell
Misty Fjords Lodge, 125 South Main St., Ketchikan, AK 99901; 888/295-5464, fax 305/296-1003.

Represented By:
Alaska's Inside Passage Resorts, 800/926-2477.

FIVE MAJOR SPAWNING STREAMS for trout and salmon come together at Boca de Quadra in the Misty Fjords National Monument. You might think that angling for steelhead, cutthroat trout and dolly varden would keep you busy, but king, coho, pink, chum and sockeye salmon are the headliners here. On Mink Bay, Misty Fjords Lodge is a modern and charming California-style resort set back in the spruce and connected to the bay by a long sweeping boardwalk.

The scenery is breathtaking. Sheer granite cliffs plunge deep into a sea that's loden green like the forest. Bear, deer, mountain goats, otters and seals are abundant. Eagles soar overhead, their cries the only sounds cutting the silence of the deep woods. That, and the sounds of water rushing down riffles and runs before settling into slick pools where trout lie. In May and June, a few spawning steelhead run these rivers. They will take flies or spinners, but angling for them requires persistence and patience. More readily hooked are cutthroats in June and July. In the streams you'll find some sockeyes and coho, but angling for them is generally done while trolling from cabined (for four anglers) and open (for two anglers) boats. Kings up to 25 pounds are prevalent in May and June. Cohos up to 10 pounds, sockeyes to eight pounds and chums upwards of 15 are all best in August. You may also fish from canoes or hike to streams and wade. You'll have the fishing to yourself, as there are no other lodges nearby.

Opened in 1990, the lodge was initially known as the Mink Bay Lodge. Today it features all the up-to-date amenities. Guest rooms are spacious, with private baths. A huge fireplace of old brick and ceiling trusses of massive pine log timbers dominate the high-ceilinged living room, and large windows add the feeling of openness. In another wing, bright and sunny, breakfast and dinner—dungeness crab, prawns, pasta and pesto—are served on small, highly polished tables for four. At this lodge everything is furnished, except the energy to catch and land the fish.

Mountaineer Lodge
Talachulitna River

*Catches of 40 to 50 rainbows per day
are possible on the upper Tal after August 25.*

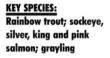

VITAL STATISTICS:

KEY SPECIES:
Rainbow trout; sockeye, silver, king and pink salmon; grayling

Season:
May through mid-September
Accommodations:
FRAME CABINS WITH SEPARATE LODGE FOR DINNING
NUMBER OF GUEST ROOMS: 3
MAXIMUM NUMBER OF GUESTS: 6
Conference Groups: No
Meals: American plan
Rates:
From $2275 per person per week, double occupancy
Guides: Included
Gratuities: 10% of package
Preferred Payment:
Credit cards, cash or check
Getting There:
Fly to Anchorage, then take a floatplane to the lodge ($200 additional round trip per person).
Other Activities:
Rafting, swimming, boating, hiking, bird watching, wildlife photography.

Contact:
**Jim Dawson
Mountaineer Lodge,
72681 Acorn Rd.,
Kimbolton, OH 43749;
614/489-9819 (winter);
PO Box 220175,
Anchorage, AK 99522-
0175; 907/733-3048
(summer).**

A**S YOU MOVE UPRIVER**, the Tal, as the Talachulitna River is called, gets skinny. Near its source, the water is clear and cold. According to Gary Young, a fishing forester and partner in the Mountaineer, the headwaters is the best place to fish for rainbows and the best time is late August. Why? Three reasons. First, rainbows are gorging on salmon eggs. They lie in the bottoms of pools and behind boulders, stumps and logs. The current brings them their diet. You can see them feed. And it's all you can do not to anticipate a strike when that six-pound rainbow turns and chases your Egg-Sucking Leech. After August 25th, you can run a powerboat up the river, and then walk to even better rainbow spots. A 40-fish day is not unusual.

Rainbows are only a fraction of the action in the Talachulitna. Equally exciting are the silver salmon. They'll hit hardware cast with spinning gear or ginger-colored flesh pattern flies. Runs are lightning fast, punctuated with somersaults. Sockeyes are acrobats but harder to catch unless you find them stacked up in a hole waiting to move upstream. In the 40- to 60-pound class, kings, whether fished with big spinners or flies (No. 2 Fat Freddies are favorites here), are the most difficult quarry. One fish per rod per day is a reasonable expectation. You can make up for the king's parsimony by fishing pinks on ultralight spin or flytackle. Or try grayling on ultralight or dries.

Mountaineer Lodge is about 17 miles up the Tal from its mouth. Its three cabins, all with private baths, are traditional white with green tin roofs, and are open and airy inside. Meals include solid, basic fare: turkey, roast beef, spaghetti. Many anglers take advantage of an option to include a two- or three-day float/tent trip from the headwaters of the Tal down to the lodge.

Self-guided fishing for Pacific salmon,
halibut, steelhead and cutthroat trout is
the order of the day at Island Point Lodge on
Kupreanof Island. — page 211.

Far up a fjord deep in the Tongass National Forest
at Yes Bay Lodge, anglers make up their own
itineraries using the lodge's floatplane and boats to find
the best salt- or freshwater fishing. — page 233.

No See Um Lodge
King Salmon

VITAL STATISTICS:

KEY SPECIES:
King, sockeye, chum, pink and silver salmon; rainbow trout; arctic char; grayling; dolly varden

Season:
June through October

Accommodations:
RUSTIC LODGE AND CABIN
NUMBER OF GUEST ROOMS: 5
MAXIMUM NUMBER OF GUESTS: 10

Conference Groups: Yes

Meals: American plan

Rates:
$4675 per person per week, double occupancy

Guides: Included

Gratuities: 10% of package

Preferred Payment:
Cash or check

Getting There:
Fly to King Salmon and a floatplane will fly you to the lodge.

Other Activities:
Hiking, bird watching, wildlife photography.

Contact:
John Holman
No See Um Lodge, 6266 Riverside Dr., Redding, CA 96001; 916/241-6204, fax 916/244-4618 (winter); PO Box 382, King Salmon, AK 99613; phone/fax 907/439-3070 (summer).

Groups of four or fewer have their own plane and pilot/guide to fly them to the best fishing.

IT'S EVENING. YOU'VE RELAXED in the sauna and the muscles at the back of your neck are loose. You, your host and your guide kick over the options for tomorrow. It won't be like this morning. A passing front with fog and drizzle grounded the floatplanes. You and your partner were disappointed. Didn't want to waste a day near the lodge. But there was no choice, so you went up the Kvichak in one of the jetboats to a gravel bar that the guide knew. He said that there might be some silvers and kings, and before the weather broke you'd had half a dozen hookups and landed three, one of them a 40-pound king on a fly. As the skies started to clear, your guide asked whether you wanted to go back to the lodge and fly out to a good stream he knew in the Iliamna Wild Trout area. If it was OK with him, you said, you'd just as soon stay here. That's when he broke out the shore lunch, and you missed one hell of a strike.

Fishing at No See Um Lodge, Jack and Sue Holman's retreat in the Bristol Bay area, is like that. Plans change. But with a floatplane and pilot/guide for every two to four anglers, you've got your choice of where to fish and what to fish for. Rainbows are available all season and average three to 10 pounds. In August and September, when they're cramming themselves full of salmon eggs, 13-pounders are occasionally caught. Salmon start their runs in June. Kings average 30 pounds; sockeyes, six pounds; chums, 10; humpies (pinks), three to five pounds; and silvers, 10 pounds but frequently up to 18 pounds. Char (three to 14 pounds), grayling (one to three pounds) and dolly varden (three to six pounds) are fishable all season. Though the season opens in early June, best fishing for salmon is generally in July and August. Rainbows become absolutely fabulous later in the season.

To provide such personal services, No See Um Lodge is small and intimate with no more than 10 guests at any given time. Of five guest rooms, all but one are in the cedar guest house on the bank of the river (furnished with two twin beds). The other is in a cabin. The guest house commands a sweeping view of the Kvichak River. The day begins at dawn with breakfast. After fishing you'll return between 5:00 and 6:00 p.m., visit the hot tub or the sauna, enjoy cocktails and hors d'oeuvres, and dine at 7:00 p.m. Then, should you still have strength in your casting arm, try fishing right in front of the lodge. Who knows?

Northwoods Lodge

S k w e n t n a

VITAL STATISTICS:

KEY SPECIES:
King, coho, pink and chum salmon; rainbow trout; grayling; northern pike

Season:
May through September

Accommodations:
TWO CABINS AND BUNKHOUSE
NUMBER OF GUEST ROOMS: 6
MAXIMUM NUMBER OF GUESTS: 16

Conference Groups: Yes

Meals: American plan

Rates:
Wide variety of packages from $550 per night to $2975 per week per person, double occupancy

Guides: Included

Gratuities: 10% of package price

Preferred Payment:
American Express, MasterCard, Visa

Getting There:
Fly to Anchorage, shuttle van or taxi to floatplane for trip to lodge.

Other Activities:
Canoeing, rafting, swimming, boating, hiking, bird watching, wildlife photography.

Contact:
Shan Johnson
Northwoods Lodge, PO Box 56, Skwentna, AK 99667; 800/999-6539, fax 907/733-3742, email nwl@matnet.com, website http://www.ala skaone.com/northwoods

Try some non-extreme fishing in the shadows of Denali.

SEVENTY-FIVE AIR MILES NORTHWEST of Anchorage is Northwoods Lodge, a small operation that provides anglers a wide range of fishing opportunities. Start in late May for grayling, pike and rainbows. In June, chinook (king) salmon come into the Yenta River and Fish Lakes Creek, the home waters of Northwoods. July brings pinks, August cohos (silvers) and chums. The best fishing, according to owners Eric and Shan Johnson, may be in the first few weeks of June when rainbows, grayling and king salmon are at the height of their runs. The northern pike fishing is also excellent at that time.

While flyfishing is spoken here—there's a fully equipped tying bench for working out local patterns—one need not be a purist to hook into good sport. Spinning tackle is the weapon of choice for chinooks up to 50 pounds, and casting gear is preferred for silvers, pinks and chums. All anglers fish with guides (on staff) and boat to hotspots on the Yenta and Sustina rivers. Tackle and hipboots are provided as part of the package price, and the lodge will obtain licenses for guests. There is no tackleshop here, however, so anglers should bring their own equipment and stock up on miscellaneous gear ahead of time. Northwoods encourages catch-and-release fishing, but will filet and package salmon for the trip home.

Set among the trees above a bend on the creek, the main log lodge is surrounded by six cabins that can accommodate 16 clients, though 12 is more typical. A log-sided chalet with queen-size bed, living room with a sofa bed, and private bath is popular with couples. Two smaller cabins contain two bedrooms each and a shared bath. Two one-bedroom cabins and a bunkhouse for up to 10 make use of a bathhouse nearby. Decor is simple Alaskan spruce, charming but not fancy.

The food, according to guests, is something to write home about. Shan and daughter Julie turn out the likes of chicken dijonaise, festive tortellini and marinated orange salmon. And guides pack a shore lunch that's apt to include local salmon or caribou. Heart healthy, vegetarian and MSG/salt free meals will be prepared with advance notice.

Reel M Inn
King Salmon

You'll get a kick out of fishing salmon and rainbows here in the center of Bristol Bay country.

VITAL STATISTICS:

KEY SPECIES:
King, sockeye, chum, pink and silver salmon; rainbow trout; grayling; arctic char

Season:
June through October
Accommodations:
New lodge of native log
Number of Guest Rooms: 4
Maximum Number of Guests: 8
Conference Groups: Yes
Meals: American plan
Rates:
Day rates from $375; packages from $1495 for 4 days and 3 nights per person, double or single occupancy
Guides: Included
Gratuities: 15% of package price
Preferred Payment:
Cash or check
Getting There:
Fly to King Salmon.
Other Activities:
Wildlife photography, hiking, bird watching.

Contact:
Nanci Morris
Reel M Inn, Katmai
Fishing Adventures, PO
Box 221, King Salmon,
AK 99613; 907/246-
8322.

RUMOR HAS IT that the alcohol tax boys are keeping an eye on Nanci Morris. For nearly a dozen years she's been the proprietress of Reel M Inn. They're not out to get her for her lousy puns. (Maybe they should.) It seems that Nanci gathers low bush cranberries and concocts a potent brew from them. No pop-skull this, it's aged in the cellar for a full year. "You never know what you are going to get," she laments. Some years it's dry, yet fruity with mellow highlights; others it's rich and full bodied. It's always robust, and just the thing to toast a 30-inch rainbow brought to net from the Naknek in front of the lodge.

The Naknek is the river that passes King Salmon, port of entry to Alaska's Bristol Bay country, famed for its five salmon, huge rainbows, deeply colored char and subtle-hued grayling. The river drains the lake of the same name, part of which is encompassed by Katmai National Park. The river is big water, 100 yards wide at the lodge. Much of it is wadeable, but some of it is not. To get around on the river, Nancy uses beamy 20-foot skiffs especially designed for flyfishers (that means little hardware to snag a cast). Rainbows up to 10 pounds fish best in June and August through October. Kings in the 20- to 40-pound class enter the system in mid-June and fade by the end of July. Sockeye, chum and pink salmon are scattered through midsummer (June 25 through August 10) and silvers up to 12 pounds are prevalent from August 10 through September 7. Numerous fishing packages from one through seven days are available, and longer stays can be arranged. Those who plan to fish four days or more can fly out to smaller, isolated streams for arctic char and grayling as well as salmon and rainbows.

Under construction in 1997 is a stunning new lodge of log and timber for up to eight guests. Facing west to catch the afternoon sun, tall windows bring views of the river into the great room dominated on the far wall by a massive stone fireplace. The north wing contains guest rooms, all with private baths; and the south, the dining room. Dinners here are sturdy works featuring regional cuisine and, even if you didn't nail that 30-inch rainbow that hammered your Muddler, a dram of Nanci's cranberry liquor.

Saltery Lake Lodge
_K o d i a k_

At Saltery, you'll find congenial hosts with lakes, creeks and a river teeming with salmon.

VITAL STATISTICS:

KEY SPECIES:
King, silver, sockeye, chum and pink salmon; dolly varden; rainbow trout; steelhead; halibut; cod

Season:
May through October
Accommodations:
WOOD CABINS
NUMBER OF GUEST ROOMS: 4
MAXIMUM NUMBER OF GUESTS: 12
Conference Groups: No
Meals: American plan
Rates:
From $1770 per person for 6 days and 6 nights
Guides: Included
Gratuities: $15 to $20 per day
Preferred Payment:
Cash or check
Getting There:
Fly to Kodiak from Anchorage and then to the lodge at no extra charge.
Other Activities:
Canoeing, boating, hiking, bird watching, wildlife photography.

Contact:
Doyle Hatfield
Saltery Lake Lodge,
1516 Larch St., Kodiak,
AK 99615; 907/486-7083, fax 907/486-3188.

SALTERY LAKE LODGE is the only one on Kodiak Island that's located on a freshwater lake. That puts anglers in the catbird seat for a number of reasons. Flowing out of the lake is the Saltery River, seldom more than 50 yards wide. It chatters over gravel bars and slides through long pools on its way to Ugak Bay, less than five miles downstream. All five salmon species use the river. So, too, do dolly varden, rainbows and steelhead. When the spawn is on, fresh waves of salmon work their way up the stream. They hold in pools, waiting for that primeval trigger to impel them over the next shallows.

You'll find that you can easily see them lying in the pools. Cast a big Mepps against the far bank, let it flutter and sink down to where the salmon lie. Work it slowly through the pool in short jerks. Getting quickly to bottom is important to flyfishers as well. Use sparsely dressed and weighted patterns, tied on a six- or seven-foot leader and aided by a couple of small split-shot. When a salmon strikes, the Saltery is shallow and open enough so you can chase the fish downstream.

Spawning salmon and steelhead school in the lake before moving on up Saltery Creek, which flows behind the lodge. After dinner, as Alaskan twilight hangs over Bread Loaf Mountain, walk down to the mouth of the creek, stand on the gravel bar and cast to sockeyes until you're tired and ready for bed.

You'll sleep in one of four cabins; two share baths and two deluxe cabins have private baths. Accommodations are a bit on the spartan side and meals are hearty but not gourmet. Heart healthy, MSG/salt free and vegetarian diets are available. Hosts Bill and Diane Franklin and Doyle and Charlotte Hatfield are warm, friendly and know Kodiak fishing inside and out. They'll bend over backwards to make your stay everything you want it to be.

In addition to fishing the Saltery system, you can arrange to fly out to other watersheds; saltwater fishing for halibut, kings, silvers and cod; and a four- or five-day raft drip down the Karluk for kings, sockeyes and steelhead. Prices for these vary.

Stephan Lake Lodge
Eagle River

VITAL STATISTICS:

KEY SPECIES:
King and silver salmon; rainbow trout; grayling

Season:
June through September

Accommodations:
WEATHERED LODGE
NUMBER OF GUEST ROOMS: 7
MAXIMUM NUMBER OF GUESTS: 14

Conference Groups: Yes

Meals: American plan

Rates:
From $1500 per person for 3 days

Guides: Included

Gratuities: 10% of package

Preferred Payment:
MasterCard, Visa

Getting There:
Fly to Anchorage. A representative from the lodge will meet you.

Other Activities:
Hunting, bear watching, hiking, wildlife photography.

Contact:
Jim Bailey
Stephan Lake Lodge, PO Box 770695, Eagle River, AK 99577; 907/696-2163, fax 907/694-4129, website http://www.alaskaone.com/stephanlake

Hook into 20 king salmon or 40 trout per day on a secret river.

FOR MORE THAN 30 YEARS, Stephan Lake Lodge has been putting guests into fine rainbows, kings and silvers, and showing them spectacular shovel-racked moose and grizzlies. Make that lots of grizzlies. When the kings run up a nearby river, the grizzlies come down, between 70 to 100 of them, and gorge on spawning salmon. If you want, you can look at a grizz up close and very personal. "Never lost a client," muses owner and master guide Jim Bailey. After a moment's reflection he chuckles, "We have had...adventures."

Kings run from the first of July to about the 13th. You'll need a 10-weight rod for these bruisers, or stout spinning or casting gear to handle hookups of 10 to 20 fish per day. Before it's time for kings, check out the rainbows. The first two weeks of June and the last two weeks of August can bring 40-fish days. We're talking 18- to 24-inch fish here. In August, rainbows are feeding on eggs from spawning king salmon and virtually any egg pattern will work. Before 'bow fishing reaches its peak, silver salmon enter the system, and you'll catch them in the six- to eight-pound range.

While the lodge is on Stephan Lake, Bailey's pretty secretive about the specific names of the rivers he fishes. They're all accessible by floatplane, and he has a fleet of Cessnas and Super Cubs that he uses to ferry guests to trophy water. He also has boats and motors cached on some of the more isolated lakes and rivers. Plus, he has a pair of cabins for anglers who want to overnight at spots that are really secluded.

Built of native spruce, now mellowed with age, the lodge sits up on a hill with a commanding view of Stephan Lake and the forest beyond. On chill evenings, a fire burns in the circular hearth and near-perpetual twilight filters through the cathedral window and glows softly on the highly polished floor. Meals are simple and substantial. While baths are shared, sinks with hot and cold water are built into each guest room.

Guests should bring their own tackle, lures and flies, though in an emergency, loaner gear is available. And you can get your fishing licenses at the lodge. That means no chasing around in Anchorage after dark looking for a license vendor.

Talaheim Lodge
Talachulitna River

Helicopters take you to pristine, seldom-fished rivers full of trout and salmon.

VITAL STATISTICS:

KEY SPECIES:
King and silver salmon; rainbow trout; grayling; dolly varden

Season:
Mid-June through August
Accommodations:
LOG LODGE AND CABIN
NUMBER OF GUEST ROOMS: 3
MAXIMUM NUMBER OF GUESTS: 6
Conference Groups: No
Meals: American plan
Rates:
From $2450 per person for 5 nights and 6 days
Guides: Included
Gratuities: 5%
Preferred Payment:
Cash or check
Getting There:
Fly to Anchorage and take a charter flight (included) to Talaheim.
Other Activities:
Bear watching.

Contact:
Mark Miller
Talaheim Lodge, PO Box 190043, Anchorage, AK 99159-0043; 907/248-6205, fax 907/243-6670.

"THERE! DOWN THERE!" the pilot yells, gesturing with pointed finger at the river winding through the trees. In the water, so clear, you see tapered shadows stacked up in the run below the frothy green fast water. Must be kings, this early in the season. "There's a gravel bar ahead. We'll put down there," the pilot says, nodding to you. You look down and smile, as you're itchy to leave the little chopper and get on the water.

Since 1988, Talaheim Lodge has been one of the few resorts in Alaska to make extensive use of helicopters to ferry guests to great fishing. While Cessnas and Beavers require somewhat smooth and straight waterways, choppers can drop in anywhere there's a few square yards of treeless, level terrain. Fly outs in rotary-winged aircraft place anglers on waters that are normally only fished by bears.

Just 85 miles west of Anchorage in the foothills of the Alaska Range, Talaheim Lodge is about halfway up the Talachulitna River. Draining into Cook Inlet, the river is a bit off the beaten path. From late June through the second week in July, king salmon averaging 20 pounds run the river. Anglers take four-day, five-night floats through wilderness devoid of other humans. From mid-July through early August, the fishing focuses on rainbows running from two to six pounds, grayling of one and a half and dolly varden of three or four pounds. You'll ride the chopper to small streams ideal for medium-weight flyrods. Salmon, this time silvers, return to the picture for the last three weeks of August. Most average between six and 15 pounds. Trout are bigger, more aggressive and are found with the salmon. You'll fly out or ride jetboats to areas where the angling is hot.

Talaheim is a family affair, owned and operated by Mark and Judi Miller and their kids Katie and Luke. The number of guests is limited to six per week, and occasionally a couple will have it all to themselves. You'll either stay in a two-bedroom log cabin with shared bath or in a one-bedroom cabin, also log, with a private bath. Meals are simple, hearty, excellent and accompanied by good conversation. Afterwards relax in the hot tub and watch the Alaskan twilight settle over this wilderness.

Talstar Lodge
W a s i l l a

Here you'll find superlative salmon and rainbow fishing, plus a flyfishing school.

VITAL STATISTICS:

KEY SPECIES:
King, sockeye, silver, chum and pink salmon; rainbow trout

Season:
June through September
Accommodations:
MODERN LOG CABINS
NUMBER OF GUEST ROOMS: 2
MAXIMUM NUMBER OF GUESTS: 8
Conference Groups: Yes
Meals: American plan
Rates:
From $995 per person for 2 days and 1 night
Guides: Included
Gratuities: $20 per day
Preferred Payment:
Visa
Getting There:
Fly to Anchorage, then air taxi to Lake Hood and fly out to Talstar—included in package.
Other Activities:
Swimming, boating, hiking, bird watching, wildlife photography.

Contact:
**Claire Dubin or Dave Simmons
Talstar Lodge, PO Box 870978, Wasilla, AK 99687; 907/688-1116 or 907/733-1672, fax 907/696-3297.**

CLAIRE DUBIN, WHO OWNS Talstar Lodge, is a lady who likes to fish. She wanted to become a better angler, though, so she hooked up with fly-fisherwoman Pudge Kleinkauf and, in 1996, hosted a school for women at this lodge on the Talachulitna River. Kleinkauf and fellow guide Sandie Arnold went through the usual stuff...casting, knot tying, leader construction, river reading and fly selection. Classmates cheered good casts and commiserated when line piled at an angler's feet. Kleinkauf and Arnold were always available to help. As the school progressed, students began to help each other too. When one hooked into a fish, congratulatory cries rang over the river. Dubin plans to include at least one school for women anglers each year at Talstar.

It is okay, of course, for men to fish at Talstar as well. The Talachulitna River is 65 miles northwest of Anchorage in the foothills of the Alaska Range. It's a high-quality fishery for all five species of salmon. Kings up to 60 pounds run from mid-June through mid-July. Sockeyes enter the river in mid-July, and chums, pinks and silvers show up by the end of that month. If a grand slam on salmon isn't your dream, think about fishing the Tal in late August or early September with light tackle—fly or spinning—for rainbows up to six pounds, and silvers. Wading is the name of the game here, though sometimes anglers will work a pool from one of the lodge's 18-foot riverboats. One guide is provided for every four anglers.

Talstar, itself, is a modern log lodge surrounded by tall stands of ferns in a spruce forest. Two cabins can sleep a total of eight, and guests share three bathrooms. Dining is close to gourmet: salmon en croute Florentine with hollandaise, marinated and alder-smoked salmon, pork medallions a la champagne; fresh fruit and vegetables; breakfasts of sourdough pancakes and reindeer sausage. Nobody starves, everyone gains weight.

[A L A S K A]

The Grand Aleutian Hotel

Dutch Harbor

Wrestle monster halibut in the clear, icy waters of Unalaska Island, far out in the Aleutians.

VITAL STATISTICS:

KEY SPECIES:
Halibut; salmon

Season:
All year

Accommodations:
FULL-SERVICE HOTEL
NUMBER OF GUEST ROOMS: 112
MAXIMUM NUMBER OF GUESTS: 386

Conference Groups: Yes

Meals: Eat in hotel restaurant

Rates:
From $945 per person per week

Guides: Included

Gratuities: Client's discretion

Preferred Payment:
Major credit cards

Getting There:
Fly to Unalaska Airport at Dutch Harbor. A hotel van will pick you up.

Other Activities:
Bird watching, wildlife viewing and photography, boating, archaeological dig.

Contact:
Tour Coordinator
The Grand Aleutian Hotel, PO Box 921169, Dutch Harbor, AK 99692; 800/891-1194, fax 907/581-7150.

Represented By:
Inside Passage Resorts, 800/350-3474.

REMEMBER THIS OLD GROANER: "Why do anglers go fishing? Just for the halibut!" Well, at Dutch Harbor, Alaska, the busiest commercial fishing port in the U.S., halibut are no joke. They are huge, as in 440 pounds huge. Here, small halibut, of a paltry 100 to 200 pounds, are almost common during the May through September season. Only when halibut begin to approach 300 pounds do people start to take notice.

When the Forgotten Army, those soldiers stationed in this archipelago to fight the Japanese in the waning days of World War II, cast around for recreation, they discovered halibut. Gear was a little primitive: rude hooks, a chunk of beef liberated from a meat locker, whatever line wasn't nailed down. Fishing from boats borrowed for important missions, Army anglers caught scores of monster halibut. And when the war was over, they took their fish tales home.

Some returned to the lovely mist-shrouded islands of the Aleutians to vacation; watch whales, shorebirds, seals and fish. But it wasn't until a few years ago that halibut came into its own here as a sportfish species. Perhaps overshadowed by salmon's classier persona, halibut is a fish that requires not so much finesse, as stamina. A No. 12/0 hook, baited with herring, is dropped over the side from a stiff boat rod with enough weight to hold it near bottom. You sit in the stern of the comfortable sportfisherman, rod in hand, rising and falling on the gentle swell, waiting for a halibut to bite. You can do nothing but wait. But when a halibut hits, you know it. You rear back on the rod for all you're worth, hoping that you've driven the hook home. That's when the halibut makes his first run and you find out whether your reel's drag is worth the money you paid for it. Then it's you and the fish. Take up five yards of line, give back three. When the skipper shouts "we've got color," you know that the end is near. With shotgun-launched harpoon or flying gaff, the halibut will be brought aboard.

The Grand Aleutian Hotel offers halibut fishing packages as well as fly outs to the black sand beaches of Volcano Bay, where you'll find salmon in the surf. Bring waders along with your fly or spinning rod. And when you're not fishing, you'll enjoy all the amenities of a first-class hotel. Modern rooms are well appointed and offer water and mountain views. Works by local artists adorn the walls, elegant dining features regional cuisine and the piano in the bar knows all the good old tunes.

The Yakutat Lodge
Y a k u t a t

**VITAL
STATISTICS:**

KEY SPECIES:
**Halibut; king, sockeye,
pink and silver salmon;
dolly varden; steelhead**

Season:
April through mid-November
Accommodations:
LODGE AND CABINS
NUMBER OF GUEST ROOMS: 22
MAXIMUM NUMBER OF GUESTS: 95
Conference Groups: No
Meals: Various packages
Rates:
From $25 to $250 (August 15
through September 30) per per-
son per night, double occupancy
Guides: From $320 for 2
per day
Gratuities: 15%
Preferred Payment:
MasterCard, Visa
Getting There:
Fly to Yakutat and walk to the
lodge.
Other Activities:
Canoeing, rafting, boating,
hiking, bird watching, wildlife
photography, glacier trips.

Contact:
**Ken Fanning
The Yakutat Lodge, PO
Box 287, Yakutat, AK
99689; 907/784-3232,
fax 907/784-3452.**

Represented By:
Rod & Reel Adventures,
800/356-6982.

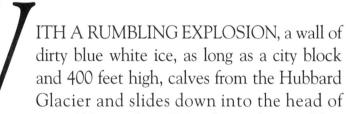

Mix and match floats, fly outs and road trips to isolated waters for a vacation tailored to your needs.

WITH A RUMBLING EXPLOSION, a wall of dirty blue white ice, as long as a city block and 400 feet high, calves from the Hubbard Glacier and slides down into the head of Yakutat Bay, only to rise again as 100 mini-icebergs. You've taken an afternoon off from fishing to make the 40-mile run from Yakutat Lodge to the glacier, one of the three largest in North America. The other two, the Yakutat and the Malaspina, are nearby.

Glaciers aren't the only thing that will humble and perhaps inspire you with awe. Hook into a spring steelhead, bright as 4140 stainless. Try to hold on as it tailwalks across the pool, then races up the run and down again. And when you tail it in the shallows, remove the hook and rest it until its gills work evenly again, you'll marvel at this fish, the supercharged relative of those rainbows you catch back home.

Yakutat is a small fishing village about 100 miles north of Cape Fairweather where British Columbia tries, but fails to squeeze through to the Gulf of Alaska. The lodge at Yakutat offers fishing, not only for steelhead in April and May and November and December, but for halibut, four species of Pacific salmon (kings, sockeyes, pinks and silvers) and dolly varden. Halibut, popular with summer guests, generally run better than 100 pounds. Kings to 30 pounds and sockeyes of five pounds run in June and July. Pinks of four pounds appear in July and are followed by silvers (12 to 15 pounds) in August. Dollies run all year. Spinfishermen as well as flyfishermen will be at home here, particularly with silvers, sockeyes and steelhead. Depending on the season and species, you may troll or bottomfish in the bay, float or wade rivers and streams that feed the bay or fly out to remote lakes.

Accommodations at Yakutat Lodge have to be among the most convenient in Alaska. You disembark from the jet from Seattle and simply walk over to the lodge which sits, with its marina, on a finger of the bay. Rooms either in the main lodge or in nearby cabins are clean and comfortable but not fancy. Lodge rooms have private baths; cabins share. Guided and nonguided fishing packages, with or without meals, allow you to create a vacation that fits your expectations and pocketbook. Whatever you need, you'll find it at Yakutat Lodge.

Waterfall Resort

P r i n c e   o f   W a l e s   I s l a n d

VITAL STATISTICS:

KEY SPECIES:
King and coho salmon; halibut; ling cod; red snapper

Season:
May through September
Accommodations:
BUNGALOWS AND TOWN HOUSES
NUMBER OF GUEST ROOMS: 40
MAXIMUM NUMBER OF GUESTS: 84
Conference Groups: Yes
Meals: American plan
Rates:
From $2645 per person for 3 nights and 4 days, double occupancy
Guides: Included
Gratuities: $25 per guide, $15 per wait staff
Preferred Payment
Major credit cards
Getting There:
Fly to Ketchikan, and meet the floatplane charter (included) to Waterfall Resort.
Other Activities:
Hiking, boating, bird watching, wildlife photography.

Contact:
Mike Dooley
Waterfall Resort, PO Box 6440, Ketchikan, AK 99901; 800/544-5125, fax 907/225-8530, email aipr@ix.netcom.com

Represented By:
Alaska's Inside Passage Resorts, 800/350-3474.

Once Alaska's premiere cannery, Waterfall is now one of its top-flight resorts.

ONCE THE STAR in the A&P Company's salmon-canning subsidiary, since 1981 Waterfall Resort has been a full-service fishing destination. At docks where commercial fishing vessels once emptied their holds of salmon, today boats of happy anglers display catches of king and coho salmon, halibut and ling cod. Unlike resorts on the Inside Passage, Waterfall is on the western shore of Prince of Wales Island. Though sheltered from the north Pacific by Suemez Island, the resort fronts on Ulloa Channel, a marine thoroughfare for salmon migrating fresh from the ocean.

Fishing is from 21-foot cruisers with heated cabins. Skippered by a guide who knows the channels, reefs, holding grounds and thoroughfares, four guests will fish from about 7:00 a.m. to 5:00 p.m. each day. Quarry and tactics depend on what's running and, of course, the weather. King salmon are most prized. You'll fish bait, perhaps with a flasher, on a long mooching rod. No heavy downriggers here. Average kings run 30 pounds but the Waterfall record is 78 pounds. Best fishing is in May and June. Coho average five to 18 pounds and are hot in July through September. Tactics are similar, except coho generally run closer to the surface. You'll go deeper for halibut, a popular fish with Waterfall guests. Halibut frequently exceed 100 pounds, but those more than that weight are normally released; they're usually females heavy with eggs. Ling cod and red snapper (a member of the rockfish family, not the one from the Gulf of Mexico) round out the range of species. Waterfall Resort cleans and packages anglers' fish for their trips home.

Old factory towns have a fascination about them, and none more so than Waterfall. Massive metal-sided cannery buildings house the resort store, tackle room and raingear room. Twin ranks of thoroughly modernized frame guest bungalows (private baths) face the channel. Four luxury beachfront town houses with two bedrooms and baths feature fireplaces, kitchens, and washer/dryers, as well as a shared spa for relaxing. Meals (Alaskan seafood and traditional fare) are served in the former home of the cannery manager, and another building nearby holds the cocktail lounge and meeting rooms. A stroll up the boardwalk will take you past the town houses, across a stream where salmon spawn and bears feed, to the waterfall. Don't forget to whistle while you walk to let the bears know you're there.

Whales Resort

Prince of Wales Island

Try a small resort that's big on service and salmon.

VITAL STATISTICS:

KEY SPECIES:
King, sockeye, silver and pink salmon; halibut; steelhead

Season:
April through October
Accommodations:
RUSTIC CEDAR LODGE
NUMBER OF GUEST ROOMS: 12
MAXIMUM NUMBER OF GUESTS: 24
Conference Groups: Yes
Meals: American plan
Rates:
From $2200 per person for 3 days and nights
Guides: Included
Gratuities: 10% of package per person
Preferred Payment:
Discover, MasterCard, Visa
Getting There:
Fly to Ketchikan and take float-plane at no additional charge.
Other Activities:
Hiking, flight seeing.

Contact:
Nani Fannemel
Whales Resort, PO Box 9835, Ketchikan, AK 99901; 907/846-5300, fax 907/846-5303, website http://www. konaweb.com/whales

Represented By:
Alaska's Inside Passage Resorts, 800/350-3474.

JETBOATS SPEED AWAY from the dock headed for that little unnamed stream loaded with cutthroats. Only a little more sedate, a 25-foot Bayliner climbs up on plane headed for the passage where salmon are running. Another Bayliner carries anglers out to drift for halibut over sea mounds, and a 4x4 is pulling out of the parking lot with a group of anglers off to a mountain lake. It's all in a morning's work at Whales Resort, on the upper end of Clarence Strait.

Tides flow vigorously through Clarence Strait, which separates Prince of Wales Island from smaller islands next to the mainland. Like the Los Angeles Freeway on a good day, the strait flows with salmon returning to home streams to spawn. Heavy tides bring fresh schools through narrow channels between forested islands. Species are season-dependent: kings (20 to 50 pounds) show up in May and fish best in the first two weeks of June. Sockeyes, averaging four pounds, are hot when the run begins in June but taper off into August. Pinks of five pounds or so come in July—best fishing is then—and leave in August. Silvers up to 10 pounds run from July through September, with August the best month. Mooching and trolling are the most popular methods for taking salmon, though silver and pinks may be taken with flies. Steelhead up to 10 pounds are very good early in the season. Try April and early May. Halibut from 30 to 100-pounds-plus are available from May through September, with the end of the season producing more big halibut of "barn door" dimension.

While not large as resorts go, Whales offers an extensive range of fishing and nonfishing activities. Bored is something you won't be here. If fishing isn't your gig, take a jetboat to Anan Creek to watch bears feed. Whales broach in the strait. Otters skitter down the boardwalk to bask in the sun on the dock and eagles cruise overhead. And inside the cedar-paneled recreation room you'll find pool, fooseball and electronic shuffleboard. A 25-foot-high cathedral ceiling spreads over a sunken lounge with rock fireplace and bay view. Dinners are very good—salmon Florentine, halibut stuffed with crab—and served in a cozy restaurant. Rooms are carpeted and modern and tasteful. Standard rooms include two twin beds; superior rooms add double beds and TV/VCRs; and suites have spacious separate sitting rooms along with everything else. All have private baths, of course.

[A L A S K A]

Wooden Wheel Cove Lodge

Point Baker

Fish for steelhead and salmon on a remote island with scores of unnamed streams.

VITAL STATISTICS:

KEY SPECIES:
King, coho, sockeye, chum and pink salmon; steelhead; halibut

Season:
Last week of April through mid-September

Accommodations:
MODERN WOODEN LODGE
NUMBER OF GUEST ROOMS: 4
MAXIMUM NUMBER OF GUESTS: 8

Conference Groups: Yes

Meals: American plan

Rates:
From $2200 per person for 5 days and 4 nights, double occupancy

Guides: Included

Gratuities: Client's discretion

Preferred Payment:
Discover, MasterCard, Visa

Getting There:
Fly to Ketchikan and a floatplane will shuttle you to the lodge. Baggage is limited to 40 pounds on the shuttle.

Other Activities:
Bear, bird and whale watching; hiking, wildlife photography.

Contact:
Robert or Patty Gray Wooden Wheel Cove Lodge, PO Box 118, Pt. Baker, AK 99927; 907/489-2288.

Represented By:
Alaska Connection, 800/288-3064.

PRINCE OF WALES ISLAND in southeast Alaska is the third largest island in the U. S. It also has very few people, which is what attracted Robert and Patty Gray. That and the salmon, the steelhead and the deer. The island has no major rivers, just hundreds of streams. The streams are not wide, seldom more than 90 feet across, nor are they particularly deep. Most bottoms are hard gravel, which is good for wading anglers and good for salmon and steelhead. Steelhead run in spring and fall, with the best fishing from mid-April to mid-May. Spinning tackle (seven-foot rods, reels spooled with 12-pound test) works well because of tight quarters on many of the streams. Try a No. 4 or 6 Blue Fox, and you'll start catching fish right away. Flyfishermen will get results with sink-tip lines and black and purple marabou flies. Polar Shrimp and various egg patterns also work well.

Bob moves anglers to the mouths of the island's streams on 22-foot boats. The craft are also used to fish for salmon in the sheltered waters of Port Protection on the northwest tip of the island. Salmon run through the pass in front of the lodge. Kings, pinks and sockeyes are best in May and June. Cohos turn up in July and peak in August and September. Jigging is the most popular method for taking salmon in salt water. After fish have entered the river, use spinners or flies. And while at Wooden Wheel Cove, don't overlook halibut up to 150 pounds.

The modern wooden lodge sits back under the spruce and looks out through the trees onto Sumner Strait. When the air is chilled, a fire crackles in the stone hearth in the sitting room. Bedrooms are cozy and decorated with antique pine reproductions. Two have private baths and the other two share. Meals are hearty and built around fresh seafood and beef.

Yes Bay Lodge

T o n g a s s   N a t i o n a l   F o r e s t

VITAL STATISTICS:

KEY SPECIES:
Steelhead; king, sockeye, pink and chum salmon; halibut; rainbow and cutthroat trout; dolly varden

Season:
Mid-May through mid-September

Accommodations:
RUSTIC WOODEN LODGE
NUMBER OF GUEST ROOMS: 15
MAXIMUM NUMBER OF GUESTS: 24

Conference Groups: Yes

Meals: American plan

Rates:
From $1965 for 4 nights and 3 days

Guides: Included

Gratuities: Client's discretion

Preferred Payment:
Major credit cards

Getting There:
Fly to Ketchikan and meet the floatplane to the lodge (included).

Other Activities:
Hiking, kayaking, bird watching, wildlife photography.

Contact:
**Stacey Hallstrom
Yes Bay Lodge, PO Box 6440, Ketchikan, AK 99901; 800/999-0784, fax 907/225-8530.**

Design your own fishing vacation at this rustic lodge deep in the Alaskan woods.

MANY ALASKAN LODGES have set fishing programs, but not Yes Bay Lodge. Two anglers and their guide decide what it'll be. Troll or mooch for salmon. Jig bottom for halibut or rockfish. Hike or fly out to streams and lakes for steelhead or trout. It all depends on the weather, and what's hot.

Far up the west arm of the Behm Canal, that twisting circular fjord-like channel that separates Revillagigedo Island from the mainland, is tiny Yes Bay. On a grassy point, the timbered lodge spreads its wings like a totem of the native peoples. A long, elevated boardwalk joins the lodge with its floating dock where 12 20-foot soft-top boats are moored, along with a DeHaviland Beaver that airlifts anglers into remote waters for steelhead, rainbows and dolly varden.

Steelheading in the rivers tumbling off the intensely forested slopes can be nothing short of fantastic. With fish averaging eight to 10 pounds, steelheading is best in the second and third weeks of May. At a price that's less than their normal rate, Yes Bay Lodge offers a special May steelhead package that includes a fly out to streams and lakes where these bright, tailwalking fighters run. And while steelheading is hot, the run of king salmon has reached its peak with thousands of 15- to 50-pounders streaming up the canal in front of the lodge.

If it's diverse angling you want, there's no time better than the second week of July at Yes Bay. Kings are still running, and rainbows and cutthroats are strong. Averaging six pounds, sockeyes are just hitting their stride, and pinks to five pounds and chums to 12 are getting good. Halibut up to 100 pounds and various rockfish up to five pounds or so are also on the bite. Chums and pinks peak in the fourth week of July; sockeyes in mid-August; and cohos from late August into September.

Accommodations at Yes Bay are gracious. Large guest rooms, carpeted and paneled in pine or cedar, are bright with large windows with views of the bay or forest. All have private baths. If you didn't get enough exercise on the boat, you can work out in the weight room complete with Jacuzzi and stationary bike. Dinner, a healthy menu of Alaskan seafood, poultry, pasta and prime rib, is served in an open and airy room overlooking the marina, and afterwards, you may want to lounge in front of the brick fireplace.

WESTERN CANADA

ALBERTA, BRITISH COLUMBIA, NORTHWEST TERRITORIES, SASKATCHEWAN, YUKON TERRITORY

W HERE the plains of central Canada will no longer sustain agriculture, the forests begin. In the north, the trees shorten to scrub and cap low stony ridges that separate the lakes. And what lakes they are; cold and brown, yielding record-size lake trout and monster northern pike. Fast rivers link the lakes and tumble over rapids filled with grayling. To the west are jagged mountains, where anglers find true native rainbow trout. Beyond are the salmon-rich waters of the Inside Passage. Far to the north, near the Arctic Circle, are camps on rivers that run red with char. Traveling here means long hours in the air, but the incredible fishing makes it all that seat-time worthwhile.

YUKON

NORTH WEST TERRITORIES

BAFFIN ISLAND

BRITISH COLUMBIA

ALBERTA

SASKATCHEWAN

Vancouver, BC, Canada V6B 2S2;
604/687-1581

References:

LAKES, LURES AND LODGES:
AN ANGLER'S GUIDE TO
WESTERN CANADA
— Jake MacDonald
Turnstone Press, 607-100 Arthur St.,
Winnipeg, MB, Canada R3B 1H3;
204/947-1555

TROUT STREAMS OF ALBERTA
— Jim McLennan
Johnson Gorman Publishers, 8680
Cambie St., Vancouver, BC, Canada
V6P 6M9; 403/342-0917

DUE NORTH OF MONTANA
— Chris Dawson
— Johnson Books, 1880 S. 57th St.,
Boulder, CO 80301; 303/443-9766

FISHING IN THE WEST
— David Carpenter
Douglas & McIntyre, 1615 Venables
St., Vancouver, BC, Canada V5L
2H1; 604/254-7191

BC FISHING: FRESHWATER
DIRECTORY AND ATLAS;
— Karl Bruhn, Editor
BC Outdoors, O.P. Publishing Ltd.,
1132 Hamilton St., Suite 202,

Resources:

TRAVEL ALBERTA,
PO Box 2500, Edmonton, AB,
Canada T5J 2Z4; 800/661-8888;
403/427-4321, website http://www.
discoveralberta.com/atp/

TOURISM BRITISH COLUMBIA,
1166 Alberni St., Suite 601,
Vancouver, BC, Canada V6E 3Z3;
800/663-6000, 604/605-8400, website
http://www.travel.bc.ca

NORTHWEST TERRITORIES
Tourism, Box 1320, Yellowknife, NWT,
Canada X1A 2L9; 800/661-0788,
403/873-7200, website
http://www.edt.gov.nt.ca/guide/
index.html

TOURISM SASKATCHEWAN,
500 - 1900 Albert St., Regina, SK,
Canada S4P 4L9; 800/667-7191,
306/787-2300, website
http://www.sasktourism.sk.ca

TOURISM YUKON,
PO Box 2703, Whitehorse, YT,
Canada Y1A 2C6; 403/667-5340,
website http://www.touryukon.com

Surrounded by towering mountains in the
southwest corner of the Yukon, Tincup Wilderness Lodge puts
visiting anglers into prime lake trout
and grayling water. — page 261.

Awaiting anglers for flights to 15 lakes where
lake trout, pike and walleyes run, the planes of
Hatchet Lake Lodge in Saskatchewan augment boats
to put anglers onto good fish. — page 258.

April Point Lodge
Q u a d r a   I s l a n d ,   B r i t i s h   C o l u m b i a

Guests come to this eclectic lodge for the food, art and music as well as for the bountiful salmon.

VITAL STATISTICS:

KEY SPECIES:
Chinook, coho, sockeye, pink and chum salmon; steelhead; ling cod

Season:
All year

Accommodations:
RAMBLING WOODEN LODGE
NUMBER OF GUEST ROOMS: 64
MAXIMUM NUMBER OF GUESTS: 110

Conference Groups: Yes

Meals: Many packages

Rates: From $375 (CDN) per person per day, double occupancy (50% discount on rooms from October through April)

Guides: Included in fishing packages

Gratuities: $25 (CDN) per day

Preferred Payment:
Major credit cards

Getting There:
Fly to Campbell River. Transfer to lodge is $15 to $20 additional.

Other Activities:
Kayaking, canoeing, hiking, bird watching, wildlife photography, horseback riding, tennis, golf, beach combing, heli-tours.

Contact:
Eric Peterson
April Point Lodge, PO Box 1, Campbell River, British Columbia, Canada V9W 4Z9; 888/334-3474, fax 604/285-2411.

ACROSS DISCOVERY PASSAGE from Campbell River lies brooding and largely unsettled Quadra Island. Hard by a little cove, where tides racing through the passage swirl and eddy and bring in salmon, lies the eclectic lodge called April Point, founded and operated by the Peterson family since 1946. It was called "Poverty Point" back then, the refuge of hard-bitten handliners who lived off what they caught from boats in the bay.

Though times have changed, the salmon are the same. Chinooks (six to 50 pounds) and cohos (eight to 18 pounds) run from May through September. Sockeyes (four to eight pounds) and pinks (three to eight pounds) show up in July and August. Chums (10 to 20 pounds) move through these waters from September to November. And what waters! Heavy tides course between stark cliffs and around jagged rocks in Seymour Narrows a few miles north of the lodge. Salmon school up in the deep rocky bays, riding the currents to the streams of their birth. Most of the fishing here is done out of Boston Whalers and similar craft, with Hootchies and flashers downrigged for depth if necessary. In June and July, chinooks are close to the surface. Then you can fish with flies. April Point also offers heli-tours to rivers for summer and winter steelhead, and bottomfishing for ling cod.

Fishing is good, guides are knowledgeable, and the personal service of the lodge alone would be enough to set it apart from others in the fishery. But what makes April Point special are its programs. A trio from the Toronto Symphony plays over Labor Day weekend during the late chinook run. Chums are running in full force during fish-printing (gyotaku) and fall cooking school. Tojo Hidekazy, whose restaurant in Vancouver is top rated by all, shares secrets in a spring cooking school in May when kings and cohos make their first appearances.

Good food is central to the April Point experience. Eggs Benedict are featured in the all-you-can-eat buffet, and if that doesn't suite, try French toast stuffed with fresh strawberries and banana. After a libation from the bar, open dinner with mussels poached with olives, tomatoes, basil and garlic; move on to blackened salmon with black bean salsa; and finish with a Caesar salad. Modern, yet weathered, the natural cedar lodge rambles around the point. Rooms in the main lodge look due west across the passage to Vancouver Island. Others face the deep-water marina. Some rooms feature Kwagiulth animal paintings, others have free-standing fireplaces and all have private baths.

Big Bay Marina & Fishing Resort

S t u a r t   I s l a n d ,   B r i t i s h   C o l u m b i a

Here, you can fish racing tides and whitewater rapids for five species of salmon.

VITAL STATISTICS:

KEY SPECIES:
King, coho, sockeye, chum and pink salmon

Season:
May through October

Accommodations:
RUSTIC CABINS
NUMBER OF GUEST ROOMS: 38
MAXIMUM NUMBER OF GUESTS: 80

Conference Groups: No

Meals: American plan

Rates:
From $395 per person for 2 days and 1 night

Guides: Included

Gratuities: Client's discretion

Preferred Payment:
Major credit cards

Getting There:
Fly to Campbell River and take a floatplane at your expense.

Other Activities:
Boating, hiking, bird watching, wildlife photography.

Contact:
Kay Knierim
Big Bay Marina & Fishing Resort, Stuart Island, British Columbia, Canada V0P 1V0;
250/286-8107.

SOME PLACES HAVE A FEEL to them that resonates, and Big Bay is one of those. A handful of cabins, sheathed with weathered shingles, are scattered under maples on the manicured lawn that slopes up from the bay to the forest above. In the middle is the low-slung great lodge of stone, cedar and glass. There you'll find a massive corner hearth where log fires chase the chill from foggy nights and mornings heavy with dew. Downhill a bit is a country store, stocked with groceries, gifts and fishing tackle. Out front spreads the dock and beyond is Big Bay, troubled twice a day with magnificent rushing tides.

The northwest entrance to Big Bay is a maze of islands and shoals turned to whitewater by 10-knot tides. Running this passage is tricky for boats as well as salmon. So the fish school up and ride the tides when it suits them best. Chinooks to 50 pounds are trolled up from May through October. Sockeyes up to 10 pounds arrive in July. Cohos in the eight-pound-range appear at the same time, and fish best in late summer and early fall. You'll also find chums from eight to 20 pounds, and pinks up to eight pounds. A favored tactic at Big Bay is to troll with herring. Artificials—flashers with Hootchies (fluorescent rubber skirts)—dropped with downriggers, also get results. At times the shoals can be fished with fly or spinning tackle. Through the lodge you can also arrange trips to isolated rivers for trout, salmon or char.

The stark gray cliffs of Mount Muehle rise over the lodge, and at its base is a little stream that drains Eagle Lake. You can hike a trail to Arran Rapids, another set of rips that reverse with the tide. Killer whales frequent Big Bay, as do otters, seals and scores of seabirds. When not fishing, you could do worse than sitting on the deck of your cabin, hands clasped behind your head, contemplating the water as the day comes to a close. Then amble over to the lodge for dinner: prawns, pasta, steaks, prime rib, chicken. Afterwards, settle into cushy sofas or chairs by the fire and swap stories in the Liar's Lounge.

Buck's Trophy Lodge

Rivers Inlet, British Columbia

Cedar cabins float on sheltered waters where kings and cohos run in midsummer.

VITAL STATISTICS:

KEY SPECIES:
King and silver salmon

Season:
June through September

Accommodations:
CEDAR CABINS
NUMBER OF GUEST ROOMS: 10
MAXIMUM NUMBER OF GUESTS: 20

Conference Groups: Yes
(10% discount)

Meals: American plan

Rates:
From $1599 per person for 4
days and 3 nights

Guides: $100 per day

Gratuities: $50 to $100

Preferred Payment:
American Express, Visa

Getting There:
From Vancouver International,
Buck's flies guests to the lodge.

Other Activities:
Bird watching, wildlife
photography.

Contact:
Shelly Lawrence
Buck's Trophy Lodge,
Box 8000-312, Sumas,
WA 98295-8000;
604/859-9779, fax
604/859-1661.

SALMON IS THE LANGUAGE of this lodge that floats on Finn Bay in Rivers Inlet, a saltwater arm that probes the mainland due north of the Queen Charlotte Strait from Port Hardy on Vancouver Island. Bright as silver, chinook (king) salmon begin their run into the bay in June. Fifty- to 70-pounders are frequently caught, and monsters of 80 pounds have been landed. The best months for chinooks are July and August. Silvers from six to 28 pounds enter the estuary in June as well, but the best angling for these slashing fighters occurs in August and September when bigger fish make their appearance. Other species include halibut up to 100 pounds, ling cod to 50 pounds and a variety of other bottomfish.

Angling at Buck's Trophy Lodge requires no guide, though you may hire one if you wish. Rather, anglers are provided with instruction on the operation of fiberglass skiffs pushed by 40-horse outboards. These boats are equipped with ship-to-shore radios, depthfinders and rain or sun tops. You'll use a long (eight- to 11-foot) rod and a direct-drive reel that works like a flyreel, only it's loaded with 20-pound-test monofilament. Buck's fishmaster will show you how to rig a herring bait or work a jig and skirt, then point you in the direction of the fish. You'll run the boat. Trolling is the name of the game in these waters, though silvers can be near the surface and may be played on conventional fly, casting or spinning gear. During the day, Buck's "Go Go" boat will bring you hot meals, fresh bait and assistance if you need it.

You may fish as much of the day as you want with only one caveat: You must be back for dinner that may include salmon, halibut, prawns and dungeness crab. Meals are family-style and 10 guests or so sit around tables and serve themselves from the lazy Susan. You'll stay in an unadorned cedar cabin on the water with a twin and a double bed, private bath, shower and drying room. At the conclusion of your stay, your cleaned catch will be packaged for shipment home. P.S. Bring a spare hat. Yours may end up on the dining room wall!

Farewell Harbour Resort

T e l e g r a p h   C o v e ,   B r i t i s h   C o l u m b i a

VITAL STATISTICS:

KEY SPECIES:
Chinook and coho salmon; halibut

Season:
June through September

Accommodations:
WATERFRONT LODGE
NUMBER OF GUEST ROOMS: 7
MAXIMUM NUMBER OF GUESTS: 12

Conference Groups: Yes

Meals: American plan

Rates:
From $1280 (US) per person for 4 days and 3 nights, double occupancy

Guides: Included

Gratuities: $25 per day

Preferred Payment:
Cash or check

Getting There:
Kenmore Air flies floatplanes to Berry Island daily from Seattle. Or take Regional Air or Pacific Coastal to Port Hardy and change to a floatplane for the trip to the lodge. The additional fee is $50 each way.

Other Activities:
Hiking, bird watching, whale watching, kayaking, wildlife photography.

Contact:
Paul Weaver,
Farewell Harbour Resort,
PO Box 3047, Carlsbad,
CA 92009; 619/438-
3681, fax 619/431-2688
(October through April);
PO Box 2-4, Telegraph
Cove, British Columbia,
Canada V0N 3J0;
250/928-3115 (May
through October).

Angling for salmon is taken seriously at this small, intimate lodge.

PERCHED ON A ROCKY POINT of Berry Island, Farewell Harbour Resort is near the top of the Discovery Passage that separates Vancouver Island from the mainland. Huge tides flush through the passage, bringing with them fresh charges of migrating salmon and baitfish on which the halibut and blackfish feed. With a season that runs June through mid-September, there are no bad times to fish. Yet species change as the weeks progress.

In early June, a few winter chinooks are still around, but an early run of blue-backs (cohos) brings out light-tackle anglers who use spinning or fly gear. Hookups are plentiful. Following the bluebacks is the first run of younger chinooks, called springs, in the 25- to 30-pound class. On their tails comes a wave of mature chinooks in the 40- to 50-pound range. By mid-July the action has gone deep. Quick-release downriggers hold lines bearing white lures or plug-cut herring in the search for resident cohos and chinooks. Also down deep are halibut. At the same time, a few pinks move in and are caught along with cohos. In late August, pinks are arriving in full force. They'll stay around until the end of September and provide steady action. The final party begins with the arrival of northern cohos. Fishing is wild: bucktails, buzz bombs, lures, herring, it's hard to miss with these slashing fighters. Chinook fishing fades, everyone's focused on the cohos until a 40-pounder grabs a bait. That's when you remember that up here big chinooks are called Tyee.

The folks at Farewell Harbour take their angling seriously. So will you. The day begins at 5:00 a.m.; you'll stoke up with coffee, fruit, rolls and juice and be on the water by 5:30 a.m. After four hours of fishing, more if there's a serious bite, you'll return to the lodge for brunch. If you can resist the urge to take a nap (and everyone can when salmon are running), you'll head back out for the afternoon. Cocktails are served at 6:30 p.m. and dinner—whitefish Florentine and cheesecake tarvana—an hour later. Then it's off to bed in one of seven guest rooms, which run, en echelon, down the deck over the waves lapping at the rock below. Here, nobody stays up late.

Frontiers Farwest

T e l k w a ,   B r i t i s h   C o l u m b i a

VITAL STATISTICS:

KEY SPECIES:
Steelhead; chinook, coho, chum and pink salmon; rainbow and cutthroat trout; grayling

Season:
April 15 through November
Accommodations:
ECLECTIC LODGE
NUMBER OF GUEST ROOMS: 7
MAXIMUM NUMBER OF GUESTS: 14
Conference Groups: Yes
Meals: American plan
Rates:
$484 per person per day, double occupancy
Guides: Included
Gratuities: 10%
Preferred Payment:
Cash or check
Getting There:
Fly to Smithers, British Columbia, and a representative from the lodge will meet you.
Other Activities:
Whitewater rafting, hiking, bird watching, wildlife photography.

Contact:
Debbie Patterson
Frontiers Farwest, PO Box 250, Telkwa, British Columbia, Canada V0J 2X0; 250/846-5391, fax 250/846-5336, email farwest@mail.netshop. net

Steelhead is the mother tongue at this eccentric lodge.

OUTSIDE, it isn't much to look at—a small weathered wooden building on an abandoned railroad grade across a dirt street from the river. But the driftboats, rafts, Suburbans, trailers and the swift current of the Bulkley fairly shout fishing. And inside, you'll find a thoroughly charming little inn of most unusual decor. Once a creamery, the building was stripped of some, but not all, of its machinery. The gabled ceiling is two stories above the main floor. Open stairs climb each end of the great dining room. To the left are guest rooms; to the right, the office. Walls are painted white and graced with original artwork. From the ceiling hang wrought-iron wheels—now painted red and trimmed in black—that once powered machinery. A massive steam valve defines a corner for the flytying bench. Walls enclose the kitchen, but not aromas from the likes of smoked salmon with glass noodles in soya vinaigrette by Yvan Sabourin (trained as a Swiss fish chef). Rooms share baths, but who cares.

Each evening at dinner, fishmaster Dave Evans hangs off the banister on the stairs to the office and says: "Listen up. Tomorrow..." and assigns guides and clients to sections of the river. Along with day floats and wading, Frontiers Farwest also does overnight floats to Twin Camp and other isolated locales on the Bulkley. Camps employ two Weatherport tents, one for sleeping, the other for cooking and eating. Sabourin packs dinner (herbed lamb chops) and breakfast, and stuff for lunches along the way.

The largest tributary of the Skeena, the Bulkley receives more than half of the Skeena's summer and fall-run steelhead. While fish will average 12 pounds, bigger fish are not uncommon, especially in the strains that run in October and November. Dry fly fishing is preferred: black and tan Bulkley mice, but wets such as the Blue or Black Bruce or the ever popular Egg-Sucking Leech take fish too. Bring two rods. Ten-foot 8 weights are fine. Rig one with a floating line for fishing dries, the other with a sinking-tip line for wets. A little diamond file to keep hooks sharp will pay big dividends. While steelheading is the game here, it isn't the only game in town. Nearby streams and ponds hold rainbows and cutthroats. Grayling inhabit some streams. Chinooks run in June, and July and August bring cohos, chums and pinks. Fishing packages span a full week. And here beneath glacier-capped Hudson Bay Mountain, in the deep loden forest where aspens flame in the fall, you'll wish it went on forever.

MacKenzie Trail Lodge

T s a c h a   L a k e ,   B r i t i s h   C o l u m b i a

VITAL STATISTICS:

KEY SPECIES:
Rainbow and lake trout; dolly varden

Season:
June through August

Accommodations:
RUSTIC LOG CABINS
NUMBER OF GUEST ROOMS/GUESTS:
MACKENZIE TRAIL: 12/6 to 8
BLACKWATER LODGE: 8/2 to 10
CHINE FALLS: 1/4

Conference Groups: Yes

Meals: American plan

Rates:
MACKENZIE TRAIL: $1699 per person for 5 days and 4 nights, double occupancy
BLACKWATER LODGE: (housekeeping), $125 per person per night, double occupancy plus $200 air fare from Nimpo Bay, British Columbia
CHINE FALLS: (housekeeping), $1995 for 4 persons for 5 days and 4 nights including airfare from Nimpo Bay

Guides: $100 per day

Gratuities: $15 per day per guest for tip pool

Preferred Payment:
MasterCard, Visa

Getting There:
Fly to Vancouver and meet the charter to the lodge.

Other Activities:
Canoeing, rafting, swimming, boating, hiking, bird watching, biking, wildlife photography, hunting, sauna, flytying instruction.

Contact:
Bill Warrington
MacKenzie Trail Lodge,
27134 NW Reeder Rd.,
Portland, OR 97231;
888/808-7688, fax
503/621-3551.

The Blackwater is one of British Columbia's most prolific rainbow rivers, and you can fish it for less than you'd imagine.

WITH MUCH angler attention focused on coastal fisheries for salmon, steelhead and sea-run cutthroats, British Columbia's fine interior fishing sometimes gets short shrift. So it is with the Blackwater River and Tsacha Lake near its headwaters. Roughly 270 miles due north of Vancouver, this river and the lakes along its route are known for its huge rainbow population.

Novice anglers will find the fishing easy. Rainbows, all natives, pounce on Royal Wulffs and Woolly Buggers. A 20-fish day is considered so-so; 50- to 70-fish days are the norm; skilled anglers hook and release more than 100; and it's said that a real type A angler—working at it from dawn to dusk—could maybe get close to 200. Tsacha Lake, 12 miles long and less than a mile wide, opens for fishing on June 1. Weighted nymphs and streamers are very effective on rainbows running two to three pounds. Fishing opens in the river on July 1. There the trick is getting your fly through the smaller 'bows to the larger fish. One suggestion: Use a bigger fly. Another suggestion: Use a small fly and fish only to rising big fish. The Blackwater is restricted to single hook, artificial flies only. Spinfishers can use weighted streamers or cast a fly with a clear bubble. The lake has no such restrictions, though pinched barbs make it easier to release fish. In addition to this lake and river, fly outs are available to more than 30 lakes and seven rivers in the area. MacKenzie Trail Lodge has cached boats on many of these.

Full-service MacKenzie Trail Lodge is the headquarters for fishing this area. Lakefront cabins for guests are comfortably appointed with private baths, wood stoves and lots of space to make yourself at home. Hop into the camp sauna after a hard day of fishing, and you'll be ready for dinner (everything from fish to flan) served in the main lodge. Boats are snugged up on the grassy lawn in front of the lodge. MacKenzie also operates two other lodges: Blackwater Lodge and Chine Falls Flyfishing Camp. The river enters the head of Tsacha Lake at the site of Blackwater Lodge. With eight log cabins that sleep between two and 10, that lodge provides common cooking and shared bath facilities. Boats, motors and gas are included. Chine Falls, 47 miles downstream from the main lodge, has a capacity of four with boats and motors on Kluskoil Lake. This, too, is a housekeeping and self-guided lodge. Bring your own sleeping bag. Don't worry about the fish; the rainbows, dolly varden, kokanees and lake trout will be waiting. And prices at Chine Falls are quite a bargain.

Moose Lake Lodge

A n a h i m   L a k e ,   B r i t i s h   C o l u m b i a

VITAL STATISTICS:

KEY SPECIES:
King, sockeye and silver salmon; rainbow trout; steelhead; dolly varden

Season:
May through October

Accommodations:
LOG CABINS
NUMBER OF GUEST ROOMS: 12
MAXIMUM NUMBER OF GUESTS: 20

Conference Groups: Yes

Meals: American plan

Rates:
From $1290 per person for 3 days and nights, double occupancy

Guides: Extra; rates vary

Gratuities: Client's discretion

Preferred Payment:
Cash or check

Getting There:
Fly to Vancouver and air shuttle to the lodge (included in package price).

Other Activities:
Riding, hiking, bird watching, wildlife photography.

Contact:
John Blackwell
Moose Lake Lodge,
Box 3310, Anahim Lake,
British Columbia,
Canada V0L 1C0;
250/742-3535, fax
250/742-3749.

Fish a different river every day or settle in on the Dean to chase steelhead fresh from the sea.

STEELHEAD, rainbows, cutthroats or salmon: They're all here for the taking. Isolated, yet little more than an hour by air from Vancouver, John and Mary Blackwell's Moose Lake Lodge offers a number of guided and nonguided programs from its base 40 miles north of the town of Anahim Lake. Nearby is the upper Dean, where 50-fish days of two-pound rainbows and dolly varden are common. Also in the vicinity is the Blackwater River, where dries raise two- to five-pound rainbows. These are barbless-hook, catch-and-release waters for both fly and spinfishers. The season generally runs from June 15 through October 15, with bigger fish showing up as summer ends and fall begins.

In addition to Moose Lake Lodge, the Blackwells also operate Dean River Lodge, three cabins and a main lodge where the river empties into Dean Channel which leads to Fitz Hugh Sound on the Pacific just north and east of the tip of Vancouver Island. It's a natural corridor for salmon, with kings of 30 pounds or so starting to show up in June. Fishing for them is best then; sockeyes arrive in August, while silvers wrap up the season later in the month and into September. Spinning gear is often used for the kings and silvers, but they and sockeyes fall prey to flies. There's nothing like a brace of tail-walking sockeyes to make your day.

Anglers come to Dean River Lodge for salmon, but the big event is the annual run of steelhead from June 15 through August 10. Fresh, bright and tipping the scales near 15 pounds, these beauties are aggressive and slam traditional patterns such as the Purple Peril, General Practitioner and Black Woolly Bugger. The Egg-Sucking Leech is good, too. Coastal rivers fish well from mid-April through mid-May, and again from September 1 through October 20.

Along with the Dean and Blackwater systems, Moose Lake Lodge provides optional fly outs, some by helicopter, to remote lakes and rivers. The lodge maintains a number of do-it-yourself outpost camps. You'll fly in with your food and gear and out again when you want. A range of packages include one- to three-day side trips with a stay at Moose Lake. With a commanding view of the lake, the main lodge, with large picture windows framing a lake view and distant mountains, serves guests in eight log cabins with private baths that sleep two to four. Meals are substantial, prepared under Mary's capable direction. She's also a master flytier, and if you're not, and are in need of a couple of local patterns, she'll tie some up for you.

Nimmo Bay Resort

P o r t   M c N e i l l ,   B r i t i s h   C o l u m b i a

Fish out of the ultimate heli-resort, tucked deep in the fjords and mountains east of Queen Charlotte Strait.

VITAL STATISTICS:

KEY SPECIES:
Steelhead; pink, silver and chinook salmon; cutthroat trout

Season:
April 15 through October 15
Accommodations:
Log chalets and lodge
Number of Guest Rooms: 10
Maximum Number of Guests: 18
Conference Groups: Yes
Meals: American plan
Rates:
From $3295 per person for 3 days
Guides: Included
Gratuities: $50 per day
Preferred Payment:
Visa
Getting There:
Fly to Port Hardy on Vancouver Island and take a helicopter or floatplane to the lodge.
Other Activities:
Kayaking, swimming, whale watching, boating, hiking, wildlife photography.

Contact:
Craig Murray
Nimmo Bay Resort,
1978 Broughton Blvd.,
Box 696, Port McNeill,
British Columbia,
Canada V0N 2R0;
250/956-4000, fax
250/956-2000, email
heli@nimmobay. bc.ca,
website http://www. nimmobay.bc.ca

Represented By:
Allied Percival International, 817/870-0300.

BANKING LIKE A BIRD, the helicopter swoops over a barren and stony ridge. Below, a river the color of coffee foams like cappuccino as it pushes through clefts in the rocks, boils in the pool below and races on through a long run. With grace, the chopper settles on a scrap of outcrop near the head of the run and the pilot kills the engine. You clamber out, rig your rods and move over to the stream. You cast, and the fly, a black Egg-Sucking Leech, lands upstream from the boulder. It washes by; nothing. Your next cast is across the eddy behind the boulder. You mend the line as best you can to slow the fly as it moves through the slack water. Good move. That's when the steelhead hits. It's not big— eight or 10 pounds—but it strips you into your backing and you palm the reel to slow it down. Twenty minutes later, you've tailed it and admired its silver flanks burnished rose and bronze spawning colors. Gently you hold it upright in the pool, watching its gills work slowly. You know its power and stamina from the way it fought. Now, as it struggles to regain equilibrium, you realize how steelhead, too, live but by a string.

Nimmo Bay is a special resort. Craig Murray has taken six yellow log chalets, a main lodge with everything in it and rolled it up into an angler's paradise deep in the fjords east of the Queen Charlotte Strait. Fishing is, as you would suspect, superb. Steelhead up to 25-pounds-plus run from April to May. Cutthroats of two to three pounds are plentiful from April into mid-October. The time for six-pound pink salmon is late July through August. Silvers of 10 to 20 pounds enter the rivers in August and chinooks, averaging 30 but running up to 60 pounds, follow in September. Fish for them both through mid-October, when the lodge closes. Each day, you and your party helicopter to water unreachable any other way. Fly and spinning tackle will be provided by the lodge, or bring your own.

Tides wash through the pilings that support the lodge and each of its red-roofed chalets, nestled against a backdrop of deep and towering spruce. Sunlight streams through half-moon windows, creating an aura of natural openness in the sitting rooms of each chalet. Sliding doors lead out onto a private deck, and a curving boardwalk joins them all with the lodge. Dinners are gourmet: prawns, halibut, salmon and lamb, with fresh baked pies and homemade ice cream. Often groups of eight or more book the entire lodge and ensure themselves of exclusive use of its helicopters and facilities.

Northern Woodsman Wilderness Resort

Westbank, British Columbia

Nobody carps about the size of the rainbows in this remote provincial park lake.

VITAL STATISTICS:

KEY SPECIES:
Rainbow trout

Season:
June through September

Accommodations:
RUSTIC CAMP

NUMBER OF GUEST ROOMS: 10

MAXIMUM NUMBER OF GUESTS: 16

Conference Groups: Yes

Meals: American plan

Rates:
$1299 per person per week

Guides: Included

Gratuities: $100

Preferred Payment:
MasterCard, Visa

Getting There:
Prince George, British Columbia is the closest airport. You'll be met and driven to the lake by a representative of the lodge.

Other Activities:
Swimming, boating, hiking, bird watching, wildlife photography.

Contact:
Les Allen
Northern Woodsman
Wilderness Resort,
Box 26025, Westbank,
British Columbia,
Canada V4T 2G3;
250/769-7642, website
http://www.northern
woodsman.com

EVERYONE'S HEARD STORIES about the fishing being so good that rainbows just jump in the boat. Well, fasten your seat belt, because for some strange reason—maybe they're aggravated with freshwater lice—the rainbows in Carp Lake Provincial Park have been known to leap a good three feet out of water without being hooked by lure to line. "When I tell people about it," says lodge owner Les Allen, "they think, well, maybe I've been in the bush too long."

OK, so if the rainbow fishing is that good, why do they call it Carp Lake? "The explorers who discovered it [Simon Fraser in 1805] saw big suckers that they thought were carp," explains Allen, who's been over it all hundreds of times. Allen is probably grateful that the adventurers didn't have their fish taxonomy straight. How could you ever run a fish camp on a lake named "Sucker?"

In fact, rainbow fishing is extremely good on Carp, MacIntire and a chain of three lakes known creatively as First, Second and Third. It doesn't make much difference how you fish or what you use. You'll catch two-pound rainbows all day long. Some guests troll gang rigs, others cast small silver and gold spinners on ultralight, others throw dark dry and wet flies (nymphs and streamers) with flyrods. "It doesn't seem to really matter what fly you use," says Allen. "If it's dark, they'll hit it." Carp Lake is large, about eight miles long and shaped like a big "H." MacIntire is about a mile by a mile and a half; and the trio of lakes, linked by small channels, are smaller. MacIntire and Third Lake have fewer fish but they run bigger, up to eight pounds in Third. Anglers fish with guides in boats. Depending on the number of guests you may have a boat and guide to yourself, but more likely you'll fish with your partner. The outflow of the lake, a wadeable river, is ideal for spin and fly anglers. Fishing is best from June through September.

Northern Woodsman Wilderness Resort is the only lodge on Carp Lake. You can drive to the lake, and then it's a short boat ride to the rustic lodge. Guests stay in two rooms in the main lodge and a pair of bunkhouses with two bedrooms each. They share a shower house, and outhouses are located at opposite ends of the camp. Home-cooked meals are served on a long pine table near a window that seems to bring the woods inside.

Painter's Lodge

C a m p b e l l   R i v e r ,   B r i t i s h   C o l u m b i a

VITAL STATISTICS:

KEY SPECIES:
Coho, sockeye, pink, chinook and chum salmon

Season:
Late March through September

Accommodations:
MODERN LOG RESORT
NUMBER OF GUEST ROOMS: 94
MAXIMUM NUMBER OF GUESTS: 220

Conference Groups: Yes

Meals: Restaurant at lodge

Rates:
Multiple packages from $144 per night

Guides: $120 per angler per half-day

Gratuities: 15%

Preferred Payment:
Major credit cards

Getting There:
Packages include round-trip airfare from Vancouver.

Other Activities:
Golf, tennis, swimming, snorkel trips, hiking, biking, whale watching.

Contact:
Harley Elias
Painter's Lodge, 1625 McDonald Rd., Campbell River, British Columbia, Canada V0P 1N0; 604/286-1102, fax 604/286-0158.

Step back to the 1920s and fish for Tyee from a rowboat on registered light tackle.

EVERY MORNING the fishmaster assigns anglers to guides and their Boston Whalers. Then they buzz off like bees, skimming across the Discovery Passage that separates Vancouver Island from the mainland. Tides course through its narrows with a velocity that rivals a whitewater river. Whirlpools eat the edge of the current, and boat handling can be tricky. A lapse can spell disaster. But with the current come the salmon—chinook, coho, chum, pink and sockeye—returning to spawn in the thousands of rivers that drain the high glacier-capped mountains to the East.

Fishing here is a straightforward affair. Two anglers to a boat. You'll fish a half or whole day, depending on your package. Guides know where the fish are running and boats tend to fish together, trolling with downriggers or not, depending on the species and their depth. Cohos run from June through October and may be taken near the surface early in the season. Sockeyes also come in June, fish best in July and fade in August. Pinks pass up the channel in July, their best month, and August. Chinooks show up in April and are still in the waters come November. They are particularly aggressive and plentiful in June, July and August.

Big chinooks, called Tyee in local lingo, are Painter's main draw, and that's the way it's been since E.C. Painter started renting rowboats from a shack on the cobble bar at the mouth of Campbell River back in the early 1920s. He built his own lapstrake boats, narrow and long like freighter canoes. Anglers fished spoons with braided line. Guides rowed them against the current, making way or dropping back to position the wavering copper or silver lure where the salmon lay. If you want, you can fish for Tyee that way today. And if the gods smile and your chinook tops 30 pounds, you'll be admitted to the exclusive Tyee Club of British Columbia.

Built in the style of a grand old hotel, Painter's has the capacity to provide fishing for 200 or more guests per day. Accommodations vary from rooms to suites to cabins, all carpeted and attractively appointed. Sauna, fitness center, swimming pool and golf all mark this as a full-service resort. Cuisine is gourmet—try the macadamia-encrusted sea bass grilled with maple-infused sweet red curry—and served banquet-style in the large dining room in the main lodge. Linger over the last of the wine and watch the setting sun turn the mainland mountains from apricot to plum, or wander upstairs to the Tyee Club and settle in with a book from the extensive fishing library.

Salmon King Lodge

Rivers Inlet, British Columbia

Catch king salmon until you can't lift your arms anymore; then relax at this cannery turned lodge.

VITAL STATISTICS:

KEY SPECIES:
King, coho, pink and chum salmon

Season:
Mid-July through mid-September

Accommodations:
REMODELED CANNERY
NUMBER OF GUEST ROOMS: 14
MAXIMUM NUMBER OF GUESTS: 28

Conference Groups: Yes

Meals: American plan

Rates:
From $1995 per person for 4 days and 3 nights, double occupancy

Guides: $200 per day for 2 anglers

Gratuities: 7% to 10% of total bill

Preferred Payment:
Visa

Getting There:
Fly to Port Hardy and a float-plane will ferry you to the lodge at no charge.

Other Activities:
Boating, bird watching, whale watching, wildlife photography.

Contact:
Lucie Drouin
Salmon King Lodge, PO Box 1237, Delta, British Columbia, Canada V4M 3T3; 800/665-0613, fax 604/278-8299, website http://www.salmon king.com

Represented By:
Fishabout, 800/409-2000.

SALMON KING LODGE is located in an old cannery, and that tells you something. Canneries were located where salmon were plentiful. While new processing methods have made small, shore-based canneries less feasible, the salmon are still running. And you can catch them yourself from this retreat on the upper end of Rivers Inlet, an arm off Fitz Hugh Sound.

This, to some degree, is a self-guided fishing vacation. When you arrive, you and your partner will be assigned a 16-foot soft-top boat with an electric start motor. Each boat is equipped with fishfinder, VHF radio and all the fishing tackle and bait you need. After a short orientation on boat and tackle operation, you're on your own. Prudent guests will invest in one day's guiding just to learn the locations and technique. Normally you'll drift over waters where your fishfinder locates salmon. Mooching with long rods and single-action reels, loaded with 20- to 45-pound-test mono, is the name of the game here. You'll bait up with a plug of cut herring, and add enough weight to get it down to where the fish are. If everything works well, and it usually does, you'll drift through schools of kings. Then you'll be busy. Like giant shock absorbers, the long rods bow deeply with every run, easing strain on terminal tackle. While the average king tips the scales between 25 and 30 pounds, 40-pounders are commonplace, 60-pounders are not unheard of, and even bigger fish are taken each year. Kings run first in July. They're followed by pinks (average five pounds), cohos (eight to 26 pounds) and chums (10 to 18 pounds). Bottomfishing for halibut up to 200 pounds—most are much lighter—is another option.

Among the factors that make this such an outstanding fishery is the number of freshwater streams that flow into Rivers Inlet in the few miles surrounding the lodge. There's the drainage of Owikeno Lake and its tributaries, and that of the Kilbella, Chuckwalla and Clyak rivers, all spawning grounds for salmon. The lodge will clean and prepare your catch for the trip home.

This is not a fancy, dolled-up place; just good and solid and very interesting, if you like factories that have changed careers. The west end of the plant is evolving into an upscale fishing lodge. Paneled rooms, some with queen-size beds and others with twins, all boast modern private baths. Maid service is provided daily. There's a lounge to while away non-fishing hours (not much of that) and the restaurant serves first-class dinners featuring prime rib and salmon. Most gear is provided, as luggage on the flight from Port Hardy to the lodge is limited to 25 pounds. Leave your rainwear at home, as the lodge will outfit you in style.

Sonora Resort

C a m p b e l l   R i v e r ,   B r i t i s h   C o l u m b i a

VITAL STATISTICS:

KEY SPECIES:
Chinook, coho, sockeye, pink and chum salmon; steelhead; dolly varden

Season:
April through October
Accommodations:
MODERN AND RUSTIC CABINS
NUMBER OF GUEST ROOMS: 25
MAXIMUM NUMBER OF GUESTS: 53
Conference Groups: Yes
Meals: American plan
Rates:
From $2395 (CDN) for 2 nights and 3 days
Guides: Included
Gratuities: $30 per day
Preferred Payment:
Discover, MasterCard, Visa
Getting There:
Fly to Vancouver, take a cab to the floatplane terminal and meet the flight to Sonora (no additional charge).
Other Activities:
Swimming, hiking, boating, bird watching, golf, tennis, wildlife photography, heli-tours, jetboating.

Contact:
Alan Moss
Sonora Resort, 625 11th Ave., Campbell River, British Columbia, Canada V9W 4G5; 604/220-9099, fax 604/220-9024.

Have it your way at this can-do luxury lodge where jetboats and choppers put you on good fish.

NESTLED INTO A FORESTED and boulder-strewn hillside, the 24 cabins of Sonora Resort merge with the lush and spectacular wilderness of its namesake island, one of scores of islands that punctuate and trouble the water between Vancouver Island and the mainland of British Columbia. Catching the rosy hue of the setting sun is snowcapped Mt. Gilbert, almost two miles high. Across the way is the gentle rise of Stuart Island and, in between, is the caldron where tides ripping south from Cordero Channel swirl with maelstrom force twice a day. Just to the north is a tortuous set of rapids where salmon school up, right off the dock at Sonora Resort.

Fishing here runs from March into October. Big chinooks (10 to 50 pounds) are the first to come. They arrive in March, with the fishing best from April into September. July brings cohos (six to 20 pounds), sockeyes (five to 10) and pinks (three to eight). Sockeyes fish best in July; cohos and pinks in September. Chums (eight to 20 pounds) run in September and October, with the former month offering the better fishing. Anglers fish from fully equipped Boston Whalers, trolling, mooching, using downriggers or casting flies—whatever works. When spring-run steelhead move up Bute Inlet into the Southgate River, you can catch them on spoons, spinners or flies. Dolly varden and cutthroats are also found in this jade-colored river turned faintly chalky by rock flour from glaciers on Mt. Gilbert. To reach freshwater species you'll ride Sonora's 30-foot, twin-jet Custom Weld, or hop a chopper to reach remote rivers and lakes. The fishing staff will put you on fish anyway you want.

A can-do, will-do spirit infuses this lodge. Make a wish out loud and it's granted. Everything (except tips for guides) is included in the price. Cabins are tastefully decorated in period style with furnishings you'd expect in a posh bed and breakfast. Meals are grand affairs of linen, china and silver, with an epicurean menu and an extensive wine list. (If you prefer a vintage not in the cellar, the staff will try to have it flown in on the next plane.) Should the fishing pale, try tennis, volleyball, swimming (one of the two pools has a swim-up bar), steam rooms (four), Jacuzzis (seven) or open bars (13). And, yes, you can work on your putting game on a nine-hole green. Sonora does a good deal of corporate business from planning retreats to incentive programs.

The Dolphins Resort

Campbell River, British Columbia

Ride the chopper to Bute Inlet, fish until you drop and return to have your favorite meal delivered to your cabin.

VITAL STATISTICS:

KEY SPECIES:
King, chum, silver and coho salmon; steelhead; cutthroat trout; dolly varden

Season:
March through October
Accommodations:
RUSTIC HOUSEKEEPING AND EXECUTIVE CABINS
NUMBER OF GUEST ROOMS: 14 cabins with 1 to 4 rooms
MAXIMUM NUMBER OF GUESTS: 50
Conference Groups: Yes
Meals: American or European plans
Rates:
From $598 per person for 3 days and 2 nights, double occupancy
Guides: Included
Gratuities: $30 to $50 (CDN) per day
Preferred Payment:
Major credit cards
Getting There:
Fly to Campbell River, and the van from the lodge will provide transportation for $10 each way.
Other Activities:
Golf, boating, hiking, bird watching, antiquing, biking, wildlife photography, skiing.

Contact:
**Clint Cameron
The Dolphins Resort,
4125 Discovery Dr.,
Campbell River, British Columbia, Canada V9W 4X6; 250/287-3066, fax 250/286-6610, email dolphins@vquest.com, website http://www. vquest.com/dolphins/**

THROUGH THE PLEXIGLASS of the helicopter's windows, you see three white mountain goats single filing it along a ledge, seemingly only inches wide, 500 feet above the green and foam river below. Obligingly they stop and pose, you click a few shots from your camera, then the pilot pulls up and you lift over a ridge, ragged and bare. He descends and settles the skids on a gravel bar of the Southgate River. Since you left Dolphins Resort an hour ago, you've been utterly absorbed by the soaring snowy peaks and steeply plunging fjords below.

Now, with spume from the rapids steaming in the air, your mind turns to the task at hand. In the Southgate, Homathko and other rivers that feed deep arms off the Inside Passage, steelhead and sea-run cutthroats begin their runs in March and continue in the rivers until October. Steelhead run between five and 25 pounds; cutts, between two and six. Sea-run dolly varden and rainbow trout also enter the system in March. Heli-fishing—taking a chopper to waters otherwise reachable only by extended wilderness hikes—is the best way to work these waters. You, three or four partners and a guide will start near the head of a river, fish a pool for an hour or so, then pack up and fly a mile or two to the next hole.

Salmon run these rivers too, but the better fishing for kings (up to 50 pounds), silvers (to 14 pounds) or chums (to 23 pounds) is by skiff. You, another angler and a guide will leave the lodge to work the swirling tides in Seymour Narrows or the gentle waters off Cape Mudge. Fight spirited cohos on flytackle when they're near the surface in May and September. Troll for kings in June, July and August with downriggers, flashers and Hootchies. Use the same tackle for chums in September and October. For a classic thrill, fish for chinooks the old-fashioned way with brass spoons and registered light tackle from a lapstrake-design rowboat.

For more than two decades, Dolphins Resort has been hosting distinguished anglers. Fourteen wooden cabins of one to four bedrooms are scattered beneath the evergreens along Discovery Passage. Each is comfortably decorated. In several, brick fireplaces are the focal point, and all have broad decks, delightful for lounging. Most have kitchens. The resort lacks a restaurant, but its chef and staff will prepare meals tailored to your specifications and deliver them to your cabin door. Or, if you prefer, you may cook for yourself. Typical packages include meals, guides and fishing from Boston Whalers in the passage. Others include a day or two of heli-fishing. Try it!

From Nimmo Bay Resort, up a fjord across from
Port McNeill, British Columbia, helicopters carry
anglers to isolated streams filled with
steelhead, salmon and cutthroats. — page 244.

For half a century, April Point Lodge on
Quadra Island, British Columbia, has offered anglers
fine salmon fishing along with concerts, art classes
and cooking schools. — page 237.

Vaseux Lake Lodge

Oliver, British Columbia

Watch a bighorn ewe and her lamb every morning while you troll for kokanee in your canoe.

VITAL STATISTICS:

KEY SPECIES:
Kokanee salmon; rainbow trout; largemouth bass

Season:
All year

Accommodations:
TOWN HOUSES
NUMBER OF GUEST ROOMS: 4
MAXIMUM NUMBER OF GUESTS: 16

Conference Groups: No

Meals: Breakfast and lunch: cook for yourself; dinner at nearby restaurants

Rates:
From $100 for 2 per night

Guides: N/A

Gratuities: N/A

Preferred Payment:
Cash or check

Getting There:
About a 250-mile drive from Vancouver.

Other Activities:
Golf, tennis, canoeing, swimming, boating, hiking, bird watching, biking, wildlife photography, skiing.

Contact:
**Peter or Denise Axhorn
Vaseux Lake Lodge,
101 Seagrit Rd., RR 1,
Sooke, British Columbia,
Canada VOS 1NO;
250/642-3930, fax
250/642-3940, email
vaseux@tnet.net, website http://vvv.com/home/vaseux**

BRITISH COLUMBIA is a fascinating province with more diverse environments than any of the others in Canada. The coast is damp and lush, mountains high and capped with glaciers and, to the east, plains with nearly desertlike conditions. A 35-minute drive from Vaseux Lake Lodge will take you through four climate zones, and the different plant and animal communities.

Part of the Okanagan (Okanogan in the U.S.) River that flows into the Columbia between Monse and Brewster, Washington, Vaseux is known for rainbows, kokanee salmon and largemouth bass. Rainbows run in the two-pound range and are best fished either in May or June, or September through November. Kokanees, up to four pounds, do best in August and September. Largemouths, like the rainbows, hit best in May and June, slump somewhat in the height of summer, and then pick up in September and October. Whitefish follow a similar pattern, as do perch. The lake is relatively small and narrow, only 1.8 miles long and .4 miles wide, and British Columbia authorities permit no outboards. You'll have to make do trolling or casting from a canoe while you watch bighorn sheep scamper on the rocky crags above the lake. In addition, you'll find rainbows and cutthroats in many of the small streams that flow into the lake and river.

The fishing can be good, but the wildlife viewing can be excellent, and that's raison d'etre for Vaseux Lake Lodge. If you visit the lodge between June and July, you are apt to see ewes leading their lambs from the lambing cave on Eagle Bluff. Marmots cavort among the bluff's boulders. Golden and bald eagles soar over the lodge, osprey plunge into the lake for fish, and 305 other bird species have been recorded in the area. At night, coyotes serenade you to sleep. This lodge is a naturalist's dream. So plentiful is the wildlife that lodge owners Peter and Denise Axhorn have placed field guides in every room.

Vaseux Lake laps at the beach in front of the lodge, which is made up of four two-story attached town houses that are staggered to provide privacy. On the main floor of each, the dining/living area with sleep sofa looks out, through floor to ceiling windows, to the mountains across the lake. You'll enjoy the view as well through the cathedral windows upstairs in the master bedroom. Or you can slide open the windows and sit on your private balcony outside. A fully equipped kitchen lets you whip up breakfast and lunch. Restaurants for dinner are nearby in Oliver or Penticton.

Frontier Fishing Lodge

S n o w d r i f t   (K u t s e l   K ' e) ,   N o r t h w e s t   T e r r i t o r i e s

VITAL STATISTICS:

KEY SPECIES:
Lake trout; grayling; northern pike

Season:
Mid-June through September 10

Accommodations:
LODGE AND LOG CABINS
NUMBER OF GUEST ROOMS: 13 plus 6 cabins
MAXIMUM NUMBER OF GUESTS: 30

Conference Groups: Yes

Meals: American plan

Rates:
From $1450 for 3 days fishing

Guides: Included

Gratuities: $15 per day

Preferred Payment:
Cash or check

Getting There:
Fly to Yellowknife, Northwest Territories, and shuttle by air (no extra charge) to the lodge.

Other Activities:
Bird watching, wildlife photography.

Contact:
**Wayne Witherspoon
Frontier Fishing Lodge,
PO Box 32008,
Edmonton, Alberta,
Canada T6K 4C2;
403/465-6843, fax
403/466-3874.**

Represented By:
Paul Merzig, 312/782-4756.

Lake trout come fast and furiously at this lodge on world-famous Great Slave Lake.

GREAT SLAVE LAKE, just below the Arctic Circle, is among the world's finest lake trout locales. The biggest allegedly ran 74 pounds and the lodge record is 58 pounds. Roughly 285 miles wide and more than 2000 feet deep in places, Great Slave stays icy cold even in the height of summer. That keeps the lake trout near the surface but slows their growth. A 20-pound fish, a little better than average, may be 20 years old, and a 50-pounder older than 40. Anyone can catch lake trout here (a 9-year-old landed a 35-pounder) and lots of them.

Trolling big bright spoons, like the ubiquitous Five 'o Diamonds with its five red diamonds on a bright yellow background, consistently takes good lakers. Plugcasters have success with anything that resembles the ciscoes on which lakers feed. Early in the season, and late, when lakers are highest in the water column, flyfishermen hammer them (or rather the lakers hammer the flyfishers) with big streamers such as the Dahlberg Diver in white, yellow or chartreuse or Peterson's Eel on a 2/0 hook. When fish are deep, bouncing heavy (five ounce!) white jigs on bottom produces some of the biggest trout of the year.

If all that work for lake trout wears you out, unlimber your light rod and traverse mosquito alley to the bank of the Stark River, where you can wade in and fish for grayling. Every eddy seems to hold a handful and each, in turn, seems willing to take your ultralight spinner or fly (dry or wet). They run about two pounds each; a really good one tops four. The water here is easily wadeable and lake trout (and a few whitefish) hold at the river's mouth just downstream.

While at Great Slave, don't miss out on the fast fishing for pike in the 10- to 20-pound range. A few shallow, grassy bays are found close to the lodge, and in these you can catch pike on almost every cast.

Frontier Fishing Lodge is on a little bay a quarter mile from the mouth of the Stark River. Six comfortable guests rooms and a lounge with fireplace are found in the main lodge. Seven more bedrooms are attached to a second large building, the conference center. And six log cabins provide accommodations for anglers desiring more privacy. Baths are shared. Meals are served in a third building that houses the dining room and kitchen. Food is hearty and abundant.

Kasba Lake Lodge

K a s b a   L a k e ,   N o r t h w e s t   T e r r i t o r i e s

VITAL STATISTICS:

KEY SPECIES:
Northern pike; lake trout; grayling

Season:
Late June through August

Accommodations:
RUSTIC LODGES
NUMBER OF GUEST ROOMS: 22 in main lodge with 3 outpost camps
MAXIMUM NUMBER OF GUESTS: MAIN LODGE: 45

Conference Groups: Yes
Meals: American plan, plus outpost packages

Rates:
From $2195 per person for 5 days in the main lodge, outposts slightly less

Guides: Included at main lodge only

Gratuities: $200 to $400 per week

Preferred Payment:
MasterCard, Visa

Getting There:
Fly to Minneapolis or Winnipeg and meet the chartered jet.

Other Activities:
Canoeing, rafting, hiking, bird watching, wildlife photography.

Contact:
Reservations
Kasba Lake Lodge
PO Box 96, Parksville, British Columbia, Canada V9P 2G3;
800/663-8641, fax 250/248-3572, email rhill@qb.island.net, website http://www. kasba.com

Get off the jet, walk over to the harbor, jump into a boat and go catch trophy lake trout.

AT THE HEIGHT OF SUMMER, there are 20 hours of fishable daylight at Kasba Lake, an outstanding fishery 430 miles south of the Arctic Circle. While guides at the lodge work from 8:00 a.m to 6:00 p.m., you're welcome to use a boat and motor after hours and fish as long as you want. The kitchen will hold dinner. You can fish to your heart's content for northern pike, lake trout and grayling, and your chances of hooking into a fish with bragging rights are good. For more than 25 years, Kasba Lake Lodge has been practicing catch-and-release fishing for all species, save a few fish kept for shore lunches.

Rugged and isolated, Kasba Lake was hollowed out by glaciers. Rocky outcrops, muskeg bogs and infrequent stands of black spruce line its shores. Feeding the lake are numerous small rivers and streams. The Snowbird comes in on the west; the Hasbela, from the south; and the Schwandt—known for early season lake trout—also from the west. Kasba's structure leads anglers to specific species. Rocky points and bars are prime lake trout terrain. Pike congregate in the backs of sandy bays. Grayling favor the fast water of inlets or outlets. Fishing style is up to you, but most lake trout are caught trolling big spoons and spinners. Spoons, spinnerbaits and buzzbaits thrown with conventional casting gear work best for pike. Ultralight anglers will find that grayling love small spinners, while flyfishermen take them with wets and dries. Kasba Lodge sells licenses and tackle to those in need.

In addition to its main lodge next to the dirt jet strip, Kasba operates two outpost camps on Snowbird Lake where anglers do their own cooking and cleanup and fish without guides, though they are available at an additional fee. In 1993 Gene Thomas landed an IGFA line-test class-record 42-pound 2-ounce lake trout on Snowbird. Kasba's north camp sleeps six and the south camp nine. Located on the headwaters of the Kazan River, the Tabane Lake camp puts anglers on 40 miles of prime river where large lake trout, grayling and pike hang out. Tabane outpost sleeps six and is a do-it-yourselfer's dream.

At the main lodge you'll find 11 cabins, furnished with all the basics and all with private baths. Four are handicapped accessible. All are a short walk from the dining room where sturdy meals are served. In the lodge you'll also find a bar and tackleshop. Morning begins when the pot of hot coffee is delivered to the door of your cabin.

Plummer's Lodges: Great Bear Lake / Great Slave Lake / Neiland Bay / Tree River Camp / Trophy Lodge

G r e a t   B e a r   L a k e ,   N o r t h w e s t   T e r r i t o r i e s

VITAL STATISTICS:

KEY SPECIES:
Arctic char; lake trout; arctic grayling; northern pike

Season:
GREAT BEAR, NEILAND, TREE AND TROPHY:
July through August
GREAT SLAVE:
July through September
Accommodations:
GREAT BEAR, GREAT SLAVE, NEILAND AND TROPHY: Cabins and rooms
TREE: Wood-floored tents
NUMBER OF GUEST ROOMS/ GUESTS:
GREAT BEAR: 30/65
GREAT SLAVE: 22/44
NEILAND: 8/16
TREE: 4/8
TROPHY: 22/44
Conference Groups: Yes except at Tree
Meals: American plan
Rates:
GREAT BEAR, NEILAND AND TROPHY: $3295 per person per week
GREAT SLAVE: $2795 per person per week
TREE: $395 per person additional to Great Bear rate

Want to have a go at a world-record lake trout, arctic char or grayling? Take your pick.

YOU CAN CHECK IT OUT in the IGFA book of world-record fish: Plummer's on Great Bear Lake is the place for world-record lake trout, arctic grayling and arctic char. The all-tackle world records for these three species are held by anglers fishing from Plummer's. So too are all of the line-class records for arctic grayling, and seven out of 10 for lake trout. The all-tackle record for lake trout, set by Rodney Hartback's 66.5-pounder in 1991, may not stand. Bill Dodson landed a 70-pound behemoth in July, 1996. His tackle: 17-pound-test Trilene and a red and white Lucky Strike half-wave spoon fished in about 25 feet of water.

Big fish are common in the waters surrounding the five lodges that Chummy Plummer runs on the fringe of the Arctic Circle:

GREAT BEAR: Arctic char, arctic grayling, lake trout. The lodge is on the northeast side of the lake, 47 miles above the Arctic Circle. The lake is shallow so fly-fishermen as well as anglers using casting and spinning gear have equal shots at record-size lake trout. The season is short: July and August. Two anglers per guide in a V-hulled boat. Fly outs to remote waters are available. The lodge's white buildings with red roofs spread low along the shore. Guests stay in utilitarian cabins with private baths, and dine on prime rib and baked Alaska. To work it off, jog the two-mile road to the jet strip, or forget it and lounge in the whirlpool overlooking the lake.

GREAT SLAVE: On the north side of Taltheilei Narrows, which separates McLeod Bay from the rest of the lake, sprawls the signature white buildings of Plummer's camp. Great Slave produces huge lake trout, grayling and pike from July through September. They migrate through the narrows. Here you'll fish with another angler and a guide in a boat, trolling or casting spinners or spoons. Flyfishers have fun with grayling on dries and dark nymphs. Modest cabins with private baths provide accommodations, and the main lodge includes the dining room for substantial meals, a trading post with proven lures and other tackle and a bank of leather easy chairs for relaxing.

NEILAND BAY: This rustic lodge on Great Bear Lake is smaller than its sibling, but the fishing and food are as good. You'll find lakers up to 60 pounds, grayling in the four-pound range and pike to 20 pounds. Guests stay two to a cabin and share baths.

TREE RIVER: Arctic char of world-record class populate the Tree River that flows into Coronation Gulf, an arm of the Arctic Ocean. Plummer's is the only camp on the river, so there are no crowds here. You'll fly out from Great Bear Lake, fish for two days and spend the night in between at the camp, set on a treeless rise overlooking the narrow river. Accommodations are four-person tents with wooden floors. Hearty meals are served in the main lodge building, and then it's back to catch char as colorful as the arctic sunsets. The overnight to Tree River adds $395 to your tab at Great Bear. And if you're serious about arctic char, Plummer's offers a week-long package split between Tree River and the Coppermine for $3895.

TROPHY LODGE: Sited on a sweeping beach that hooks into Ford Bay, Trophy Lodge is surrounded by trees and flowers. It's pretty, but trophy fish are the attraction here. Four IGFA records for lake trout, two for grayling and one for char on a fly have been set by anglers staying at Trophy. Water is shallow here, a flyfisher's dream for big lakers. Pike up to 25 pounds are a bonus. Guests fish two to a boat with Dene guides and stay in modern, carpeted rooms with private baths.

Though Plummer's five lodges are close to the Arctic Circle, temperatures in summer frequently nudge the mid-80s. And while climate is semi-arid in summer, fronts with lots of moisture move through (fairly quickly). Bring a thick Polarfleece pullover, a set of long underwear (synthetic fiber) and a hooded Gore-Tex rainjacket. A pair of rubber-bottomed L.L. Bean-style boots will pay dividends, as will a billed cap, a small bottle of bug dope and a soft tackle satchel that you can swing over your shoulder. Prepare for the worst, think layered and travel light.

Guides: Included
Gratuities: Client's discretion
Preferred Payment: MasterCard, Visa
Getting There:
Fly to Winnipeg and meet chartered 737 to lodges.
Other Activities:
Hiking, bird watching, wildlife photography.

Contact:
Cameron Baty
Plummer's Lodges,
950 Bradford St.,
Winnipeg, Manitoba,
Canada R3H ON5;
800/665-0240,
fax 204/783-2320,
email plummers@
canadianarcticfishing.
com, website http://
canadianarticfishing.com

Athabasca Fishing Lodges

O t h e r s i d e   R i v e r ,   S a s k a t c h e w a n

VITAL STATISTICS:

KEY SPECIES:
Northern pike; lake trout; walleyes; arctic grayling; whitefish

Season:
June through September

Accommodations:
CABINS AND WILDERNESS CAMPS
NUMBER OF GUEST ROOMS:
OTHERSIDE: 10 cabins with 2 bedrooms each
ENGER LAKE: 5 2-person cabins
MAXIMUM NUMBER OF GUESTS:
OTHERSIDE: 48
ENGER LAKE: 10

Conference Groups: Yes

Meals: American plan

Rates:
OTHERSIDE: $2695 per person per week
ENGER: $2095 per person per week

Guides: Included at Otherside

Gratuities: $15 to $25 per day

Preferred Payment:
MasterCard, Visa

Getting There:
Fly to Saskatoon, overnight, and meet Athabasca's chartered jet.

Other Activities:
Canoeing, boating, eco touring, wildlife photography.

Contact:
Cliff Blackmu
Athabasca Fishing Lodges, PO Box 7800, Saskatoon, Saskatchewan, Canada S7K 4R5; 306/653-5490, fax 306/653-5525.

Fish out of a lodge or cabin for record-size northern pike and lake trout.

NORTHERN SASKATCHEWAN is country barren of all but boreal forest and hundreds of lakes and connecting rivers. The forest flows over low, rocky hills, and ridges of bouldery sands left by the glaciers. The waters, deeply tannin, hold record-class northern pike and lake trout as well as walleyes, whitefish and arctic grayling. The largest body of water in the province is Lake Athabasca, and its easternmost arm is called Fond du Lac. It is here, at the mouth of the Otherside River, that you'll find the headquarters of Athabasca Fishing Lodges.

Anglers come to Athabasca for big fish. Northern pike (five to 30 pounds) readily hit spoons and big spinnerbaits from June through August. You'll find lake trout (five to 60 pounds) up top early on and deeper as summer progresses. As days grow short and water cools in the fall, the lakers rise and provide great light tackle sport. Walleyes (two to four pounds) are probably the most popular fish because of their utterly delectable flesh, and you can fish them all summer long. Grayling hit ultralight lures, dry flies and nymphs fished in the eddies of fast moving water.

With several types of accommodations ranging from full-service to outpost camps scattered in the vicinity of the eastern end of the big lake, Athabasca Fishing Lodges provides a range of experiences for anglers with varying interests.

OTHERSIDE RIVER LODGE: With 10 suite-style cabins, each with a living room, two bedrooms, private bath and daily maid service, the lodge provides a comfortable, functional home base for fishing Fond du Lac, the river or a number of hotspots on the Athabasca's east end. A 32-foot cabin cruiser ferries anglers and guides to fishing boats cached in the bush. Two anglers fish with each guide, normally Dene Indians who have worked with the lodge for many years. Fly outs in the lodge's Otter to small lakes and bays are available at extra cost (about $180 additional). Meals of steak, turkey and prime rib are family-style.

ENGER LAKE CAMP: More a mini-lodge than a camp—five wooden cabins, hot showers in a central bathhouse, home-cooked meals and 24-hour electricity—Enger Lake is the place for experienced anglers to fish on their own. You'll have a 16-foot aluminum boat, motor and all the gas you need at your disposal. A camp manager provides advice and assistance. Then you're off on your own to explore the lake and the portage to Rious, the next lake up the chain. This is a slightly less expensive alternative to the main lodge on Otherside River.

Camp Grayling

Black Lake, Saskatchewan

Friendly and not at all pretentious, Camp Grayling excels in service and first-class fishing.

VITAL STATISTICS:

KEY SPECIES:
Grayling; lake trout; northern pike; walleyes

Season:
June through September

Accommodations:
WOODEN CABINS WITH PORCHES
NUMBER OF GUEST ROOMS: 16
MAXIMUM NUMBER OF GUESTS: 32

Conference Groups: Yes
Meals: American plan
Rates:
Packages from $875 (US) per person for 3 days, double occupancy

Guides: Included
Gratuities: $30 per day per guide
Preferred Payment:
Visa or personal check

Getting There:
Stoney Rapids, Saskatchewan has commercial service. A bus from the lodge will meet your flight.

Other Activities:
Rafting, swimming, hiking, boating, bird watching, biking, wildlife photography.

Contact:
Margy Michel
Camp Grayling, 111 Gathercole Crescent, Saskatoon, Saskatchewan, Canada S7K 7J3; 306/249-2655 (winter); General Delivery, Stony Rapids, Saskatchewan, Canada S0J 2R0; 306/439-2178 (summer).

THE LAND THAT'S NOT CARPETED with pine scrub in northern Saskatchewan is covered by lakes and rivers. An incredibly rich fishery, these waters boil with pike, walleye, lake trout and grayling. The camp, established about 40 years ago, sits at the outlet of Black Lake. This is not a pretentious place, but what it may lack in fancy decor, its service makes up for. A half dozen Dene guides, the native people of this northland, skipper aluminum boats powered by Honda outboards. The guides speak fluent English and know where the fish are. The fishing is among the best in Canada, and owners Ed White and Margy Michel work hard to keep it that way. They insist on catch-and-release and rotate fishing from lake to lake so that each body of water has a chance to rest.

White has established outpost camps—single cabins for four with boat, motor, kitchen and bedding—on two smaller lakes, Rious and Dodge. Water warms more quickly there than on bigger Black Lake. Northern pike exceeding 30 pounds and lake trout in the 40-pound range move into the shallows in June. Less than half an hour's floatplane flight from the main lodge puts you over these fish. One-day fly outs are available, or you can book these outposts for four days at a stretch. In addition, White runs a mini-camp—complete with guide and cook and all the comforts—on Selwyn Lake, a few hundred yards from the Northwest Territories border.

The main lodge is command central for a host of activities. Beavers and Cessnas depart for fly-out floats on rivers that feed Black Lake and Fon du Lac. Others head downriver to fish the Fon du Lac at Middle Lake for grayling and walleyes. But the main event is the departure of the AluMarine fleet for coves on Black or Giles Lake for northerns. Baitcasting is the tackle of choice here, with most successful anglers using big yellow Five 'o Diamond spoons. Johnson weedless spoons work well, as do buzz and spinnerbaits.

Back at camp, Michel will be fixing dinner. Meals run no set rotation here and the fare is substantial. You'll find plenty of chicken and pasta on the menu as well as grilled steak and roast beef. Breads and pastries are homemade and Michel will assure you that her desserts have absolutely no calories. You can sleep it off in your cabin which has a private bath and hot shower. But before you hit the sack, pick up your rod, walk down to the lake outlet and cast for grayling. It's good for the digestion.

Hatchet Lake Lodge

H a t c h e t   L a k e ,   S a s k a t c h e w a n

**VITAL
STATISTICS:**

KEY SPECIES:
Northern pike; lake
trout; grayling; walleyes

Season:
June through September
Accommodations:
LOG CABINS
NUMBER OF GUEST ROOMS: 22
MAXIMUM NUMBER OF GUESTS: 60
Meals: American plan
Conference Groups: Yes
Rates:
From $2095 per person for 5
days and 4 nights
Guides: Included
Gratuities: $100
Preferred Payment:
Major credit cards
Getting There:
Fly to Minneapolis and connect
with charter jet to lodge.
Other Activities:
Hiking, bird watching, wildlife
photography.

Contact:
**George Fleming
Hatchet Lake Lodge,
PO Box 262, Elk River,
MN 55330; 800/661-
9183, fax 306/922-5446,
email gofish@hatchet
lake.com, website
http://www.hatchet
lake.com**

*Fish as long and eat as much as you want
at this first-class North Country lodge.*

THE POT OF COFFEE has been delivered to your room and a fire lit in your wood stove. Both help shake the morning chill. You're up and dressed when the Highlander strolls by, piping Scottish airs, reminding you of breakfast. An hour later you'll either be in an AluMarine boat headed to a hotspot on Hatchet Lake, or taxiing in a floatplane prior to takeoff for one of 15 surrounding lakes and streams. Fly outs are optional at additional cost.

The attractions in this remote region of northeast Saskatchewan are northern pike, lake trout, grayling and walleyes. An average pike will range from six to 15 pounds, though the lodge record is a 35-pounder. Spincasters generally use medium-action rods and reels spooled with 10- to 12-pound-test line. Casting reels carry 17- to 20-pound line. Six- to nine-inch steel leaders are essential. Favorite lures include the ever-popular Five 'o Diamonds, Johnson's Silver Minnows and No. 3 and 4 Mepps. Flyfishers will want a nine- or 10-foot rod for an 8 weight, steel leader material and a selection of big white, chartreuse and yellow streamers.

Just after ice-out in June, lake trout cruise the shallows feeding. In July and August they retreat to deep holes and come September they move to rocky reefs to spawn. Fly anglers will find outstanding action early and late with them, using the same streamers they use for pike. Anglers favoring spin or casting gear will do better trolling early and late and can take several fish in just a few hours by vertical jigging with two- to four-ounce spoons in midsummer. Arctic grayling also frequent these lakes and the streams that feed them. They are easily taken in moving water with small spinners cast with ultralight tackle or on a 5-weight flyrod. Grayling are not choosy when it comes to flies, but tend to favor dark dries and nymphs. Walleyes round out the action with average fish in the three- to six-pound range. You'll have them for your shore lunch.

Located on an island on the northern end of the lake, the three-level main lodge is built of hand-peeled log and has a dining room, bar, game room and conference room, plus a fully-stocked tackleshop. Scattered in the trees nearby are woodsy, comfortable guest cabins with private baths for parties of two to four. Meals give new definition to "hearty." Bacon, eggs, steaming Red River Cereal, French toast and pancakes start you off. Dinners include steak, ham, turkey, fresh salads and vegetables, all topped off by a definitely high-cal dessert. And there are seconds on everything. Afterward, if you're so motivated, you can check out a boat and fish some more.

Reindeer Lake Trout Camp
Southend, Saskatchewan

VITAL STATISTICS:

KEY SPECIES:
Northern pike; lake trout; walleyes; grayling

Season:
June through September
Accommodations:
LOG CABINS
NUMBER OF GUEST ROOMS: 12
MAXIMUM NUMBER OF GUESTS: 45
Conference Groups: Yes
Meals: American plan
Rates:
Packages from $825 per person for 4 nights and 3 days, double occupancy
Guides: Included at main camp, additional at outposts
Gratuities: $20 per day
Preferred Payment:
MasterCard, Visa, check
Getting There:
Direct flights to LaRonge, Saskatchewan from Denver and Minneapolis. Flight to Southend may or may not be included in your specific package.
Other Activities:
Swimming, hiking, bird watching, wildlife photography.

Contact:
Ron or Cindi Holmes Reindeer Lake Lodge, Rt. 1, Box 81, Sargent, NE 68874; 800/272-6359, fax 308/527-4364.

A meteor crater seven miles wide provides shelter for amazing populations of lake trout.

IN THIS LAND OF LAKES, Reindeer Lake stands out from all the others. A meteorite once slammed into the earth here, and its seven-mile-wide, 700-foot-deep crater is now known as Deep Bay. The icy waters of the bay provide a haven for lake trout when the high summer sun warms the lake. Ron and Cindi Holmes' Reindeer Lake Trout Camp lies amongst birches and maples on a cusp of shore three miles across the lake from the bay.

As is the case in most lakes in northern Saskatchewan, northern pike, lake trout, walleyes and grayling comprise most of the sporting species. In comparison to other lakes, lake trout and northerns are not huge here. Lakers run in the four- to six-pound range, and pike, six to 10. But don't lose heart. These are average sizes, and much bigger fish are taken from these waters where, increasingly, guides are trained in CPR—"Catch, Photo and Release." Both pike and trout frequent shallow waters as the season opens in June. That's the best time to nail them on a big streamer—such as a three-inch Tabory's Snake Fly in chartreuse or white. Otherwise you'll fish weedbeds for pike with big spoons and spinners, and go deep with jigs for trout. Both make cameo appearances near the surface in September before sounding for the winter. Grayling from one to three pounds fall to small spinners and dark dry and wet flies. Pack along an ultra-light spinning or 4-weight flyrod for these northwoods sailfish.

While walleyes are caught near the main lodge, the better fishing is found at remote outpost camps where you and your party hole-up for a week of self-guided fishing. The Holmeses have cabins at Harriot (trophy lakers in spring and fall), Kyaska (big northerns) and Johnson (northerns) lakes. At each you'll find a cabin completely stocked with all the cooking and camping gear you'll need except sleeping bags and towels. You'll have unlimited use of boats and motors. If you know a little about lake fishing, here's a place to solo at a reasonable rate. If you're new to the game, hire a guide for a day, go to school on his advice and then do it yourself. Baggage including food is limited to 60 pounds per person on outpost trips. Travel light and eat well.

At the main lodge, guests stay in contemporary yet rustic log cabins, each with private bath, refrigerators and decks. In the central log lodge, you'll lounge in front of a wood stove and look out over the lake before dinner...your basic rib-sticking home cooking. Afterwards shoot a game or two of pool.

Selwyn Lake Lodge

S e l w y n   L a k e ,   S a s k a t c h e w a n / N o r t h w e s t   T e r r i t o r i e s

VITAL STATISTICS:

KEY SPECIES:
Lake trout; northern pike; grayling

Season:
June through September

Accommodations:
Rustic cabin suites
Number of Guest Rooms: 4
Maximum Number of Guests: 8
Conference Groups: Yes
Meals: American plan
Rates:
From $2395 per person for 3 days, double occupancy
Guides: Included
Gratuities: 10% to 20%
Preferred Payment:
Major credit cards
Getting There:
Fly to Saskatoon, Saskatchewan. A charter will carry you to Stony Rapids and a floatplane on to the lodge.
Other Activities:
Canoeing, swimming, hiking, bird watching, wildlife photography.

Contact:
Gordon Wallace
Selwyn Lake Lodge,
1105-620 Spadina Cres. E., Saskatoon, Saskatchewan, Canada 57K 3T5; 800/667-9556, fax 306/664-3445, email selwyn@sk.sympatico.ca, website http://www.vsource.com/selwyn

Represented By:
Gage Outdoor Expeditions, 800/896-2200.

Lake trout run large at a wilderness lodge on Canada's lake of a million islands.

IT SHOULD HAVE BEEN CALLED the lake of a million islands. Selwyn's 135,000 acres are mottled with islands of long and intricate shape. Rocky points, reefs, drop-offs, shallow weedy bays, unnamed streams tumbling down from feeder lakes, deep holes...all abound on this 45-mile-long, 18-mile-wide body of water that spreads across the wilderness border between Saskatchewan and the Northwest Territories.

For anglers, this is the land of opportunity when it comes to fishing. Lake trout typically range in the 20-pound class, although occasional 40- and even 50-pounders are caught each year. Early in the season, you can take lake trout on flies when they are feeding on baitfish near the surface. Floating lines and lines with varying sink rates should be in the kits of flyfishermen looking for lakers. Dahlberg Divers, Cotton Candies and other three- to four-inch minnow imitations work well. Spinfishermen will find success with crankbaits and spoons early, but the biggest lakers are caught by trolling or vertical jigging with casting gear and flashers, often tipped with belly meat.

The shallows teem with northern pike averaging 20 pounds. Five 'o Diamonds and similar spoons, as well as spinners and buzzbaits, will provoke strikes from these alligators of the North. Flyfishers will want a bit of fine steel tippet. Dahlbergs, especially the mega and rabbit varieties, are effective, as are Clousers and similar streamers in red and white, yellow, chartreuse and pure white. Grayling are prevalent in the swift, short rivers that feed Selwyn. They rise readily to small Mepps or Panther Martin spinners (use a black body), and to dark dry and wet flies. Along with your other gear, pack an ultralight spinning rig with 2- or 4-pound-test line; or take a 4- or 5-weight flyrod. With luck, you may also tie into a whitefish in the four- to five-pound range.

Selwyn lake offers anglers two styles of accommodations. The long, low, wood-sided main lodge sits in the trees on a rise over the lake. Here are a pair of comfortable, but not fancy, two-room suites for four anglers apiece. Each suite enjoys a private bath. Meals, family-style American cuisine with European accents and prepared by a Swiss chef, are served in the sunny country dining room that overlooks the lake. The main lodge also includes a lounge with complimentary beverages and a tackleshop. At the foot of the hill, the lodge's fleet of 16- and 18-foot Lunds is moored to the dock. Experienced anglers might consider the lodge's outpost camp at the other end of the lake. Two tent cabins sleep eight anglers, who serve as their own cooks and guides. Boats and motors are provided.

Tincup Wilderness Lodge

Tincup Lake, Yukon Territory

Stay in a wilderness lodge, in the home of lake trout, grayling, northern pike and wonderful European cuisine.

VITAL STATISTICS:

KEY SPECIES:
Lake trout; grayling

Season:
Mid-June through mid-September

Accommodations:
CEDAR CABINS
NUMBER OF GUEST ROOMS: 4
MAXIMUM NUMBER OF GUESTS: 8

Conference Groups: Yes

Meals: American plan

Rates:
$2695 per person per week

Guides: $50 per day

Gratuities: $20 per day

Preferred Payment:
MasterCard, Visa

Getting There:
Fly to Whitehorse, Yukon Territory, and the lodge's aircraft will shuttle you to Tincup.

Other Activities:
Hiking, bird watching, wildlife photography.

Contact:
Larry Nagy
Tincup Wilderness Lodge, 3641 Park Dr., RR 4, Victoria, British Columbia, Canada V9C 3W3; 250/391-0400, fax 250/391-0841.

Represented By:
Fishabout, 800/409-2000.

LARRY NAGY IS A GEOLOGIST, a guy who understands mountains and glaciation and the flow of surface water. He's poked around in many of the world's corners, and when it came time to hang up his rock hammer and Brunton compass, he picked a little lake on the lee of the St. Elias Mountain Range at the doorstep of Kluane National Park. With 25 miles of shoreline, Tincup has ample shallow bays, rock bluffs, drop-offs and stony reefs to provide structure for lake trout (lake char in Tincup parlance), and the odd pike. (Not that there's anything wrong with the pike, it's just somewhat strange to find them in this particular lake.)

Lake trout are the main event, and fishing for them is stellar as soon as Tincup becomes free of ice in mid-June. Drawn to warmer waters in shallow bays in search of the first active baitfish, five-pounders are plentiful and behemoths of 40-pounds-plus are not all that infrequent. Early in the season, fly anglers with 8- or 9-weight rods casting big saltwater streamer patterns like Tabory's Sea Rats or Snakes ought to find themselves hooked into trophy lakers. So, too, for spinfishermen. Spinners and spoons fished with medium to heavy rods through weedy cover in six to 10 feet of water often produce bragging-size fish.

Bring an ultralight rig, too. Small spinners will seduce grayling in Tincup and lakes and rivers in the Kathleen drainage, reachable by the lodge's DeHaviland Beaver. Grayling rise to dries, particularly dark patterns of No. 14 and smaller, and they'll hit dull or dark-colored weighted nymphs as well. A 5-weight system is about right. The Kathleen also holds rainbows up to 20 inches. In addition to one-day fly outs, Tincup offers overnight adventures to outcamps as well. Guests have use of motorboats and the first two days of guiding are included.

In the 1960s and 70s, Tincup became a destination for international anglers in the know. But the old lodge burned in 1981. For a decade it was all but abandoned. Then Larry and his brother Ernie bought the place and built four new cabins and a main lodge, all of cedar. Red roofed and the color of dark toffee, they're located facing the lake on a little alluvial plain where a stream enters Tincup. Inside the stylish cabins you'll find all the modern conveniences: private baths, ample closets, a wood stove to shake the morning chill and 24-hour electricity. Ethnic dishes from Germany, Hungary and France are featured as well as good Canadian beef and fish. After dinner, a stroll up the mountain behind the lodge may be just the tonic you need for a good night's sleep in this land of the midnight sun.

EASTERN CANADA

MANITOBA, NEW BRUNSWICK, NEWFOUNDLAND/LABRADOR, NOVA SCOTIA, ONTARIO, QUEBEC

THROUGH DEEP and brooding forests flow slender streams alive with bright native brook trout. The streams grow into the rivers that draw Atlantic salmon to spawn in summer and early fall, and return to the oceans in spring, what some consider to be the heartiest stock. To the north, in the barren tundra lands, rocky rivers are thick with char and brook trout. Inland waters teem with smallmouth bass, and lakes are heavy with pike and walleyes. Much of this region's better angling is no more than a two-day drive from the cities of the eastern U.S. Visit remote fly-in lodges and you'll find more trophies, however. And if you're headed to Quebec or the Maritimes, brush up on your French.

Lodges:

Manitoba

1 GANGLER'S LODGES
2 NUELTIN FLY-IN LODGES

New Brunswick

3 CHICKADEE LODGE
4 MIRAMICHI GRAY RAPIDS LODGE
5 MIRAMICHI INN
6 PINKHAM'S LODGE
7 PONDS...ON THE MIRAMICHI
8 UPPER OXBOW OUTDOOR ADVENTURES
9 WADE'S FISHING LODGE
10 WILSON'S SPORTING CAMPS

Newfoundland/Labrador

11 BIG RIVER CAMPS
12 COOPER'S MINIPI CAMPS
13 GANDER RIVER OUTFITTERS
14 RIVERKEEP LODGE
15 TUCKAMORE WILDERNESS LODGE

Nova Scotia

16 BIG INTERVALE SALMON CAMP

Ontario

17 HAWK LAKE LODGE
18 KESAGAMI WILDERNESS LODGE
19 LAKE OBABIKA LODGE
20 LAKE OF THE WOODS HOUSEBOATS
21 MANOTAK LODGE

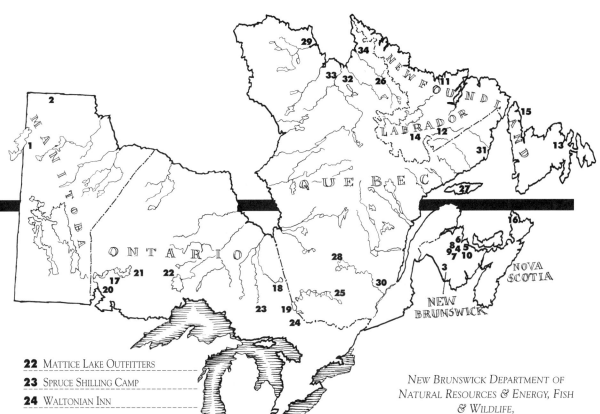

References:

ATLANTIC SALMON FISHING
— Bill Cummings
International Marine/McGraw-Hill
Companies, Customer Service Dept.,
PO Box 547, Blacklick, OH 43004;
800/822-8158

BUGGING THE ATLANTIC SALMON
— Michael Brislan
CURRENTS IN THE STREAM
— Wayne Curtis
FISHING THE MIRAMICHI
— Wayne Curtis
HOME POOL
— Philip Lee
RIVER GUIDES OF THE MIRAMICHI
— Wayne Curtis
Goose Lane Editions, 469 King St.,
Fredericton, NB, Canada E3B 1E5;
506/450-4251

Resources:

TRAVEL MANITOBA,
700-155 Carlton St., Winnipeg, MB,
Canada R3C 3H8; 204/945-3796,
800/665-0040, website
http://www.gov.mb.ca/Travel-Manitoba

NEW BRUNSWICK DEPARTMENT OF
NATURAL RESOURCES & ENERGY, FISH
& WILDLIFE,
PO Box 6000, Fredericton, NB,
Canada E3B 5HI; 506/453-2440

NEWFOUNDLAND/LABRADOR
DEPARTMENT OF
TOURISM & CULTURE,
PO Box 8730, St. John's, NF, Canada
A1B 4K2; 709/729-3813, 800/563-
6353, website http://www.gov.nf.ca

TOURISM NOVA SCOTIA,
PO Box 519, Halifax, NS, Canada
B3J 2M7; 902/424-5000, 800/565-
0000, website http://www.gov.ns.ca

TRAVELINX ONTARIO,
1 Concorde Gate, Don Mills, ON,
Canada M3C 3N6; 416/314-0944,
800/668-2746, website
http://www.travelinx.com

TOURISME QUEBEC,
PO Box 979, Montreal, PQ, Canada
H3C 2W3; 800/363-7777, website
http://www.tourisme.gouv.qc.ca

*At Tuckamore Wilderness Lodge near Main Brook, Newfoundland,
anglers may hook up to four Atlantic salmon a day,
then go whale watching. — page 280.*

*Superlative smallmouth fishing brings anglers to Lake Obabika Lodge
at River Valley, Ontario, where they find delightful
accommodations with a distinctive Austrian ambiance. — page 284.*

Gangler's Lodges
N o r t h e r n   S a s k a t c h e w a n   &   M a n i t o b a

VITAL STATISTICS:

KEY SPECIES:
Lake trout; northern pike; walleyes

Season:
June through August

Accommodations:
CABINS WITH VARYING AMENITIES
NUMBER OF GUEST ROOMS: From 2 to 8 cabins
MAXIMUM NUMBER OF GUESTS: From 4 to 28

Conference Groups: Yes

Meals: American plan or cook for yourself, depending on location

Rates:
From $1895 (US) per person per week at Reilly Lake to $2695 (US) at Reindeer Lodge, single occupancy

Guides: Provided at Reindeer Lake, but not at other locations

Gratuities: Client's discretion

Preferred Payment:
American Express, MasterCard, Visa

Getting There:
Jet charter from Winnipeg to Lynn Lake. Floatplane to lodges and outposts (price varies depending on package).

Other Activities:
Swimming, hiking, wildlife photography, bird watching.

Contact:
**Wayne Gangler
Gangler's Lodges, 1568
E. Wedgewood Lane,
Hernando, FL 34442;
352/637-2244, fax
352/637-2240 (winter);
PO Box 848, Lynn Lake,
Manitoba, Canada R0B
0W0; 600/700-0964
(summer).**

Lake trout, northerns and walleyes will nail your baits from this series of northwoods lodges.

AT REINDEER LAKE YOU'LL FIND two million acres of fishable water on the northern border between Saskatchewan and Manitoba. Deep in this boreal forest, Reindeer is the largest of hundreds of lakes, linked by a web of tumbling coffee-colored rivers and streams. The lakes are prime habitat for pike, lake trout and walleyes. You'll also find walleyes and grayling in the rivers.

As you'd expect, 90 percent of the fishing is from deep V boats. All feature carpeted casting decks and pedestal seats. Depending on the size of the lake, motors will range from 15 to 55 horsepower, with a trolling motor mounted on the stern. Most also carry Bottom Line fishfinders. Most important, the boats are skippered by native guides. Most have grown up on the lakes, know the moods of the lake and the fish as well. They are also schooled in catch-and-release fishing. The only fish you'll keep are a few walleyes for your lunch, cooked over an open fire on the beach.

You'll need to bring at least two rods. Make them seven-footers with fast retrieve casting reels. Twelve-pound-test line is ample, but you might want to spool one of the reels with 17-pound-test. Your tacklebox should include a variety of floating/diving stickbaits in orange and green and black and silver; spinnerbaits in chartreuse and white; large bucktail spinners such as Blue Foxes (bring some that are undressed as well); and spoons such as the Five 'o Diamonds and Johnson's weedless silver minnows. Flyfishers will take pike and lake trout on big white and chartreuse streamers and grayling on Adams and bead-head Woolly Buggers. Take a 10-foot 8 weight for the pike and a 5 for the grayling.

Gangler's operates five lodges and camps on and around Reindeer Lake. Reindeer Lake Lodge is top-flight, offering 28 anglers accommodations in eight log cabins with private baths. After a day's fishing, you'll find a plate of hors d'oeuvres in your room to tide you over until dinner. On nearby Reilly Lake is an outpost camp with two cabins where guests provide their own food and do their own cooking. Across the border in Manitoba, Gangler's Maria Lake mini-lodge provides full service for eight with four cabins with private baths, and its Steven's/Nicklin outpost hosts eight in two cabins with private baths. Here all food is provided, but you'll cook it yourself. Rounding out the quintet is Burnie Lake Lodge, with two cabins where up to eight anglers rough it in sleeping bags. Food is provided and guests flip to see who'll be chef du jour.

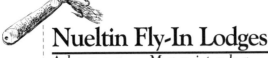

Nueltin Fly-In Lodges
Alonsa, Manitoba

Catch big lake trout and pike in the shallows
as you follow the seasons north on Nueltin Lake.

VITAL STATISTICS:

KEY SPECIES:
Northern pike; lake trout; walleyes; grayling

Season:
June through early September

Accommodations:
RUSTIC LODGES
NUMBER OF GUEST ROOMS: About 20
MAXIMUM NUMBER OF GUESTS: 10 at each outpost, 24 at the main lodge

Conference Groups: Yes

Meals: American plan and other options

Rates:
From $1995 to $2895 per person per week depending on location

Guides: Included at Treeline Lodge only

Gratuities: $100 to $150 per week

Preferred Payment:
Cash or check

Getting There:
Fly to Winnipeg and catch the turbo-prop shuttle to Nueltin Lodge's private strip at no additional charge.

Other Activities:
Boating, hiking, bird watching, wildlife photography.

Contact:
Shawn Gurke
Nueltin Fly-In Lodges, Box 500, Alonsa, Manitoba, Canada ROH 0A0; 800/361-7177, fax 204/767-2331, website http://www.outdoors.net /online/nueltin

IF YOU DON'T BELIEVE that catch-and-release can make a difference on big waters, just talk to Shawn Gurke at Nueltin Fly-In Lodges. Gurke's dad, Gary, was among the pioneers of the catch-and-release policy on Nueltin, a huge lake about 120 miles long by 35 miles wide that straddles the Manitoba/Northwest Territories border. Lake trout more than 50 pounds, northern pike of 30 pounds plus and grayling in excess of four pounds are caught in this vast wilderness. You'll also find plenty of walleyes in the six-pound range. In the cold lakes, it takes time to grow big fish, and the number of trophies in these waters is testimony to the success of catch-and-release, which has been in effect here since 1979.

The Gurkes offer anglers a choice of three locations. Treeline Lodge, with modern, utilitarian accommodations for up to 24 guests, is the southernmost. Guests stay in individual paneled cabins complete with private baths. The main lodge includes a congenial lounge, well-stocked tackleshop and family-style dining room overlooking the water. Pike fishing is best at Treeline, although anglers catch a lot of lake trout between 20 and 45 pounds and a number of grayling. Guides take anglers, two to a boat, out for the species that's hitting and fire up a shore lunch of walleye. Dinners consist of hearty fare such as steak, shrimp and Cornish hens.

Draining from south to north, Nueltin constricts near its middle to an area called The Narrows. The steady current sweeps through myriad channels with shoals and pools, shallows and runs. These troubled waters offer excellent cover for feeding and spawning fish. There is an outpost camp here, staffed by a couple who serve as camp managers. A maximum of 10 guests are provided with everything they need: 16-foot Lunds with new 15-horse outboards, safety gear, and groceries, including fresh meats and vegetables. Divided among three redwood sleeping cabins, guests share two bathhouses. The managers will direct you to the best fishing water and, for a fee, will serve as chefs.

It's the same story up at the third and northernmost camp, at the mouth of the Windy River. Set on a rocky hill above the river, camp managers can be prevailed on to handle cooking and K.P. for an additional stipend. Guests bunk in four bedrooms and share two baths. The fishing here tends to peak three weeks later than at Treeline. Lakers and pike will still be shallow into July after they've gone deep down south. The mouth of the river provides big-water flyfishing for grayling and walleyes.

Chickadee Lodge

Prince William, New Brunswick

The St. John and surrounding lakes will spoil smallmouth fans forever.

VITAL STATISTICS:

KEY SPECIES:
Smallmouth bass;
Atlantic salmon

Season:
May through October
Accommodations:
LAKEFRONT HOUSE
NUMBER OF GUEST ROOMS: 5
MAXIMUM NUMBER OF GUESTS: 12
Conference Groups: Yes
Meals: American plan
Rates:
$390 per person per week
Guides: $370 per day for 2
Gratuities: 10% to 15%
Preferred Payment:
MasterCard, Visa
Getting There:
Fly into Fredericton, rent a car
and drive to the lodge.
Other Activities:
Canoeing, swimming, hiking.

Contact:
**Vaughan Schriver
Chickadee Lodge, Prince
William, New Brunswick,
Canada EOH 1SO; 506/
363-2759 (summer);
506/363-2288 (winter).**

SMALLMOUTH BASS are the raptors of New Brunswick's rivers and lakes. From rocky lairs, they'll race across the current, smash a bait then lunge for the sky as if they're trying to fly. Those who fish these waters for smallmouths with anything but light tackle do themselves and their quarry disservice. Four-pound-test line is enough. The rod should be supple enough to flip-cast light lures into pockets under brush. Flyfishermen should arm themselves with 5- or 6-weight rigs. If you fish this way, you'll feel everything a smallmouth has to offer, and smallmouth bass in the St. John and lakes near Chickadee Lodge offer a lot.

From May through October, the average fish runs about three pounds, although four- and five-pounders are netted and released with regularity. The fishery is diverse. A power dam 10 miles downstream from Chickadee Lodge turns the St. John into long, narrow Lake Mactaquac. This section of the St. John fishes well from the middle of May through the June spawn. Then the water warms and fish go deeper. As fishing in the river loses momentum, action picks up in four lakes. Lake George is the shallowest of the quartet. It teems with two- to three-pounders and fishes well throughout the season. Lakes Harvey and Magaguadavic are the largest, and they consistently yield fish more than four pounds. Topwater fishing is hot early in the season, then crankbaits and spinnerbaits take over. Little Magaguadavic rounds out the quartet. Vaughan Schriver, who owns Chickadee Lodge, will recommend guides with fully-rigged bassboats for day trips to these lakes as well as excursions on the St. John.

Chickadee also offers guided float trips on 12 miles of the Meduxnekeag River, which crosses from Maine into New Brunswick south of Bloomfield and joins the St. John at Woodstock. Ideal for flyfishing, the river's record is a five-pound 12-ounce bronzeback taken on a streamer. Gentle riffles and clear pools make this an idyllic trip, and as a bonus you may pick up a brown trout or two. Many area rivers also have Atlantic salmon runs, fished for with flies only.

When you see the price, you won't believe it. Chickadee offers lakefront room and board for less than $400 per week. Rooms share baths, and meals are substantial: roasts, turkey, baked ham. For the quality of its accommodations and services, Chickadee has earned a 3 1/2 star rating from Canada Select.

Miramichi Gray Rapids Lodge
O r o m o c t o ,   N e w   B r u n s w i c k

Just upstream from salt water, here your odds of catching salmon are better than average.

VITAL STATISTICS:

KEY SPECIES:
Atlantic salmon; sea-run trout

Season:
All year

Accommodations:
COMFORTABLE HOUSE AND CABIN
NUMBER OF GUEST ROOMS: 5
MAXIMUM NUMBER OF GUESTS: 12

Conference Groups: Yes

Meals: American plan

Rates:
From $780 per person for 3 days and nights

Guides: Included

Gratuities: 3% to 7%

Preferred Payment:
Visa

Getting There:
Fly to Miramichi or Fredericton, rent a car or arrange for the lodge to pick you up for an additional fee.

Other Activities:
Canoeing, hiking, bird watching, antiquing, wildlife photography.

Contact:
**Guy A. Smith
Miramichi Gray Rapids Lodge, 326 MacDonald Ave., Oromocto, New Brunswick, Canada E2V 1A7; 506/357-9784, fax 506/357-9733.**

TED WILLIAMS AND HIS GUESTS used to fish the run of the Main Southwest Miramichi in front of this convivial salmon lodge. Today, Guy Smith owns the property, and from mid-April through mid-October, you'll find 10 to 12 rods a week working his private pools on this river and the Renous a few miles away.

Just upstream of the maximum tidal flow, Miramichi Gray Rapids Lodge has an advantage over others. Virtually every salmon that enters the vast watershed swims past Smith's front porch. The converse is equally true. In April and May, spring salmon—those that ran up the previous fall, survived the spawn and are now returning to salt—have nowhere else to go other than by the lodge. The closer spring salmon get to salt water, the more aggressively they feed. Some guests hook up with 10 or more spring salmon in the 10-pound-or-better class per day. Some of these will run up to 40 pounds.

Come July, the first bright or summer salmon enter the river. Though many are grilse, immature fish of less than 25 inches in length, there are plenty of adult salmon. They fish best when they enter the river system. The farther up they run and the longer they remain in the river, the less likely they are to take a fly. You want to get them while they're fresh. Bigger and better runs of salmon (10 to 20 pounds) begin their spawn in late September and October. The percentage of salmon to grilse is higher in the fall. Lest this leave the wrong impression, fall salmon are not easily caught. One fish per rod per day is not a bad average, and to do better is phenomenal. Smith's clients average four fish in three days. Most anglers and their guides wade, although fishing from canoe or boat is available.

The lodge is neither fancy nor spartan. Guest rooms in the main house and in the nearby cottage are clean and comfortable. In the main house, three of the guest rooms have private baths and two share. From the dining room (family-style meals of good traditional fare with excellent breads and pastries), you can watch salmon roll, as you can from the screened porch—that is if you can stand it without making a dash for your rod.

Miramichi Inn
Red Bank, New Brunswick

*Fish for salmon on a crisp October morning,
then hunt grouse and woodcock in the afternoon.*

VITAL STATISTICS:

KEY SPECIES:
Atlantic salmon

Season:
Late April through October
Accommodations:
RUSTIC LOG LODGE AND CABIN
NUMBER OF GUEST ROOMS: 8
MAXIMUM NUMBER OF GUESTS: 14
Conference Groups: Yes
Meals: American plan
Rates:
From $295 per person per day,
double occupancy
Guides: Included
Gratuities: 10% of package
Preferred Payment:
Cash or check
Getting There:
Fly to Chatham, New Brunswick,
and be met by the van from the
lodge.
Other Activities:
Bird and bear hunting.

Contact:
**Andre Godin
Miramichi Inn, RR 2, Red
Bank, New Brunswick,
Canada EOC 1W0;
506/836-7452, fax
506/836-7805.**

BUILT OF RUSTIC PINE LOGS, the Miramichi Inn and its adjacent cabin are tucked in the trees on the Little Southwest Miramichi. Don't confuse this with the Southwest Miramichi River, a river three times the size that points southwest from its mouth in the city of Miramichi. The Little Southwest flows east from Tuadook Lake to Sunny Corner, where it flows into the Northwest which joins the Southwest at Derby Junction.

In the early 1960s, Andre Godin bought 100 acres on the Little Southwest for a private fishing and hunting camp. Salmon fishing was good, but crashed in the 1970s due to heavy commercial fishing pressure off the coast. Despite seasonal cycles, grouse and woodcock hunting remained excellent. So did fishing for freshwater and sea-run brook trout. As the salmon started to come back in the 80s, Godin made innkeeping his full-time business, and committed himself to running one of the best camps in the Maritimes.

On the Little Southwest, the salmon seasons are three. The season for kelts or spent salmon—salmon that came up in the fall, spawned, wintered over under the ice and returned to the ocean in the spring—runs from mid-April to late May. Since these fish are feeding, an angler will hook an average of 10 a day. Salmon that are 25 inches and more must be released. Salmon less than 25 inches are called grilse; two may be kept per day, although most flyfishers release them as well. Bright salmon, fresh from the sea, charge up the river from mid-June until the end of July. These fish, in the 10- to 20-pound range, are as silver as newly minted coins and are difficult to catch. When you do, they'll run you down to backing in nothing flat. After August 20 or so, the fall season begins. This is when the biggest fish of all (20 to 30 pounds) enter the river, which is literally full until the season closes October 15. That's when Godin gets in trouble.

Salmon are his love, but his passion is hunting grouse and woodcock over Irish setters. The two come together in the first two weeks of October. Fish for salmon in the cool bright mornings and after noon, tote a 12 gauge choked skeet for grouse and woodcock through woods turned scarlet and gold. You may flush 20 to 30 grouse and woodcock in four hours. Afterwards, fill up on the likes of fiddlehead chicken soup, scallops and gingerbread with rum raisin sauce. Tumble off to bed and dream of casts and coverts.

Pinkham's Lodge

F l a t l a n d s ,   N e w   B r u n s w i c k

VITAL STATISTICS:

KEY SPECIES:
Atlantic salmon

Season:
May 15 through August 15
Accommodations:
WOODEN LODGE AND CABIN
NUMBER OF GUEST ROOMS: 5
MAXIMUM NUMBER OF GUESTS: 10
Conference Facilities: Yes
Meals: American plan
Rates: From $1200 per angler (shared rod) per week, double occupancy
Guides: Included
Gratuities:
$10 to $20 per day
Preferred Payment:
Cash or check
Getting There:
Fly to Charlo, New Brunswick, which is an hour's drive from the lodge. Pinkham's will provide transportation for $35 each way. Or, fly to Presque Isle, Maine, three hours from the lodge. Transportation is $100 each way.
Other Activities:
Canoeing, swimming, boating, bird watching, antiquing, biking, wildlife photography.

Contact:
Virginia Pinkham
Pinkham's Lodge, PO
Box M, Ashland, ME
04732; 207/435-6954,
fax 207/435-2451 (winter); RR1, Group 8, Box
5, Tide Head, New
Brunswick, Canada E0K
1K0; 506/573-3644
(summer).

Share the rod and spoil the angler for $1200 per week.

LUMBERMAN, CONSERVATIONIST and salmon fisher, Thomas Pinkham had always wanted a place on a salmon river. His first camp was below Renous Bridge on the Miramichi. The water there is tidal, suitable only for spring fishing. In 1978, he bought the Bensinger (founder of Brunswick Bowling and the International Atlantic Salmon Foundation) Lodge and freehold fishing rights on the Restigouche. Pinkham died in 1982, and ever since, the lodge and its four miles of private pools have been in the gentle and capable hands of his wife, Virginia. Mrs. Pinkham, elderly yet spry (she casts a long line and entered a 40-pounder in the camp's log in 1994), assures guests that their surroundings will be comfortable and serene, that food will be ample and of good quality and that service from guides will be knowledgeable, friendly and courteous.

The Restigouche is one of New Brunswick's premiere salmon rivers. Upwards of 25,000 salmon enter the main river each year. Larger salmon appear first, generally in June. July and August see more grilse. Still, during the season from June 1 through August 15 (trout opens May 15), the chances of hooking into a salmon are good. This is flyfishing-only water. Salmon are caught and released. Anglers may take two grilse of less than five pounds per day if they wish, and Pinkham's will prepare an angler's catch for the trip home. However, most fishers release grilse as well and settle for a few pounds of smoked salmon as a memento of their trip on the Restigouche. Except during periods of low water when wading is possible, anglers fish in pairs from freighter canoes with outboards. The guide will position the canoe at the head of a drop, and the first angler will lengthen each cast and drift by three feet until he's covered the water on the right side of the canoe. The second angler in the boat will then do the same on the other side. The guide then drops the canoe down 10 feet in the pool and the fishing begins again.

If ever there was a lodge set up for anglers to fish together and enjoy each other's company, this is it. A solitary angler will shell out $2310 for six days of fishing. But two anglers will pay only $1200 apiece for the same six days if they agree to share a rod. If you want, the guides will teach flycasting. The main wood-sided lodge with four guest rooms and shared baths overlooks the river. An adjacent cabin with private bath houses two anglers. Pinkham's lodge is handicapped accessible, and Mrs. Pinkham stresses that "such anglers are very welcome."

Pond's...on the Miramichi
Ludlow, New Brunswick

VITAL STATISTICS:

KEY SPECIES:
Atlantic salmon

Season:
April 15 through October 15
Accommodations:
CABINS, MOTEL ROOMS AND 5-ROOM LODGE
NUMBER OF GUEST ROOMS: 24
MAXIMUM NUMBER OF GUESTS: 60, but only 20 can fish
Conference Groups: Yes
Meals: American plan
Rates:
Numerous packages from $370 (CDN) per person per day
Guides: Included
Gratuities: $30 per day
Preferred Payment:
Major credit cards
Getting There:
Fly to Fredericton, New Brunswick, and either rent a car or arrange for the lodge van to pick you up.
Other Activities:
Golf, tennis, hiking, bird watching, biking, wildlife photography, snowmobiling, volleyball, horseshoes, corporate challenge courses.

Contact:
Keith Pond
Pond's, 91 Porter Cove Rd., PO Box 73, Ludlow, New Brunswick, Canada E0C 1N0; 506/369-2612, fax 506/369-2293, email flyfish@nbnet.nb.ca, website http://www.cygnus.nb.ca/ponds/homepond.html

Represented By:
Fishing International, 800/950-4242; Go Fishing (London), 0181 742-3700.

With its four-star rating and a persona to match, Pond's is in the first rank of salmon lodges.

THE HIGHWAY BRIDGE crosses the river, the Southwest Miramichi, at Pond's home pool. On your left, you can see the river, shallow and running down a cobbly channel cutting around an island before widening, deepening and running under the bridge. Atlantic salmon hold in the pool below the channel before moving upstream. If traffic on the bridge is stopped, you can bet someone's fighting a salmon.

Pond's has been hosting anglers for more than 75 years. With exclusive access to nine miles of this, one of the prime Atlantic salmon rivers in Canada, third-generation owner Keith Pond can guarantee that clients will fish productive water. He can forecast when the fish will be in the river system (heck, you can see them rising in front of your cabin), but he can't tell you whether they'll bite. His guides are competent, and will rig your fly and put you over water that holds fish. Long casts aren't necessary here, but you've got to stay with it. Atlantic salmon are not feeding when they're running upstream. They strike out of frustration, perhaps, or from some deeply imprinted memory of feeding in the river as smolts. Each morning after breakfast, you and your guide will work a section of the river best suited to your abilities and the current run of salmon. If you like, you can take a two-day float down the upper reaches of the river, stopping overnight at a rustic log cabin in the backwoods.

Salmon season opens on April 15 and closes on October 15. In the first part of the season, kelts or black salmon, those which came upriver in the fall and are now returning to sea, are legal quarry. But the better angling begins in July with the first runs of salmon, bright from salt water. The run slows a bit in August, but picks up in September and October, when maples and birch along the river color up and the air takes on that unmistakable nip of impending winter.

That's when the fire in the chunk stove in your 1930s vintage "Jack Russell" log cabin feels so good. If it's really late and you've missed dinner and the bar's closed, you may find hors d'oeuvres—fiddleheads and smoked salmon on cocktail rye spread with cream cheese—in your refrigerator, along with soup, salad and warm rolls on the side. These folks know how to take care of starving anglers. If your taste runs more to contemporary accommodations, you'll enjoy the modern paneled rooms in the main lodge or in a separate five-bedroom lodge. Orvis-endorsed, Pond's has a full-service flyshop on-site and offers, in addition, guided overnight trips for native brook trout.

Upper Oxbow Outdoor Adventures
S i l l i k e r s ,   N e w   B r u n s w i c k

For kelts or bright Atlantic salmon, this small lodge offers big service at a fair price.

VITAL STATISTICS:

KEY SPECIES:
Atlantic salmon

Season:
April through October
Accommodations:
HILLSIDE CABINS
NUMBER OF GUEST ROOMS: 9
MAXIMUM NUMBER OF GUESTS: 14
Conference Groups: Yes
Meals: Housekeeping or American plan
Rates:
From $387 (American plan) per person for 3 days and 2 nights, single occupancy
Guides: Included
Gratuities: $20 per day
Preferred Payment:
Visa
Getting There:
Fly to Chatham and the lodge van will pick you up.
Other Activities:
Golf, whitewater rafting, swimming, hiking, bird watching, wildlife photography.

Contact:
Debbie Norton
Upper Oxbow Outdoor Adventures, 11042 Rt. 430 Hwy., Trout Brook, New Brunswick, Canada E9E 1R4; 506/662-8834, fax 506/622-2027.

THE LITTLE SOUTHWEST MIRAMICHI rises on the flanks of Mount McNair and North Pole Mountain and flows southeast for about 40 miles before hooking sharply to the northeast to join the larger Southwest Miramichi at Derby Junction. Upper Oxbow Outdoor Adventures and their three well-appointed cabins are located at Sillikers, a mile before the river turns tidal. Good runs of kelt and bright salmon pass Upper Oxbow's 40 acres on the river, which includes the well-known Bogan Pool.

For those who are not prejudiced against angling for kelts—some oppose interfering with spawned salmon that winter in the river and return to the sea in spring—the early part of the year can produce outstanding fishing. Traditionally, the season opens on April 15 and continues through May 15. Kelts, or black salmon as they are also called, are streaming downriver and feeding voraciously. While the average hookup during spring and fall runs of "bright" salmon is one per day or less, anglers in the spring consistently connect with eight or 10 black salmon each day when the water is not discolored. Kelts range upwards of 30 inches, though most run about 20. The Little Southwest Miramichi is flies-only water. Fishing is generally by boat or canoe, and a guide must accompany nonresident anglers. Sinking or sink-tip lines are used.

The first runs of bright salmon enter the Little Southwest Miramichi in mid-June and another batch, generally larger, follows in September and October. These fall salmon are the fish that have made the Miramichi famous. Anglers are permitted to keep two grilse (salmon of less than 25 inches) but many release these as well. Tackle required is the same, a No. 8 or 9 rod with a reel that has a smooth drag, except that floating lines and smaller flies are the order of the day. Wading is the name of the game in fall until the season closes October 15.

Upper Oxbow operates four modern cabins (two three-bedroom, one two-bedroom and one one-bedroom, respectively), each set on hillsides with views of the river. All have full kitchens and private baths. The larger have wood stoves. Guests may prepare their own food or eat delicious home cooking; chicken, steak, roast beef and salmon. Numerous packages are available at this lodge rated 3 1/2 stars by Canada Select.

Wade's Fishing Lodge

Blackville, New Brunswick

*Fish from a lodge at the junction of
two of the province's finest salmon rivers.*

VITAL STATISTICS:

KEY SPECIES:
Atlantic salmon

Season:
April 15 through October 15
Accommodations:
RUSTIC CABINS AND LODGE
NUMBER OF GUEST ROOMS: 18
MAXIMUM NUMBER OF GUESTS: 20
Conference Groups: Yes
Meals: American plan
Rates:
From $360 (CDN) per person
per day, single occupancy
Guides: Included
Gratuities: $10 per day
Preferred Payment:
Visa
Getting There:
Fredericton, New Brunswick is
the closest airport. Wade's will
provide transportation for $150
additional. Renting a car is an
alternative.
Other Activities:
Canoeing, swimming, boating,
hiking, bird watching, wildlife
photography, golf.

Contact:
Joyce Holmes
**Wade's Fishing Lodge,
Blackville, New
Brunswick, Canada E0C
1C0; 506/384-2229, fax
506/843-2334.**

OF ALL THE RIVERS in the Maritime Provinces that are enjoying a salmon rebirth, none is more celebrated than the Miramichi. It is New Brunswick's quintessential salmon river which, with its tributaries, encompasses 500 miles of runs and pools. The water on the main river at Wade's is relatively large. Pools are long, open and easily accessed from submerged gravel bars. Wading is not difficult. The Cain, which joins the Miramichi at the lodge, is a smaller, tighter stream. While the Atlantic salmon season opens on April 15, the best and biggest run of bright fish begins about June 20 and continues for a month. These are days of piercing blue skies, where the sun on the back of your flannel shirt feels good. And these fish are the most aggressive of the year and fight gallantly.

But the best time of year to fish the Miramichi is the fall. Fish are in excellent condition, air temperatures are ideal and the woods have turned gold and scarlet. September and early October are the prime weeks. Take an 8- or 9-weight rod, and load your reel with 150 yards of backing. If you don't have enough flies—Blue Charms, Bombers, Butterflies, Cossebooms, Green Butts, Rat-Faced MacDougals or Silver Doctors—don't worry. You can buy all you need at Wade's or W.W. Doak's, an excellent flyfishing shop in nearby Doaktown.

Set at the junction of the Cains and Miramichi, Wade's main lodge hosts up to 20 guests in five rustic wood cabins set under the trees on a high bank overlooking the river. A mile upriver, Wade's recently opened the Cains River Camp, a rustic log cabin with a fireplace and screened porch. Cains can accommodate six. Two more outpost camps are downriver. Meals at the camps and main lodge include entrees of steak, turkey, Cornish hens, lobster and baked stuffed shrimp. In addition, Wade's runs overnight canoe trips on the rivers. Everything except a sleeping bag is provided. Book the river float in advance. Wade's has a four-star ranking by Canada Select.

Wilson's Sporting Camps

M c N a m e e ,   N e w   B r u n s w i c k

Since 1929, the Wilsons have hosted anglers fishing the Southwest Miramichi.

VITAL STATISTICS:

Key Species:
Atlantic salmon

Season:
April through October

Accommodations:
RUSTIC CABINS AND FARMHOUSE
NUMBER OF GUEST ROOMS: 14
MAXIMUM NUMBER OF GUESTS: 12

Conference Groups: Yes

Meals: American plan

Rates:
From $400 (CDN) per person per day (minimum 3-day stay)

Guides: Included

Gratuities: $40 (CDN) per day

Preferred Payment:
MasterCard, Visa

Getting There:
Fly to Fredericton. Round-trip fare from the airport is $125 (CDN).

Other Activities:
Golf, canoeing, swimming, boating, hiking, bird watching, biking, wildlife photography.

Contact:
Keith Wilson
Wilson's Sporting Camps,
303 McNamee,
McNamee, New
Brunswick, Canada E0C
1P0; 506/365-7962, fax
506/365-7106.

Represented By:
Angler Adventures, 860/434-9624, fax 860/434-8605.

FOR MORE THAN FOUR GENERATIONS, the Wilsons have been running a sporting camp on the Southwest Miramichi. Sporting means the Wilsons have an interest in other game, namely grouse and woodcock. But it's salmon that anglers seek and service that's made this lodge famous.

Wilson's owns 16 pools scattered along five miles of the river. Duff Pool is the farthest upstream and Lyon's Rapids marks the lowest. The camps are set in the middle, and each day anglers and their guides take to wood and canvas canoes. No outboards here, except in the spring season (mid-April to mid-May) for kelts or black salmon that have wintered over and are returning to the sea. During the summer and fall runs, guides pole or paddle your canoe to good water, and you'll fish from the canoe or wade the cobbled riverbottom, casting to salmon lying in pools, pockets or runs.

Summer brings bright salmon into the river. These fish are fresh from the sea. Angling is best early in the day and later in the afternoon. To accommodate the schedule, Wilson's fishes from 8:00 a.m. until noon, brings anglers in for dinner (as in the main meal of the day, with lobster or prime rib, hot rolls and homemade pie), allows them a nap, and then returns them to the river at 4:00 p.m. Over an open fire, guides whip up a shore supper at about 6:00 p.m. During summer, shad up to five pounds also run the river, as do sea-run brook trout. The fall salmon run begins in late August and continues into October. The last weeks of the fall run are magic. Maples are crimson, ocher and amber, and birch leaves flutter gold against smoky green spruce. Salmon have colored up too, iridescent in plum and rose. The wind has a nip to it. The water is low and you can sight-cast to salmon. Fish are bigger in September and October. In the fall, dinner again becomes the evening meal.

There's nothing pretentious about Wilson's accommodations, but you'll have everything you need. Eight guest cabins are scattered under the trees across the road from the white farmhouse where you'll eat family-style. The cabins have private baths and hooks for waders and rods on their front porches. The farmhouse also has four guest rooms. Tackle, licenses and flies are available from the excellent W.W. Doak fly-shop in Doaktown, 10 miles away.

Big River Camps

Pasadena, Newfoundland

Two lodges form this camp on the Big River, where it brawls and where salmon and sea-run trout hang out.

VITAL STATISTICS:

KEY SPECIES:
Atlantic salmon; sea-run trout; arctic char

Season:
Second week in June through late August

Accommodations:
RUSTIC LOG LODGES
NUMBER OF GUEST ROOMS:
MAIN: 6
GREAT WHITE: 4
MAXIMUM NUMBER OF GUESTS:
MAIN: 12
GREAT WHITE: 8

Conference Groups: No
Meals: American plan
Rates:
$3250 (CDN) per person per week, double occupancy
Guides: Included
Gratuities: $100 per week (minimum)
Preferred Payment:
MasterCard, Visa
Getting There:
Fly to Goose Bay and take a floatplane to the lodge at no extra expense.
Other Activities:
Boating, hiking, bird watching, wildlife photography.

Contact:
Bob Skinner
Big River Camps, PO Box 250, Pasadena, Newfoundland, Canada AOL 1K0; 709/686-2242, fax 709/686-5244.

ABOUT 120 MILES NORTH of Goose Bay, Big River swirls out of White Bear Lake and begins a tortuous 40-mile journey to the Atlantic. Wild and remote, with numerous falls, deep gorges, long rapids and slick pools, Big River sees excellent runs of Atlantic salmon, sea-run trout and arctic char, later in the season. So, too, does Rattling Brook, which joins the Big at its mouth.

Located on a bench on the north side of the river, the log lodge has a commanding view of a major turn in the course of the Big. The main river hooks south around a small island, carving its deepest channel against the far bank. Between the island and the lodge are gravel flats and myriad little sloughs that change each time the river floods. You can wade this area. Atlantic salmon run up to 22 pounds, sea-run trout top six, and arctic char can reach seven. Char are fished here only in the last two weeks of August. The fishing is similar five miles upstream at the base of a three-mile-long rattle (rapid) known as the Great White Way, site of the second lodge, built in 1990. To get there, you'll hike for 45 minutes through the barrens and then board native-designed Gander Bay boats with hulls patterned after the cross sections of fish. The boats will carry you up to fishable pools. A set of falls a short distance up Rattling Brook from its mouth limits the number of rods to four each day, but the fishing here for sea-run trout can be extremely good.

More than 30 years ago Bob Skinner caught his first Big River salmon. The following year, he came back and caught more, sought and received permission to build a lodge, hauled in a portable sawmill and, with the help of guides, constructed the main lodge. Eight anglers are usually in the informal but comfortable camp, staying two to a room and sharing four baths. Great White Way sleeps six. Camps are staffed with one guide for every two anglers, a handyman and a cook. That's Gloria Hancock, who's been head chef at the main camp for a dozen years. But once a week she goes on strike. That's the night the guests host the guides in a farewell party.

Cooper's Minipi Camps
H a p p y   V a l l e y ,   L a b r a d o r

VITAL STATISTICS:

KEY SPECIES:
Brook trout

Season:
June through September

Accommodations:
THREE WOODEN LODGES
NUMBER OF GUEST ROOMS: 18
MAXIMUM NUMBER OF GUESTS: 36

Conference Groups: Yes

Meals: American plan

Rates:
$2995 (US) per person per week, double occupancy

Guides: Included

Gratuities:
Angler's discretion

Preferred Payment:
American Express, MasterCard, Visa

Getting There:
Fly to Goose Bay, Labrador and a floatplane will ferry you to Minipi Camps at no additional charge.

Other Activities:
Bird watching, wildlife photography.

Contact:
Jack E. Cooper
Cooper's Minipi Camps,
PO Box 340, Station B,
Happy Valley, Labrador,
Canada A0P 1E0;
709/896-2891, fax
709/896-9619, email
103453.226@Compu
serv.com, website http:
//mgfx.com/minipi//

Represented By:
Angler Adventures, 860/434-9624, fax 860/434-8605.

At Cooper's, brook trout grow as big as Southern largemouths.

YOU CAN CATCH BROOK TROUT almost any-where. Natives in the lower 48 are dainty as a jeweled broach, colored with blues and reds and yellows like the wildflowers along the banks of the high mountain streams and beaver creek bogs where they live. Most put-and-take brookies are muted and dull in color, a reminder, if you need one, that the waters where you find them may never sparkle again. The farther north you go, the bigger the brookies and the bolder and brighter their colors. The world's record brook trout was taken in 1916 on the Nipigon River in Ontario. It weighed 14 pounds 8 ounces. If there's a place in North America where that record might be broken, it's probably the Minipi watershed in Labrador.

Here brook trout are similar in size to lunker largemouths caught in the South. Three- and four-pounders are common enough so that, after the first day, anglers try to avoid them. It's hard. When they reach six pounds, and take you down to the backing a time or two, they attract your attention. At seven or eight pounds they hold it for quite a while. In 1966 Lee Wulff discovered that Minipi brook trout would readily rise to dry flies. So too do northern pike; a 26-pounder was taken on a dry not too long ago. Larger pike have been taken on spinning tackle. Pure water, abundant aquatic insects and crustaceans, and restricted access combine to ensure that the fishery does not decline.

Fishing in the Minipi watershed's two lakes, their feeder streams and the Minipi River is restricted to guests of Cooper's Minipi Camps. The season is open from June through September, and the best brook trout fishing runs through mid-August. Anglers fish by wading or from canoes and powerboats. To call the lodging "camps" does not do it justice. The largest of the three, Minipi Lodge, has 10 bedrooms and four baths. Its two-story glass prow opens the lodge to the lake and lights the anglers' library in the second-floor loft. Anne Marie Lodge is log and rustic and sleeps half a dozen who share a bath. Ranch-style Minonipi Lodge is a little bigger. Meals are first class. But, after-wards, before you go to sleep, there's something you must do: Fish the twilight caddis hatch under dancing northern lights.

Gander River Outfitters

VITAL STATISTICS:

KEY SPECIES:
Atlantic salmon; brook trout

Season:
May through mid-October

Accommodations:
Log lodge with 2 cabins
Number of Guest Rooms: 2 in lodge, 2 in cabins
Maximum Number of Guests: 12

Conference Groups: Yes

Meals: American plan

Rates:
From $250 per person per day; $1500 per week (US), single occupancy

Guides: Included

Gratuities: Client's discretion

Preferred Payment:
Diner's Club, MasterCard, Visa

Getting There:
Fly to Gander International. Taxi and boat service to lodge included in price. Also offered are packages including airfare from St. John's, Halifax, Boston, New York and London.

Other Activities:
Sight-seeing, hiking, bird watching, canoeing.

Contact:
Terry Cusack
Gander River Outfitters,
PO Box 21017, St. John's
Newfoundland, Canada
A1A 5B2; 709/753-9163,
fax 709/753-9169,
website www.netfxinc.
com/flyfish

Try for a 20-pound salmon this fall in the reborn Gander River.

OVERALL, ATLANTIC SALMON streams in Canada's Maritime Provinces are undergoing a renaissance. One water where the rebirth is evident is the Gander River in Newfoundland. In 1991 the annual run of wild salmon was 7000; in 1995 the run hit 27,000. Says Terry Cusack, owner of Gander River Outfitters, "Everyone of those salmon runs by our door." While most of the run consists of grilse, about 20 percent are adult salmon and the ratio appears to be increasing. Fishing success averages out at one salmon per rod per day. Better anglers catch more fish, obviously.

The Gander itself is 37 miles long. Outboard-powered 25-foot freighter canoes, run by the guides, carry anglers to pools where the salmon are and other fishermen are not. Pressure from local fishermen falls off sharply in August, and the fall run of salmon (mid-September to mid-October) may offer the best chance for joining Gander's 20 Pound Plus Club. And while the focus is primarily on salmon—you can often count upwards of 100 jumping in front of the lodge—don't overlook brook trout in the two- to three-pound range.

Whether your quarry is trout or salmon, flyrods and reels are the tackle of choice at Gander River. Plan on taking 6- and 8-weight rods. If you're buying a new salmon rod, consider a 10-foot for an 8, an ideal combination for big open salmon water. Load both reels (make sure they have good, smooth drags) with at least 100 yards of backing. Why a 6 as a second rod? It may be a little heavy for the big brookies, but if the salmon are really hitting, you might want to fight one on a light rod. Gander River Outfitters supplies licenses, raingear and flotation jackets. If you forget anything, you can buy what you need at the lodge.

The log lodge is unpretentious but comfortable. It includes two guest rooms, one with a private bath. Guests also stay in two nearby cabins. All are under the trees in the woods by the river. Meals are straightforward, home-cooked affairs: dijon chicken with rice, baked cod with Hollandaise sauce, roast beef. Because this lodge is close by the river, seniors and anglers who have difficulty walking will have little trouble fishing here.

Anglers after Atlantic salmon may stay
in "Jack Russell" cabinsthat line the home
pool at Pond's . . . on the Miramichi
at Ludlow, New Brunswick. — page 271.

Flyfish for trophy brook trout, plus
landlocked salmon and northern pike, out of
Matt Libby's new Riverkeep Lodge in
western Labrador. — page 279.

Riverkeep Lodge
Atikonak, Labrador

VITAL STATISTICS:

KEY SPECIES:
Brook and lake trout; landlocked salmon; northern pike

Season:
June 15 through September 10
Accommodations:
RUSTIC CABINS
NUMBER OF GUEST ROOMS: 4
MAXIMUM NUMBER OF GUESTS: 8
Conference Groups: Yes
Meals: American plan
Rates:
$2700 per person for 7 days, double occupancy
Guides: Included
Gratuities: $300 per angler per week for staff and guides
Preferred Payment:
MasterCard, Visa
Getting There:
Fly to Wabush/Labrador City, Newfoundland. You'll be shuttled to the lodge via seaplane at no additional expense.
Other Activities:
Boating, hiking, wildlife photography.

Contact:
Matt Libby
Riverkeep Lodge, PO Box V, Ashland, ME 04732-0561; 207/435-8274, fax 207/435-3230.

One hundred miles from the nearest town, the Libbys have established a new camp for serious flyfishermen.

MATT AND ELLEN LIBBY built an angling tradition with their Libby Camps in Maine. For years, Matt had fished Labrador when he had a chance, and he kept his eye open for a spot where he could offer clients the same excellent service for which the Maine camp is so highly regarded. He found the fishing he wanted—landlocked salmon, brook trout, lake trout and pike—on the Atikonak River in western Labrador. There, too, he found the site for a first-class lodge.

A new main house with kitchen and dining facilities sits above the river at the edge of the forest. Adjacent are the lodge's guest cabins, green and roofed in red. Guests choose from one cabin with three bedrooms and shared bath or a one-bedroom cabin with private bath normally reserved for couples. A full breakfast opens the day at 8:00 a.m., but nobody lingers over coffee. They're headed down to the boats—25-foot square-stern cedar canoes—and either up or down the river in search of fish. Along the way, one may see woodland caribou, black bear and moose.

Mainly catch-and-release, anglers can retain one trophy of each species if they desire, and a few pan-size brookies are kept for the shore lunch. At the height of summer, dinner back at camp interrupts the fishing at 6:00 p.m., and then it's back on the water for more angling until 10:00 p.m. or so. Rarely does anyone stay up late after a day like that. In September, shorter days eliminate evening angling. Instead, the aurora borealis may put on a show.

Orvis-endorsed, angling at Riverkeep is flyfishing only. Large stoneflies and mayflies emerge in late June. Caddis come off in July and the evening hatch can approximate a blizzard. August sees more mayflies and a few large tan caddis. In September, the water has cooled and streamers turn on big fish. Brook trout run in the two- to eight-pound range and are most active in June and July. Landlocked salmon (two to 12 pounds) and lake trout (10 to 30 pounds) fish best in June and September. July and August are prime months for northern pike from five to 25 pounds and whitefish from two to six pounds. On a given day, you may drift the river in a MacKenzie boat, wade and fish riffles and runs or work slower waters from a canoe. It all depends on what you want to catch and how you want to do it. Matt, son Tyler, and partner Scott McArthur have assembled an eclectic and gregarious group of guides whose mission in life is to make your stay everything you want it to be.

Tuckamore Wilderness Lodge
M a i n   B r o o k ,   N e w f o u n d l a n d

VITAL STATISTICS:

KEY SPECIES:
Atlantic salmon; brook trout; arctic char

Season:
All year

Accommodations:
WOODEN CHALET AND ADJACENT COTTAGE
NUMBER OF GUEST ROOMS: 9
MAXIMUM NUMBER OF GUESTS: 18

Conference Groups: Yes

Meals: American plan

Rates:
$1500 (CDN) per person for 7 days and nights, double occupancy

Guides: Included

Gratuities: $100 per week

Preferred Payment:
Visa

Getting There:
Fly to St. Anthony and a representative of the lodge will pick you up.

Other Activities:
Canoeing, boating, hiking, bird watching, wildlife photography, whale watching, eco touring, snowmobiling, cross-country skiing.

Contact:
Barb Genge
Tuckamore Wilderness Lodge, PO Box 100, Main Brook, Newfoundland, Canada A0K 3N0;
709/865-6361, fax 709/865-2112, website http://www.nucleus. com/~fitz

When you're spent catching salmon, this is the place to watch whales and icebergs.

A
S IS THE CASE ALMOST EVERYWHERE in the Canadian Maritimes, Atlantic salmon are running in numbers almost unknown in the past 50 years. Sportfishing for salmon has never been better and the odds are that, as long as the moratorium on commercial fishing is maintained, angling will continue to improve. Such is certainly the case on the Salmon River, which drains a vast watershed in northern Newfoundland and flows unmolested into Hare Bay south of St. Anthony. The tiny town of Main Brook sits at the mouth of the river. Tuckamore is located a mile or so from the town on Southwest Pond.

The lure of this lodge is found in its wilderness setting and in the fishing nearby. The short spring and summer blankets the floor of this northern boreal forest with wildflowers. Moose, caribou and bear are frequently seen by anglers, as are eagles, eiders and loons. Icebergs drift south past the coast. Puffins with their improbable bills of vermillion and yellow strut on the rocky beach. Whales and orcas broach offshore.

With all of this, it may be hard to keep your mind on fishing. From 12,000 to 15,000 Atlantic salmon, many of them grilse, spawn in the river. The typical recreational fishing season runs from late June through the first days of September. Hooked-and-released salmon have been averaging three pounds, but Tuckamore's logs show increasing numbers of six- to eight-pound fish with an occasional 10-pounder. Unlike many other Atlantic salmon fisheries where one hookup per day is considered par, fishermen in this river generally raise several fish and play three or four. Not to be overlooked are brook trout and arctic char. The former are common and run in the two- to three-pound range; char are fewer and slightly larger in size. Angling here can be a year-round proposition. In winter, the lodge offers icefishing as well as snowmobiling and cross-country skiing.

Home base for angling and eco sight-seeing is Tuckamore Wilderness Lodge, a large A-frame chalet with four guest rooms and a recently built pine and cedar cottage with five guest rooms. All have private baths, and you'll find a sauna and whirlpool in the chalet. Meals are built around local seafood and desserts feature fresh blueberries and raspberries.

Big Intervale Salmon Camp

Margaree Valley, Nova Scotia

VITAL STATISTICS:

KEY SPECIES:
Atlantic salmon; brook, brown and rainbow trout

Season:
May through October

Accommodations:
FRAME CABINS
NUMBER OF GUEST ROOMS: 6
MAXIMUM NUMBER OF GUESTS: 12

Conference Groups: No

Meals: American plan

Rates:
From $100 (CDN) for 2 with breakfast per day

Guides: $150 (CDN) for 2

Gratuities: Client's discretion

Preferred Payment:
Visa

Getting There:
Fly to Halifax, rent a car and drive to the lodge.

Other Activities:
Hiking, bird watching, wildlife photography.

Contact:
Ruth Schneeberger
Big Intervale Salmon Camp, RR 1, Margaree Valley, Nova Scotia, Canada BOE 2C0;
902/248-2275.

Represented By:
Kaiser Reisen, Zurich, 01-252-5212.

This old lodge is now owned by an angling couple who've fallen in love with the Margaree.

RUTH AND HERMAN Schneeberger arrived on the Margaree River in the fall of 1996 at the same time as a run of bright salmon. They caught fish. They fell in love with the clear river, the maples brilliant in reds, oranges and yellows, the friendly Nova Scotians, the gentle valley. It was all so different from Switzerland and the crowds of people there. They soon bought the Big Intervale Salmon Camp on the Margaree. "Oh, it was a quick decision, yes!" says Ruth, laughing, in her lilting German accent.

The couple has picked one of Canada's finest salmon rivers. It rises on the flanks of mountains at the north end of Cape Breton Island and flows south through the quaint river town of Margaree Valley. At Margaree Forks it turns north, and then west at Belle Cote before entering the Gulf of St. Lawrence at Margaree Harbor. Ernest Schwiebert, in *The Traveling Angler*, reports that the river is "gin-clear and deceptively swift." Riffles and some 40 salmon pools characterize the river's 20 miles of fishable water. The first run of salmon occurs in early summer, with fish tending to stay in the lower section. Each rainstorm charges the river with fresh cool water and impels the fish to migrate up to the next pool. But it is in September that the Margaree receives its largest run of salmon. And at that time, the river valley is decked out in vibrant fall colors. The best fishing is for salmon fresh from the sea. They have the greatest propensity to take both dries and wets and somersault as they strip away your backing. Only flyfishing is permitted on the Margaree and regulations prohibit the use of weighted flies lest they be used to snag fish. The river also holds brook, brown and rainbow trout. Guides are available through the lodge for an additional, quite reasonable, fee.

With .6 miles of frontage on the lower Margaree, Big Intervale is a great spot from which to fish the river. Guests stay in three riverside cabins, a five-minute walk from the main lodge. Each cabin contains two rooms with a pair of double beds and a private bath. Chef Ruth adds a continental flare to solid meals of beef and potatoes and salmon. Anglers are sent fishing with a lunch bucket, packed with thick sandwiches, a boiled egg, fruit, chocolate and hot coffee or tea. In the evening, sit on the spacious front deck, or work up new patterns at the three-station flytying bench. Though the couple is new to running a lodge, they're experienced anglers, and that makes Big Intervale worthy of consideration.

Hawk Lake Lodge

K e n o r a ,   O n t a r i o

VITAL STATISTICS:

KEY SPECIES:
Smallmouth bass; lake trout; northern pike

Season:
May through September

Accommodations:
MODERN LOG CABINS
NUMBER OF GUEST ROOMS: Cabins with 1 to 4 bedrooms
MAXIMUM NUMBER OF GUESTS: 24

Conference Groups: Yes

Meals: American plan

Rates:
$245 per person per night, single occupancy

Guides: $100 per day

Gratuities: 6% to 8% of package

Preferred Payment:
MasterCard, Visa

Getting There:
Drive or fly to Kenora from Winnipeg.

Other Activities:
Canoeing, swimming, boating, hiking, bird watching, biking, wildlife photography.

Contact:
**Gary Delton
Hawk Lake Lodge, Box 142, Kenora, Ontario, Canada P9N 3X1;
807/227-5208, fax 807/226-1228 (summer); 9 7th Ave. North, Hopkins, MN 55343;
612/881-7578 (winter), website http://www. hawk-lake.com**

Where the lodge and fishing for smallmouth bass earn five stars and the bill is no surprise.

BASS LAKE, KNOWN FOR trophy smallmouths, is just one of 15 lakes that Hawk Lake Lodge fishes. It's the only lodge on these lakes and, taking 24 or fewer guests at a time, there are no crowds. Anglers seldom see each other during the day. Each pair of anglers is assigned a boat, with outboard and electric trolling motors and plenty of gas, a chart of the lake showing structure and bag lunch (breakfast and dinner too, if they want). They're then turned loose. Rocky outcrops, bluffs and boulder-strewn beaches provide cover for smallmouths in the one- to six-pound range. Fish them with flies, stickbaits or spinners, or bait. Best action is in July and August, when fish that are usually deep hug the shore.

While smallmouths are the predominant species, northern pike to 25 pounds also inhabit these waters. June and September are the months for trophies, and spoons and big spinners produce the most. In May and June, lake trout also fall for hardware; you'll have to jig them up from deep holes later on. Walleyes round out the bill of fare on these lakes, but they are difficult to catch. Jig and minnow or leech rigs work reasonably well.

You don't need a guide to fish this lake system, as owners Gary and Sandy Delton have developed a self-guiding program that puts anglers on fish. When you arrive, you'll tour the lakes for orientation. And each night you'll discuss plans for the next day. The log lodge, one of the few to receive Tourism Ontario's five star rating, is warm, comfortable and scrupulously maintained. Guests stay in spacious waterfront cabins with decks and private baths. A huge stone fireplace dominates the lodge's great room, full of rustic ambiance with log walls and wagon wheel chandeliers, where dinners (walleye, prime rib, Cornish hens) are served. Guests have a choice of two entrees, and seconds are not a problem. The dinner hour is preceded by complimentary cocktails and hors d'oeuvres. Most lodges would lose money on this but the Deltons aren't worried, as even free drinks rarely lure smallmouth anglers off the water.

Kesagami Wilderness Lodge
L a k e   K e s a g a m i ,   O n t a r i o

VITAL STATISTICS:

KEY SPECIES:
Northern pike; walleyes

Season:
Late May through mid-August

Accommodations:
LOG LODGE AND CABINS
NUMBER OF GUEST ROOMS: 16
MAXIMUM NUMBER OF GUESTS: 50

Conference Groups: Yes

Meals: American plan

Rates:
From $979 per person per week

Guides: $125 for 2 per day

Gratuities: Client's discretion

Preferred Payment:
Major credit cards

Getting There:
Fly or drive to Cochrane, Ontario. The shuttle flight to the lodge is included.

Other Activities:
Canoeing, hiking, swimming, bird watching, wildlife photography.

Contact:
Charlie McDonald
Kesagami Wilderness Lodge, 371 Airport Rd., Naples, FL 34104; 800/253-3474, fax 941/643-7312.

Fish for record pike as far out in the wilderness as you can go.

IF YOU ASKED A DOZEN outdoor writers to pick the best place in North America to catch big northern pike and walleye consistently, you'd get three dozen opinions. But near the top of everyone's list would be Kesagami Lake, a provincial park some 60 miles south of James Bay. Days of 100 walleyes up to six pounds and two dozen pike in the neighborhood of 20 pounds each are not uncommon.

Here's why. Road access to Kesagami Lake isn't just limited, it doesn't exist. There are only three ways to get there. Fly, paddle through on the wilderness canoe route or walk. Nobody walks in, and few mosquito-hardened souls float through on the way to James Bay. The lodge is the only game in this corner of the country, so the number of anglers on this lake is limited to 50 for each of the 12 weeks in the season. Finally, Kesagami is unusually shallow, averaging seven feet deep with holes to nearly 30. Thus, it warms earlier than other lakes in similar latitude, and that means a longer growing season for everything in the food chain that supports pike and walleyes. A strict policy of catch-and-release with single, barbless hooks is enforced.

Surrounded by peat bogs and quaking muskeg, Kesagami is deeply tannin colored. Some say that the dark water gives anglers more cover, allowing them to get closer to big fish. Others believe that the tannin somehow adds to the pikes' ferocity. Makes little difference, but the fact is that if you cast a Power Spin or chrome and red Mepps Syclops over the weedbeds, you'll get thrashing strikes, time after time. You don't have to be a flycasting champ to reach big fish, but it helps if you've figured out how to knot monofilament and steel leader materials. Generally speaking, the bigger the fly, the bigger the pike. Walleye anglers can pick up fish all day with grub-tipped jigs (no live bait allowed), and flyrodders will do reasonably well with Clousers and sink-tip lines. You'll fish, guided or unguided, from 24-foot freighter canoes, pushed by outboards.

The lodge welcomes kids and goes out of its way to ensure that they not only catch fish, but learn about pike, the lake and the environment. The classroom is the canoe and the teachers are mom, dad, guide or, as 13-year-old Jeff Brenchley from Bloomsburg, Pennsylvania discovered, a 45.5-inch pike. Brenchley's fish set a Canadian "Live Release" record for northern pike when he caught the fish on June 16, 1995.

Ten rooms in the log lodge and the six cabins stretched along the lakefront that can accommodate up to eight are attractive and comfortable, all with private baths. The lodge has a bar, and you can even get in a game of pool.

Lake Obabika Lodge
River Valley, Ontario

VITAL STATISTICS:

KEY SPECIES:
Smallmouth bass; lake trout; northern pike

Season:
May through October

Accommodations:
CHALETS
NUMBER OF GUEST ROOMS: 13
MAXIMUM NUMBER OF GUESTS: 20

Conference Groups: Yes
Meals: American plan
Rates:
From $660 (CDN) per person for 3 nights
Guides: $130 for 2 per day
Gratuities: 10%
Preferred Payment:
American Express, MasterCard, Visa

Getting There:
Sudbury is the closest airport. Round-trip air shuttles cost $640 for 3. Or rent a car and enjoy the 2-hour scenic drive.

Other Activities:
Canoeing, swimming, boating, hiking, bird watching, wildlife photography.

Contact:
**Peter or Margit Herburger
Lake Obabika Lodge,
PO Box 10, River Valley,
Ontario, Canada P0H
2C0; 705/858-1056,
fax 705/858-0115,
email obabika@
sympatico.ca, website
http://www.obabika.com**

The Family Herburger has created a lodge with Austrian flare in the heart of smallmouth country.

ABOUT HALFWAY BETWEEN Sudbury and North Bay is the town of River Valley, gateway to the Lake Obabika region of central Ontario. In this land of many lakes, Obabika has a growing reputation for the quality of its smallmouth fishing, and the only lodge on the lake, run by Peter Herburger and his family, is nothing short of exquisite. Here, amid flowers and landscaped walks, is a place where families can relax in pampered comfort while anglers in the group do their thing.

The thing to do on Obabika is catch bronzebacks. The lake, scooped out by advancing continental glaciers, is dotted with islands and studded with bays. Points are numerous, as are rock reefs. Habitat is outstanding, but fishing pressure is not. Generally, the smallmouth season runs from July through October, with fishing best in the first three months. The bass tend to be deep, so jigs are the order of the day. Crankbaits can also be effective, as are topwater plugs and flyrod poppers at dawn and dusk. The size of the fish is surprising: Every angler should connect with one or more three- to four-pounders as well as a bunch in the two-pound range. Bigger fish are more common in late August and September. Obabika also has healthy populations of northern pike (four to 16 pounds) and lake trout (four to 12 pounds). Pike are good from May through October, and lake trout are best in May, June and September. In addition to Obabika, nearby Upper Bass and Wawiagama lakes hold smallmouths, lake trout and pike. Clearwater Lake, also close by, contains primarily smallmouths and lakers. Speckled trout (brookies) populate Sarah Lake.

The fishing package at Obabika includes use of a 16-foot boat, 25-horse motor, gas and bait. Canoes are also included. Keep one smallie for your shore lunch and release the others.

Back at the lodge you'll find modern log chalets with vaulted living rooms and fireplaces, complete baths and screened porches. You even get free movies from the main lodge channeled to your television. Meals are of the best caliber, with six-course gourmet dinners served on Wednesday and Saturday nights. On other nights you'll have to make do with standard four-course affairs. Flowers accent the lodge both inside and out and boardwalks wind through the trees linking chalets, the lodge, marina and miscellaneous recreational amenities.

Lake of the Woods Houseboats

Sioux Narrows, Ontario

Try angling out of a lodge that takes you to smallmouths and walleyes.

WANT TO GET AWAY FROM IT ALL? Want unspoiled fishing for smallmouths, walleyes, saugers, northern pike, lake trout, crappies, perch and maybe a muskie? Want to captain your own ship? Here's the deal. Rent a houseboat on Lake of the Woods. With 65,000 miles of shoreline and 14,000 islands, Lake of the Woods is loaded with isolated bays, coves and headlands where you can spend a week with no intrusion aside from that of a curious loon.

Fishing in this huge lake system between Minnesota and Ontario is quite good. Use jigs and minnows for walleyes. Throw big spoons (Five 'o Diamonds or Dardevles) for northern pike. Cast crankbaits and spinners or break out the flyrod and fish streamers, poppers or big nymphs for smallmouths. Minnows take crappies and trolling can be effective for lake trout and muskies. The nice thing about renting a houseboat is that there's room for all of your tackle: spinning rods, flyrods, casting rods. Bring it all, and if you don't have what you need, get it from the marina. Depending on the species you seek, and the time of year, you may work the shore, drift over submerged bars or troll. Each houseboat is equipped with a 14-foot Lund and oars. A 10-horse outboard can be rented for $150 per week and it's worth it. Canoes are also available for $65 per week.

Houseboats come in various sizes, from the 40-foot Pioneer for two to four up to the 52-foot Voyageur that sleeps 12. Staff at the marina will check you out on the boat's operation and handling, provide maps and directions to waters that hold your favorite species and will resupply your boat if you want to stay out longer than the standard week. All houseboats have showers, ship-to-shore radios and complete kitchens. All you need to provide are the groceries and any libations. You'll reimburse the marina for gas and oil, typically about $150, used during your trip. The closest major airport is 90 miles away at International Falls, Minnesota. If you fly, Lake of the Woods Houseboats will provide transportation for $100 round trip.

Manotak Lodge

P e r r a u l t   L a k e ,   O n t a r i o

VITAL STATISTICS:

KEY SPECIES:
Walleyes; northern pike; smallmouth bass; muskies; whitefish; perch

Season:
Mid-May through September

Accommodations:
RUSTIC LOG CABINS
NUMBER OF GUEST ROOMS: 16
MAXIMUM NUMBER OF GUESTS: 60

Conference Groups: Yes

Meals: Various plans

Rates:
$900 for 2 per week

Guides: $100 for 2 per day

Gratuities: 15%

Preferred Payment:
MasterCard, Visa

Getting There:
Dryden, Ontario has commercial service; a lodge representative will pick you up for $25.

Other Activities:
Canoeing.

Contact:
Rej Roy
Manotak Lodge, Perrault Lake, Perrault Falls, Ontario, Canada P0V 2K0; 800/541-3431, fax 807/529-3190.

Once a retreat for oil company moguls, now it's yours for less than $500 per week.

IN THE MID-1940S, an American oil company sought a wilderness setting, not too far from an airfield but on an isolated lake where the fishing was better than good. Settling on Perrault Lake, the company built a log lodge and a number of cabins, a rustic hideaway for upper-echelon executives and top customers. The lodge is Manotak. Today it is among the more affordable fishing resorts in Ontario.

Perrault Lake's 50 miles of shoreline contain scores of secluded bays, rocky headlands, drop-offs and shallows. A navigable stream connects to Cedar Lake, which has another 67 miles of structure. A warmwater fishery, the lakes produce good walleyes (to 12 pounds), northern pike (four to 20 pounds), smallmouths averaging three-pounds-plus, muskies between 20 and 45 pounds, whitefish to five pounds and perch. Walleyes hit best in May and June and again at the end of the season in August and September. Pike are hot in June and July. The smallmouths fish well from July through September, and muskies are at the top of their form from August to September. You'll hook whitefish in September as well, and you can take perch pretty near anytime. Guides are not included in most packages, but are available, and many guests take advantage of their knowledge of the lakes and their fish. You can also take fly outs to other lakes.

Manotak's packages include 14- to 16-foot Naden boats, pushed by 20-horse Yamahas, that contain everything you need: cushions, bait buckets, anchors, paddles and nets. You'll start the morning with five gallons of gas. Buy your bait of choice and you're on your way. At night, after a full day of fishing, amble over to the main lodge, its log walls hung with pelts, to play pool or watch TV. You'll stay in one of 16 simple log cabins that sleep from two to 12, all with private baths and lake views. Most have kitchenettes. You may cook as little or as much as you like. Manotak offers a full American plan, a supper-only plan and a housekeeping plan. Sit around the picnic tables for substantial breakfasts and dinners. For lunches, the lodge will provide you with all the fixings (including pots, pans and Coleman stove) for a shore lunch. If you'd rather eat on the run, opt for a bag of sandwiches.

Mattice Lake Outfitters

A r m s t r o n g ,   O n t a r i o

Catch walleyes and big pike in the river and lake system that feeds Nipigon.

VITAL STATISTICS:

KEY SPECIES:
Walleyes; northern pike; sturgeon

Season:
May through September

Accommodations:
OUTPOST HOUSEKEEPING CABINS
NUMBER OF GUEST ROOMS: Varies with each location
MAXIMUM NUMBER OF GUESTS: Varies with each location

Conference Groups: No

Meals: Cook for yourself

Rates:
From $575 per person for a party of 4 for 3 days

Guides: $100 per day

Gratuities: Client's discretion

Preferred Payment:
Visa, cash, traveler's checks

Getting There:
Fly to Thunder Bay, Ontario, rent a car and drive 250 kilometers to Armstrong.

Other Activities:
Canoeing, hunting in the fall.

Contact:
Don or Annette Elliot Mattice Lake Outfitters, PO Box 157, Armstrong, Ontario, Canada P0T 1A0; 807/583-2483, fax 807/583-2114.

IN THE 1930S AND 1940S, the Ogoki river was impounded below Ogoki Lake and the water diverted by channel via Lake Mojikit into Lake Nipigon. As a result, Ogoki Lake became a huge, 34,290-acre, 35-mile-long reservoir offering endless opportunities for walleye and pike anglers. So do Mojikit and Whitewater Lake up the river from the big lake. On these lakes, Don and Annette Elliot operate a series of four fly-in housekeeping camps where self-guided parties of anglers cook their own meals. Boats and motors are provided at all camps.

WHITEWATER LAKE: This 25-mile-long lake of 26,000 acres brims with two- to three-pound walleyes, just right for eating, and yields a northern topping 30 pounds at least once a season. Bring a light rig for the walleyes and heavier gear for northerns. The camp is comprised of three, two- to six-person cabins, log sauna, hot showers and a white sandy beach. It's staffed by an attendant.

OGOKI RESERVOIR: The biggest lake has thousands of rocky reefs, shallow weedbeds and deep holes. The camp is located on an island two miles from Eight Flume Falls where the Ogoki River enters the lake. Fast water in the falls area provides an alternative to lake fishing and can be particularly good for walleyes that tend to run between three and four pounds. You'll also find pike, whitefish and sturgeon in Ogoki. Five cabins for two to six anglers are scattered on the island's east and north beaches. Here too you'll find a log sauna, hot showers and camp attendant.

SHORT LAKE: Short Lake's walleyes and pike are similar in size and number to those at the lodge on the upper end of the reservoir. The lodge here is a single cabin for six to 10 anglers. Groups find privacy and all the amenities that the other sites have, without an attendant.

MOJIKIT LAKE: Linked by the channel to the reservoir, Mojikit is similar in size to Whitewater, though the walleyes run in the three- to four-pound range. Also offering solitude without attendant, Mojikit's single cabin provides four to eight anglers with all the comforts of a rustic home and an icy freshwater spring for drinking water.

Use coolers to pack in food and bring out filets. Rates include flights from Armstrong to the camps, gas, ice, service flights and housekeeping gear. A two-way radio at each site provides communications with home base.

Spruce Shilling Camp

S h i n i n g   T r e e ,   O n t a r i o

Fish out of a down-home housekeeping camp on the banks of a little lake that's full of walleyes, smallmouths and pike.

VITAL STATISTICS:

KEY SPECIES:
Walleyes; smallmouth bass; lake, rainbow, brook, splake and Aurora trout; pike

Season:
All year

Accommodations:
RUSTIC WOODEN CABINS
NUMBER OF GUEST ROOMS: 9
MAXIMUM NUMBER OF GUESTS: 60
Meals: Housekeeping
Conference Groups: No
Rates:
From $30 per person per day, double occupancy
Guides: On special request
Gratuities: Client's discretion
Preferred Payment:
Visa
Getting There:
Eight-hour drive from Buffalo, 10-hour drive from Detroit.
Other Activities:
Canoeing, swimming, boating, hiking, wildlife photography, skiing, snowmobiling, icefishing.

Contact:
**Gary or Verva Gaebel
Spruce Shilling Camp
Hwy. 560, Shining Tree,
Ontario, Canada P0M
2X0; 705/263-2082.**

IF YOU'RE LOOKING FOR a low-price housekeeping camp where the fishing is as good as it is diverse, then Spruce Shilling Camp north of Sudbury may be for you. For $150 each, you and your partner can rent a clean one-bedroom cabin for a week on the banks of Cryderman Lake near Shining Tree. Bring your own boat, motor and groceries. No boat? Not a problem. You can rent what you need.

You'll fish little lakes, linked by channels or streams, for walleyes, smallmouths, pike and five species of trout. Flyrodders may find some success, but most anglers use spinning or casting gear. The big draw here is walleyes. Angling is best in late May and June when fish feed at the mouths of rivers flowing into the lakes. Anchor just down from the tail of the rapids. Cast a jig and minnow up into the fast water and bounce it back along bottom. Later in summer, you'll jig for walleyes in 15 to 20 feet of water. Good fish run in the three- to four-pound range. Smallmouths here average better than three pounds and are found along the shore of two or three isolated ponds that feed the main lake. You'll have to portage a canoe a short ways to get in, but once there you stand a chance of catching the bronzeback of a lifetime on small, jointed crankbaits. Northern pike, not as big as in other lakes but still running in the 15-pound range, are thick. Lake trout in the seven-pound neighborhood can be trolled up in the spring, but really dive deep in summer. These lakes also have populations of rainbows, brookies, Auroras and splake. Trout fishing is limited in summer and is generally best through the ice.

Gary Gaebel runs the fishing side and his mother, Verva, handles lodging and the camp store. Four of the cabins feature two beds, hot showers, electricity, heat, stove, refrigerator and kitchen utensils. The other four cabins (and a room in the main building) are similarly decked out, but lack private showers. A shower house is provided, and all share sanitary facilities. Licenses and productive lures are available at the camp store. If you plan to come, be sure to stock up on groceries before you leave Sudbury. The shopping beyond is mighty slim.

Waltonian Inn
Callander, Ontario

VITAL STATISTICS:

KEY SPECIES:
Walleyes; northern pike; smallmouth bass; white perch; whitefish; cisco herring

Season:
All year

Accommodations:
RUSTIC LODGE WITH NEARBY CABINS
NUMBER OF GUEST ROOMS: 58
MAXIMUM NUMBER OF GUESTS: 120

Conference Groups: Yes

Meals: American plan or modified American plan

Rates:
Numerous packages from $65 per person per night

Guides: Not usually needed, but available on request

Gratuities: Client's discretion

Preferred Payment:
MasterCard, Visa

Getting There:
North Bay, Ontario, is 45 minutes north of the lodge, which is about 3 hours north of Toronto.

Other Activities:
Swimming, boating, hiking, bird watching, wildlife photography, snowmobiling.

Contact:
Nadia Day
Waltonian Inn,
Waltonian Dr., RR 1,
Callander, Ontario,
Canada P0H 1H0;
705/752-2060, fax
705/752-4260.

A winter and summer fishing resort, the Marusich's place is right for the whole family.

FRANK MARUSICH HAD A PROBLEM. In 1970 he and Thea, his wife, sold their real estate business in Hamilton and bought the Waltonian Inn on Lake Nipissing. Once prime water for walleyes, the lake had declined dramatically by 1973. Nipissing, it was said, was fished out. Marusich organized lodge owners and engineered a campaign to convince the provincial government to initiate a restoration project. He and a group of friends built a walleye hatchery. He convinced other lodge owners to adopt the catch-and-release philosophy of letting the big ones go. The results are evident. Walleyes of five pounds are frequent, those in the three-pound class are abundant and smaller ones are plentiful. On this lake you can have 30- to 50-fish days.

Fishing is a year-round proposition. Ice leaves the 65-mile-long, 22-mile-wide lake in April, and walleyes begin to spawn in May. While the season runs from May through October, fishing begins to fall off after mid-July. Smallmouths open at the end of June and continue through October, with the end of the season generally better than the beginning. You'll also find northern pike up to 18 pounds. The best fishing, with spoons cast over weedbeds, is in May and June and again in September and October.

Ice comes to Nipissing in November and December and winter fishing hits full stride with the new year. Marusich's 1950s-vintage Bombardiers—tracked, enclosed, heated snow machines carrying 12 anglers—ferry anglers out to ice huts over Waltonian Reef, a mile or so from the lodge. Jig for walleyes, pike, white perch, whitefish and cisco herring through mid-March. When you arrive at your hut, you'll find it warmed by a gas heater with holes already drilled in the ice and a stock of minnows laid in. Lunch will be delivered to your door around noon.

Summer at the Waltonian is family-oriented. A long beach in front of the two-story log inn and its cabins is an ideal place for kids to play. Cookouts are frequent. And when breezes keep mosquitoes at bay, dinner on the deck with the setting sun is a fine way to end the day. The Marusiches are natives of Trieste and the menu features "peasant food," as Frank calls it. Don't miss the Heavenly Pickerel. Guests stay either in the eight rooms in the lodge, or in 22 cottages scattered along the lake. Some of the cottages have kitchen facilities. The lodge also operates a full-service marina.

Air Melancon

S t e . - A n n e - d u - L a c ,   Q u e b e c

VITAL STATISTICS:

KEY SPECIES:
Brook trout; northern pike; walleyes

Season:
Mid-May through September

Accommodations:
RUSTIC CABINS
NUMBER OF GUEST ROOMS: 33
MAXIMUM NUMBER OF GUESTS:
From 2 to 12 depending on cabin site

Conference Groups: Yes

Meals: European plan

Rates:
$390 per person for 3 days, double occupancy

Guides: $80 for 2 per day

Gratuities: Client's discretion

Preferred Payment:
Cash or traveler's check

Getting There:
Drive to Ste.-Anne-du-Lac, about 3 hours north of Montreal.

Other Activities:
Spring bear and moose hunting, canoeing, swimming, hiking, bird watching, wildlife photography.

Contact:
Francine Melancon Milot
2 Chemin Tour du lac,
Ste.-Anne-du-lac,
Quebec, Canada J0W 1V0;
819/586-2220, fax
819/586-2388.

Remote lakes in the highlands of Quebec teem with fish, and the only way to get there is by air.

WITH 33 CABINS scattered on 18 lakes, this air charter outfitter offers anglers so many different kinds of water that it would take a lifetime to get to know them all. More then 40 years ago, Real Melancon began exploring lakes in the highlands of central Quebec and opened the flying service to carry anglers to the best fishing he found. Daughter Francine and son-in-law Gary Milot are continuing to expand and refine the operation with the same goals in mind: safe access to the best hunting and fishing, and exemplary service at a price within everyone's reach.

This is pike, walleye and speckled (brook) trout country, with a few lake trout on the side. In the Moselle territory, between the Gatieau and Coucou rivers, Air Melancon operates 20 camps on 14 lakes. If you're seeking big lake trout as well as pike and walleye, try Sand Lake in mid-May just after ice-out; a short, but steep climb over "Cardiac" Hill will bring you to a delightful brook trout pond where Milot has stashed a canoe and rowboat. On the other hand, brookies up to two pounds hang out with walleyes and big pike in Natakim Lake. To the north and east, the Sauterelle territory covers a trio of lakes in a maze of rugged, wooded hills. Fish the lakes or streams or hike to nearby ponds with cached boats. Wild brook trout are everywhere from small, gaily colored fish in flowages between ponds to thick two-pounders dredged up from the lakes. Farther north, about 120 air-miles from the base at Ste.-Anne-du-Lac, are eight camps scattered on two bays on Gouin Reservoir, one of Quebec's best walleye lakes. Ten-fish limits are easy even for novices. And the chances for big pike are good too.

Air Melancon's camps are clean frame cabins. More than half have running water and indoor showers. You'll fly-in your own sleeping bags and food (perishables can be purchased at a grocery in Ste.-Anne-du-Lac). All camps have propane refrigerator/freezers and stoves, a wood stove with plenty of firewood and boats (14-foot Lunds) with 6.5- or 8-horse outboards. Gary is installing solar lighting systems, and several of the camps now feature electric lights without the noise of generators. Guests, usually in parties of two, four or six, are flown into camp by one of the line's four Beavers, turbo Otter or Cessna. Because Air Melancon owns the aircraft as well as the camps, guests don't have to fit their schedules to a rigid Saturday to Saturday schedule, but can begin packages anytime they wish. And, while cooks and guides are not really needed here, both are available at some camps if desired.

George River Lodge
St.-Augustin, Quebec

VITAL STATISTICS:

KEY SPECIES:
Atlantic salmon; brook and lake trout; char

Season:
Mid-June through September
Accommodations:
Log, frame or tent cabins (varies with location)
Maximum Number of Guests:
MAIN CAMP: 12
HIGH CLIFF: 6 (group only)
FALCON: 6 (group only)
CHATEAUGUAY: 6 (in each camp)
Conference Groups: No
Meals:
MAIN CAMP and CHATEAUGUAY: American plan
HIGH CLIFF and FALCON: Housekeeping
Rates:
From $2150 per person for housekeeping and $3450 per person American plan per week. Discounts available.
Guides: Included
Gratuities: $200 per week
Preferred Payment:
Cash or check
Getting There:
Transportation provided from Montreal.
Other Activities:
Wildlife photography.

Contact:
Pierre Paquet
George River Lodge, PO Box 88, St.-Augustin, Quebec, Canada G3A 1V9; 418/877-4650, fax 418/877-4652 (year-round); 418/585-3477 (mid-June through mid-October); 800/473-4650 (reservations only, October through May).

Combine caribou and ptarmigan with salmon and brook trout in the barren Ungava tundra.

THIN FORESTS RISE from this almost barren tundra, cut here and there by streams that rush north to Ungava Bay. It is the land of caribou, black bears and arctic foxes. The rivers that cut through the rolling plain and the gentle, stony streams that fill them run with brook trout, char and Atlantic salmon. Other anglers are few on the George and Chateauguay. Basically it's you, your guide and the fish.

While fish are plentiful, the season is short: June 20 through the end of September. Atlantic salmon (12 to 15 pounds) are found in the George from mid-June to mid-July (kelts) and from mid-August into September (bright). Brook trout and arctic char (three-pounds-plus) and lake trout up to 15 pounds run from June through August. Salmon and brook trout fish best in late August and September. Lakers are strongest in July, char in August. While spinfishing is permitted in some waters, most of the angling here is by fly-rod. You'll need two: an 8 or 9 for salmon and a 6 for trout and char.

Pierre Paquet operates three camps on the George River. His main camp—log cabins and a lodge—is about halfway up the river. Here you'll fish for salmon, primarily, with brook trout, lake trout and char as bonuses. Twenty-foot canoes powered by 20-horse outboards transport you to salmon runs and shoals where you'll wade and cast. High Cliff Camp, a collection of housekeeping cabins, is 30 miles farther upriver. Here one guide serves as camp manager and guide for a group of six or so. You'll bring your own groceries and use 18-foot canoes with 9.9-horse motors to fish for trout, char and salmon. The operation is similar at Falcon Camp, which is 15 more miles upriver.

To the west, on the Chateauguay River, are the main and satellite outpost camps, both with wood-floored wall tents. This river and its lake are known for outstanding runs of brook trout and lakers. Early in the season, mid-July, flyfishing for lake trout in the upper pools of the Chateauguay River is superb. In late August, the lakers turn on again, this time on their spawning beds in Chateauguay Lake. Brook trout are the mainstay at this camp, however. You'll hook between 30 and 50 per day. In addition to fixed camps, Paquet also takes anglers on six-day float-fishing trips down the George River.

As well as holding a fine fishery, the northern Quebec tundra sees tremendous migrations of caribou and is thick with ptarmigan. Trophy bulls abound in the massive George River caribou herds. And Paquet, ever flexible, books combination fishing and hunting trips when seasons open in August.

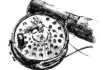

Jupiter 12

A n t i c o s t i ,   Q u e b e c

**VITAL
STATISTICS:**

KEY SPECIES:
Atlantic salmon; sea-run
trout

Season:
June 15 through August 15
Accommodations:
RUSTIC LODGE ON RIVER
NUMBER OF GUEST ROOMS: 6
MAXIMUM NUMBER OF GUESTS: 12
Conference Groups: Yes
Meals: American plan
Rates:
$3850 (CDN) per person for 5
days in June and July and 6
days in August
Guides: Included
Gratuities: Client's discretion
Preferred Payment:
American Express, MasterCard,
Visa
Getting There:
Fly to Port Mender on Anticosti,
where your guide will meet you.
Stock up on last-minute inciden-
tals here; then ride to the lodge
with your guide.
Other Activities:
Wildlife photography.

Contact:
**Gilles Dumaresq
SEPAQ-Anticosti, 801
Chemin St. Louis, Bureau
125, Quebec, Quebec,
Canada G1S 1C1;
418/686-6313, fax
418/682-9944 (winter);
CP 139 Port Menier, Ile
Anticosti, Quebec,
Canada G06 2Y0;
418/535-0156, fax
418/535-0289 (summer).**

*Catch and release salmon while staying at
a plush lodge in the middle of the wilderness.*

INDING SOUTH through the thick
conifer forests of Anticosti Island, the crys-
tal-clear Jupiter River runs with Atlantic
salmon from mid-June through mid-August.
The season is short yet fabulous. Here are the rules: During June, when the run is
strong, anglers may hook a maximum of four salmon and are permitted to keep two.
Two grilse may also be kept. In July and August, all adult salmon must be released, but
two grilse may be kept. That's the law. Think of it. In many of Canada's Atlantic
salmon fisheries, you're lucky to hook one salmon per day!

Part of the success of the Jupiter River stems from steps that ensure reduced pressure on the fish. While the river is 40 miles long, only eight rods may fish it each week.
During the 10-week season, only 80 anglers can fish salmon in the river. Not only do
the salmon seldom see flies, but anglers almost never see anyone else. You'll fish two to
a 22-foot cedar canoe. You, your partner and guide will plan the day's float over breakfast. With the canoe loaded on a four-wheel-drive pickup, and lunch and gear stowed
in the back, you'll drive upstream to your put-in for the day. The float through low
spruce-capped hills and rocky canyons is idyllic and serene. You'll see deer that have
made this island a hunter's paradise. And you will see salmon in the bottle-glass green
river. You may work pools and runs from the canoe or wade and fish as the water dictates. Bring two rods, an 8 for salmon and a 6 for sea-run trout that frequent the river.
Patterns that work well include Black Ghosts, Mickey Finns, Silver Cossebooms,
Muddlers, Brown or Blue Bombers, White Wulffs and Stoneflies.

Twelve miles from the rivermouth, Jupiter 12 Lodge is a collection of low and
rustic wooden buildings on a rise over the river. Operated by the provincial government, the main lodge accommodates 12 guests in six rooms that share two baths. After
fishing, slump into an easy chair in the pine-paneled lounge with a cocktail. Dinner will
be ready soon and will be accompanied with wine from the lodge's cellar. Special diets
are easily accommodated.

Oasis du Gouin

R e p e n t i g n y ,   Q u e b e c

VITAL STATISTICS:

KEY SPECIES:
Walleyes; northern pike; speckled brook trout

Season:
May through September

Accommodations:
LODGE, HOUSEBOATS AND CABINS
NUMBER OF GUEST ROOMS: 5 in lodge; 8 in cabins
MAXIMUM NUMBER OF GUESTS: 35

Conference Groups: Yes

Meals: American plan and a la carte

Rates:
$832 (US) per person for 8 days and 7 nights

Guides: $132 for 2 per day

Gratuities: $20 per day

Preferred Payment:
MasterCard, Visa

Getting There:
Round-trip airfare from Montreal is $335 per person (groups of 4) or you may drive to Parent (350 miles from Montreal) and take a 45-minute boat ride to the island.

Other Activities:
Bear hunting, swimming, boating, bird watching, wildlife photography.

Contact:
Jackie Leblanc
Oasis Du Gouin,
17 Champlain St.
Repentigny, Quebec,
Canada J6A 5L5;
819/974-8825 (sum-
mer); 514/984-4158, fax
514/585-0974 (winter);
email oasis@sympatico.
ca, website http://www.
sportstravel.com/oasis
en.htm

Enjoy a private island lodge in the middle of one of Quebec's hottest walleye lakes.

HOW WOULD YOU LIKE to catch 100 walleyes a day? Not just little ones, but stickbenders of two to six pounds? Or, if that doesn't whet your whistle, how about big northern pike? Still no takers? What about native speckled trout, as bright as bracelets? And what if you did it from a 16-square-mile island where the only civilization is a comfortable lodge, a handful of housekeeping cabins and a private airstrip?

That's just what you'll find at Oasis du Gouin, a full-service resort owned and operated by Bernard Leblanc and his wife, Jackie. Surrounded by Reservoir Gouin, a 125-long impoundment 200 miles north-northwest of Montreal, Leblanc's island sits in the middle of what is one of the best walleye fisheries in Canada. All that's needed for walleye is a medium-weight spinning rod and 6-pound monofilament on your reel. The best fish are caught jigging over reefs or holes, depending on weather and water temperature. They'll also hit crankbaits and spoons. Heavier gear is needed for northerns that can reach 35 pounds, especially in early summer. Best action here is with big spoons, spinnerbaits and buzzbaits in the shallows.

Don't forget your 8-weight flyrod, either. Five-inch mice and streamers in white, yellow or chartreuse, fished among the weeds and grasses, can provoke vicious strikes from northerns. But remember that wire leader is essential, or it's bye-bye fly. And if you've got room in your duffel, slip in a 5-weight packrod with floating and sink-tip lines. Leblanc has this little pond up the hill where squaretails can give you a tussle, although you may need to dredge deep to get the bigger ones.

Oasis du Gouin offers a variety of simple accommodations. In the rustic log lodge just off the beach are five bedrooms with shared baths. Guests with rooms in the lodge take meals in the restaurant as part of their package. Do-it-yourselfers can avail themselves of eight cabins spotted among the spruce on the hill behind the lodge. You'll need to bring provisions and sheets, blankets and towels, as you will for Leblanc's rental houseboats and outpost camps. All packages include use of a boat and motor.

Payne River Fishing Camp

U n g a v a   B a y ,   Q u e b e c

VITAL STATISTICS:

KEY SPECIES:
Arctic char; brook and lake trout

Season:
June through September

Accommodations:
CABINS
NUMBER OF GUEST ROOMS: 4
MAXIMUM NUMBER OF GUESTS: 10

Conference Groups: No

Meals: American plan

Rates:
$2300 per person for 6 nights and 5 days, double occupancy

Guides: Included

Gratuities: $50 per guide, $25 per cook

Preferred Payment:
MasterCard, Visa

Getting There:
Fort Chimo, Canada, has commercial air service; the camp plane will ferry you from there.

Other Activities:
Bird watching, wildlife photography.

Contact:
Steve Ashton
Payne River Fishing Camp, 19950 Clark Graham, Baie D'Urfe, Quebec, Canada H9X 3R8; 800/465-9474 or 514/457-9371, fax 514/475-4626, website http://www.arctic adventures.ca

Represented By:
Creative Outdoor Adventures, 413/596-3876.

Catch arctic char until your arms fall off, then go for brook and lake trout in the high tundra.

SOMETIMES ARCTIC CHAR are as fiery red as a sunset after a storm. And like a howling three-day blow, char fight long and hard with the drive and determination, if not the dash, of Atlantic salmon. Unlike their better known and respected cousins, arctic char are not "fish of 1000 casts." When you find them schooled, as often is the case in the Payne River, catching them is like eating peanuts—one right after the other until your arms ache.

Draining the boggy tundra of the central Ungava Peninsula, roughly 1000 miles north of Montreal, the Payne flows due east into a fjord off Ungava Bay. Forty-five-foot tides flush the lower river system with incredible runs of capelin, smeltlike fish that char devour in an unceasing frenzy. When char move up into fresh water, they become rapacious, striking anything that resembles food. You can catch them on spoons, spinners, big light-colored streamers and nymphs, or virtually anything that is silver, slender and looks like a smelt or sand eel. When they are near the surface, you can take them on No. 8 light-colored Wulffs. The average size of char is not large, seven pounds or so, but they can run up to 15, and will burn the heel of your hand when they strip line from your flyreel. An 8-weight rod with a reel (a good drag is essential) spooled with a fast sinking-tip or sinking line is ample. Spinfishers will want a medium-heavy rod with eight- to 10-pound-test line. Fishing is generally from shore or by wading. You'll ride outboard-powered 24-foot freighter canoes guided by Inuits who can read the river, its fish and their moods.

The Payne River Camp, operated by the Inuits, is 25 miles upstream from Kangirsuk, a village at the mouth of the fjord. The main lodge contains the dining room, a lounge, bathrooms and showers. Adjacent are metal cabins that are warm and insect free, if Spartan (sleeping bags). Optional on the week-long package to Payne River is an overnight stay at a spike camp upriver. Here you'll find brook trout, with most in the two- to three-pound range. Lake trout also abound. While average fish run five to seven pounds, the lodge record 40-pounder came from these waters and during every trip, someone usually lands one in excess of 15 pounds. The wind blows up here, but when it stops you'll think that every mosquito in the world wants your flesh. A headnet and bug dope are recommended.

Pourvoire Lac du Blanc

S t e . - A l e x i s - d e s - M o n t s ,   Q u e b e c

Spend some time at a family fishing resort with spacious guest houses and a little inn with Quebec country flare.

GASTON PELLERIN'S FATHER was a logger and a sportsman. For the pulpwood, in 1975 he bought 6000 acres of land with low rolling hills, small ponds and numerous bogs. They harvested the wood leaving the forest intact around the ponds, thinking that maybe someday they would do something with it. In 1995, the younger Pellerin opened Pourvoire Lac Blanc, a full-service resort that includes 12 three-bedroom cottages, eight lakes with more to be opened, a five-stand sporting clays course, miles of trails for snowmobiling and cross-country skiing and a small inn for six with a very good restaurant.

Scooped out by glaciation, Lac Blanc is the largest of the lakes. Beneath its granite bluffs in the dark tannin-stained waters you'll find smallmouth bass up to four pounds. Fish crankbaits among submerged boulders, over the rocky reefs, and in the mouths of shallow, boggy bays. The lake is tranquil, and no outboards are permitted. You'll paddle a canoe or ride a rowboat pushed by a trolling motor. Lac Blanc is also heavily stocked with brook trout of 10 to 12 inches. The trout fall prey to spinners and nymphs. The other lakes are really woodland ponds like the ones so typical of New England's foothills. They, too, receive heavy infusions of fish from May through September.

This is purely a catch-and-eat fishery. Families come here to catch fresh trout. Everybody fishes—mom, dad, kids, grandma and grandpa, aunts and uncles—and they typically stay for a weekend or a week. Most use nightcrawlers, trolled behind the boats. They fish one lake in the morning and another in the afternoon.

They cook their catches in the modern kitchen of one of the 12 cottages tastefully sighted on points above Lac Blanc. These are really complete homes, built in traditional style with dormers, with three spacious bedrooms, two baths, a large combination living and dining room and a sunroom with windows on three sides. A porch fronts on the lake, and adjacent is an outside fireplace for grilling dinner or for sitting around and talking when the night has a chill. For those who are taking a vacation from cooking, the inn's small dining room with a fireplace looks out across a porch toward the lake. Dinners feature trout: amandine, meuniere, provencale, forestiere or any other way you'd like it prepared. The chef is skilled and the meals quite good.

St. Paul's Salmon Fishing Club

B l a n c   S a b l o n ,   Q u e b e c

VITAL STATISTICS:

KEY SPECIES:
Atlantic salmon

Season:
July to mid-September

Accommodations:
RUSTIC LODGE
NUMBER OF GUEST ROOMS: 5
MAXIMUM NUMBER OF GUESTS: 10

Conference Facilities: No

Meals: American plan

Rates:
$4000 (CDN) per person per week, double occupancy

Guides: Included

Gratuities: $200 (CDN) per week

Preferred Payment:
Cash or check

Getting There:
Fly to Deer Lake, Newfoundland and the club will provide a floatplane to the lodge.

Other Activities:
Bird watching, wildlife photography, hiking.

Contact:
**Jules Goodman
St. Paul's Salmon Fishing Club, PO Box 47096, Sillery, Quebec, Canada G1S 4X1; 418/527-4877, fax 418/688-4920.**

Flyfish for Atlantic salmon in the braided channels and emerald waters of Quebec's easternmost river.

RISING CLOSE TO THE BORDER with Labrador, the St. Paul River has many of the characteristics of its neighbor's famed salmon streams. Water is seldom fished by others than those staying at select salmon clubs. Most is shallow and easily waded. Guides transport anglers in freighter canoes propelled with small outboards. On Quebec streams, flyfishing is the only legal sporting method for taking salmon.

Salmon run into the St. Paul in June and by early July have made the 40 miles from the mouth up to club waters. Half a mile above the club, the river braids through a series of small islands interlaced with half a dozen small channels. Each channel contains riffles, runs and pools that hold salmon. Fishing here is delightful. You'll see fish in water as green as bottle glass. You'll start at the top of a channel and fish it down, casting to individual fish or over holds where they are lying. The average size of salmon in the waters before the camp ranges from four pounds for grilse to more than 20. Though the club advocates catch-and-release fishing, anglers are allowed to keep three salmon per day with a total possession limit of 10. Here, the season runs from July through mid-September, when the provincial government closes it down. In the last month of the season, the river fills with sea-run trout, a bonus at this strictly salmon camp.

Set on a bench, the club overlooks a wide pool in the river. Behind it rises a hill dark with spruce. Guests fly in to the club in Beaver aircraft from Deer Lake, Newfoundland, or Blanc Sablon, Quebec. During their week's fishing, they stay in one of five rooms (shared baths) in the log lodge.

Meals are simple, good and based on roast beef, turkey, salmon, cod and pork. The price includes licenses and air transfer from the commercial airport. Be sure to bring ample spare flies and a backup rod and reel.

Tunulik River Fishing Camps
Ungava Bay, Quebec

Outgoing Inuit are eager to show you the fish and share their culture at these two camps.

VITAL STATISTICS:

KEY SPECIES:
Arctic char; brook and lake trout

Season:
TUNULIK: June through September
TUNULIK II: Mid-August through early September

Accommodations:
CABINS
NUMBER OF GUEST ROOMS/GUESTS:
TUNULIK: 4/16
TUNULIK II: 2/6

Conference Groups: No
Meals: American plan
Rates:
TUNULIK: $2000 per person for 6 nights and 5 days
TUNULIK II: $1800 per person for 5 nights and 4 days
Guides: Included
Gratuities: $50 per guide, $25 per cook
Preferred Payment:
MasterCard, Visa
Getting There:
Fort Chimo, Quebec, has commercial air service; the camp plane will ferry you from there.
Other Activities:
Bird watching, wildlife photography.

Contact:
Steve Ashton
Tunulik River Fishing Camps, 19950 Clark Graham, Baie D'Urfe, Quebec, Canada H9X 3R8; 800/465-9474, fax 514/457-9371, website http://www.arctic adventures.ca

Represented By:
Sportravel, Ltd., 514/669-1309.

HIGH UP IN WILD QUEBEC where the tundra meets arctic seas, rivers flowing into Ungava Bay provide some of the best fishing for arctic char, sea-run brook trout and lake trout in North America. The land is primitive, but not quite barren. Scattered scrub pines struggle for altitude and low bushes sprawl where the thin soil allows. It is the land of caribou, a land of rushing brackish rivers where tides may fall 40 feet or more only to surge back upstream with a fresh cargo of fish.

Arctic Adventures of Baie D'Urfe, Quebec has two camps on the southeast side of Ungava Bay. Near the mouth of the river of the same name, Tunulik River Camp is known for its char and sea-run brookies. Char average seven pounds but 10-pounders are regularly taken and one of 20 pounds or more is not an accident. The camp record is 32-plus-pounds. Saltwater brookies average five pounds, and above the tidal zone, you'll find them in the two- to three-pound class. Char and brook trout are voracious, insatiable feeders. Twenty-fish days are the norm, weather cooperating (which, of course, it may not). The camp is operated by Inuits, warm and friendly native people who will guide you in 22-foot freighter canoes pushed by 35-horse outboards. If you ask, they'll be delighted to prepare meals of traditional regional fare. Heated cabins sleep four each and the main lodge has plenty of hot water for showers.

Tunulik II Fishing Camp is perched on a granite bluff, exposed and swept by the wind. This is a good thing; not only is the view of the Lagreve River spectacular, but the breeze keeps the mosquitoes away (almost). The river is narrow, about 100 feet wide. Above camp the river spreads and becomes Tunulliup Lake. Below, it races over boulders and a cobbly bed, in a dash for Ungava Bay, a mile and a half downstream. Most of the section, and an additional eight miles of water upstream, is wadeable. You can get yourself into a good position to cast to sea-run brook trout of four to six pounds and arctic char that are a little bigger. Once in a while someone hooks into an Atlantic salmon. That's when the fun really begins. The camp operates for only three weeks each year, when the fishing is at its peak. You'll stay in wooden cabins with two other anglers, and bathe in the main lodge where hearty meals are served.

Ungava Adventures

P o i n t e   C l a i r e ,   Q u e b e c

Try some extreme angling in the wild and wonderful tundra in sub-arctic Quebec.

VITAL STATISTICS:

KEY SPECIES:
Brook and lake trout; Atlantic salmon; char

Season:
June through September

Accommodations:
FRAME CABINS AND TENT CABINS
NUMBER OF GUEST ROOMS: Varies per site
MAXIMUM NUMBER OF GUESTS: 6 or 8 per site

Conference Groups: Yes

Meals: American plan (optional at mobile camps)

Rates:
From $3250 (CDN) per person for 5 days and 6 nights

Guides: Included in permanent camps

Gratuities: 5% of total package

Preferred Payment:
Cash or check

Getting There:
Fly to Fort Chimo, Quebec and then by private charter to camp (included)

Other Activities:
Caribou, bear and bird hunting, hiking, wildlife photography.

Contact:
**Sammy Cantafio
Ungava Adventures, 46 Ste. Anne St., Suite 3A, Pointe Claire, Quebec, Canada H9S 4P8; 514/694-4424, fax 514/694-4267.**

Represented By:
Cabela's Outdoor Adventures, 800/346-8747; Jim McCarthy Adventures, 717/652-4374.

IN NORTHERNMOST QUEBEC, where incessant winds sweep unimpeded across the tundra, facilities are few and primitive. Anglers don't mind. Rivers, cutting down through these barren lands of caribou, wolf and ptarmigan, race toward the Arctic Ocean and are fished by fewer than 100 anglers per year. They are the fortunate ones. Angling for lake trout, brook trout, Atlantic salmon and arctic char can be, and usually is, fantastic in the extreme. Fifty to 100 fish per day, most in the three- to 10-pound-plus category and some much bigger, will strip line from your reel and make the drag howl. The fishing is great, no question. But the weather may not cooperate, so bring Polarfleece, Neoprene and Gore-Tex.

Fishing isn't the only game in this town. Black bears become legal game in early June and caribou season starts in mid-August. Most hunters pack in a spinning or fly-rod, and a number of anglers go home with a set of trophy racks. A grand slam in these parts is a caribou and Atlantic salmon, and it's reasonably available, thanks to Sammy Cantafio who, in 1954, became the first guide licensed to hunt and fish these Inuit lands.

Cantafio, in partnership with the Inuit, operates three fixed and three mobile camps in the area south of Ungava Bay. Of the three, the camp at Helen's Falls offers the best shot at Atlantic salmon. They begin running in late July and congregate at the base of the falls, waiting for that primal urge to propel them upstream. Twelve- to 18-pounders are taken consistently, with larger ones up to 25 pounds always a possibility. Located on the east shore of Ungava Bay, Weymouth Inlet Camp specializes in arctic char up to 15 pounds. At Wolf Lake, the camp to the west of Fort Chimo, lake trout (to 40 pounds), landlocked char and native brook trout will fill your day. All three camps have similar facilities: Eight anglers reside in rustic cabins. A bathhouse provides hot showers and indoor washrooms. Dinners are served in a cabin that offers a panoramic water view of the river. Guided freighter canoes carry you and one or two other anglers to the best fishing water.

Three mobile tent camps (six anglers per week) have been erected at lakes Napier, Lemoyne and Sabrina. Anglers are free to prowl the lakes and the rivers that feed them in search of landlocked char, brook trout and lake trout. You'll do your own cooking from groceries that are provided and guide yourself unless you engage the services of the camp manager. There's no better way to rough it in this wilderness.

Wedge Hills Lodge
Schefferville, Quebec

Fish a remote tundra river for Atlantic salmon, brook trout, lakers and char.

VITAL STATISTICS:

KEY SPECIES:
Atlantic salmon; brook and lake trout; arctic char

Season:
June 14 through September 30

Accommodations:
RUSTIC LODGE AND CABINS
NUMBER OF GUEST ROOMS: 3 rooms, 9 cabins
MAXIMUM NUMBER OF GUESTS: 24

Conference Groups: No

Meals: American plan

Rates:
From $2395 per person per week

Guides: Included

Gratuities: $50 per week

Preferred Payment:
En Route, MasterCard, Visa,

Getting There:
Fly to Schefferville. Packages include lodging overnight in Schefferville (if necessary) and the flight to the lodge. Guests are limited to 70 pounds of luggage for the trip in.

Other Activities:
Hiking, bird watching, wildlife photography, caribou and bear hunting.

Contact:
Diane Fortier
Wedge Hills Lodge, PO Box 280, Schefferville, Quebec, Canada G0G 2T0; 418/585-2605, fax 418/585-3555.

THERE'S MORE TO QUEBEC than the strip with those great salmon and trout rivers that drain into the St. Lawrence and its gulf. The province stretches due north for more than 1000 miles from its border with New York to the tip of the Ungava Peninsula. Follow it on a map. To the east is Ungava Bay. The easternmost major river feeding the bay flows north along Labrador's coastal highlands. The river is the George, and it's a first-class fishery. You won't find brawling rapids here. Rather, this gravel-bottomed river winds gently across the tundra.

In the river swim Atlantic salmon, brook trout, lake trout and arctic char. The season for all four runs from mid-June through September. Angling is from 23-foot freighter canoes powered by 40-horse Yamahas. There is some wading available, and anglers may fish without guides if they like. A seven-foot medium-weight spinning rig loaded with 10- to 15-pound-test line is needed for lake trout and salmon, which run up to 20 pounds. Bring a lighter rod for brook trout and char. Among the most effective lures: Dardevles, Mepps, Veltic, Rapalas and red and orange Pixies. Flyfishermen should pack two rods: an 8 for salmon and lake trout and a 6 for brookies and char. Best patterns for these waters are green Cossebooms, Mickey Finns, Black Bears, Green Butts, Blue Charms, Muddlers, Butterflies, Bagog Smelts, Mouses and Bombers. Wedge Hills sells tackle, lures and licenses.

Above the beach fronting the river, the red wooden buildings of the lodge add color to the loden landscape of spruce and dark pine. A maximum of 24 guests have their pick of nine cabins along the river or three rooms in the main lodge. As you'd suspect, when the closest town is more than 300 miles across roadless wilderness, accommodations are not fancy, but they are clean and comfortable. Baths are shared. Dinners feature seafood and have a reputation for excellence: coquille St. Jacques, smoked salmon and shrimp. Wedge Hills also operates several outpost camps. Each is staffed with a camp manager, but cooking and guiding is strictly on your own.

If you hunt as well as fish, you may want to plan your trip for August through September. Caribou and black bear seasons are open and the fishing is excellent. The combined hunting and fishing package is only $300 (CDN) more than the normal fare.

CARIBBEAN BASIN

BAHAMAS, BELIZE, COSTA RICA, GUATEMALA,
HONDURAS, MEXICO, PANAMA

BEACHES blazing bright as summer sun, aquamarine waters darkening to blue as they deepen; hibiscus, fragrant in the night: No wonder so many Northerners flock to the Caribbean Basin and adjoining areas to escape winter's chill. But that may not be the best time for fishing in this broad area. April into June and September through November are often the better months for Caribbean angling. Light-tackle enthusiasts chase bonefish, permit, snook and roosterfish. Those with heavier gear aim for tarpon and such bluewater species as sailfish and marlin. Inland lakes frequently hold large bass. Lodging is laid back but food is generally of gourmet quality.

Lodges:

Bahamas

1 DEEP WATER CAY CLUB

2 MOXEY'S GUESTHOUSE & BONEFISHING CLUB

3 NORTH RIDING POINT CLUB

4 PEACE & PLENTY BONEFISH LODGE

5 WALKER'S CAY HOTEL AND MARINA

Belize

6 BELIZE RIVER LODGE

7 TURNEFFE ISLAND LODGE

Costa Rica

8 EL OCTAL

9 RAIN GODDESS

10 RIO COLORADO LODGE

11 ROY'S ZANCUDO LODGE

12 SILVER KING LODGE

Guatemala

13 FINS 'N FEATHERS INN

Honduras

14 POSADA DEL SOL

Mexico

15 CASA BLANCA

16 HOTELS PLAMAS DE CORTEZ, PUNTA COLORADO, PLAYA DEL SOL

Panama

References:

*Bonefish, Tarpon, Permit
Fly Fishing Guide
— Al Raychard
Frank Amato Publications, PO Box
82112, Portland, OR 97282;
503/653-8108*

Resources:

*Note: For the best information on
angling in Caribbean Basin countries,
contact the lodges themselves or
reputable booking agents.*

*Bahamas Ministry of Tourism,
PO Box N3701, Nassau, Bahama;
242/322-7500, 800/422-4262,
website
http://www.interknowledge.com/
bahamas*

*Belize Tourist Board,
83 N. Front St., Belize City, Belize;
501-27-7213; 800/624-0686,
website http://www.belize.com*

*Costa Rica Tourist Board,
PO Box 777-1000, San Juan, Costa
Rica; 011-506-223-1733*

*Instituto Guatemalteco
de Turismo,
78 Avemida 1-17, Zona 4, Cintro
Civico, Quatemala City, Guatemala;
502/331-1333, 305/442-0651*

*Honduras Institute of Tourism,
PO Box 140458, Coral Gables, FL
33114-0458; 800/410-9608, website
http://www.hondurasinfo.hn*

*Mexico Tourism Office,
405 Park Ave., Suite 1401, New York,
NY 10022; 212/421-6655, 800/446-
3942, website http://mexico-travel.com/*

*Panama: IPAT,
Box 4421, Panama 5, Republic of
Panama; 507/226-7000,
website http://www.pa/turismo.*

Fish the Gulf of Papagayo for marlin, sailfish and tuna, while staying in spacious air-conditioned cottages, all with views of the bay, at El Octal near Guanacaste, Costa Rica. — page 310.

Anglers serious about their flats fishing stay at The Bonefish Lodge, one of three inns operated by Peace & Plenty out of George Town, Exuma in the Bahamas. — page 306.

Deep Water Cay Club

Deep Water Cay, Bahama

VITAL STATISTICS:

KEY SPECIES:
Bonefish; permit

Season:
All year

Accommodations:
ANGLING RESORT AND COTTAGES
NUMBER OF GUEST ROOMS: 12
MAXIMUM NUMBER OF GUESTS: 23

Conference Groups: Yes

Meals: American plan

Rates:
From $1140 per person for 3 nights and 2 1/2 days of fishing, double occupancy

Guides: Included

Gratuities: $30 to $50 per day

Preferred Payment:
Cash or check

Getting There:
Fly to Freeport, take taxi and ferry to lodge at $125 additional each way. Also charter flights from Florida.

Contact:
Shari Hall
Deep Water Cay Club, Deep Water Cay, Bahama; 809/353-3073, fax 809/353-3095; U.S. address: 1100 Lee Wagener Blvd., Suite 352, Ft. Lauderdale, FL 33315; 954/359-0488, fax 954/359-9488, website http://www.spav.com/progc/deepwater cay

One of the oldest and classiest resorts in the Bahamas offers great fishing for bonefish (and a few big permit).

PUFFS OF GRAY MARL STREAM in the tide behind the mudding bone. You cannot see the fish, only the stain in the water. Crouching as low as you can on the bow of the gently rocking skiff, you delay as long as you dare. Double-hauling for distance, you fire the line hard forward. A gust of ever-present wind plays tricks on your cast. Your Clouser lands with a splat 10 feet from where you wanted it. OK. You wait. "What's he doing," you whisper to the guide as if the bone can hear you. "Turning, mon, cast more to the right," comes the reply. And you do. And when this fish fails to take, you find another. Same story. And another and, again, another. And you're casting your arm out. You start to think of the swimming pool and an eight-pound bone picks up your fly and heads for Freeport at flank speed.

That's bonefishing at Deep Water Cay, one of the oldest and best flats resorts in the Bahamas. Only 112 miles east of Palm Beach, Deep Water Cay sits in the midst of 250 square miles of fishable flats. Close to the club, the fish are more finicky; they've seen all the patterns before. But a 20-minute ride in a 16-foot skiff can take you to flats unfished for months. There your chances are better. Fish from the bow of the skiff or, better yet, stalk bones where the bottom's hard. You'll get closer that way.

Deep Water Cay Club is on a private island just off Grand Bahama. Twelve guest rooms with private baths, air-conditioning and refrigerators are scattered in cottages with wide porches under the trees facing west to catch the winds. Were it not for the bones and permit (the club record is better than 46 pounds), it would be tempting to sit on the porch and do nothing. As you'd expect, meals are superb: cracked conch, snapper and rack of lamb complemented by a good cellar.

If you're inclined to fish both bones and permit, book a week between September and November or in May or June. Neoprene wading shoes with arch supports are best for wading the flats. Long-sleeve shirts, light trousers and a wide-brimmed hat provide protection from the sun. Bring 7- and 9-weight systems. Flies can be bought at the lodge.

Moxey's Guesthouse & Bonefishing Club

A n d r o s   I s l a n d ,   B a h a m a

VITAL STATISTICS:

KEY SPECIES:
Bonefish; tarpon; permit

Season:
All year

Accommodations:
ISLAND RESORT
NUMBER OF GUEST ROOMS: 10
MAXIMUM NUMBER OF GUESTS: 14
Conference Groups: Yes
Meals: American plan
Rates:
$1150 per person for 3 days, double occupancy
Guides: Included
Gratuities: Client's discretion
Preferred Payment:
American Express, Visa
Getting There:
Fly to Nassau and take a charter to South Andros Island. You'll spend $400 additional round trip. Congo Air also provides commercial service.
Other Activities:
Swimming, boating, bird watching, biking.

Contact:
Joel Moxey
Moxey's Guesthouse, Moxey Town, Mangrove Cay, Andros, Bahama; phone/fax 242/369-0023, email pax@baha mas.net.bs, website http://www.bahamas. net.bs/clients/moxeys

Represented By:
Westbank Anglers, 800/922-3474.

Everybody here is named Moxey and they all speak bonefish with great fluency.

IN MOXEY TOWN on Mangrove Cay you'll find a small, laid-back bonefishing club where the fishing is quite good. The two-story club, its white stucco with yellow trim quintessentially islands, is 50 feet from the gentle waters of Middle Bight on the east coast of Andros Island. As the sun sets, sea breezes ruffle the surrounding palms and wash the day's heat and humidity from the wide front deck that faces the beach across a narrow road. A cool drink tastes good there, as you watch the sky streak pink and talk about the fishing.

Guides, normally one per angler but couples and friends can fish together if they wish, have 800 square miles of bonefish flats at their disposal. You may fish Moxey Creek or Big or Little Loggerhead creeks, or any one of 100 tidal sloughs through the maze of mangroves on these nearly endless flats. Anglers depart the lodge at 7:00 a.m. and fish to 4:30 or 5:00 p.m. If need be, you can boat to distant flats where bones have not been disturbed by other anglers. Your chances of hooking up with eight to 10 good fish in the six-pound-plus range are very good. Some anglers tie into 15 to 20 fish per day, and once in a while there's a 10-pounder or better in the bunch. The club record, set in 1983, is 13 pounds.

The most comfortable bonefishing is in October and November, and again in March and April. Despite the heat, summer can provide very good angling too. According to Loundy Moxey, the high sun angle under cloudless skies makes bonefish easier to spot. Obviously lots of sunscreen, long-sleeve shirts and long pants, and hats with long bills are necessities. Yet the ever-present breeze will keep you surprisingly cool. And the months of late spring and early summer are the best for a grand slam: bonefish, tarpon and permit all in one day. While a few anglers use spinning gear, bait-fishing here has become passe and flyrodding is the name of the game.

Accommodations are pleasant. Upstairs in the main house, two air-conditioned, two-bedroom apartments with private baths have a sitting room that opens to a porch. Behind the main lodge is a second building with six guest rooms upstairs that share three baths. Meals feature indigenous Bahamian cuisine ably prepared by Pearl Moxey, Loundy's mother. She's justly famous for her minced lobster, peas and rice, steamed grouper or steamed conch. You'll eat on the deck when the nights are velvet and inside, in an air-conditioned dining room, when they are not.

North Riding Point Club

B u r n s i d e   C o v e ,   G r a n d   B a h a m a   I s l a n d

VITAL STATISTICS:

KEY SPECIES:
Bonefish; permit

Season:
All year
Accommodations:
LODGE AND COTTAGES
NUMBER OF GUEST ROOMS: 5
MAXIMUM NUMBER OF GUESTS: 10
Conference Groups: No
Meals: American plan
Rates:
From $1195 per person for 3
days, double occupancy
Guides: Included
Gratuities: $30 to $35 per
boat per day
Preferred Payment:
Cash or check
Getting There:
Fly to Freeport; the van from
the lodge will meet you.
Other Activities:
Swimming, casinos in Freeport.

Contact:
Jerry Uleborn
North Riding Point Club,
PO Box F. 43665,
Freeport, Bahama;
242/352-3211.

Represented By:
Kim Dawes, 330/337-6531.

A new and exclusive club opens bonefishing on the north shore of Grand Bahama Island.

THOUGH THE CLUB is relatively new, the staff at North Riding Point Club—20 miles due east of Freeport—has more than a century of cumulative experience at long established bonefish clubs such as Deep Water Cay. Managed by Ben and Judy Rose, long-time Bahamian hands, the club has the exclusive rights to operate in the Freeport vicinity. Located on the south side of the island, boats are trailered each morning to discrete launching points on the north side to put anglers over bones that have seldom seen a fly. The permit under which the club operates allows no more than five boats and 10 anglers.

Riding 16-foot Dolphin Super Skiffs pushed by 70-horse engines (with one 18-foot 90-horse outfit for longer hauls), anglers zip out into the maze of white sand flats, mangrove cays and tidal inlets. Because this area has not been heavily fished, the bones here tend to spook less readily than their mates elsewhere in the islands. Fish in the four- to six-pound range are plentiful and provide warm-ups for 10- to 12-pounders that are somewhat frequent. This is a flyfishing-only club, and 9-weight rods with floating lines are recommended. A range of flies in Sizes 4 to 8 would include Gotcha Bonefish Clousers, Mini Puffs, Horrors and Crazie Charlies. Bright colors—pink, orange, white, gold—work well. You'll cast from the skiff or wade, depending on where you spot the bones. Tarpon and permit are also available. Al Raychard reports that a grand slam is certainly possible here, though somewhat unlikely. Best months for bones are October and November, and March through July. Permit fish best in October and November, May and June. Tarpon are always around.

Because of all the action, the lodge has arranged for two masseuses to be on call. After a day on the water, arrive back at your airy seafront cottage or room in the lodge (two queen beds, private bath, wall safe), take a shower then have a massage. The only reason to move afterwards is to walk over to the main lodge for dinner prepared by Judy, who specializes in island fare with a continental twist. Afterwards, visit the library or lounge if you're able. If not, toddle back to your cottage and collapse.

Peace & Plenty Bonefish Lodge

G e o r g e   T o w n ,   E x u m a ,   B a h a m a

VITAL STATISTICS:

KEY SPECIES:
Bonefish; permit; shark; barracuda

Season:
All year

Accommodations:
MODERN YET TRADITIONAL ISLANDS LODGE
NUMBER OF GUEST ROOMS/GUESTS:
BONEFISH LODGE: 8/16
THE BEACH INN: 16/32

Conference Groups: Yes
Meals: American plan
Rates:
$2326 per person for 7 nights and 6 days, double occupancy
Guides: Included
Gratuities: $25 to $50
Preferred Payment:
American Express, MasterCard, Visa
Getting There:
Fly to Exuma, and the lodge van will meet you.
Other Activities:
Swimming, tennis, snorkeling, diving, boating, biking, wildlife photography.

Contact:
**Magnolia Morley
Peace & Plenty Bonefish Lodge, PO Box 29173, George Town, Exuma, Bahama; 809/345-5555, fax 809/345-5556, email ppbone@baha mas.net.bs, website http://www.peace andplenty.com**

Roll them bones down Bahama way.

WHEN THE BOTTOM FALLS OUT of the thermometer in northern climes, every angler dreams of fishing Bahamas flats for bonefish. Azure skies, turquoise water, wading along with the velvet bay lapping at your knees, rod cocked, peering ahead through polarized sunglasses from under a long-billed cap, ready to cast to a tailing bonefish. What wind there is caresses you, and for once it comes from behind. Dead ahead, 50 feet, a school, coming toward you. The cast, five feet in front. The pickup, tightline!

Where to go? Peace & Plenty on Grand Exuma has been in business for years. But it wasn't until Bob Hyde, a Key's guide, and his wife, Karen, came aboard that the club became really serious about anglers. That's because the waters here have excellent populations of bonefish averaging five pounds, and some much bigger. Hyde initiated a training program for guides, teaching them the intricacies of flyfishing and the eccentricities of American anglers. Peace & Plenty has three properties—Club Peace & Plenty in George Town, The Beach Inn about nine miles from town, and The Bonefish Lodge a mile farther away and out on a sand spit. The third is where most dedicated anglers stay. With easy access to fishing (you can stalk the flats right off the beach), this modern wood and glass lodge with lofted and open beam ceilings has everything: a tying bench, video library, air conditioned and attractive guest rooms with private baths. Meals are islands in spirit: conch chowder, steamed lobster, broiled grouper and a Bahamian specialty that varies each night. When the Bonefish Lodge is full, anglers also stay at the larger Beach Inn with 16 rooms and a freshwater pool.

Two anglers fish with each guide in a 16-foot skiff. While the lodge caters to flyfishers, anglers who fish spinning tackle are also welcome. Bring a pair of rods, generally nine or 10 feet, No. 8 or 9 with weight-forward lines and at least 150 yards of backing. Reels must have good, smooth drag systems. Flies are the usual: Clousers, Crazy Charlies, Gotchas and Puffs in white, orange and pink. Bring a few Merkins and McCrabs for permit. Long-sleeve, light-colored cotton shirts, a good long-billed fishing cap with a cape for the back of your neck, and a pair of booties for wading the flats (old tennis shoes will do) should be in your gear. Don't forget a lightweight slicker. If you're missing something, you can find it in George Town.

Walker's Cay Hotel and Marina

A b a c o ,   B a h a m a s

On the edge of the blue Atlantic, Walker's offers big game and bonefish 12 months a year.

VITAL STATISTICS:

KEY SPECIES:
Marlin; sailfish; wahoo; dolphin; tuna; bonefish; groupers; snappers

Season:
All year

Accommodations:
TROPICAL OCEAN RESORT
NUMBER OF GUEST ROOMS: 65 plus 4 villas
MAXIMUM NUMBER OF GUESTS: 130

Conference Groups: Yes

Meals: Modified American plan

Rates:
From $137.50 per person per day, double occupancy

Guides: Flats or reef fishing: $300 per day for 3 anglers; big-game fishing: $700 per day for 3 anglers

Gratuities: $30 to $50 per boat

Preferred Payment:
Major credit cards

Getting There:
Take the Pan Am Airbridge seaplane from Ft. Lauderdale, Florida.

Other Activities:
Scuba diving, tennis, sailing, swimming, boating.

Contact:
Joanne Robinson Walker's Cay Hotel and Marina, Abaco, Bahamas. U.S. address: c/o Walker's Aviation Services, Inc., 700 SW 34th St., Ft. Lauderdale, FL 33315; 800/925-5377, fax 954/359-1414, website http://www. walkerscay.com

LOCATION IS EVERYTHING. Tucked on the tip of the northernmost major island in the Bahamas, Walker's Cay lies but a mile across the shallows from the blue-water Atlantic. Twelve miles out is the 1000-fathom curve and beyond a rugged bottom of sea mounts and canyons. Easterly currents wash against the Abaco Wall, as the eastern edge of the reef is called, rising plumes of nutrients that feed organisms at the base of the food chain. At the top of the chain are white and blue marlin, for which Walker's has gained worldwide renown.

Bluewater fishing is good all year. White marlin are best from January through March. Blue marlin are strongest from March through August. Sailfish are hot from May through July and again from October through December. Overall, anglers who fish in April or May see the best action: blue marlin, sailfish, wahoo, tuna (yellowfin, bluefin and blackfin), dolphin, king and Spanish mackerel, groupers, snappers and bonefish. In addition to trolling for big-game species, bottomfishing wrecks and reefs for snappers and groupers is very productive, as is riding a skiff off to the bonefish flats. At Walker's, no matter what your preference—heavy boat tackle, bass-weight casting or spinning gear, or flyrods—you'll find fish any time during the year.

Enveloping the docks like the clutch of a crab's clay, Walker's marina is home to one of the most diverse sportfishing fleets on the Atlantic. Fifty-foot Hatterases and similar Bertrams bob in their slips. Riding their tethers are flats boats and skiffs. Walker's employs a number of guides. You'll have no trouble finding one who's knowledgeable and experienced in the kind of fishing you want to do. And, of course, the marina offers dockage for private boats.

Guests stay in comfortable ocean-view hotel rooms or in rental guest villas; dine in an airy restaurant that features islands fare such as conch, fresh fish and lobster; exercise with a round or two of tennis; and lounge around a pair of swimming pools—one fresh and the other salt. Diving on exquisite coral reefs and exploring submerged caverns, as well as sailing, round out activities here. It's all just a short flight from Florida, 45 minutes west. Private aircraft use the 2500-foot paved runway and seaplanes taxi into the harbor.

Belize River Lodge

B e l i z e   C i t y ,   B e l i z e

VITAL STATISTICS:

KEY SPECIES:
Bonefish; tarpon; permit; snook

Season:
All year

Accommodations:
CABINS AND MOTOR YACHTS
NUMBER OF GUEST ROOMS/GUESTS:
CABINS: 8/16
YACHTS: From 2 to 6/from 1 to 6

Conference Groups: Yes

Meals: American plan

Rates:
CABINS: From $1504 per person for 6 nights and 5 days
YACHTS: From $1992 per person for 7 nights and 5 days fishing, all double occupancy.

Guides: Included

Gratuities: $30 per day

Preferred Payment:
Cash or check

Getting There:
Fly to Philip Goldson International Airport in Belize City. You'll be met by a van.

Other Activities:
Eco tours, Mayan ruins, bird watching, wildlife photography.

Contact:
Marguerite Miles
Belize River Lodge, PO Box 459, Belize City, Belize; 011-501-25-2002, fax: 011-501-25-2298, email bzelodge@ btl.net, website http:// belize.com/belizeriver lodge.html

Represented By:
Angler Adventures, 203/434-9624; Frontiers International, 412/935-1577; Pan Angling, 312/263-0328; Sea & Explore, 504/366-0041; Sporting Charters, 512/458-8900.

The big decision here is whether to fish from the lodge or book a light-tackle cruise.

HERE, BENEATH THE PALMS on the bank of the river, you have alternatives. You may choose to stay at the lodge and fish from skiffs for tarpon, snook, bonefish, snapper, jacks or barracuda. With a guide, you'll fish the Belize, Sibun and Manatee rivers, Black Creek, and a number of channels and lagoons. You'll work flats, the coast and mangroves using casting, spinning or flyfishing tackle. Along the way you'll see monkeys, manatees, iguanas and maybe a crocodile. Fishing is as lazy or intense as you want to make it. Those who are more manic grab a quick coffee, fruit and roll and are on the water at dawn. The laid back enjoy the breeze with their breakfast and start fishing after the sun's cleared the horizon.

That's one way. The other is to book one of three light-tackle cruises. A solo angler or a couple can charter the *Permit,* a 40-foot Santa Barbara conversion, for five days. You and a captain cum guide will consider the weather and the tides and follow your insights to the kind of fishing you want. The yacht tows a 23-foot skiff that you'll use to work shallow waters. Your schedule is set by the fish, and afterwards you'll return to the yacht, shower, lounge in the air-conditioned stern cabin and sip something cold as dinner is prepared in the galley.

In addition to the 40-footer, Belize River Lodge operates two larger live-aboard motor yachts: the *Blue Yonder,* a 52-foot Chris Craft, and the *Christina,* a 58-foot Hatteras. Normally carrying four guests, these floating lodges will comfortably handle six, and they are ideal for families or groups of serious anglers. As with the *Permit,* anglers fish from 23-foot skiffs. Angling is best for permit in August; tarpon, February through October; snook, March through October; and bonefish, snapper and barracuda are good all year.

The lodge itself is a main house where meals are prepared and served, with eight guest rooms with private baths located in cabins nearby. Two of the rooms are handicapped accessible. Belize River Lodge caters to groups of up to 16 and has something of a reputation as a family vacation spot. While visiting these waters, you may want to snorkel the reef, scout remote cays and enjoy deserted beaches. In addition side trips can be arranged to Mayan ruins and tropical rainforests.

Turneffe Island Lodge

Turneffe Island, Belize

An old bonefish lodge has new owners, a new look and a good shot at getting you a grand slam.

VITAL STATISTICS:

KEY SPECIES:
Bonefish; permit; tarpon

Season:
All year
Accommodations:
TROPICAL CABINS
NUMBER OF GUEST ROOMS: 12
MAXIMUM NUMBER OF GUESTS: 24
(but only 8 anglers at a time)
Conference Groups: Yes
Meals: American plan
Rates:
$1950 per person per week, double occupancy
Guides: Included
Gratuities: $15 to $25 per day
Preferred Payment:
MasterCard, Visa
Getting There:
Fly to Belize City, and board Bodacious for the 1 1/2-hour ride to the lodge.
Other Activities:
Scuba, snorkeling, kayaking, sailing, swimming, bird watching, wildlife photography.

Contact:
Tommy Gay
Turneffe Island Lodge,
PO Box 2974,
Gainesville, GA 30503;
800/874-0118, fax
770/534-8290, email
info@turneffelodge.com,
website http://www.
turneffelodge.com

TURNEFFE IS AN ATOLL, one of only four in the Western Hemisphere. About 30 miles off Belize City, the atoll is surrounded by extensive and easily wadeable flats which, together with the nearby reef, creates an incredibly rich marine environment. Baitfish abound, and game species thrive on this abundance. The fishery was once on the decline, but a government moratorium on native netting and a catch-and-release policy at the lodge are bringing it back. It's not unusual to cast to schools of 50 or more tailing bonefish in the three- to six-pound range, or smaller schools of bones from six to 12 pounds. Permit are becoming plentiful and many anglers who've never fished for them before get their first at Turneffe. Tarpon in the 30- to 150-pound range are also prevalent. If you fish in September or October, you have a reasonably good shot at a grand slam—all three in a single day. In addition, you'll find barracuda, snook, kings, groupers, wahoo, tuna, snappers and jacks.

Unlike other lodges that rely on long boat rides to put clients over fish, at Turneffe the flats, reef and mangrove cays are in your front yard. You and your guide will sit down in the morning and plan a strategy based on your expectations, capabilities and local conditions. Then it's off in one of the Dolphin skiffs. Most anglers fish flytackle, but spinning gear is OK too. A dockside tackleshop sells replacements for anything—flies, lures, stuff you left at home.

Since the Gay family bought the lodge in 1995, it has undergone extensive renovation. Light and airy guest rooms have new beds, furnishings and air conditioning (optional). Windows open to water views, and all baths are private. The lounge (dinners feature local seafood or steaks) has been expanded and redecorated with woods native to Belize, and there's a new deck off the bar that overlooks the Caribbean. In addition to fishing, Turneffe Island is a popular destination for divers. The Gays have rebuilt the three dive boats and upgraded the 43-foot *Bodacious* that transfers guests from the mainland to the island. If diving isn't the diversion you need from fishing, take out a sea kayak, sailboat or wind surfer, or hang out in a hammock in the shade.

El Octal

G u a n a c a s t e ,   C o s t a   R i c a

VITAL STATISTICS:

KEY SPECIES:
Black marlin; yellowfin tuna; sailfish; roosterfish

Season:
All year

Accommodations:
TROPICAL CABINS WITH PORCHES
NUMBER OF GUEST ROOMS: 43
MAXIMUM NUMBER OF GUESTS: 86

Conference Groups: Yes

Meals: Included in fishing packages

Rates:
From $895 per person for 4 days, 3 nights and 2 days fishing, double occupancy

Guides: Included in packages

Gratuities: $25 to $40 per day

Preferred Payment:
Major credit cards

Getting There:
Fly to Liberia, Costa Rica. El Octal's van will take you to the resort. Transportation will be provided from San Jose for $125 for 1 to 4 persons.

Other Activities:
Tennis, biking, scuba, swimming, bird watching.

Contact:
Rick Wallace
El Octal, PO Box 1,
Playas del Coco,
Guanacaste, Costa Rica;
011-506-670-0321, fax
011-506-670-0083,
email elocotal@sol.
rasca.co.cr

Represented By:
Adventure Sport Fishing, 619/792-8172; Fishing International, 707/539-1320; Pan Angling Travel Service, 312/263-0328; Rod and Reel Adventures, 209/524-7775.

The West Coast story for Costa Rica is big billfish.

ANGLERS IN SEARCH OF marlin and sailfish know about El Octal, a resort as dedicated to boating, reviving and releasing billfish as it is to providing first-class accommodations. First, the fishing: The Gulf of Papagayo provides more than two dozen varieties of sportfish. Combine angling for black marlin in the 300- to 500-pound class in May through July with sailfish of 100-pounds-plus. They reach their peak from May through September. You can also work in yellowfin tuna of up to 200 pounds (the resort record is a 221-pounder taken in January, 1995). If you're after blue marlin, January through March are the hot months and fish run between 200 and 400 pounds. Forty- to 60-pound roosterfish are taken on live bait all year long.

You'll fish from a fleet of five boats: four 32-foot sportfishermen and a 43-foot yacht. All boats are powered by twin engines to cut running time to fishing grounds and for security. Heads and bunks, as well as complete marine electronics, are standard on all boats. Boats also carry a range of trolling rigs loaded with 20- to 80-pound line. In addition, spinning tackle is available. A limited stock of terminal tackle is maintained at El Octal's marina. Bring what you think you'll reasonably need. If you need more, you can get it there. Flyfishing for sailfish is a different matter. Best to arrive fully equipped. This resort prides itself on its catch-and-release record. It is impressive: Of 1542 sailfish boated in 1994, 1511 were released. That same year, 189 marlin were landed and 175 were released.

El Octal provides a range of fishing packages from two days on the water to six. Included are room, meals, fishing boat, tackle, ground transfer and airport pick up. Tips bar bills, and personal expenses are up to you. You'll stay in air-conditioned cottages that climb the hill above the white sand beach and blue gulf beyond. Each has a private terrace, refrigerator and satellite TV. Three freshwater pools and a Jacuzzi round out amenities. And you'll find a sweeping view of the bay from the resort's hilltop restaurant where dinners feature local fish. If you wish, you can simply book a room and take meals at El Octal's restaurant or at others in the tiny fishing village of Playas del Coco two miles away.

Rain Goddess

E s c a z u ,   C o s t a   R i c a

VITAL STATISTICS:

KEY SPECIES:
Snook; tarpon; dorado; tuna; jacks

Season:
All year

Accommodations:
HOUSEBOAT
NUMBER OF GUEST ROOMS: 6
MAXIMUM NUMBER OF GUESTS: 12

Conference Groups: Yes

Meals: American plan

Rates:
From $1620 per person for 5 days with 3 days of fishing, single occupancy

Guides: Included

Gratuities: $10 per person per day

Preferred Payment:
MasterCard, Visa

Getting There:
Fly to San Jose. Overnight accommodations and the flight to the Rain Goddess are included at no additional charge.

Other Activities:
Bird watching, wildlife photography.

Contact:
Dr. Alfredo Lopez
Rain Goddess, P. O. Box 850-1250 Escazu San Jose, Costa Rica;
506/231-4299, fax 506/231-3816,
email blue wing@sol.racsa.co.cr,
website http://www. magi.com/crica/tours/ bluewing.html

Represented By:
Pan Angling Adventures, 312/263-0328.

For luxurious living and fast fishing, take a houseboat deep into Costa Rica's northeast waterways.

THE PROBLEM WITH MOST LODGES is that they're located in one spot, and can't move to where the fish are. A boat can solve the mobility problem, but folks over six feet tall usually can't stand up in their cabins. Enter the *Rain Goddess,* which may be a boat, but which is posh and spacious inside. The salon and staterooms are paneled with deeply polished tropical woods. Traditional period chairs and tables grace the salon where guests dine on china and sip wine from crystal. No Melmac and plastic glasses on this boat. Filet mignon and lobster are on the menu. Staterooms feature queen or double beds. Sixty-five feet long and 18 feet wide, the *Rain Goddess* has room for a maximum of 12 guests, and it's fully air-conditioned.

While accommodations count, it's the fishing that's important. Operating out of Barra Colorado near the mouth of the Rio Colorado, the *Rain Goddess* cruises the brackish waters of northeastern Costa Rica. You may run up the Rio San Juan, nosing into lakes and rivers that are inaccessible by road, angling for fish that seldom see lures. Or you may cruise to the Gulf, then up the Rio Colorado or into the Totuguero or Parismina. You and your fellow anglers will decide the route based on season, species and your preference.

The *Rain Goddess* tows a pair of 16-foot johnboats and two 23-foot skiffs. You'll use the johnboats to fish backwaters for snook, tarpon, rainbow bass and mojarra. The 23-footers come into play in the heavier water at rivermouths for big tarpon, and in the Gulf, tuna, jacks, dorado and maybe a sailfish. Blue Wing International, operators of the *Rain Goddess,* provides guides who know the waters and the fish. You can use their tackle, but it's far better to take your own. Best months for snook are September and December, and February and March are tops for rainbow bass, mojarra and tarpon.

At Walker's Cay, at the northern tip of the Bahamas, moor your craft in the sheltered harbor that's a short run from deep blue water or shallow flats. — page 307.

Big schools of bonefish, increasing numbers of permit and enough tarpon to keep things interesting are close by Turneffe Island Lodge on an atoll off the coast of Belize. — page 309.

Rio Colorado Lodge

Rio Colorado, Costa Rica

VITAL STATISTICS:

KEY SPECIES:
Tarpon; snook

Season:
All year
Accommodations:
TROPICAL RIVERSIDE LODGE
NUMBER OF GUEST ROOMS: 17
MAXIMUM NUMBER OF GUESTS: 34
Conference Groups: Yes
Meals: American plan
Rates:
From $1367 per person for 6
days, 5 nights and 3 full days of
fishing, double occupancy
Guides: Included
Gratuities: Client's discretion
Preferred Payment:
Cash or check
Getting There:
Fly to San Jose, Costa Rica.
Overnight accommodations and
transfer to the lodge are
included.
Other Activities:
Swimming, bird watching,
wildlife photography.

Contact:
Diann Wise
Rio Colorado Lodge,
PO Box 5094, 1000 San
Jose, Costa Rica;
800/243-9777, fax
813/933-3280, email
tarpon4u@cyberspy.
com

Fish out of a tropical riverfront lodge where tarpon are huge and plentiful.

A THIN BAR OF DARK SAND, on which tropical grasses cling tenuously, forces the mouth of the Rio Colorado northward and nearly parallel to Costa Rica's Caribbean Coast. At times the mouth of the river seems to choke with sand, but its power always pushes through. Tarpon and snook run the mouth of the river and far upstream into the jungle, where orchids, parrots and monkeys distract you from the business at hand.

That business is tarpon fishing, doing battle with a beast as big as a person and that fights with every ounce of its being. Hook one and you'll see. Head shaking, it leaps clear of the water, lands with a crash and bores away with incredible speed. Fighting a tarpon isn't for the faint of heart. You think you've got it whipped, and it thrashes into the air at boatside, so close you can almost count the age rings on its scales. Refreshed, it races away, your drag screams and you thank God that 125 pounds of writhing fish muscle did not land at your feet.

Tarpon average 70 to 80 pounds in Rio Colorado. From January through May they move upriver to spawn in the jungle backwaters. In fall you'll find them in the surf off the mouth of the river. There, in the fall surf, they mix with snook, and trolling or casting can be fabulous for both species. Smaller snook move into the river in November and December and hookups of 30 fish per day are fairly typical. Most of these fish run about five pounds, but larger ones are to be expected. For snook, a medium casting or spinning rig loaded with 8- to 12-pound-test line is ample. An 8-weight flyrod is about right, though you'll want at least a 10 for tarpon.

Founded by Archie Fields, Rio Colorado Lodge has been the standard-bearer on these waters for years. Your room of richly varnished native wood feels cozy yet open with many windows that catch the breeze from the veranda. All have private baths. Meals are served family-style, and a lounge with billiards and other games provides after-dinner entertainment. The fishing day begins early and runs into late afternoon. You and your partner will fish from 23-foot skiffs or smaller craft with a trained guide who most likely grew up in the village, speaks fluent English and knows the river and its fish.

As with other remote Caribbean lodges, baggage is limited to 25 pounds. And by all means include a good rainjacket. Showers in the tropics brew up quickly, and May through October are known locally as the rainy season.

Roy's Zancudo Lodge

Golfito, Costa Rica

VITAL STATISTICS:

KEY SPECIES:
Blue and black marlin; sailfish; yellowfin and big-eye tuna; permit; snook

Season:
December through September

Accommodations:
SHADED CABINS

NUMBER OF GUEST ROOMS: 14

MAXIMUM NUMBER OF GUESTS: 20

Conference Groups: No

Meals: American plan

Rates:
From $325 per person per day and $1355 for 3 days, double occupancy

Guides: Included

Gratuities: $20 to $30 per day

Preferred Payment:
American Express, Discover, MasterCard, Visa

Getting There:
Fly to San Jose, air shuttle to lodge. NOTE: Severe baggage restriction, 25 pounds only, on flight from San Jose to lodge.

Other Activities:
Swimming, bird watching.

Contact:
Martha Fields
Roy's Zancudo Lodge, 8406 Lopez Dr., Tampa, FL 33615; 800/551-7697, fax 813/889-9189.

Twenty world records are on the books. Could yours be next?

ON THE SOUTHERNMOST TIP of Costa Rica is a bay named for the village of Golfito, a small town that is the center of a growing sportfishery. Around the bay to the east and south is Zancudo Beach. Under palms by the beach sit the four cabins and the main house of Roy's lodge. Fishing here is for blue and black marlin (June through September), sailfish (December through May), dorado, yellowfin and big-eye tuna, permit, snook (May through September), wahoo, barracuda, roosterfish, pompano, Sierra mackerel, treuelly, jack cravelle, corvina, amberjack, triple tail, rainbow runner, grouper, and red and yellow snapper. Tackle, of course, depends on the species and the lodge furnishes all you'll need, with the exception of flyfishing gear. If that's your game, bring your own.

Over the years Roy's guests have chalked up a number of IGFA world records; 20 are current as of this writing, and three more are pending. You'll fish from 22- to 25-foot center-console boats rigged for the species of your choice. Although some fish may be kept for dinner, most angling here is catch-and-release, so bring a camera.

Depending on the number in your party, you'll have your choice of suites with bedroom, sitting room with wet bar and refrigerator, and private baths or a private room with a bath. All are air-conditioned. Meals are served family-style, and the menu revolves around local specialties and, of course, fresh fish. Heart healthy and vegetarian diets are no problem. And for relaxing after a day of fighting the big ones, there's a beach-side pool and hot tub.

Guests fly to San Jose, Costa Rica, overnight in a hotel (dinner is on you), and the next morning will fly in a light plane to Golfito. Baggage on this flight is limited—no more than 25 pounds per passenger—so travel light. Temperatures average 80°F; light pants, long-sleeve shirt and a broad-brimmed hat make up the uniform of the week. Be prepared for rain and pack an extra pair of sneakers. Mosquitoes are not usually a problem because of the constant breeze, but a bottle of bug dope won't weigh much and it may be very welcome.

Silver King Lodge
Rio Colorado, Costa Rica

VITAL STATISTICS:

KEY SPECIES:
Tarpon; snook; wahoo; dorado; yellowfin; guapote

Season:
All year

Accommodations:
TROPICAL BUNGALOW
NUMBER OF GUEST ROOMS: 10
MAXIMUM NUMBER OF GUESTS: 20

Conference Groups: Yes

Meals: American plan

Rates:
$2080 per person for 7 days and 5 days of fishing, double occupancy

Guides: Included

Gratuities: $10 to $20 per day

Preferred Payment:
Major credit cards

Getting There:
Fly to Juan Santa Maria Airport in San Jose, Costa Rica. A representative of the lodge will meet you and conduct you to a hotel (included), where you will spend the night before flying to the lodge in the morning.

Other Activities:
Canoeing, boating, hiking, bird watching, wildlife photography.

Contact:
Shawn Feliciano
Silver King Lodge, PO Box 02516, Suite 1597, Miami, FL 33102; 800/847-3474, fax 209/526-3007; Costa Rica: 800/309-8125, fax 011-506-381-1403.

Tarpon aren't finicky in the murky water of the Rio Colorado.

TARPON ARE THE HEAVYWEIGHTS and snook the warm-up bouts at Silver King Lodge near the mouth of Rio Colorado on Costa Rica's northeast coast. The river carries a heavy load of suspended sediments and is generally cloudy. It drains Barra del Colorado, a wildlife preserve rich with tropical birds and orchids. Fingers of the river reach back into the mangrove jungle, a nursery for sportfish such as tarpon, snook, guapote and mojarra. Like some of the tidal rivers in the western Everglades, when there's been a storm the Rio Colorado is often murky.

You won't sight-cast for tarpon here. Instead you'll let your fly or lure work down to bottom. You'll retrieve in short, choppy strips. The rhythm of the retrieve, the gentle rocking of the skiff, the sun, pleasantly warm on your shoulders, will lull you. That, of course, is when the tarpon strikes and makes for Cuba. Tarpon here are plentiful. The average fish weighs 70 pounds; the record is a 207-pounder. Heavy casting rods and 12-weight flyrods are required. Best times are February through May, and October.

Snook also burn up the waters in the Rio Colorado. Twenty-pounders are average, and the lodge record topped 53 pounds. You'll find them up in the mangroves and also down where the river meets the sea. Use bass tackle, either casting, fly or spinning. For guapote and mojarra, the bass tackle will do, but bring a stock of spinnerbaits and poppers. Guests who book five or more days receive a free offshore trip for wahoo, yellowfin, sails, marlin and dorado. Heavy tackle is provided. Snook fish best from August through December; the other species in spring and fall.

Fishing days begin early. You're rousted out of bed at 5:00 a.m. and have breakfast half an hour later. Guests headed up the river will fish from Carolina skiffs, while a 23-foot closed-transom deep V carries anglers to the rivermouth. Canoes are used in shallow lagoons where powerboats can't go. Generally two anglers fish with a guide. You'll return to the lodge for lunch about 11:00 a.m. and a nap, then there's more fishing from 1:30 until 5:00 p.m.

Highly regarded for its fishing, the lodge also earns top marks for its accommodations...spacious, paneled guest rooms with two queen-size beds, high ceilings and private tiled baths. Langostinos, filet mignon, chicken cordon bleu and fresh fish highlight the menu, which is served buffet-style and complemented by good wines. A Jacuzzi awaits those with aching muscles. A note of caution: Guests are permitted only 25 pounds of luggage on the flight from San Jose to the lodge.

Fins 'n Feathers Inn

Iztapa, Guatemala

VITAL STATISTICS:

KEY SPECIES:
Sailfish

Season:
All year
Accommodations:
STUCCO VILLAS
NUMBER OF GUEST ROOMS: 8
MAXIMUM NUMBER OF GUESTS: 16
Conference Groups: Yes
Meals: American plan
Rates:
From $2590 per person for 3 nights and 3 days, double occupancy
Guides: Included
Gratuities: 15%
Preferred Payment:
Cash or check
Getting There:
Fly to Guatemala City; Fins 'n Feathers will provide ground transportation to the lodge.
Other Activities:
Swimming, bird watching.

Contact:
Tim Choate
Artmarina, 1390 S. Dixie Hwy. 2221, Miami, FL 33146; 305/663-3553, fax 305/666-6445, email fishguat@ icanect.net, website http://artmarina.com

The world's best billfishing may be found off the southwest coast of Guatemala.

THE PACIFIC off Guatemala may be the hottest billfish water in Central America. The story goes like this: Tim Choate, Miami entrepreneur, sailfish fanatic and owner of Artmarina, had maintained a fleet of sportfishermen in Costa Rica. Ever on the prowl for bigger and better billfish, he heard from local anglers about large numbers of sails in the waters south of Puerto San Jose, about halfway down Guatemala's coast. They are found in big meanders of blue water that break off from the California Current and surge landward. Depending on weather and season, some day's they'll be within six miles, on others 30. The average is about 20 miles offshore.

Large sailfish—usually running more than 100 pounds—work these waters from October through December. In terms of sheer numbers of fish, the best month to go is January. If the seas are right, and they usually are, you can expect 20 to 30 bites per day. Anglers who use conventional reels with revolving spools stand a reasonable chance of landing most that they solidly hook. Choate's captains specialize in flyfishing, and anglers so equipped will be presented with plenty of opportunities to play sails. Bringing them to boat is another matter. While sailfish are the prime quarry here, offshore blue marlin and Allison tuna occupy summer months, along with tuna and dolphin closer in, and roosterfish along the coast. Four cruisers from 31 to 37 feet constitute the offshore fleet and a 20-foot center console outboard carries anglers after roosterfish. Boats are ready at 7:00 a.m. each day, skippered by captains who know where the billfish are and how to induce them to slam your bait or fly.

In 1995, Choate's company, Artmarina, opened Fins 'n Feathers, a lushly landscaped white stucco resort of four villas with two air-conditioned rooms each. Clean, spacious and comfortable, each villa features two bedrooms, two baths, Jacuzzi, central living room and kitchenette. Sliding doors open onto the pool. Fine dinners of local seafood (which you caught yourself) and prime steaks are served in the restaurant that fronts on the river. Sit and linger as long as you wish. In addition to Fins 'n Feathers, other accommodations are available in a private three-bedroom home or in the Hotel Martita or Hotel Princes in town.

Posada Del Sol

Guanaja Bay Islands, Honduras

Snug in a grove of orchids and palms, this full-service island resort books no more than six anglers per week.

VITAL STATISTICS:

KEY SPECIES:
Bonefish; permit; tarpon; snook

Season:
All year

Accommodations:
SMALL RESORT HOTEL
NUMBER OF GUEST ROOMS: 23
MAXIMUM NUMBER OF GUESTS: 46
(but only 6 anglers per week)

Conference Groups: Yes

Meals: American plan

Rates:
From $1695 per person for 7 nights and 6 days of fishing, double occupancy

Guides: Included

Gratuities: Client's discretion

Preferred Payment:
Credit cards or cash

Getting There:
Fly to Guanaja via San Pedro Sula, Honduras. A boat will meet your plane and take you to the lodge.

Other Activities:
Tennis, rafting, swimming, hiking.

Contact:
Kimberly Luba
Posada Del Sol, 1201 W. US Hwy. 1, North Palm Beach, FL 33408; 800/642-3483, fax 561/624-3225.

THREE ISLANDS JUT UP through the flats off the north coast of Honduras. The largest is Rotan, the smallest Utila, and the other, Guanaja, is where Columbus anchored in July 1502 during his fourth, final and most disappointing voyage. Under intense pressure to find a route to the Indies, Columbus tarried but a short time at this rugged nine-mile-long pine-forested island before sailing 30 miles across the strait to the Honduran mainland. He never knew that his landfall on the continent would lead to Spanish conquest of the Mayans in 1540 and bring great wealth to Spain. But ever the keen observer, Columbus must have made mental note of bonefish and permit gliding across the flats over which his caravels sailed.

The flats off Guanaja fill the bill as fine bonefish water. Bottom ranges from hard sand to soft sand and some, but not much, marl. Anglers wade and sight-fish, casting to tailing bones or those leaving cloudy water as they root along bottom. Fish are not particularly big (running between two and six pounds or so), but they are there in numbers. And once in a while a larger (eight- to 10-pound) fish picks up a Clouser or Crazy Charlie and takes off for Cozumel. Skilled anglers will play 120 fish during a week-long stay. Permit are plentiful as well, but hookups are not as frequent as they are with the bones. The secret to this piece of piscatorial paradise is the offshore coral reef that protects the flats that surround the island. In addition to bonefish and permit, there are some snook and tarpon. To get a handle on the dynamics of the fishery, lodge owner George Cundiff has commissioned Texas A&M University to study the fish population around Guanaja. Results should be available in 1998.

While Posada Del Sol only books six anglers per week to limit impact on the environment, the tile-roofed Spanish-style resort contains 23 guest rooms that front on the ocean, forest or pool. With the coral reef, diving is a big attraction here. Also popular are walks through the orchid-rich rainforest to a freshwater falls. Two white sand beaches, a tennis court, an Orvis Pro-Shop, and an excellent restaurant round out amenities.

Casa Blanca

Q u i n t a n a   R o o ,   M e x i c o

You might have your best shot at a saltwater grand slam right here.

VITAL STATISTICS:

KEY SPECIES:
Bonefish; permit; tarpon

Season:
All year

Accommodations:
ANGLING RESORT
NUMBER OF GUEST ROOMS:
CASA BLANCA: 10
ESPIRITU SANTO: 5
MAXIMUM NUMBER OF GUESTS: 28

Conference Groups: No

Meals: American plan

Rates:
From $1647 per person for 4 nights and 3 days, double occupancy

Guides: Included

Gratuities:
$40 to $100 per week

Preferred Payment:
Cash or traveler's checks

Getting There:
Time your flight to Cancun, Mexico, to connect with private air charter-to the lodge (no additional cost).

Other Activities:
Snorkeling, bird watching, wildlife photography.

Contact:
David Settles
Outdoor Travel Inc.,
1973 W. Gray St., Suite
9, Houston, TX 77019;
800/533-7299, fax
713/526-4306, email
outdoor@insyc.net

ACCORDING TO ANGLING WRITER Lefty Kreh, "...Casa Blanca offers the very best shot at a 'grand slam'...a bonefish, a permit and a tarpon all in one day." That's probably so, but it will take furious dedication on your part. You'll be distracted by the abundance of bones and permit. You may be so busy that you forget about tarpon.

In the flats of Ascencion Bay and Espiritu Santo Bay down the coast, scores of bonefish ghost across the sandy bottom, given away by their fleeting shadows and flicking tails. Anglers who have never fished bones before can practice on school fish of two to six pounds. Your fingers will be rapped by the handle of your madly spinning reel as a bone does its best to spool you. After this happens once, twice, three times, you're ready for the big singles of 12 to 15 pounds. That's when the fun begins. Permit, more elusive, are plentiful here. It isn't all that unusual to be in casting range of a couple dozen. And then there are tarpon. While not primarily tarpon grounds, this area does have numbers of fish in the 30- to 50-pound class. Migratory fish begin to enter the bay in April and the population peaks in July. If you want to go for the slam, it's best to reserve a trip or two to the tarpon pools when you book.

Take at least two rods (7 weight, 9 weight) and a pair of corrosion-resistant saltwater reels with good drags, loaded with weight-forward saltwater tapers and at least 100 yards of backing. If you're going at the height of the season for big tarpon, take a 10 weight. And remember, four-piece rods travel more conveniently than longer two-piece numbers. You can't buy any tackle on the island, though effective patterns and lures (yes, you can fish with spinning or casting tackle) are stocked at the lodge. So are a few loaner rods, in case "you break all your tackle."

Accommodations at Casa Blanca are superlative. The main lodge at Casa Blanca has 10 rooms with tile floors and plenty of windows opening onto shady verandas fronting the Caribbean. A second lodge with five cottages is located 10 miles down the coast at Espiritu Santo (open only from February to May). Accommodations are similar and at both locations, dining is exquisite; native fruits and vegetables complement the day's catch.

Hotels Plamas de Cortez, Punta Colorado, Playa del Sol

Baja California Sur, Mexico

VITAL STATISTICS:

KEY SPECIES:
Marlin; sailfish; tuna; dorado (dolphin); roosterfish

Season:
All year

Accommodations:
SPACIOUS HOTEL ROOMS
NUMBER OF GUEST ROOMS/GUESTS:
PLAMAS DE CORTEZ: 60/157
PUNTA COLORADO: 29/72
PLAYA DEL SOL: 26/64

Conference Groups: Yes
Meals: American plan
Rates:
PLAMAS DE CORTEZ: From $70
PUNTA COLORADO: From $55
PLAYA DEL SOL: From $60;
all per person per day, single occupancy
Boats/Guides: From $195 for a skiff with skipper to $300 with skipper and mate per day
Gratuities: 15% of charter
Preferred Payment:
Cash or check
Getting There:
Fly to San Jose del Cabo or La Paz and the lodge's van will provide transfers to hotel for an additional fee.
Other Activities:
Swimming, snorkeling, scuba diving, sailing.

Contact:
Reservations
Hotel Plamas de Cortez, Punta Colorado or Playa del Sol, PO Box 9016, Calabasas, CA 91372; 800/368-4334, fax 818/591-9463, website http://www.successnet. net/bajafishing

Looking for great value in big-game fishing?
Check out these three hotels at the tip of the Baja.

LIKE THE PENDANT FOOT of a mollusk, Baja California pokes more than 800 miles south, separating the Pacific from the Gulf of California. Here, from Cabo San Lucas north and east along the coast to La Paz, you'll find some of the finest billfishing waters in North America. The waters of the Gulf of California, like its eastern sibling, the Gulf of Mexico, are gentle. A string of reefs parallels the coast in spots, providing a nursery for baitfish and a magnet for big game species that feed on them.

Marlin are available year-round, with striped marlin the main event in January. Blue marlin of 600 pounds make their appearance in April, and are joined by similar-size black marlin in July. The best months to fish these waters are May through October. Along with marlin, you can catch sailfish, tuna, amberjack, roosterfish, jack cravelle, groupers, cabrilla and dorado. This is a big-game fishery: Angling is mostly done from 30-foot cruisers or center console skiffs or pangas measuring 20 feet or more. Light-tackle anglers will be happy fishing the surf or in the shallows near the reef. Where else could you catch a world-record tuna on 2-pound-test line? Sound weird? It's possible.

Three first-class hotels, all served by excellent charter fleets, provide outstanding accommodations. Hotel Playa del Sol is located up the coast from East Cape on Bahia de Las Plamas. The Cerralvo, Oulmo Reef and Los Frailes are within a short boat ride. Just south of East Cape, Hotel Punta Colorado faces the Sea of Cortez. You can see fish on the reef through the windows of your ocean-front room. The southernmost member of the trio is Plamas de Cortez. Mirroring the style of old Mexico, yet thoroughly modern, all three offer light and spacious air-conditioned rooms with private baths, exquisite restaurants featuring regional cuisine, deep shady verandas, sparkling freshwater pools lined with palms and miles of white sand beaches. Snorkel, scuba, sail or just swim. What you won't find is golf and tennis or the incessant hustle of other tourist towns. Here you'll find serenity and more than a few fish.

Rancho Mariposa—
Jimenez and San Lorenzo

T a m a u l i p a s ,   M e x i c o

VITAL STATISTICS:

KEY SPECIES:
Largemouth bass

Season:
September through May

Accommodations:
JIMENEZ: ROUND ADOBE COTTAGES
SAN LORENZO: ADOBE MOTEL ROOMS
NUMBER OF GUEST ROOMS/GUESTS:
JIMENEZ: 8/16
SAN LORENZO: 28/41

Conference Groups: Yes

Meals: American plan

Rates:
JIMENEZ: From $850 per person for 4 nights and 3 days
SAN LORENZO: From $1100 per person for 4 nights and 3 days

Guides: Included

Gratuities: Client's discretion

Preferred Payment:
Cash or check

Getting There:
Fly to Harlingen, Texas. Anglers headed for San Lorenzo will fly; those for Jimenez will ride in a motor coach or van. Neither pays anything additional.

Contact:
Mark Bailey
Rancho Mariposa, 3025 Oak Ridge Rd., Crawford, TX 76638; 817/932-6503.

Down Mexico way, you'll stay in adobe villas, dine on fajitas and chili rellenos and catch bass that top 10 pounds.

CHANCES OF LANDING a 10-pound-plus largemouth are very good at this pair of Mexican lodges. Fishing runs from September through May. The best, though, is in the cooler months, November through March. While the lodges are of different styles, and the lakes of different character, the fishing packages are the same.

Rancho Mariposa Lorenzo is on San Lorenzo Lake about 60 miles west of Tampico on the Gulf Coast. The lake is similar in structure to Bull Shoals in Arkansas. Mountains come right down to the lake and the water is deep. Vertical jigging with worms is an effective tactic, as is fishing spinnerbaits and topwaters when conditions are right. Rancho Mariposa Jimenez is about 15 minutes from Lake Guerrero, which resembles and fishes like a typical Texas lake: lots of grassbeds, submerged timber and shallow points. Ten-inch blue fleck power worms work here, as do spinnerbaits, jerkbaits and jumpers. A 19-pound largemouth came out of Guerrero in 1995 and 10-pounders, while not an everyday event, happen with some frequency.

Anglers fish from old-style triple-V bass boats with 40-horse Yamahas and trolling motors mounted on the transom. They are not equipped with fishfinders. Why the low-tech approach? Simpler is better where repair facilities are limited. The guide piloting the boat has fished this water for a decade or more and knows it well. He sits in the stern running the boat, leaving the bow seat open for one of the two anglers aboard. He who sits in the bow seat is first to the fish.

With 28 guest rooms in a white adobe-style motel, Rancho Lorenzo is more than three times larger than Rancho Jimenez with its eight round adobe thatched-roofed villas for two. All are air-conditioned and have private baths. The regimen is the same at both: You're awakened at sun-up when freshly squeezed orange juice and coffee are delivered to your door. You'll fish until 10:30 or 11:00 a.m., return to the lodge for a snack of nachos or ceviche, lunch at 1:00 p.m., enjoy a siesta, then head back to the lake to fish until dusk. Dinners are Mexican, of course.

Tropic Star Lodge
Pinas Bay, Panama

VITAL STATISTICS:

KEY SPECIES:
Black, blue and striped marlin; sailfish; roosterfish; tuna; dolphin

Season:
December through July

Accommodations:
TROPICAL OCEANFRONT RESORT
NUMBER OF GUEST ROOMS: 18
MAXIMUM NUMBER OF GUESTS: 36

Conference Groups: Yes

Meals: American plan

Rates:
From $2100 per person
(4 anglers, 1 boat) per week,
single occupancy

Guides: Included

Gratuities: $250 per person
per week

Preferred Payment:
Cash or traveler's checks

Getting There:
Fly to Panama City, Panama
and overnight at hotel
recommended by lodge (at your
expense). Charter flight to Pinas
Bay ($225, additional), and
panga to lodge.

Other Activities:
Swimming, hiking, wildlife
photography.

Contact:
Don Crandall
Tropic Star Lodge, 635 N.
Rio Grande Ave.,
Orlando, FL 32805;
407/423-9931, fax
407/839-3637.

Discover Zane Grey's secret marlin hole off Panama's rugged and exotic Darien Jungle.

ISOLATED WHERE THE MOUNTAINOUS Darien Jungle meets Pinas Bay 150 miles south of Panama City, Panama, Tropic Star Lodge is the place for Pacific grand slams—a combo of black, blue or striped marlin, and sailfish. More than 140 world records have been set here, and 40 of them still stand. Fishing here was pioneered by Zane Grey, who in the 1920s discovered a reef that slopes from 120 to 350 feet, providing an abundance of bait upon which bigger fish feed.

Tropic Star is devoted to big-game species: black marlin, blue marlin, striped marlin, tuna, sailfish and roosterfish. Marlin season runs from December to mid-April, and it's best in January and February. Sails, tuna and roosters pick up in mid-April and run through July, with the better angling for sails in May and the other species in June. In the mouth of the Pinas River and off the rocky islands, you'll find dolphin, rainbow runners, snappers, groupers, amberjacks and mackerel. Though infrequent, tarpon are also taken.

You and your party will fish with a mate and captain on a 31-foot Bertram with tackle and baits provided. While this lodge caters to traditional big-game anglers, flyfishing is increasingly spoken here, and the lodge offers an excellent chance to hook into blue-water species. Landing them is another matter. If flyfishing is your preference, take your own tackle.

Tropic Star may be as remote as any of the lodges in the Alaskan bush, but it knows how to lay on the luxury. Built by Texas oilman Ray Smith in the early 1960s, the lodge and adjacent cabins offer twin beds, private baths with dressing areas, air conditioning and views of the bay. Or you can stay 150 steps up the mountain at El Palacio, Smith's winter retreat with three bedrooms, sunken living room and panoramic view. Before dinner, take a swim in the lushly landscaped pool, then sit down to a five-course dinner with complimentary wine.

Because travel to the lodge requires an hour's charter flight from Panama City on a twin Otter or similar aircraft, each guest is permitted only one suitcase 40 pounds max, a carry-on bag of 15 pounds and one rod tube. Excess baggage will be transported on a space available basis for $1.50 per pound and may not arrive at the lodge the same day you do.

While fishing is on everyone's mind here, guests also enjoy trips up the river in native dugouts to trade with indigenous peoples. Many guests bring cloth, needles and thread while others bring candy or school supplies to barter for baskets or carvings. Tides dictate upriver travel, and these trips should be planned in advance.

INDEX

(Here are some of the major water and land features that are
not included in lodge names or addresses)